D0226150

FOURTH EDITION

OBJECTIVES, METHODS, AND EVALUATION FOR SECONDARY TEACHING

Michael A. Lorber
Illinois State University

Allyn and Bacon
Boston • London • Toronto • Sydney • Tokyo • Singapore

Dedicated to Ellen Jane and David Marcel

Senior Editor, Education: Virginia Lanigan
Editorial Assistant: Nihad Farooq
Senior Marketing Manager: Kathy Hunter
Editorial-Production Administrator: Donna Simons
Editorial-Production Service: Matrix Productions, Inc.
Composition and Prepress Buyer: Linda Cox
Manufacturing Buyer: Aloka Rathnam
Cover Administrator: Suzanne Harbison

Library of Congress Cataloging-in-Publication Data

Lorber, Michael A.
  Objectives, methods, and evaluation for secondary teaching /
Michael A. Lorber.—4th ed.
    p.   cm.
  Includes bibliographical references and index.
  ISBN 0–205–19392–7
  1. High school teaching. I. Title
LB1737.A3L65 1995
373.11'02—dc20   95–33143
                                CIP

Printed in the United States of America

10 9 8 7 6 5 4 3 2   00 99 98

CONTENTS

PREFACE

This book is based on the idea that prospective teachers can acquire certain skills and knowledge that will help them become more humane and effective teachers. Because this era emphasizes factors such as technology, reflective thinking, and competency-based instruction, you will find, incorporated into the content and the structure of the text itself, principles central to each of these factors. For example, each chapter begins with a rationale and a set of suggested instructional objectives and ends with a section entitled "So How Does This Affect My Teaching?" You will also find explanations and models of problem-based learning, course syllabi, unit plans, and lesson plans, as well as an in-depth look at the increasingly varied ways in which computers can be used to enhance the teaching–learning process.

While there is much of value in the competency-based movement, the teaching–learning process is not as precise or clear-cut as some proponents of the movement imply. A teacher's success depends, to a large degree, on the success of his or her students. To help students succeed, teachers must not only develop a range of pedagogical skills, they must also develop the personal characteristics conducive to effective teaching. A good teacher must, for example, be tolerant of individual differences and opinions, be fair with people, and be receptive to new ideas. Characteristics such as these are as crucial to good teaching as any of the skills and procedures about to be presented.

I gratefully acknowledge the time, effort, and ideas that others contributed to this book. Dr. Walter D. Pierce, Professor Emeritus of Education at Illinois State University, provided the initial incentive and encouragement to complete the book. Dr. Sally Pancrazio, Dean of the College of Education at Illinois State University, provided encouragement and support. It was she who compiled the list of tasks, included in Chapter 1, that have been given to educators over the years. Dr. Morton Waimon, Professor Emeritus of Education at Illinois State University, adapted Ralph Tyler's three sources of instructional objectives into the "Knowledge Structure" described in Chapter 4. Mr. Kenneth Lovett developed the model knowledge structure and unit plan used in this text. Dr. Edward Streeter, in a commencement address at the Illinois State University in 1988, clearly enunciated the idea of "educating all the children of all the people." Dr. Clifford Edwards, Professor of Education at Brigham Young University, and Drs. Larry Kennedy and Frank Lewis, both Professors of Education at Illinois State University, provided many of the insights that found their way into this text.

Dr. Joe Parks, Assistant Professor of Education at Illinois State University, wrote Chapter 15, Multicultural Concerns. Dr. Parks has had both personal and professional experience with respect to multicultural concerns and, particularly, with biracialism. His willingness to share his expertise is greatly appreciated.

My appreciation also goes to the following reviewers for their valuable comments: Douglas D. Hatch, Georgia Southwestern, Ann W. Karaffa, Baylor University, Eugene Kim, California State University, Sacramento, Bob Mayer, Moravian College, John Mack Welford, Roanoke College, and John R. Zalazek, Central Missouri State University.

I want to express special thanks to my son, David Marcel Lorber. His expertise with word processing, library searches, Internet, and spreadsheets was crucial to compiling the data and completing the manuscript.

Finally, I want to thank my wife, Ellen Jane, for her never-ending encouragement, patience, and support. Her smiles and Toll-House cookies saved the day more than once.

NOTE TO INSTRUCTORS AND STUDENTS

In this text, there is a discussion of how computer networks can be used to enable people to share ideas easily with one another. As author of this text, it would be my pleasure to respond to questions concerning anything in the text, and/or to exchange ideas with students and other instructors. My e-mail address is: **malorber@ilstu.edu.** If you would prefer to correspond by conventional mail, my address is:

Michael A. Lorber, Ph.D.
Department of Curriculum and Instruction—5330
Illinois State University
Normal, IL 61790–5330

1

EDUCATIONAL PHILOSOPHIES AND WHY YOU NEED ONE

RATIONALE

Two of the most basic questions in education are (1) what should students know and be able to do, and (2) how can we determine if they know and can do those things? You may not have thought deeply about these questions yet, but now is a good time to start. You are likely to be asked these questions during job interviews and, whether you are asked or not, your views will largely determine what you do in your classroom. Your views will reflect your philosophy of education.

Differences among educational philosophies are central to most controversies in education. Much of what educators write is intended to persuade readers to accept and support a particular philosophic stance and the practices that follow from it. Understanding philosophic starting points will help you better understand why different people advocate different practices.

Sometimes prospective teachers do not recognize the fundamental importance of philosophy. They want to skip over it and get on with the task of learning how to teach their subject-area content. What they soon discover is that they need to make choices about what to teach and how to teach—they need to think about their philosophic position. This chapter will give you a basis for examining your own, probably tentative, philosophic position and the positions advocated by others. It will also help you make decisions about what and how you will teach, and it will help you understand why education always seems to be in a crisis.

SAMPLE OBJECTIVES

You will be able, in writing, to:
1. Given quotations by people such as Hutchins, Adler, Bagley, Bestor, Rickover, Dewey, and Neill, explain at least one characteristic that identifies the quotation as reflective of Perennialism, Essentialism, Progressivism, or Existentialism.
2. Create a comparison chart, perhaps a Venn diagram, depicting the common and unique characteristics of Perennialism, Essentialism, Progressivism, and Existentialism.
3. Based on your own experiences, select the educational philosophy that seems most appropriate to you and describe two reasons why that view seems more appropriate than each of the others.
4. Examine at least two of the tests or other evaluation instruments or procedures used by two high school teachers and: (a) explain which educational philosophy is most clearly reflected, and (b) cite two characteristics of the evaluation instruments/procedures that support your assessment.

WHAT IS A PHILOSOPHY OF EDUCATION?

Educational philosophies represent basic theories and viewpoints, which eventually acquire labels such as Perennialism, Essentialism, Progressivism, and Existentialism. John Dewey, one of America's greatest educational theorists, warned against 'isms. He said that "in spite of itself, any movement that thinks and acts in terms of an 'ism becomes so involved in reaction against other 'isms that it is unwittingly controlled by them."[1] Nonetheless, the 'isms are alive and well and understanding them will help you make more informed choices.

When educational philosophies in their "pure" forms are discussed, the differences among them are fairly clear. When these philosophies are actually applied in school settings, however, compromises are often made and some of the differences disappear. Further, most philosophies have at least one goal in common: the production of educated people who can live happy and productive lives. The problem is that the terms *educated, happy,* and *productive* mean different things to different people. Still further, many educators are eclectic; they pick and choose elements from different philosophies as they develop their own. You are likely to do the same, but the task will be easier if you first know something of four basic philosophies.

A WORD OF ADVICE

Educational philosophies are usually stated with great conviction and are often supported with strong, cause-effect arguments. You might, therefore, want to consider the following advice offered by Gautama **Buddha** (563?–483? B.C.):

Believe nothing because a so-called wise man said it.
Believe nothing because a belief is generally held.
Believe nothing because it is written in ancient books.
Believe nothing because it is said to be of divine origin.
Believe nothing because someone else believes it.
Believe only what you yourself judge to be true.

LEARNING FROM THE ANCIENT GREEKS

Virtually all philosophies of western education are rooted in ancient Greek thought, so pulling back the curtain of history just a little will shed a great deal of light on today's controversies in education. As you read, keep in mind that when we are talking about the ancient Greeks, we are talking about a relatively small number of people. **Sparta,** at its height in the fifth century B.C., had a population of about 250,000, of which about 25,000 were full citizens.[2] At about the same time, **Athens** had a population of about 335,000, of which about 35,000 were full citizens.[3] What is said about education in ancient Greece pertained only to full citizens. The other 90 percent of the population—the females, foreigners, serfs, and slaves—were excluded, partially or altogether, from formal education.

The numbers are relevant because although ancient Greece is often cited as the source of democracy, when it came to education, it was not so democratic. The Greeks saw education as necessary, but only for the children of citizens. Educating all the children of all the people is an idea born in the New England colonies. With a system educating about 42 million students (as of Fall 1992),[4] student diversity and sheer logistics become problems of a magnitude never encountered by smaller societies then or now.

A look at the views of the Elder Sophists, Socrates, Plato, and Aristotle will suffice to expose the roots of modern educational philosophies. Much of their thinking is still valid today.

The Elder Sophists—The First Professional Teachers

The Elder Sophists were a group of itinerant teachers who, at about 450 B.C., went from city-state to city-state operating "as freelance teachers in competition with each other, accepting fees for their work."[5] Among the best known of these outstanding teachers were Protagoras, Gorgias, Prodikos, Hippias, and Thrasymachus. Since success in ancient Greece depended largely on one's ability to speak in public, the Sophists met the needs of their students by specializing in the teaching of rhetoric.

The idea of meeting students' needs was evidently a good one. **Protagoras,** the best known of the Elder Sophists, was "able to charge 10,000 drachmas for a two- or three-year course of instruction at a time when 1 drachma was a skilled worker's daily wage. By 350 B.C., however, the price of such a course had fallen to about 1,000 drachmas."[6] Despite this, it should be noted that the Sophists' ideal was the polymath, a person expert in all areas of knowledge.

Protagoras had some ideas that are clearly parts of modern philosophies. For example, Plato attributes to him the idea that "Of all things, the measure is Man."[7] This is the root of the modern philosophy of Existentialism and of "situation ethics," the idea that what is right is dependent on time, place, and circumstance. His view that "Art without practice, and practice without art, are nothing,"[8] is central to Progressivist thinking. He also believed that "all men were capable of intelligent, socially responsible self-rule, but that they could not achieve their potential without education."[9] The idea that all children can learn is accepted in all philosophies today. **Gorgias,** with his idea that nothing (absolute) exists, also helped lay the foundation for Existentialism.

Until the time of the Sophists (the fifth century B.C.), instruction had been mostly tutorial. The Sophists, however, modified the tutorial system and taught groups of students rather than individuals. "It was the first recorded instance of mass instruction."[10]

It is likely that the Sophists introduced the technique of analysis in teaching. "By analyzing exemplary models of writing and speaking, they formulated rules for effective writing and speaking.... They also combined theory and application. First, the Sophists taught their students the rules (theory) of the spoken and written word. Then they prepared a model speech for them to copy, analyze, discuss, and present in actual spoken practice.... Because the Sophists' procedures were inherently systematic, the student always knew what was of expected of him, how he might achieve his goals, and how well he was progressing."[11] Most educators today still think those are good things for students to know. The way the Elder Sophists taught helps explain why they are often regarded as the first professional teachers.

Socrates—Knowledge Is Inborn; Questioning Can Draw It Out

Socrates (c. 470–399 B.C.) believed that knowledge was good in and of itself, that the main purpose of education was to guide and motivate moral conduct, and that much knowledge was inborn and could be drawn out by skillful questioning. As it happens, recent research supports the idea that the minds of babies are far more developed than previously suspected. For example, at three months of age, babies can not only remember visual sequences, but can also foresee and predict four-step sequences. Children as young as five months have been found to have rudimentary abilities to add and subtract and to have a built-in sense of how objects behave. The research results make it increasingly difficult to deny the existence of some kinds of innate knowledge.[12]

The questioning used by Socrates, which came to be called the **Socratic Method,** required that each question lead to a definite point and that the questioner build only on the facts students already knew. If the student had to collect data in order to reach a new conclusion, the teacher had strayed from the original Socratic technique.[13] The Socratic Method is typically easier to use with younger, rather than older, children because when dealing with older children, adults tend to make assumptions about what the children know and ask inappropriate questions.

Keep in mind what happened to Socrates. When his educational views and practices conflicted enough with those thought to be proper by the city administrators, they sentenced him to death. We are kinder today, but if your educational views and practices differ enough from those thought to be proper by the administrators of your district, you might not be rehired after your first year.

Plato—The Ideal World of Ideas; Learn by Thinking

Plato (c. 427–347 B.C.) contributed many ideas still revered today. For example, he believed that the world we see is illusory and that the real world exists as pure "Forms" or "Ideas" which never change. He also believed that education should concern itself with helping people comprehend these never-changing Truths. The idea of eternal Truths is central to most religions and to the twentieth-century philosophy of Perennialism.

Plato was among the first to formally recognize individual differences. In *The Republic,* Plato described how social harmony could be achieved in an ideal society by requiring all citizens to begin formal education, but allowing those least able or least inclined to profit from instruction to leave. They would become menial workers. Those who could profit more from instruction would continue with military training and would become the warriors and guardians of the state. The most able, the intellectual elite, would go on to further study and become the philosopher-kings who would rule. This awareness of, and concern for, individual differences is important to Progressivism. We also see the roots of a tracked educational system and the resulting stratified society.

Aristotle—World Ruled by Natural Laws; Learn by Experience

Aristotle (c. 384–322 B.C.) agreed with most other ancient Greeks that the state's welfare depended on an educated citizenry and that the state should take an active role in guiding education. As you will see in the following chapters, Congress has taken an active interest in, and has heavily influenced, education in the United States.

The thinking of Plato and Aristotle concerning education differed in at least one respect. Plato believed that thought, pure cognition, was the major tool of learning and that knowledge was its own reward. Aristotle believed that little or nothing was in the mind other than what got there through the senses. **John Locke** (1632–1704) echoed that idea when he said that the mind was a *tabula rasa*, a blank tablet, on which all that we know is written via our experiences.[14] Aristotle also saw knowledge as having more utilitarian purposes than did Plato.

Aristotle's interest in examining new things and in scientific investigation was well known to his students. One of them, Alexander the Great, remembered his teacher's interest and sent to him a steady stream of plants, animals, and artifacts as he went about conquering most of the world known at that time. This concern for scientific investigation is central to Essentialism and to Progressivism.

Plato and Aristotle also believed that the mind was made up of separate powers or "faculties" such as memory, judgment, and reasoning; and that these faculties could be strengthened by rigorous mental exercise.[15] This "faculty theory" was not disproved until Edward L. Thorndike's study in 1922–23 (more on this in Chapter Two).

Despite his genius, Aristotle was unable to resolve the educational problems of his day. He observed that:

> *Education should be regulated by law and should be an affair of state.... Since there is a single end for the city as a whole, it is evident that education must necessarily be one and the same for all.... but at present there is a dispute concerning its tasks. Not everyone conceives that the young should learn the same things either with a view to virtue or with a view to the best way of life, nor is it evident whether it is more appropriate that it be with a view to the mind or with a view to the character of the soul. Investigation on the basis of the education that is current yields confusion, and it is not at all clear whether one should have training in things useful for life, things contributing to virtue, or extraordinary things; for all of these have obtained some judges (supporters). Concerning the things relating to virtue, nothing is agreed. Indeed, to start with, not everyone honors the same virtues, so it is reasonable to expect them to differ as well in regard to the training in it.[16]*

After more than 2,000 years, the questions are still open. Should everyone know certain things? The Goals 2000: Educate America Act, with its call for national standards, certainly seems to point in that direction. What about the focus of education? Should it be on "training in things useful for life," such as making our students first in the world in science and math, or should it be more on "a view to the mind," focusing more on the liberal arts? The issues that Aristotle observed in his day are alive and well today.

"TRADITIONAL" PHILOSOPHIES— PERENNIALISM AND ESSENTIALISM

Of all the educational philosophies that could be explored, four—Perennialism, Essentialism, Progressivism, and Existentialism—seem to be most pervasive. We will look first at Perennialism because it focuses on the seven liberal arts (grammar, rhetoric, logic, arithmetic, geometry, music, and astronomy). These subjects have been the foundation of western education since the Middle Ages and, to a large extent, they still dominate the secondary curriculum.

Perennialism

Perennialism reflects Plato's belief that Truth (with a capital T to denote its eternal nature) and values are absolute, timeless, and universal. The goal of education should be to help all students discover and understand these Truths, and the study of mankind's accumulated knowledge is the best way to accomplish this goal. Perennialists are often cited as advocating a separate-subjects curriculum, but the Truths sought cut across time, place, and the subject-matter lines that educators establish to manage instruction. Viewed from this perspective, Perennialism seems very much concerned with curricular integration or, as it is sometimes called, interdisciplinary studies. The work of Robert Hutchins and Mortimer Adler will help further delineate the basic tenets of Perennialism.

Robert Hutchins and Mortimer Adler
Robert M. Hutchins (1899–1977) was 30 years old when he became president of the University of Chicago. He served as president for 22 years (1929–1951) and his views are often associated with Perennialism. He wrote that:

> *One purpose of education is to draw out the elements of our common human nature. These elements are the same in any time or place. The notion of educating a man to live in any particular time or place, to adjust him to any particular environment, is therefore foreign to a true conception of education.*[17]
>
> *If education is rightly understood, it will be understood as the cultivation of the intellect. The cultivation of the intellect is the same good for all men in all societies.*[18]

Hutchins also believed that schools are called upon to teach too much. Many educators agreed with him then, and many more would agree now. What follows is a listing of some of the functions that have been assigned to, or assumed by, the schools. Many of these had once been the primary responsibility of the home, church, or workplace, while others emerged from concerns at the state and federal levels.

1640–1900

Basic reading, writing, and arithmetic
Transmission of values and knowledge associated with a democratic society (includes history of the United States and our form of governance)

1900–1930 (Due to immigration of Europeans to America in early 1900s)

Nutrition
Immunization
Health

1930s

Vocational Education
Practical Arts
Physical Education
School Lunch Programs

1950s

Sex Education introduced (topics escalating through the 1990s)
Foreign Languages (strengthened)
Driver Education
Safety Education (strengthened in succeeding decades)

1960s

Consumer Education
Career Education
Peace Education
Leisure/Recreational Education
Early Childhood Education/Pre-School programs for at-risk children

1970s

Drug and Alcohol Abuse Education
Parent Education

Character Education/Values Clarification
Special Education (mandated by the federal government)
School breakfast programs added

1980s

Bilingual Education
Global Education
Ethnic Education
English-as-a-Second-Language
Multicultural Education
Full-day kindergarten
After-school programs for children of working parents
Stranger/Danger—Sexual Abuse Prevention Education
Child Abuse Monitoring (legal requirement for teachers)
Keyboarding and computer literacy

1990s

HIV/AIDs Education
Death Education
Geography (re-emergence as a separate subject)
Inclusion of special education students[19]

The problem here is not the value of the topics. The problem is that teachers who were prepared to teach in particular disciplines are not well prepared to provide meaningful instruction in many of these other areas. Further, neither the school day nor the school year have been lengthened to accommodate the new inclusions. As Alfred North Whitehead noted:

Lack of time is the rock upon which the fairest educational schemes are wrecked. It has wrecked the scheme which our fathers constructed to meet the growing demand for the introduction of modern ideas. They simply increased the number of subjects taught.[20]

Further, as new topics were added, the function of schools became less clear and teachers less sure of what was expected of them. Hutchins seems to have made a good point. More of his views, including his view that undergraduate education should be the same for doctors, lawyers, and prospective teachers, are included in Appendix A.

With the Perennialist conviction that much of our cultural heritage was already written and was available for study, Hutchins, working with another educator with Perennialist views, **Mortimer J. Adler** (1902–), compiled and edited the 54 volumes of *Great Books of the Western World.* Published by Encyclopedia Brittanica in 1952, these volumes contained the Bible and the works of people such as Homer (*Odyssey, Iliad*), Archimedes, Galileo, Shakespeare, Spinoza, Huygens, Sir Isaac Newton, Leibnitz, John Locke, and many others. They are often central to courses of study and are sometimes the center of controversy. For example, in 1988, a small group of students at Stanford University objected to the *Great Books* as the focus of a highly popular program entitled the Western Culture Program. They thought the program should be broadened to include more works by blacks, Hispanics, and women. Some changes were made, but the *Great Books* remain central to the program.[21]

Adler took the principles of Perennialism (and some principles of Progressivism), and put them into practice first at the high school level and then K–12, with the **Paideia** (py-dee-a) Project. A basic premise of the project, and one that Adler credits to John Dewey, is that if democracy is to succeed then all children must be given the same educational opportunities, the same quantity of public education, and the same quality of education.[22] Adler quotes Hutchins's statement that "the best education for the best, is the best education for all."[23] As might be expected, this position raised questions by those concerned with individual differences.

Adler argued that in order to provide the general and liberal education he saw as necessary for all students, "all sidetracks, specialized courses, or elective choices must be eliminated. Allowing them will always lead a certain number of students to voluntarily downgrade their own education."[24] The curricular model he advocated was laid out in three columns, and is shown in Figure 1.1.

Distinguishing Characteristics of Perennialism in Its "Pure" Form
1. The role of education is to help students understand perennial Truths, rather than to meet contemporary, often transitory, needs.
2. To accomplish this goal a single curriculum should exist for all students.
3. The curriculum should consist of separate courses, principally the most general and abstract subjects such as philosophy and logic, since they cut across time, place, and circumstance, but it should emphasize the integration of that knowledge.
4. The curriculum should include the study of original sources such as the *Great Books*.

Points of Contention
1. The role of education should be broader than simply cultivating the intellect and studying ideas of the past.
2. Curricular choices must exist to accommodate differences in abilities and interests among students and students should help determine what they will learn.

FIGURE 1.1   Curricular Model for the Paideia Project

Goals	Acquisition of Knowledge	Development of Intellectual Skills—Skills of Learning	Enlarged Understanding of Ideas and Values
	by means of	*by means of*	*by means of*
Means	Didactic Instruction, Lectures, Responses, Textbooks, and other aids	Coaching, Exercises, and Supervised Practice	Maieutic or Socratic Questioning and Active Participation
	In the three areas of subject matter	*in the operations of*	*in the*
Arenas, Operations, and Activities	Language, Literature, and the Fine Arts; Mathematics and Natural Science; History, Geography, and Social Studies	Reading, Writing, Speaking, Listening, Calculating, Problem-solving, Observing, Measuring, Estimating, Exercising critical judgment	Discussion of books (not textbooks) and other works of art and involvement in artistic activities, for example, music, drama, visual arts.

The three columns do not correspond to separate courses, nor is one kind of teaching and learning necessarily confined to any one class. Adler, Mortimer J., *The Paideia Project, An Educational Manifesto* (New York: Macmillan Publishing, 1982), p. 23.

3. Focusing on the past does not prepare students for today or tomorrow as effectively as focusing on modern scientific studies and the changing state of knowledge.

Essentialism

Essentialism is the philosophy that underlies virtually all of today's secondary school curriculums. When people speak of the "traditional" curriculum, what they typically mean is an Essentialistic curriculum. One of the main goals of Essentialists is to pass on the cultural and historical heritage to each new generation of learners, beginning with a strong foundation in the "basics." It is primarily subject centered and it sees the teacher as a master of a particular subject field.[25] However, there are two other, less frequently mentioned, characteristics that cause Essentialism to seem "right" to so many.

One characteristic is that Essentialism emphasizes clear, measurable goals. One of those goals is to help students acquire a common and strong knowledge-base (English, math, social studies, and science) that they can use to make judgments, deal with the world, and solve problems. Using this knowledge-base, students can move on to new discoveries and perhaps develop new solutions to existing problems. Students can build on what others have learned and experienced. They do not have to learn by trial and error. The fact that some students might not recognize the value of this approach is of little concern to Essentialists. They believe that students, because of their lack of experience, are not aware of what they need to know. Therefore, they should trust their elders and apply themselves to the prescribed studies.

A second characteristic is that Essentialists believe that competition is inherent in the human species and is a driving force in virtually all human endeavors. They accept the fact that people compete with each other for power, status, goods, and services and that nations do the same. Essentialists seek to prepare students, and the country, to compete successfully in the global economy. Cooperative learning is not excluded, but neither is it a major characteristic of Essentialism.

Think back to the courses you were required to take, or to choose from, when you went to elementary and high school. The chances are good that you had to take a certain number of history, math, English, and science courses. A specification of disciplines or courses to be studied is typical of Essentialistic curriculums. The words of three Essentialists will give you a fairly good idea of that philosophy.

William S. Bagley (1874–1946)

Gripping and enduring interests frequently grow out of learning efforts that are not intrinsically appealing or attractive.

The control, direction, and guidance of the immature by the mature is inherent in the prolonged period of infancy or necessary dependence peculiar to the human species.

While the capacity for self-discipline should be the goal, imposed discipline is a necessary means to this end.[26]

Arthur Bestor (1908–)

...the curriculum should consist essentially of disciplined study in five great areas: (1) command of the mother tongue and the systematic study of grammar, literature, and writing; (2) mathematics; (3) sciences; (4) history; and (5) foreign language.[27]

Liberal education is designed to produce self-reliance. It expects a man to use his general intelligence to solve particular problems. Vocational and "life-adjustment" programs, on the other hand, breed servile dependence.[28]

Concern with the personal problems of adolescents has grown so excessive as to push into the background what should be the school's central concern, the intellectual development of its students.[29]

Hyman G. Rickover (1900–1986)

For all children, the educational process must be one of collecting factual knowledge to the limit of their absorptive capacity. Recreation, manual or clerical training, etiquette, and similar know-how have little effect on the mind itself and it is with the mind that the school must solely concern itself. The poorer a child's natural endowments, the more does he need to have his mind trained. . . . To acquire such knowledge, fact upon fact, takes time and effort. Nothing can really make it fun.[30]

Distinguishing Characteristics of Essentialism in Its "Pure" Form

1. The roles of education are to perpetuate the culture and to teach students the knowledge, skills, and values needed to become contributing members of society.
2. To accomplish its goals, the subject-centered curriculum should focus first on teaching that which is known, and then on helping students build on that knowledge to explore the unknown, particularly via scientific investigation.
3. Non-academic subjects such as vocational courses, physical education, and the fine arts, should be excluded from the curriculum or, at most, be a very minor part of it.
4. Progress in education should be measurable at the end of some reasonable timeframe and one useful tool in this measurement is the standardized test.

Points of Contention

1. The role of education should be to introduce students to, and help them acquire, the skills and understandings needed to appreciate all aspects of life. Since life includes cognitive and physical activities, creative endeavors and recreational endeavors, the curriculum should include all of these things.
2. A separate-subjects curriculum fragments knowledge whereas the intent of a curriculum should be to help students integrate knowledge.
3. It is better to focus on the process of learning rather than on learning specific content.
4. Education should be a life-long endeavor and efforts to "measure" it, particularly via tests, are misguided.

NONTRADITIONAL PHILOSOPHIES— PROGRESSIVISM AND EXISTENTIALISM

Progressivism

Progressivism is the philosophy most often cited in contrast to Perennialism and Essentialism. Most Progressivists believe that the curriculum should be more student-centered than subject-centered, more focused on activities than on passive learning, and more aimed at long-term rather than short-term goals. Most Progressives also believe that since knowledge is continually changing and expanding it is more important to learn *how* to think than to learn *what* to think.

John Dewey

John Dewey (1859–1952) is perhaps the most often cited Progressivist. He had an abiding faith in the link between an educated citizenry and the flourishing of democracy and thought that schools should be a place where students could learn the skills needed to live in a democratic society. He believed that students had an innate desire to know and grow, and that the best way to capitalize on those desires was to give students tasks and materials they saw as relevant to their own needs. He also believed that the curriculum should be interdisciplinary. Students would learn elements of math, science, and English, etc., as they needed those elements to do certain things and solve relevant problems. Further, he saw cooperation and standards established for individuals as more beneficial than competition and standards established for groups.

As early as 1938, Dewey saw that some educators had taken his ideas well beyond his intent and from that point forward he spent a good deal of time pointing out that he did *not* agree with those who wanted to "make little or nothing of organized subject-matter... or to proceed as if any form of direction or guidance by adults was an invasion of individual freedom."[31] With respect to the project method, often cited as a hallmark of Progressivism, Dewey said. "I do not urge it as the sole way out of educational confusion, not even in the elementary school, though I think experimentation with it is desirable in college and secondary school."[32] A few quotations from Dewey's *Democracy and Education* are included in Appendix A. They may help you judge for yourself what Dewey advocated.

One of Progressivism's most distinguishing characteristics, and one that clearly differentiates it from Perennialism and Essentialism, is the view that the curriculum should be **student-centered** rather than **subject-centered.** In thinking about student-centered versus subject-centered curricula, consider the characteristics of the whole K–12 curriculum, not just the secondary curriculum. When viewed from this perspective it becomes clear that there is a gradual shifting from student-centeredness at the lower levels to subject-centeredness at the higher levels. The shift may not be as linear as depicted in Figure 1.2, but the gradual change in emphasis is evident in all K–12 curriculums.

There are sound reasons for the change in emphasis. When students are young they need the kind of nurturing, structure, and consistency that a single teacher in a self-contained classroom can provide. Their need to learn how to act in a group and to master fundamental skills is greater than their need for learning about particular subject matter. Teachers can more easily plan lessons that cut across subject-area lines because the students are with them for a whole day, not for just an hour. For example, a first-grade teacher can use an interdisciplinary approach when teaching about dinosaurs by having students count dinosaurs, draw them, write short stories about them, and think about the fact that they are extinct.

As students move through the grade levels they are typically able to profit from increasingly detailed knowledge. To provide this knowledge and guide student learning, teachers need to be increasingly knowledgeable about particular subjects. This, in turn, results in departmentalization and a subject-centered curriculum. These factors make curricular integration easier at the elementary level than at the secondary level.

Theodore R. Sizer

Since the 1970s, Theodore Sizer (1932–) has been working to reform and restructure schools, largely along Progressivist lines. In 1984, he published *Horace's Compromise: The Dilemma of the American High School,*[33] in which a fictional teacher, Horace Smith, explains what he believes is wrong with today's high schools and suggests ways the schools might be restructured and improved. In 1984, Sizer launched a movement known as the Coalition of Essential Schools. He, and the movement, are based at Brown University, in Rhode Island.[34]

FIGURE 1.2   Emphasis Distribution

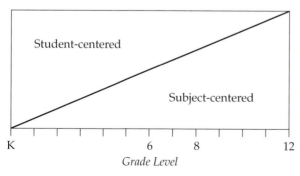

In 1992, Sizer authored a sequel to *Horace's Compromise,* entitled *Horace's School: Redesigning the American High School.*[35] In *Horace's School,* Horace Smith has been appointed chair of a committee whose charge is to review the purposes and practices of the fictitious Franklin High School. In portraying the committee meetings, Sizer's arguments are sometimes hard to follow. For example, he argues that one indicator of the need to reform schools is the poor performance of U. S. students in comparison to students internationally.[36] Shortly thereafter, however, he raises the valid question of whether the tests are appropriate measures of learning.[37] What is left unexplained is why, if the tests are inappropriate measures, their results should be considered at all.

In true Progressivist fashion, Sizer has Horace arguing that when it comes to high school diplomas, "no one should be left out...."[38] He also argues that students be directly involved in all aspects of school life: "Students who eat meals at school should help prepare them."[39] Ideas such as this have been tried, and they failed. For example, in 1916, educators in Gary, Indiana, implemented what came to be called the **Gary Plan.** Among other features, students did much of the work of the school. They ordered and distributed lunch room supplies, kept accounts, and did some of the maintenance and repair work in the school. Unfortunately, the students required so much adult checking and supervision, and the time required so detracted from academic pursuits, that the plan was soon abandoned.[40]

Other ideas suggested by Horace's committee, such as differentiated diplomas, have also been tried before and found wanting. If advocates of educational reform thoroughly reviewed the history of American education, perhaps fewer mistakes would be repeated. There is nothing wrong with trying to improve on ideas that have failed. However, if an idea did not work well, before trying it again, it is a good idea to determine what factors caused it to fail, and how to change one or more of those factors so the idea has a reasonable chance of working now. Ironically, Sizer points out that one reason that previous reform efforts failed was the lack of "a fresh and ambitious research effort...."[41] Not much has changed since.

At times, Sizer has Horace's committee making suggestions similar to one attributed to Will Rogers (1879–1935), an American humorist, actor, and author. Legend has it that when Rogers was asked what he would recommend to get rid of German submarines, he suggested that they boil the ocean. When asked how that could be done, he said that he had given them a solution and it was up to them to work out the details. Many Progressive ideas, including some suggested by Horace's committee (such as class sizes of about 15 students, an ideal school year of 240 days, and spending $150,000–$250,000 per year for five years for staff development), leave similar "details" to be worked out.

It is not likely that the public will rush to fund ideas such as Sizer's after having spent large amounts of money on other "crucially important" efforts—schools without walls, educational television, language labs and computers—with little significant improvement. Many taxpayers now see education's requests for more money as insatiable. No matter how much is provided, it is never enough. Further, some of the ideas Sizer advocates, such as focusing on academics and competence, have been standard operating procedure for many teachers for many years.

In fairness, it should be pointed out that while some of Sizer's ideas seem to be impractical in today's schools, he is arguing for a fundamental restructuring of American education. What follow are the nine basic principles of the Coalition of Essential Schools:

1. The school should focus on helping adolescents learn to use their minds well. Schools should not attempt to be "comprehensive" if such a claim is made at the expense of the school's central intellectual purpose.
2. The school's goals should be simple: each student should master a number of essential skills and be competent in certain areas of knowledge. Although these skills will, to varying degrees, reflect the traditional academic disciplines, the program's design should be shaped by the intellectual and imaginative powers and competencies that students need, rather than by conventional "subjects." The aphorism, "less is more" should dominate: curricular decisions are to be directed toward the students' attempt to gain mastery rather than by the teacher's effort to cover content.
3. The school's goals should apply to all students, but the means to these goals will vary as these students themselves vary. School practice should be tailor-made to meet the needs of every group of adolescents.
4. Teaching and learning should be personalized to the maximum feasible extent. No teacher should have direct responsibility for more than eighty students; decisions about the course of study, the use of students' and teachers' time, and the choice of teaching materials and specific pedagogies must be placed in the hands of the principal and staff.
5. The governing metaphor of the school should be student as worker rather than the more familiar metaphor of teacher as deliverer of instructional services. Accordingly, a prominent pedagogy will be coaching, to provoke students to learn how to learn and thus to teach themselves.
6. Students embarking on secondary school studies are those who show competence in language and elementary mathematics. Students of traditional high school age who do not yet have appropriate levels of competence to start secondary school studies will be provided with intensive remedial work so they can quickly meet those standards. The diploma

should be awarded on a successful demonstration of mastery for graduation—an Exhibition. This Exhibition by the student of his or her grasp
of the central skills and knowledge of the school's program may be
jointly administered by the faculty and higher authorities. Because the
diploma is awarded when earned, the school's program proceeds with
no strict age grading and with no system of credits earned by time spent
in class. The emphasis is on the students' demonstration that they can
do important things.

7. The tone of the school should explicitly and self-consciously stress the
values of unanxious expectation (I won't threaten you, but I expect
much of you), of trust (unless it is abused), and decency (the values of
fairness, generosity, and tolerance). Incentives appropriate to the
schools' students and teachers should be emphasized, and parents
should be treated as essential collaborators.

8. The principal and teachers should perceive of themselves first as gener-
alists (teachers and scholars in general education) and next as specialists
(experts in a particular discipline). Staff should expect multiple obligations (teacher–counselor–manager) and a sense of commitment to the
entire school.

9. Administrative and budget targets should include substantial time for
collective planning by teachers, competitive salaries for staff, and an
ultimate per-pupil cost not more than 10 percent higher than that at traditional schools. Administrative plans may have to show the phased
reduction or elimination of some services now provided for students in
many traditional comprehensive high schools.[42]

Few educators would argue with the logic of most of these principles,
but some, such as Principles 6 and 7, are questionable. For example, part of
Principle 6 says that, "Students of traditional high-school age who do not yet
have appropriate levels of competence to start secondary-school studies will
be provided with intensive remedial work so they can quickly meet those
standards." If remediation was that simple, quick, and sure, it would be
common practice. The fact is that it is easier to talk about remediation than
to accomplish it. The same is true about treating parents as "essential collaborators," as called for in Principle 7. Teachers have been trying to do that for
years; it is the majority of parents who have been reluctant collaborators.

All ideas about educational reform ultimately come down to what it is
that students are expected to know and be able to do. Aristotle noted the lack
of agreement in his day and we have the same lack of agreement today. Each
group of reformers is simply one more group who thinks that the current
emphasis is wrong and that it should be something else. No matter how
things change, it is a good idea to keep in mind that teachers can only do so
much. In trying to do one thing they must, because of time restrictions, do

less of something else. For example, in X amount of time, content breadth must come at the expense of content depth. Loading more expectations on teachers will decrease, not increase, the effectiveness of schools.

Distinguishing Characteristics of Progressivism in Its "Pure" Form

1. The role of education is to prepare students to live in a democratic society.
2. The curriculum should be interdisciplinary and structured so that students work at solving relevant problems and find it necessary to acquire certain skills and understandings in order to solve those problems. Students should learn how to think rather than what to think.
3. Textbooks, memorization, and other traditional tools and techniques should be replaced, as much as possible, with actual experiences and problem solving.

Points of Contention

1. The main goals of education should be to pass on the cultural and historical heritage of the society and to prepare people to compete successfully in life and in the job market.
2. A subject-centered curriculum allows teachers to develop the expertise needed to help students learn in-depth. Time spent trying to integrate knowledge must come at the expense of time spent acquiring more knowledge.
3. While the application of knowledge is critical, students cannot apply what they do not know. Good classroom instruction saves time by helping students profit from what others learned by trial and error.
4. Progressivism ignores the basic competitive nature of our society and tends to sacrifice high standards for good feelings.

Existentialism

Existentialism is built on Protagoras's idea that man is the measure of all things. It takes the position that all people are unique individuals and must define, and find, happiness for themselves. **Ivan Illich,** a noted Existentialist, maintained, in *Deschooling Society*,[43] that we did not need schools at all. He believed that education should take place throughout society, not just in school buildings. In 1921, **A. S. Neill,** another Existentialist, started a boarding school in Suffolk, England. The name of the school was **Summerhill** and it had a maximum enrollment of about 50 students aged five through 15, most of whom were children of wealthy Americans. In his book, *Summerhill,* Neill describes his Existentialist views and the operating philosophy of Summerhill.

> *My view is that a child is innately wise and realistic. If left to himself without adult suggestion of any kind, he will develop as far as he is capable of*

developing.... We set out to make a school in which we should allow children freedom to be themselves. In order to do this we had to renounce all discipline, all direction, all suggestion, all moral training, all religious instruction.[44]

Another educator with Existentialist views is **John Holt.** He wrote that:

Learning is not everything, and certainly one piece of learning is as good as another.... In short, the school should be a great smorgasbord of intellectual, artistic, creative, and athletic activities, from which each child could take whatever he wanted, and as much as he wanted, or as little.[45]

Distinguishing Characteristics of Existentialism in Its "Pure" Form
1. Each person should have the freedom and the responsibility to choose what, when, and how to learn.
2. Any planned curriculum will, by definition, infringe on the freedom of individuals to make choices.

Points of Contention
1. Learners are not aware of what they do not know and therefore cannot make wise choices about what to learn.
2. Society as a whole is often called upon to help individuals deal with the consequences of poor choices so it has a vested interest in doing what it can to teach people how to make wise choices.

SUMMARY

Since the time of the ancient Greeks, people have debated what students should learn and why they should learn it. The debate continues today with the different positions reflecting different philosophies of education.

Perennialism focuses on acquiring knowledge for its own sake. Perennialists see the knowledge, skills, and understandings that have been developed by mankind over the centuries as being the richest source of knowledge. They would make the study of original writings that have withstood the test of time, the classics, the *Great Books of the Western World*, the focal point of the curriculum. Robert M. Hutchins and Mortimer J. Adler are educators often associated with Perennialism.

Essentialism also sees great value in learning from the past and, like the Perennialists, would have a single, rigorous, subject-centered curriculum for everyone. Students would have few, if any, curricular choices. Typically, Essentialists see knowledge as being more utilitarian than do Perennialists and they advocate clear and measurable goals. William Bagley, Arthur Bestor, and Admiral Hyman G. Rickover are educators often associated with Essentialism.

Progressivism stands in contrast to Perennialism and Essentialism. Schools are seen not as places where students simply prepare to live in a democratic society, but as places where they follow democratic principles every day. School is not preparation for life, it is life. The curriculum is typically student-centered and more concerned with process, particularly with problem solving, than with content. John Dewey, William Kilpatrick, and Boyd Bode are educators often associated with Progressivism.

Existentialism remains a fringe philosophy. Few people are willing to grant students the kind of freedoms advocated by Existentialists for fear that our cultural heritage would be lost and that students would be ill prepared to take their places as productive members of society. Ivan Illich and A. S. Neill are educators often associated with Existentialism.

SO HOW DOES THIS AFFECT MY TEACHING?

Your beliefs about what students should learn and be able to do, and how they can be best helped to learn, will largely determine what you do in your classroom. Those beliefs will reflect your philosophy of education. Further, understanding philosophic positions will make it easier to deal with colleagues, students, parents, and administrators, each of whom may be operating from a different philosophic position. By understanding their starting points you can better understand where they are headed and why, and you can better decide which, if any, of them, you want to join. Ultimately, you need to determine what you want your students to know and be able to do and you need to have some valid way to determine whether they know and can do those things.

KEY TERMS, PEOPLE, AND IDEAS

Educational Philosophy
Elder Sophists, 450 B.C.—First Professional Teachers—Rhetoric
Socrates—Socratic Method—Inborn Knowledge
Plato—Truth through thought—Individual Differences—Faculty Theory
Aristotle—Learn via the senses—Syllogistic Reasoning
John Locke—*Tabula Rasa* (Blank Sheet), 1690
Perennialism—Hutchins, Adler
Essentialism—Bagley, Bestor, Rickover
Progressivism—Dewey, Sizer
Gary Plan
Student-centered, Subject-centered
Existentialism—Illich, Neill, Holt

ENDNOTES

1. Dewey, John, *Experience and Education* (New York: Collier Cooks, 1938), p. 6.

2. Swain, Joseph., and William H. Armstrong, *The Peoples of the Ancient World* (New York: Harper and Row, 1959), p. 191.

3. Perry, Marvin, *A History of the World* (Boston: Houghton Mifflin, 1985), p. 69.

4. Farnighetti, Robert, ed., *The World Almanac and Book of Facts: 1995* (Mahwah, N. J.: Funk & Wagnalls, 1994), p. 219.

5. Saettler, Paul, *The Evolution of American Educational Technology* (Englewood, Colo.: Libraries Unlimited, 1990), p. 24.

6. Saettler, p. 48.

7. From Plato's dialogue entitled "Protagoras," as cited in Kaufman, Walter (ed.), *Philosophic Classics: Thales to St. Thomas* (Englewood Cliffs, N. J.: Prentice-Hall, 1961), p. 72.

8. Kaufman, p. 73.

9. Saettler, p. 25.

10. Saettler, p. 24.

11. Saettler, pp. 25–26.

12. Grunwald, Lisa, and Jeff Goldberg, "The Amazing Minds of Infants," *Life,* July 1993, pp. 46–60.

13. Saettler, p. 26.

14. Locke, John, "Essay Concerning Humane Understanding," 1690, under "Locke, John," in *Encyclopedia Brittanica* (Chicago: Encyclopedia Britannica, Inc., 1960), Vol. 14, pp. 273–274.

15. Morse, William C. and G. Max Wingo, *Psychology and Teaching*, 2nd ed. (Chicago: Scott, Foresman, 1962), p. 242.

16. Aristotle (384–322 B.C.), *The Politics*, Book 8, Chs. 1 and 2, trans. by Carnes Lord. (Chicago: The University of Chicago Press, 1984), pp. 229–30.

17. Hutchins, Robert M., *The Higher Learning in America* (New Haven: Yale University Press, 1936), p. 66.

18. Hutchins, p. 67.

19. Pancrazio, Sally B., Dean, College of Education, Illinois State University, "Functions Assigned to Public Schools," Personal letter dated Oct. 22, 1993.

20. Whitehead, Alfred North, *Essays in Science and Philosophy* (New York: Philosophical Library, 1947), p. 176.

21. Bennett, William J., "Why the West?," *National Review*, Vol. 40 (May 27, 1988), pp. 37–39.

22. Adler, Mortimer J., *The Paideia Project, An Educational Manifesto* (New York: Macmillan Publishing, 1982), p. 4.

23. Adler, p. 6.

24. Adler, p. 21.

25. Ellis, Arthur K., John J. Cogan, and Kenneth R. Howey, *The Foundations of Education*, (Englewood Cliffs, N. J.: Prentice-Hall, 1981), pp. 85–86.

26. Bagley, William C., "The Case for Essentialism in Education," *NEA Journal*, Vol. 30, no. 7 (1941), pp. 201–202.

27. Bestor, Arthur, *The Restoration of Learning* (New York: Knopf, 1956), pp. 48–49.

28. Bestor, p. 79.

29. Bestor, p. 120.

30. Rickover, Hyman G., "European vs. American Secondary Schools," *Phi Delta Kappan,* Vol. 40 (November 1958), p. 61.

31. Dewey, John, *Experience and Education* (New York, Collier Books, 1938), p. 22.

32. Dewey, John, *The Way Out of Educational Confusion* (Cambridge, Mass.: Harvard University Press, 1931), p. 36.

33. Sizer, Theodore R., *Horace's Compromise: The Dilemma of the American High School* (Boston: Houghton Mifflin, 1984).

34. Coalition of Essential Schools, Box 1969, Brown University, Providence, Rhode Island 02912.

35. Sizer, Theodore R., *Horace's School: Redesigning the American High School,* (Boston: Houghton Mifflin, 1992).

36. Sizer, *Horace's School,* p. 109.

37. Sizer, *Horace's School,* pp. 110–111.

38. Sizer, *Horace's School,* p. 117.

39. Sizer, *Horace's School,* p. 123.

40. Flexner, Abraham, and Frank Bachman, *The Gary Schools* (New York: General Education Board, 1918).

41. Sizer, *Horace's School,* p. 11.

42. Sizer, *Horace's School,* pp. 207–209.

43. Illich, Ivan, *Deschooling Society* (New York: Harper and Row, 1971).

44. Neill, A. S., *Summerhill* (New York: Hart Publishing, 1960), p. 4.

45. Holt, John, *How Children Fail* (New York: Dell, 1964), pp. 177–180.

2

WHY THE SCHOOLS
ARE AS THEY ARE

RATIONALE

There are over 2.4 million teachers in the United States, and each one has his or her own philosophy of education. Further, they teach over 42 million K–12 students[1] with widely varying cultural and socio-economic backgrounds. Critics would have us believe that this diversity contributes to chaos and ineffectiveness in our schools. There is, however, evidence that shows that our schools are not nearly as chaotic or ineffective as the critics claim and there are logical explanations for why our schools are as they are.

This chapter will, first, present evidence concerning the effectiveness of schools. You can compare this evidence with that presented by critics of the schools and then reach your own conclusions. The chapter will then examine, in chronological order, a few of the ideas and ideals that seem central to most secondary schools in the United States and which account for the high degree of curricular consistency. Many of these ideas and ideals were expressed in national legislation and in reports and studies of national renown. This information, in conjunction with your personal, evolving, philosophy of education, will help you decide what to teach and how to teach it.

SAMPLE OBJECTIVES

You will be able, in writing, to:

1. Explain how ideals such as educating all the children of all the people, providing for individual differences, and preparing virtually all students for college, got started in the United States and why they persist.

2. Describe at least two events that strengthened the idea that time, rather than competence, should be used to measure education in the United States.
3. Describe the provisions of at least two federal legislative acts that directly affected education.
4. Take a position for or against the typical practice in schools of holding time stable and allowing achievement to vary, and support that position with at least two cause–effect reasons.

THE EFFECTIVENESS OF OUR SCHOOLS

While few would argue that our schools are perfect, they are far more effective than critics would have us believe. One piece of evidence is the declining dropout rate. In 1967, the dropout rate was 17 percent. In 1990, it was down to 12.1 percent.[2] If schools were as bad as some critics claim, it is unlikely that increasing numbers of students would stay in them. In large cities the dropout rate typically is higher than in other locations.

A second piece of evidence is found in the 26th Annual Phi Delta Kappa/Gallup Poll of "The Public's Attitudes Toward the Public Schools." The researchers considered one of the most revealing questions to be "What grade would you give the school your oldest child attends?" In the 1994 poll, 70 percent of the parents rated the schools A or B. When asked to rate public schools *nationally,* only 22 percent of the respondents graded them A or B. "Parents' responses made it clear that the more one knows about a school, the more likely one is to think well of its performance."[3]

A third piece of evidence is the mean scores on the Scholastic Aptitude Test (SAT) and the American College Testing Program Test (ACT). As Tables 2.1 and 2.2 show, those scores are fairly stable, as are the number of students taking the tests.

Finally, judging from the scores, and despite the differences in educational philosophies and student backgrounds, our schools seem to be teaching content that is fairly consistent from coast to coast and from border to

TABLE 2.1   SAT Mean Scores and Number of Participants 1990–1993*

	1990	1991	1992	1993	1994
Verbal	424	422	423	424	423
Math	476	474	476	478	479
Participants	1,033,000	NA	1,034,000	1,109,000	1,050,000

Maximum scores are 800 for verbal and 800 for math
**World Almanac,* 1994, p. 198, and 1995, p. 223.

TABLE 2.2   ACT Mean Scores and Number of Participants 1990–1993*

	1990	1991	1992	1993	1994
Composite	20.6	20.6	20.6	20.7	20.8
English	20.5	20.3	20.2	20.3	20.3
Math	19.9	20.0	20.0	20.1	20.2
Participants	817,000	796,000	832,000	875,000	891,700

Maximum scores are 36 for English and 36 for math
*World Almanac, 1994, p. 199, and 1995, p. 223; also 1993 data provided directly by
ACT via telephone on July 14, 1994.

border. The consistency itself is important because it reflects a general agreement among millions of people about certain basics that our schools should
be teaching. More important, however, are the factors that account for the
curricular consistency. Knowing about them will help you better understand
why our schools are as they are, and where we seem to be headed. Further,
the information will help you identify which of the many proposed curricular and structural changes are most likely to succeed, and why.

FROM PILGRIMS TO PROGRESSIVES

How and Why Secondary Schools Were Established

In 1635, the village of Boston, in the Massachusetts Bay Colony, established
the **Boston Latin Grammar School,** the first secondary school in the New
World. In establishing this school the Pilgrims also established the subject-
centered, liberal arts curriculum as the standard model for secondary
schools. This happened because the main purpose of the Latin Grammar
School was to prepare students to go on to colleges and universities. Harvard was established in 1636 so students could continue their education here
rather than having to go back to England and Europe. In order to properly
prepare students, the secondary curriculum was largely based on the
entrance requirements and expectations of colleges and universities. At this
time this meant students needed to know Greek and Latin, rhetoric, mathematics, and philosophy. They got this liberal arts background via a Perennialist, subject-centered curriculum.

When the "lower" schools were established later, they accepted, as one
of their main roles, the preparation of students for secondary schools. To do
this, they followed essentially the same subject-centered, liberal arts curriculum. A look at a typical K–12 curriculum today will show that, for the most
part, the initial power structure is still with us. When colleges change their

entrance requirements, high schools change their curriculums to prepare their graduates to meet those requirements. Those changes, in turn, prompt changes in the K–8 curriculum.

The State's Interest in Education—Educating All the Children at Public Expense

In 1642, the General Court of the Massachusetts Bay Colony, the colonial legislative body, passed a law requiring that parents ensure that their children could read and understand the Bible and the laws of the colony. This law was reinforced in 1647, with the passage of the "**Old Deluder Satan**" law. This law said that:

> *It being one chief project of the old deluder, Satan: to keep men from the knowledge of the Scriptures . . . it is therefore ordered that every township in this jurisdiction, after the Lord hath increased your number to 50 householders, shall then forthwith appoint one within their town to teach all such children as shall resort to him to write and read . . . and it is further ordered, that where any town shall increase to the number of 100 families or householders they shall set up a grammar school, the master thereof being able to instruct youth so far as shall be fitted for the university.*[4]

The law established two more precedents that are still with us. One was that **all the children of all the people should be educated.** This is noteworthy because until this time, societies had restricted formal education either to males, to citizens, or to children of the wealthy or powerful. A second precedent was that the state had the right to pass laws concerning education including curricular focus, attendance, and public support. The **public support** precedent was challenged in 1872, when some citizens in **Kalamazoo,** Michigan, challenged the right of the city to use taxes to support secondary education. The issue was settled when the Supreme Court of Michigan ruled that the City of Kalamazoo had the right to establish, and support by taxation, schools at any level.[5]

College Preparation versus General Education

By 1750, it was clear that not everyone went on to college and that the secondary curriculum needed to be broadened. **Benjamin Franklin** was one of the first to argue that schools should prepare students for vocations as well as for college, and it was at his suggestion that the first **Academy,** the model for later comprehensive high schools, was started in Philadelphia in 1751. In addition to the courses required for college preparation, such as mathematics, Greek, Latin, and philosophy, the Academy offered courses in vocational areas such as carpentry, surveying, and bookkeeping. Part of that academy became the University of Pennsylvania. While comprehensive high schools are now the most common type of high school, their curriculums are still centered on preparation for college. The reason is as follows.

Since colonial times, higher education has been seen as the surest way to a "good life." While we know that all students do not go on to college, most parents hope that their children will and, in 1991, about 60 percent of all high school graduates did enroll in two- or four-year colleges immediately after graduation.[6] It seems reasonable to assume that as long as parents see a college education as a goal for their children, high schools will continue to make preparation for college a central part of their curriculums. Critics of this ideal should be asked two questions: (1) would they like their own children to go on to college, and (2) do they know many parents who do not hope that their children will go on to college? Preparation for college, with all that it implies for the high school curriculum, is likely to remain a central curricular factor for a long time.

Land Ordinance of 1785—First Federal Action Concerning Education

The Land Ordinance of 1785 specified that land in the Northwest Territories (the present states of Ohio, Indiana, Illinois, Michigan, Wisconsin, and parts of Minnesota) be surveyed into townships six miles on a side; that each township be divided into 36 sections each containing 640 acres; and that one section in each township, or the proceeds from the sale of it, be used for public education.[7]

This act is significant because it marks the beginning of federal involvement in education—an area not mentioned in the Constitution and therefore an area reserved for the states. It also establishes the precedent for federal aid to education, aid that is always accompanied by certain conditions and constraints. Federal aid to education is a clear example of the economic Golden Rule—he who has the gold, makes the rules. The person or people who control the money also control how it is spent.

The Morrill Land Grant Act of 1862— Vocational Education Emerges

In 1630, the total colonial population was about 4,600. By 1860, the population in the United States had grown to about 31 million, and in 1993 it stood at about 250 million.[8] As the population increased, so did the demand for all kinds of goods and services. Lawmakers in Washington recognized the need for greater efficiency in agriculture and manufacturing and they also recognized that the Perennialist curriculums of the colleges and universities were not addressing this national need. Consequently, Congress passed, and in 1862 President Lincoln signed into law, the **Morrill Land Grant Act.**

The act granted public lands to the states for the specific purpose of providing for the foundation and maintenance of colleges,

> *where the leading object shall be, without excluding other scientific and classical studies, and including military tactics, to teach such branches of learning as are related to agriculture and the mechanic arts ... in order to promote the liberal and practical education of the industrial classes in the several pursuits and professions of life.*[9]

Today there is a land-grant university in each state with Purdue, the Massachusetts Institute of Technology, Cornell, Michigan State, Ohio State, Pennsylvania State, and the universities of California, Illinois, and Wisconsin being among the largest.[10] The act is included here because it marked the first time that Congress specified curricular content. Vocational education became a legitimate part of the curriculum for higher education and the long dominance of the Perennialist philosophy was directly challenged. In time, vocational education was included in the curriculums of secondary schools.

Passage of the Morrill Act in 1862 did not end the debate about what to teach and why to teach it. In the last half of the 1800s, the curriculums of most high schools were still primarily intended to prepare students for college, but there was growing diversity. Schools were trying to provide a satisfactory curriculum for the many students who did not go on to college.

The diversity was causing problems because, in order for their college-bound students to get into colleges, the high schools had to specify what subject-area content they had completed. If high schools could agree on a common curriculum that would satisfy most colleges, advisement would be simplified.

Committee of Ten Report, 1893—Essentialism and Instructional Time

In 1892, the National Education Association (NEA) appointed the **Committee of Ten** (officially, The Committee on Secondary School Studies). The purposes of the Committee were to: (1) try to bring order to the diverse secondary education programs, (2) reconcile the demands of those who saw high school in terms of preparation for college with those who saw high school as preparation for the world of work, and (3) increase articulation between high schools and colleges. Its deliberations were heavily influenced by men such as Charles Eliot, chair of the committee. Eliot was president of Harvard University and, like most of his peers, had attended schools with predominantly Perennialist curriculums.

The report began with the premise that while not all students went on to college, all students would benefit from studying the same subjects. The Committee then considered nine subjects: (1) Latin; (2) Greek; (3) English; (4) other modern languages; (5) mathematics; (6) physics, astronomy, and chemistry; (7) natural history (biology, including botany, zoology, and physiology); (8) history, civil government, and political economy; and (9) geography (physical geography, geology, and meteorology). It concluded that these subjects were equally valuable if well taught. It did *not* consider the subjects of art, music, physical education, and vocational education because these subjects were not required for admission to college.[11] The inclusion of "modern" subjects such as physiology and geology, and the exclusion of art, music, physical education, and vocational education are characteristic of Essentialism.

The Committee also recommended that all pupils who studied a given subject study it in the same way and to the same extent, and it exemplified its thinking by proposing four high school programs: Classical, Latin Scientific, Modern Languages, and English. The Modern Languages and English programs did not require Latin, so they were considered by the committee to be inferior.[12] For each program, the Committee proposed specific courses and, of importance here, a specific number of class periods per week for each subject. This last element had the effect of formally equating learning with time under instruction rather than with competence.

Time under Instruction and the Carnegie Unit

The idea of equating time under instruction with learning was strengthened in 1895, when the **Committee on College Entrance Requirements** recommended that high schools assign credits for various subjects in order to systematize the college admission process. The ideas of specifying a given number of instructional periods per week, and assigning credits to subjects for the purpose of college admission, were brought together in 1906. In that year, the Carnegie Foundation for the Advancement of Teaching recommended a way of standardizing measures of instructional time. It recommended that instructional time be divided into "units" and it defined a unit as satisfactory completion of a subject that met five days per week, a minimum of 40 minutes per period, and a minimum of 120 clock hours for the school year.[13] The **Carnegie Unit** was born.

The Carnegie unit fit well with the operation of our schools. Since colonial times schools have operated on the basis of time. Teachers are paid for teaching a given number of days per year and schools receive state funding on the basis of the number of students in daily attendance. Education is assessed in terms of instructional time, with learner competence being assumed on the basis of a passing grade. The Education 2000 Act suggests the establishment of national competency standards, and those standards are being developed by national councils in the various subject areas. However, even when the standards are fully developed, compliance with them will be voluntary.

A switch to assessing education on the basis of learner competencies rather than time under instruction would require, at the least, the development of broadly accepted competencies, a new basis for paying teachers, and a new basis for funding schools. Such changes will not be made easily. Teachers need to balance all that they would like to do with the time available and, most often, there is more to do than time allows.

In addition to establishing time, rather than competence, as the measure of education, the various committee reports at the beginning of the 1900s had other long-lasting effects. One was to perpetuate traditional subjects and methods. This included not only organizing curriculums on the basis of separate subjects, but also the idea that student interests were of little importance. Further, the use of whole-class instruction was established as standard rather than individualized or small-group instruction.

The effects of the committee reports in the early 1900s did not satisfy those who saw a need to expand the traditional high school curriculum and methods. In fact, they had just the opposite effect; they perpetuated the status quo. The status quo, at a time when the industrial base of the country was growing faster than at any previous time, was not acceptable. The country needed people who could take their place in the workforce and it looked to the schools to prepare those workers.

The Smith–Hughes Act

In 1917, Congress responded by passing the Smith–Hughes Act. The purpose of the act was to provide federal aid for education in vocational areas such as home economics, agricultural, trade, and industrial subjects in high schools. It accomplished this goal and, in addition, it strengthened the role of the federal government in establishing curricular goals for the country as a whole. The National Education Association (NEA), which is now the largest teacher organization in the United States, was not wholly supportive of this legislation. It pointed out that the establishment of vocational education as an alternative to the traditional curriculum might have the effect of establishing a two-tracked system with the vocational track always seen as inferior to the college preparatory track.

Commission on the Reorganization of Secondary Education

In 1918, another NEA committee, the Commission on the Reorganization of Secondary Education, issued its recommendations about how to best resolve the continuing problems of preparing students for college and for life. Its report, heavily influenced by the thinking of Abraham Flexner and John Dewey, stated that:

> *Secondary education should be determined by the needs of the society to be served, the character of the individuals to be educated, and the knowledge of the educational theory and practice available.*[14]

The Seven Cardinal Principles

The Commission saw the main purpose of secondary schools as giving "flesh and blood reality to the ideal of democracy." To help do this, the Commission listed seven **Cardinal Principles of Secondary Education.** In summary, those principles called for secondary school curriculums to include:

1. *Health*—Good health habits need to be taught and encouraged by the school. The community and school should cooperate in fulfilling the health needs of all youngsters and adults.
2. *Command of fundamental processes*—The secondary school should accept a responsibility for continuing to teach and polish the basic tools of learning, such as arithmetical computation, reading, and writing, that were begun in the elementary school.
3. *Worthy home membership*—Schools should give students an understanding of the interrelationships of the family in order for the give and take to be a healthy, happy affair. Proper adjustment as a family member will lead to proper acceptance of responsibility as a family leader later in life.
4. *Vocation*—The secondary school should teach students to appreciate all vocations. The basic skills of a variety of vocations should be made available to students who have the need or desire for them.
5. *Citizenship*—The students' basic commitment to proper citizenship must be fostered and strengthened during the adolescent years. The secondary school needs to assume this responsibility not only in the social sciences classes but in all subjects.
6. *Proper use of leisure time*—The students should be provided opportunities while in secondary school to expand the available possibilities of leisure time. (The Commission felt that using leisure time properly would enrich the total personality.)
7. *Ethical Character*—The secondary school should organize its activities and personal relationships to reflect good ethical character, both to serve as an exemplar and to involve the student in a series of activities that will provide opportunities to make ethically correct decisions.[15]

Where to draw the line in balancing the Progressivist goals exemplified in the Cardinal Principles against the more traditional goals of preparing students for college remains a major point of contention. Time and money are two of the limiting factors.

Edward L. Thorndike—Discrediting the Faculty Theory

One of the ideas that persisted since ancient Greek times was that the mind consisted of specific "faculties" which, like muscles, could be developed by specific exercises, such as the study of particular subjects. It was largely because this idea was accepted so widely and for so long that subjects such as Greek and Latin remained in the secondary curriculum. In 1924, **Edward L. Thorndike** (1874–1949) conducted a study that did much to discredit the "faculty" theory.

Using a sample of 8,564 students, Thorndike compared gains in general intelligence (as reflected by intelligence quotient (IQ) scores) of students who studied English, history, geometry, and Latin, with those who studied English, history, geometry, and shopwork. If the faculty theory was valid, students who studied Latin should have scored higher than those who studied shopwork. They did not. Thorndike concluded that, "the expectation of any large difference in general improvement of the mind from one study rather than another seems doomed to disappointment."[16] Nonetheless, there are still some who believe that studying certain subjects, such as math or computer programming, will help develop certain mental skills, such as logic.

The Eight-Year Study

The great social and economic changes occurring during the early 1900s (mass immigrations and the flourishing of the Industrial Revolution, for example) made it a time ripe for experimentation in the schools. It was the golden age of Progressivism. It was during this period that the Progressive Education Association (which adopted its name from the Progressive branch of the Republican political party) commissioned what remains today as one of the best controlled, long-term, studies in education—**The Eight-Year Study.**

After a year-long study, the Progressive Education Association identified a number of weaknesses in the secondary schools. Critics of education today claim that many of these weaknesses still exist. Among the weaknesses identified were that schools:

1. did not have a clear-cut, definite, central purpose;
2. failed to give students a sincere appreciation of their heritage as American citizens;
3. did not prepare students adequately for the responsibilities of community life;

4. seldom challenged the student of first-rate ability to work up to the level of his intellectual powers;
5. neither knew their students well nor guided them wisely;
6. seldom provided opportunities for students to release or develop their creative energies;
7. had curriculums far removed from the real concerns of youth;
8. taught subjects that had lost much of their vitality and significance; and
9. had principals and teachers laboring earnestly, often sacrificially, but usually without any comprehensive evaluation of the results of their work.[17]

The Progressivists wanted to know how students who went to high schools with "Progressive" curriculums would compare, after four years of college, with students who had gone to high schools with "traditional" curriculums. To find out, the Progressive Education Association (PEA) persuaded more than 300 colleges and universities to release 30 secondary schools from the restrictions of college entrance requirements. The graduates of these high schools would not have to meet Carnegie Unit requirements for college entrance (120 clock hours in a subject during a school year with 16 units in specific subject areas required for graduation).

A Commission appointed by the PEA selected the 30 public and private secondary schools, large and small, urban and rural, and coast to coast, on the basis of their willingness to implement a "progressive" curriculum. Each graduate of one of the 30 schools was matched with a graduate of a "traditional" high school (who had therefore met the usual college entrance requirements) on the basis of age, sex, race, scholastic aptitude scores, home and community background, and interests. This matching was done by the colleges and resulted in 1,475 matched pairs of subjects. The results of the study were published in 1942, and showed, among other things, that graduates of the thirty schools:

1. earned a slightly higher total grade average;
2. earned higher grade averages in all subject fields except foreign languages;
3. received slightly more academic honors in each year;
4. were more often judged to possess a high degree of intellectual curiosity and drive;
5. were more often judged to be precise, systematic, and objective in their thinking; and
6. more often demonstrated a high degree of resourcefulness in meeting new situations.[18]

With such promising results from a carefully controlled longitudinal study, one would expect a flood of proposals for developing more Progressive curriculums. It did not happen. In 1942, the country was embroiled in

World War II. Attention was focused on Germany and Japan, not on America's public schools. The results of the Eight-Year Study were largely ignored.

The study did have its critics and at least one of their points is difficult to ignore. Despite the careful matching and tracking of the students, it was virtually impossible for the investigators to document the specific commonalties of the "Progressive" curriculums implemented by the schools. Some schools said their curriculum was "experimental" while others simply said theirs was "nontraditional." This problem meant that the study's findings could not be easily generalized. There was no single "Progressive" curriculum that could be credited with the success of the students so there was nothing that could easily replace the existing "traditional" curriculums.

The results of the Eight-Year Study did have some impact. An increasing number of educators accepted the Commission's conclusions that: (1) "success in the college of liberal arts does not depend upon the study of certain subjects for a certain period in high school, and (2) there are many different kinds of experience by which students may prepare themselves for successful work in college."[19] Further, some educators began to seriously consider alternatives to traditional content and methods. They were, for example, willing to look at content with respect to its relevance, or lack of relevance, to students—something of little concern to traditionalists. Some were also willing to replace textbooks, to one extent or another, with instructional materials that they, themselves, developed or organized. Still others began to de-emphasize rote memorization and to increase active student participation. The Eight-Year Study did have an effect, but primarily for those who already accepted at least some Progressivist ideas.

POST-WORLD WAR II TO THE PRESENT

The Supreme Court—Separate Is Not Equal

In comparison to the activities in education from 1890 through the 1930s, the 1940s and 1950s were relatively quiet. High school curriculums remained largely conservative and traditional with occasional experiments with Progressive ideas. In 1954, however, the Supreme Court, in *Brown* v. *Board of Education of Topeka*, overturned *Plessey* v. *Ferguson* (1896), and ruled that separate schools for blacks and whites were inherently unequal. The ruling set in motion massive efforts at school integration including the allocation of millions of dollars for school bussing. Whether the money spent on bussing could have been used in better ways is debatable. What is less debatable is that, as the number of students being bussed increased: (1) the size of schools increased (in part, to minimize bussing problems); (2) the intimacy of neighborhood schools where teachers, parents, and students knew each other fairly well, was greatly reduced, and (3) fewer students were able to take advantage of time before and after school to get extra help from teachers. As is often the case, the solution to one problem caused other problems.

Sputnik and the National Defense Education Act

On October 4, 1957, the Soviet Union launched **Sputnik I,** the first man-made earth satellite. This was the time of the Cold War between the United States and the Soviet Union, so the launching, and the message that Sputnik continually beeped to Earth, "Communism is all powerful," did not sit well with the American public. A large number of Americans, used to seeing the United States first in everything, feared that we were losing our technological edge. Congress responded in 1958 by passing the **National Defense Education Act** (NDEA). This act did two major things. First, it provided millions of dollars for the development of new programs in math and science and, later, in foreign languages. Second, it caused many people who had embraced Progressivist ideas to change their minds and return to the subject-centered, Essentialist curriculum, which they saw as more rigorous and more accountable.

The Great Society and Compensatory Education

In 1965, the federal government again exerted its influence on education. With the same kind of national vision exhibited by President Franklin Roosevelt when he unveiled his New Deal program in 1933, President Lyndon B. Johnson unveiled his **Great Society** program in 1965. As part of that program Congress passed the **Elementary and Secondary Education Act.** One of the main provisions of this act was to allocate $1.3 billion to improve education for poor and minority children. Chief among these compensatory education programs was, and is, the **Head Start** program. This program was designed to provide special help for children aged three to five who were poor and disadvantaged. It is mentioned here to demonstrate a point.

In 1968, Westinghouse Learning Corp., under contract with the U. S. Office of Economic Opportunity, conducted a national-level evaluation of the Head Start program. It concluded that "Head Start children did not differ significantly in the elementary grades on most intellectual and socioemotional variables from their peers who had not enrolled in the program."[20] In 1985, a second national-level study was conducted, this one by CSR (McKey et al.). The results of this study were more positive than those of the earlier study, but the conclusion was that any gains children might make in the Head Start program were short-term and "washed out" by the end of the first or second grade.[21] Despite evidence that the Head Start program is not effective in promoting significant academic achievement, it is politically popular and each year receives millions dollars that might be spent more wisely. Political expediency sometimes supersedes empirical data.

The government continued to exert its influence on behalf of disadvantaged students. In 1968, the **Bilingual Act** was passed. This act required that schools take steps to help non-English-speaking students learn. In most cases this meant providing these students with extra help in learning English and many teachers were trained to teach **English-as-a-Second-Language (ESL).** In a few cases, people argued that the act required schools to provide instruction in the students' native language. That view is rapidly losing ground to the majority view that schools should help all students learn to speak standard English.

In 1975, Congress passed the **Education for All Handicapped Children Act** (Public Law 94–142). This act became law because some states, finding that educating the handicapped was expensive, wanted to limit the opportunities they had to provide. PL 94–142 required that public schools: (1) evaluate the status of students with special needs at least once each year, (2) develop an Individualized Educational Plan (IEP) for every handicapped student, and (3) place each handicapped student in the least restrictive environment (which means that, whenever possible, students should be placed in the classrooms in which they would normally be placed if they were not handicapped). This law was strengthened in 1986, by passage of Amendment 99–457, which extends the rights and protections provided in PL 94–142 to handicapped children ages three to five.

The significance of PL 94–142 and PL 99–457 is threefold. First, it demonstrates, once again, strong federal involvement in education. Second, the mandating of Individualized Educational Plans means that teachers need to think about the extent to which the objectives, content, instructional procedures, and experiences of their courses might be modified to accommodate students with special needs. Third, the fact that teachers might have severely disabled students in their classrooms raises questions about their preparation for dealing with severely handicapped students and the extent of their legal liability. Solving one problem sometimes causes others.

A Nation at Risk

By the end of the 1970s, the economies of countries such as Japan, West Germany, and Korea, countries that the United States had helped rebuild after World War II and the Korean War, were strong and getting stronger. American businessmen complained that American workers were not as well prepared as their counterparts in Europe and Asia. Terrell H. Bell, then U. S. Secretary of Education, formed the **National Commission on Excellence in Education** and asked it to investigate the quality of education in the United States. In 1983, the Commission issued its report and the title, *A Nation at*

Risk, provided an idea of the results. Among other findings, the Commission reported that:

1. International comparisons of student achievement, completed a decade ago, reveal that on 19 academic tests American students were never first or second and, in comparison with other industrialized nations, were last seven times.
2. Some 23 million American adults are functionally illiterate by the simplest tests of everyday reading, writing, and comprehension.
3. About 13 percent of all 17-year-olds in the United States can be considered functionally illiterate. Functional illiteracy among minority youth may run as high as 40 percent.
4. Average achievement of high school students on most standardized tests is now lower than 26 years ago when Sputnik was launched.
5. Over half the population of gifted students do not match their tested ability with comparable achievement in school.
6. The College Board's Scholastic Aptitude Tests (SAT) demonstrate a virtual unbroken decline from 1963 to 1980. Average verbal scores fell over 50 points and average mathematics scores dropped nearly 40 points.
7. Both the number and proportion of students demonstrating superior achievement on the SATs (those with scores of 650 or higher) have also dramatically declined.
8. Many 17-year-olds do not possess the "higher order" intellectual skills we should expect of them. Nearly 40 percent cannot draw inferences from written material; only one-fifth can write a persuasive essay; and only one-third can solve mathematics problems requiring several steps.
9. Business and military leaders complain that they are required to spend millions of dollars on costly remedial education and training programs in such basic skills as reading, writing, spelling, and computation. The Department of the Navy, for example, reported to the Commission that one-quarter of its recent recruits cannot read at the ninth grade level, the minimum needed to understand written safety instructions. Without remedial work they cannot even begin, much less complete, the sophisticated training essential in much of the modern military.[22]

The Commission also found that while "the public understands the primary importance of education as the foundation for a satisfying life, an enlightened and civil society, a strong economy, and a secure nation, it . . . has no patience with undemanding and superfluous high school offerings."[23] Further, it found that:

> *Secondary school curricula have been homogenized, diluted, and diffused to the point that they no longer have a central purpose. In effect, we have a cafeteria-style curriculum in which appetizers and desserts can easily be*

*mistaken for the main course. It also found that this curricular smorgas-
bord, combined with extensive student choice, explains a great deal about
where we find ourselves today.*[24]

In light of its findings, the Commission made five broad recommendations, which were followed by detailed explanations. The first three were that:

1. State and local high school graduation requirements be strengthened
   and that, at a minimum, all students seeking a diploma be required to
   lay the foundation in the Five New Basics by taking the following curriculum during their 4 years of high school: (a) 4 years of English; (b) 3
   years of mathematics; (c) 3 years of science; (d) 3 years of social studies;
   and (e) one-half year of computer science. For the college-bound, 2 years
   of foreign language in high school are strongly recommended in addition to those taken earlier.
2. Schools, colleges, and universities adopt more rigorous and measurable
   standards, and higher expectation for academic performance and student conduct, and the 4-year colleges and universities raise their requirement for admission.
3. Significantly more time be devoted to learning the New Basics. This will
   require more effective use of the existing school day, a longer school day,
   or a lengthened school year.

The fourth recommendation had to do with teachers and teacher preparation. It called for higher standards for teachers, 11-month contracts, financial incentives to attract outstanding students to the teaching profession, and
greater involvement by teachers in planning programs. The fifth recommendation had to do with leadership and fiscal support. Among other things it
said that "The Federal Government has *the primary responsibility* to identify
the national interest in education."[25]

A Nation at Risk profoundly affected education in the United States.
Many high schools adopted the "New Basics" and adjusted their curriculums accordingly. Many elective subjects were deleted and time and
resources reallocated to subjects in the New Basics. In the subject areas themselves, courses such as Pre-Algebra, Consumer Math, and Ecology were
deleted and additional sections of Algebra, Geometry, Trigonometry, Biology, Chemistry, and Physics were provided. High school curriculums
became increasingly subject-centered and academically oriented (Essentialist) and they remain mostly that way today.

America 2000

In 1991, President George Bush released *America 2000, An Education Strategy,*
his vision of what education should be like by the year 2000. Six goals were
central:

1. All children in America will start school ready to learn.
2. The high school graduation rate will increase to at least 90 percent.
3. American students will leave grades four, eight, and twelve having demonstrated competency in challenging subject matter including English, mathematics, science, history, and geography; and every school in America will ensure that all students learn to use their minds, so they may be prepared for responsible citizenship, further learning, and productive employment in our modern economy.
4. U. S. students will be first in the world in science and mathematics achievement.
5. Every adult American will be literate and will possess the knowledge and skills necessary to compete in a global economy and exercise the rights and responsibilities of citizenship.
6. Every school in America will be free of drugs and violence and will offer a disciplined environment conducive to learning.[26]

The goals for America 2000 are far broader than those of earlier goal statements. However, like its predecessors, America 2000 focuses primarily on traditional academic subjects. Further, conspicuous by their absence in *A Nation at Risk* and *America 2000* are recommendations concerning the Fine Arts, Physical Education, Vocational Education, or any of the many other topics and subjects various groups would like to see in the curriculum. Clearly, this does not please everyone, so the debate about what students should learn and why they should learn it continues. There is one difference now, however.

Both *A Nation at Risk* and *America 2000* focus on American students, as a group, reaching higher standards. Since we are talking about millions of students, there is likely to be an increased dependence on the use of standardized tests to determine if students are meeting those higher standards. The focus will shift from what students are taught to what they are able to do. This means there is likely to be an increased emphasis on relatively short-term, measurable, goals. Being able to specify meaningful and measurable goals will be crucial to your success in the classroom.

SUMMARY

Over the years, federal legislation and national reports have been important in shaping education in the United States. Even before the Constitution was written, some colonists had passed laws providing for the education of all the children of all the people, and providing public funding for this purpose. In establishing the secondary school first, the colonists unintentionally established a curricular power structure that remains with us today. In that structure, the entrance requirements of colleges and universities largely dictate what courses the secondary schools will offer. This, in turn, largely dictates what is taught in grades K–8. This structure is unlikely to change as long as most parents want their children to have the opportunity to attend college.

As did the ancient Greeks, U. S. citizens believe that the state, in this case the national government, should be involved in education and they supported the following legislation:

1647   Old Deluder Satan—provided for the education of all the children of all the people in Massachusetts, at public expense.

1785   Land Ordinance—provided for the division of land in the Northwest territories, or proceeds from the sale of that land, for education.

1862   Morrill Act—provided for land-grant colleges, which would include agriculture and the mechanical arts in their curriculums.

1917   Smith–Hughes Act—provided money for vocational education at the secondary level.

1958   National Defense Education Act—provided money for new programs in math, science, and foreign language.

1965   Elementary and Secondary Education Act—provided money for compensatory education. The Head Start program is one of the most popular of these programs and receives continued funding even though it is not effective in promoting long-term academic gains.

1968   Bilingual Act—provided money for English-as-a-Second-Language (ESL) programs.

1975   Education for All Handicapped Children Act (Public Law 94–142)—provided for the education of all handicapped students, at public expense, in the least restrictive environment, and with Individualized Educational Plans (IEP).

1986   Amendment 99–457—extended provisions of PL 94–142 to children as young as three years of age.

1991   *America 2000*—Established goals such as increasing the high school graduation rate to at least 90 percent, and making U. S. students first in the world in science and mathematics achievement. Did not include reference to the Fine Arts, Physical Education, or Vocational Education.

Our current educational practices were also shaped by national reports and studies. Among the more important of these were the following:

1892   Committee of Ten Report—resulted in the continuation and strengthening of the traditional, subject-centered curriculum and group instructional methods. Did not include reference to the Fine Arts, Physical Education, or Vocational Education.

1895	Committee on College Entrance Requirements—called for assigning credits to subjects for purposes of college admission.
1906	Carnegie Foundation for the Advancement of Teaching—proposed dividing instructional time into units with one unit being credited for the satisfactory completion of a subject that met five days per week, a minimum of 40 minutes per period, and a minimum of 120 clock hours for the school year. Became known as a Carnegie Unit.
1918	Commission on the Reorganization of Secondary Education—proposed the Seven Cardinal Principles.
1924	Edward L. Thorndike—discredited the faculty theory of learning, which held that areas of the mind could be strengthened by studying particular subjects.
1933	Eight-Year Study—showed that students who went to high schools with Progressive curriculum did at least as well as, and in most cases better than students who went to traditional high schools. Results were minimized due to timing (they were released in 1942 when attention was focused on World War II), and because of the inability of investigators to describe a single Progressive curriculum that could replace existing traditional curriculums.
1954	*Brown v. Board of Education of Topeka*—Supreme Court ruled separate schools are inherently unequal. Resulted in greater racial integration in schools, but increased school size and educational costs while reducing time available before and after school for students to get extra help.
1983	*A Nation at Risk*—Commission on Excellence in Education found that the United States was at risk because of increasingly ill-prepared students. Recommended, among other things, that the high school curriculum focus on the New Basics: four years of English; three years of mathematics; three years of science; three years of social studies; and one-half year of computer science. For the college-bound, two years of foreign language in high school were strongly recommended in addition to those taken earlier. Did not include reference to the Fine Arts, Physical Education, or Vocational Education.
1991	*America 2000*—Outlined six broad goals focusing on increased responsibilities on the part of parents, higher academic standards, and safer schools.

SO HOW DOES THIS AFFECT MY TEACHING?

The trail of legislation, studies, and reports indicates that the nation, as a whole, is primarily interested in having schools educate all students and produce citizens who can help the nation compete successfully in the global economy. Most often these interests result in support for subject-centered, academically oriented, Essentialist, curriculums that focus on relatively short-term, measurable objectives. The Progressive idea of an integrated (cross-disciplinary) curriculum focusing on problem-solving and including a wide range of "non-academic" options is still alive, but it is usually seen as less practical than Essentialist curriculums, particularly at the high school level.

As you find your way through the various currents in the river of education, keep in mind that Americans are increasingly concerned with what students can actually do. The mainstream Essentialist curriculums reflect the belief that there is more rigor and accountability with this approach than with the Progressive approach. We are, however, a pragmatic people, and any curriculum that can demonstrate consistent success in graduating students who can compete successfully in the job market and in higher education is likely to be widely supported. This means that you need to think beyond what you want your students to know. You need to think about what you want them to be able to do.

KEY TERMS, PEOPLE, AND IDEAS

Education in United States today is good but could be even better
Boston Latin Grammar School, 1635
Harvard, 1636
Old Deluder Satan Law, 1647
Kalamazoo, Michigan, 1872—Tax money can be used for secondary education
Benjamin Franklin, 1751—First Academy, Prototype for comprehensive high schools
Land Ordinance, 1785—First federal action concerning education
Morrill Land Grant Act, 1862—Vocational Education emerges
Committee of Ten Report, 1893—Essentialism and instructional time
Carnegie Unit, 1906—One class, five days a week, 40 minutes per period, 120 clock hours per year
Smith–Hughes Act, 1917—Federal support of vocational education
Commission on the Reorganization of Secondary Education, 1918—Seven Cardinal Principles
Edward L. Thorndike, 1924—Discredited the faculty theory
The Eight-Year Study, 1933–1942
Brown v. Board of Education of Topeka, 1954—Separate is inherently unequal
Sputnik I, Oct. 4, 1957—First man-made satellite
National Defense Education Act (NDEA), 1958—Math and Science
Lyndon Johnson, 1965—Great Society, Compensatory Education—(Project Head Start)

Education for All Handicapped Children Act (Public Law 94–142), 1975
A Nation at Risk, 1983—Back to basics, higher standards
America 2000, 1991

ENDNOTES

1. Farnighetti, Robert ed., *The World Almanac and Book of Facts, 1994* (Mahwah, New Jersey: Funk & Wagnalls, 1993), p. 196. Actual numbers are 42,000,343 students and 2,431,622 teachers.

2. Mattson, Mark T., *Fact Book on Elementary, Middle and Secondary Schools—1993* (New York: Scholastic, Inc., 1993), p. 5.18.

3. Elam, Stanley M., Lowell C. Rose, and Alec M. Gallup, "The 26th Annual Phi Delta Kappa/Gallup Poll of the Public's Attitudes Toward the Public Schools," *Phi Delta Kappan,* Vol. 76, no. 1 (Sept. 1994), p. 45.

4. Dumas, Wayne, and Weldon Beckner, *Introduction to Secondary Education* (Scranton, Penn.: International Textbook Co., 1968), pp. 5–6.

5. Dumas and Beckner, p. 27.

6. *The National Education Goals Report, Volume One: The National Report* (SSOP, Washington, D. C.: U. S. Government Printing Office, 1993), p. 134.

7. Boorstin, Daniel J., and Brooks Mather Kelly, *A History of the United States* (Lexington, Mass.: Ginn and Co., 1981), p. 101.

8. *World Almanac and Book of Facts* (Mahwah, N. J., 1994), pp. 359–360. Actual numbers were 31,443,321 in 1860 and 248,709,873 in 1990.

9. "Morrill, Justin Smith," *Encyclopedia Britannica* (Chicago: Encyclopedia Britannica, 1960), Vol. 15, p. 820.

10. "Land-Grant Colleges," *Encyclopedia Britannica,* 1960 ed., Vol. 13, p. 648B.

11. Tanner, Daniel, and Laurel N. Tanner, *Curriculum Development,* 2nd. ed., (New York: Macmillan, 1980), p. 233.

12. Tanner and Tanner, pp. 233–234.

13. Oliva, Peter F., *Developing the Curriculum* 2nd ed. (Glenview, Ill.: Scott, Foresman and Co., 1988), p. 319.

14. Commission on Reorganization of Secondary Education, *Cardinal Principles of Secondary Education,* Bulletin No. 35 (Washington, D. C.: U. S. Government Printing Office, 1918), p. 7.

15. Commission on Reorganization, pp. 5–10.

16. Thorndike, Edward L., "Mental Discipline in High School Studies," *Journal of Educational Psychology,* Vol. 15 (January 1924), p. 98.

17. Aiken, Wilford M., *Adventure in American Education, Volume I: The Story of the Eight-Year Study* (New York: Harper & Brothers, 1942), pp. 4–10.

18. Aiken, pp. 111–112.

19. Aiken, p. 117.

20. Alkin, Marvin C., ed., "Compensatory Education," *Encyclopedia of Educational Research,* Vol. 1, (New York: Macmillan, 1992), p. 208.

21. Alkin, p. 213.

22. Commission on Excellence in Education, *A Nation at Risk* (Washington, D. C.: U. S. Government Printing Office, 1983), pp. 8–9.

23. *Nation at Risk,* p. 17.

24. *Nation at Risk,* p. 18.

25. *Nation at Risk,* pp. 32–33.

26. *America 2000, An Education Strategy* (Washington, D. C.: U. S. Government Printing Office, 1991), p. 19.

3

LEARNING THEORIES AND INSTRUCTIONAL MODELS

RATIONALE

No one yet knows how people learn or how we store memories such as math facts, events, a hug, or the taste of Mom's apple pie. As teachers, however, we are charged with helping students learn, so it is to our advantage to examine some of the best researched learning theories and instructional models. The examination will reveal some of the strengths and weaknesses of each theory and model, and will give you a better idea of how and why the theories and models differ.

The information about learning theories and instructional models, together with your tentative conclusions about a philosophy of education, should help clarify your thinking about what you will do in your classroom and why you will do it. The large number of variables involved makes it difficult to pin down what you hope to accomplish as a teacher in both the short and the long terms. Nonetheless, the more clearly you can explain what you are doing and why, the more effective you are likely to be. The information in this chapter is intended to help.

SAMPLE OBJECTIVES

You will be able, in writing, to:

1. Explain at least one distinguishing characteristic of Behaviorism, Field theories, and Cognitive theory.
2. Given a specific instructional task (such as teaching students the stages of the water cycle or how to defend a point of view), explain whether

principles of behaviorism, field theory, or cognitive theory would be most applicable and use cause–effect reasoning and examples to explain your answer.

3. Explain the purpose of each of the four stages common to virtually all instructional models.

4. Explain at least one strength and one inherent weakness of the systems approach.

LEARNING THEORIES

By definition, a theory is "a system of assumptions, accepted principles, and rules of procedure devised to analyze, predict, or otherwise explain the nature or behavior of a specified set of phenomena."[1] As you read, keep in mind that all learning theories attempt to explain how people learn. However, researchers are just beginning to explore the intricacies of the human mind. Each of the theories may be partly or wholly correct or all may be totally wrong; we simply do not know. Researchers are working to learn more and the following theories represent some of the best documented explanations of how people learn. Large numbers of educators have found them worthy of serious consideration and they are presented here for your consideration.

Behaviorism

In its simplest form **behaviorism** holds that by appropriately manipulating the environment, all living things can be made to behave in designated ways. For example, the direction an amoeba takes can be manipulated by laying down a line of salt. The amoeba will avoid the salt. **Ivan Pavlov** (1849–1936) demonstrated that dogs could be conditioned to salivate at the sound of a bell.[2] When you are driving and see a red light, do you stop? You probably do, and without much thought. That kind of action demonstrates one of the key principles of behaviorism, namely, that humans, like all other living things, can be conditioned to behave in designated ways.

John B. Watson (1878–1958) was one of the first psychologists to describe behaviorism as a unique aspect of psychology. His article, "Psychology as the Behaviorist Views It," published in 1913,[3] is regarded by some as the formal beginning of behaviorism. He was so convinced of the effectiveness of behaviorism that he said,

> *Give me a dozen healthy infants, well-formed, and my own specified world to bring them up and I'll guarantee to take anyone at random and train him to be any type of specialist I might select—doctor, lawyer, artist . . . and yes, even into a beggarman and thief, regardless of his talents, . . . abilities, vocations, and race.*[4]

The work of behaviorists such as **Edward L. Thorndike** (1874–1949)[5] and **B(urrhus) F(rederic) Skinner** (1904–1990)[6] did much to promote behaviorism during the 1940s and 1950s. Behaviorism was widely accepted for a number of reasons. First, it was clearly demonstrable. You do not need an advanced degree to recognize that people can be induced to behave in particular ways by the use of appropriate rewards. As we get older those rewards change from smiles and hugs, to gold stars and As on report cards, to important titles and salary increases (we do, of course, still like the hugs). The principle remains the same. We have learned that to get certain rewards we must exhibit certain behaviors and, to the extent that we want the rewards, we are willing to modify our behavior accordingly.

A second reason many teachers apply behavioristic principles is that it puts them in charge. It is the teacher who determines what is to be learned and what the standards of behavior will be, and it is the teacher who manages the reward system to bring about the desired learning and behaviors. Behaviorism typically requires an external locus of control, and that locus of control is the teacher.

Behaviorism also assumes that learners are inherently neutral and passive, but we know that students, at least when they are young, are inherently curious and active. Nonetheless, in an era when classroom control is a major concern of teachers, it is understandable why many of them adopt behavioristic strategies.

A third reason for the continued strength of behaviorism is that it has been shown to be effective in many applications, and especially in programmed instruction. Behaviorists found that some complex behaviors could be learned more easily by breaking them into smaller, less complex, segments and helping students learn the segments sequentially. Learning in this fashion is analogous to building a structure by adding brick after brick until the structure is completed. In education, for example, we first teach letters and simple words, then how to combine words into sentences, sentences into paragraphs and, finally, paragraphs into whole essays, reports, and other documents. This idea of dividing complex information or tasks into simpler, less complex units is particularly evident in tutorials and in drill and practice computer-assisted instruction programs.

Most behaviorists would agree that students come to school with different backgrounds, abilities, and interests. They would say, however, that by the appropriate structuring of the information and skills to be learned, and the appropriate use of incentives, these students can be taught the same things and will leave the educational process much more alike than when they began. A diagram of this viewpoint might look like Figure 3.1.

Problems with Behaviorism
Behaviorism has its critics. They point out that when the teacher provides an external locus of control, students are deprived of the opportunity to think

FIGURE 3.1   Behavioristic View

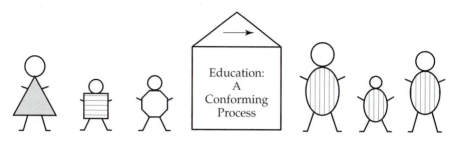

for themselves. In fact, in many situations students are unaware that their behavior is being manipulated. They go on to argue that if we want citizens who can think for themselves and control their own behavior, we need to help them develop those skills in school, and that behaviorism does not lend itself well to those goals.

Critics also point out that while principles of behaviorism may be effective in helping students learn factual information, sequences of events, and discreet facts, it is less effective in fostering creativity or the ability to solve problems. While students are in school, it is useful for them to have command of a large database of facts, figures, names, and places. However, unless that database is developed with an eye toward how, or whether, students will use that information after graduation, much of the information remains unused and is eventually forgotten. Clearly, behaviorism has its strengths and weaknesses.

Gestalt Theory

In the early 1900s, a group of German psychologists [**Max Wertheimer** (1880–1943), **Kurt Koffka** (1886–1941) and **Wolfgang Kohler** (1887–1967)] argued that learning takes place "when the individual sees the overall pattern (or Gestalt) in a situation and changes his behavior accordingly. Thus the learner responds as a whole organism and not automatically, or mechanically, through specific reflexes."[7] **Gestaltism** holds that the whole is more than the sum of the parts, that the learning process may, indeed, be more complex than suggested by the behaviorists.

However, the behaviorists were more able than the Gestaltists to dramatically demonstrate the efficacy of their principles so, for many years, behaviorism was the most commonly accepted learning theory.

Cognitive Field Theory

Field theories were an outgrowth of Gestaltism. Like the Gestaltists, **Kurt Lewin** (1890–1947) believed that human activity was the result of complex psychological factors rather than simple environmental factors. He refined the broad view of Gestaltism by arguing that regardless of how the teacher presents information, students perceive and interpret that information on the basis of their own experiences, needs, and abilities—their own **perceptual or cognitive fields.**[8]

A visit to any high school will quickly verify that students do, in fact, have widely different backgrounds, interests, and abilities. Unlike the behaviorists, however, the field theorists did not think that schooling would make all students alike. To the extent that their theory is correct, students would come to school with widely different backgrounds, abilities, and interests; but differences in cognitive fields would work against uniformity among the exiting students. A diagram of this viewpoint might look like Figure 3.2.

Cognitive Psychology

Cognitive theory focuses on how learners acquire information and how they use that information to deal with new experiences and situations. Although **cognitive psychology** did not emerge as a separate branch of psychology until the early 1960s, it has deep roots. For example, **John Dewey,** in describing the educational practices typical of his day, said they could, "be compared to inscribing records upon a passive phonograph disk to result in giving back what has been inscribed when the proper button is pressed in recitation or examination."[9] He certainly did not equate memorization with learning. He held that learning, and particularly reflective thinking, took place only under certain conditions.

> *They are first that the pupil have a genuine situation of experience—that there be a continuous activity in which he is interested for its own sake; secondly, that a genuine problem develop within this situation as a stimulus to thought; third, that he possess the information to make the observations needed to deal with it; fourth, that suggested solutions occur to him which he shall be responsible for developing in an orderly way; fifth, that*

FIGURE 3.2   Cognitive Field Theorist View

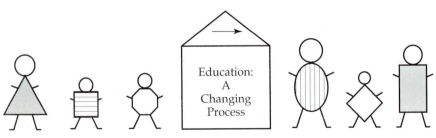

Education:
A
Changing
Process

he may have the opportunity and occasion to test his ideas by application, to make their meaning clear and to discover for himself their validity.[10]

Jean Piaget (1896–1980) was another early cognitive theorist. Piaget is perhaps best known for his description of how the human intellect develops in phases.

Phase One	Sensory-motor (birth to about age 2)
Phase Two	Preoperational (about ages 2–7)
	A. Preconceptual thought (about ages 2–4)
	B. Intuitive thought (about ages 4–7)
Phase Three	Concrete operations (about ages 7–11)
Phase Four	Formal operations (about age 11 onward).[11]

These phases, because of the ages they span, are most relevant to preschool and elementary school teachers. However, one of the key points underlying the phases is relevant to secondary-school teachers and is central to cognitive psychology.

To the extent that cognitive psychologists are correct, cognitive development takes place as a consequence of the interaction of learners with their environment. Neither maturation alone, nor instruction alone, is sufficient; interaction is necessary. John Dewey explained this view when he defined education as "that reconstruction of experience which adds to the meaning of experience and which increases ability to direct the course of subsequent experience."[12]

If cognitive psychologists are correct, teachers can maximize the learning potential of their students if they structure situations in which students must solve new problems. It is while thinking about these new experiences that learners assimilate new information and reorganize their knowledge-base. The theory holds that people learn best if they are challenged to use information and skills. More will be said of problem solving as a learning strategy in Chapter 8.

Comparison of Learning Theories

A comparison of these theories will highlight some of their respective strengths and weaknesses. Behaviorism, for example, views the learning process in a very mechanical way—find the right system of rewards and present the information in appropriate blocks, and learning will occur.

The validity of the theory can be seen when its principles are followed to help students learn basic facts and information, particularly via programmed instruction. Those techniques, however, do little to foster the development of problem-solving skills or creativity.

Field theories focus on the importance of each student's background, interests, and abilities, but they offer little practical help to teachers who may have 20–30 students in a class and who are expected to help each of those students achieve the same objectives by the end of the year. Teachers often try to use individual or group projects in the attempt to accommodate individual differences, but the attempts typically fall short of the goal. To a large extent, mass education, as we know it, requires that individuals subordinate much of their individuality to "the system." Field theorists would like the system to adapt to individual differences.

Cognitive psychology makes it clear that students learn most effectively when they are challenged to solve problems and deal with new situations. One of its weaknesses is that it does little to explain how students acquire basic knowledge in the first place. Using information and skills to learn more, to solve problems, and to deal with life, are admirable goals and should be incorporated into every teacher's objectives. However, students must *have* information before they can use it or reorganize it.

No single theory seems to adequately explain all the complexities of learning nor does any one offer principles that are useful in all situations. Researchers are still hard at work trying to learn how we learn. The wise teacher will not be too quick to adopt or reject any one theory.

INSTRUCTIONAL MODELS

Instructional models describe, sometimes graphically, various instructional strategies. They are useful because they help educators visualize those strategies as a series of steps, to see how the steps fit together, and to analyze the strengths and weaknesses of each step. Some models are more complex than others, but each can be effective for specific purposes.

The Military Model

Whether it is true or not, the military is often credited with having a clear, easy-to-follow, instructional model: (1) tell them what you are going to tell them, (2) tell them, (3) tell them what you told them, and (4) test them. The model clearly adheres to the advice offered by **William of Ockham,** that "Entities should not be multiplied unnecessarily," (known as **Ockham's razor**) and its more modern version, the **KISS** principle (*Keep It Simple, Stupid*).[13] More importantly, the model incorporates steps that contribute to student learning. For example, it calls for a preview or overview of new information. A preview can help students create a mental framework which, in turn, can help them organize information as they receive it, and remember it later. You will note that each chapter in this book includes a rationale and a set of sample objectives. The purpose of both is to give the reader a clear idea of what the chapter concerns and some of the things that they will be able to do after reading the chapter.

The model also calls for direct instruction. Direct instruction is teacher controlled and highly structured. Information is presented systematically, in small segments, and feedback concerning learning progress is continually provided. After surveying 20 years of research, **Levin** and **Ornstein** found that this kind of instruction is, indeed, effective.[14] The model also calls for the review of information to help students focus on main points and properly organize them in their minds. Finally, it calls for a determination of whether students have mastered, to an acceptable degree, the appropriate information and skills.

In many situations this model works quite well. However, its critics point out that the model fails to recognize or provide for individual differences and those differences might affect the capacity or willingness of students to benefit from the instruction. Critics also point out that the model does not provide for student involvement.

The Systems Approach

The systems approach has two basic roots, the Industrial Revolution and behaviorism. During the early 1900s, the Industrial Revolution was at its height and American industry was the envy of the world. One of the keystones of the Industrial Revolution was the idea of taking a complex task, such as building an automobile, and dividing it into a series of smaller, less complex tasks, such as building frames, body parts, and engines. Since this idea worked so well for industry, some educators thought it might also work well in schools. One educator (and behaviorist), **Franklin Bobbitt** (1876–1956), went so far as to directly compare education and manufacturing. He said that, "education is a shaping process as much as the manufacture of steel rails."[15] Some people agree, others disagree.

The second root, behaviorism, held that learning was largely a mechanical process. Students could be taught if they were presented with information that had been systematically arranged in small units, and if the teacher (or machine), appropriately manipulated the reward system. As it happened, the industrial model and behaviorism complemented each other and this encouraged educators to adapt these ideas for use in education.

At the heart of most systems models are four key steps: (1) the specification of instructional objectives, (2) preassessment of students to determine their beginning abilities relative to the objectives, (3) instructional activities intended to help students achieve the objectives, and (4) evaluation in order to determine whether students have achieved the objectives.

These steps are not very different from the steps taken to achieve any goal. For example, when you get up in the morning you have to decide what to wear so you consciously or unconsciously specify an objective—typically, to dress appropriately for some activity. Next, you consciously or unconsciously assess your current dress and determine that your pajamas or nightgown are not likely to be appropriate. Then you do something to achieve the objective—you select and put on the clothes that you think will be appropriate. Finally, you engage in the planned activity and, if you were dressed appropriately for it, you achieved your objective.

The General Model of Instruction (GMI)

Since the steps are so basic to achieving any goal, it is surprising that it was not until 1970 that they were formally depicted as parts of instructional models. It was then that **Robert Kibler, Larry Barker,** and **David Miles,** in *Behavioral Objectives and Instruction,*[16] depicted these four stages in the General Model of Instruction (GMI), shown in Figure 3.3.

FIGURE 3.3   The General Model of Instruction

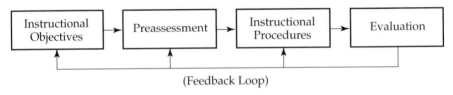

(Feedback Loop)

The Goal-Referenced Instructional Model

In the same year, **James Popham** and **Eva Baker,** in *Systematic Instruction,*[17] published a similar model, the Goal-Referenced Instructional Model, shown in Figure 3.4.

In addition to the four basic steps, each model also includes a feedback loop that shows what follows evaluation. In the GMI, the loop indicates that once the objective has been achieved, the whole process is repeated with a new objective. If the objective was not achieved, the upward arrows under each step indicate that the teacher should examine that step, see if there is a problem in it and, if so, fix the problem. In the Goal-Referenced Instructional Model, the top loop goes only to the instruction step implying that if students do not achieve the objective, the problem lies in that step and remedial instruction needs to be provided. Once the objective is achieved, the learner moves on to the next objective.

The Logical Instructional Model

The Logical Instructional Model (LIM) depicts the same four stages as the preceding models but it depicts them vertically and, more important, it

FIGURE 3.4   Goal-Referenced Instructional Model

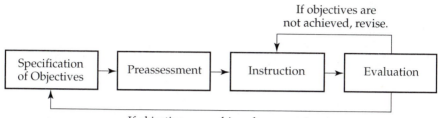

(W. James Popham and Eva L. Baker, *Systematic Instruction,*© 1970, p. 17. Reprinted by permission of Prentice-Hall, Inc., Englewood Cliffs, New Jersey.)

expands the preassessment step, as shown in Figure 3.5. Since preassessment is such an important part of both the Logical Instructional Model and the ASSURE model (featured next), it will be discussed immediately after depicting these two models.

ASSURE

The ASSURE model[18] is interesting for a number of reasons. One is that it makes use of an acronym to help students remember a process. The acronym, ASSURE, represents the following steps.

A   Same as Preassessment in the preceding models.)
S   State objectives
S   Select media and materials (Included in the Instruction step of the preceding models.)
U   Utilize materials (Included in the Instruction step of the preceding models.)
R   Require learner performance (Refers to having students practice skills and use information. Ideally it would be included in the Instruction step of the preceding models.)
E   Evaluate

PREASSESSMENT

The Logical Instructional Model and the ASSURE model highlight the importance of preassessment. The ASSURE model, by calling for the analysis of students first, indicates that the objectives and instruction that follow should take into account the abilities and interests of the students. What is meant here is that the general type of *prospective* students—freshmen or

FIGURE 3.5   Logical Instructional Model

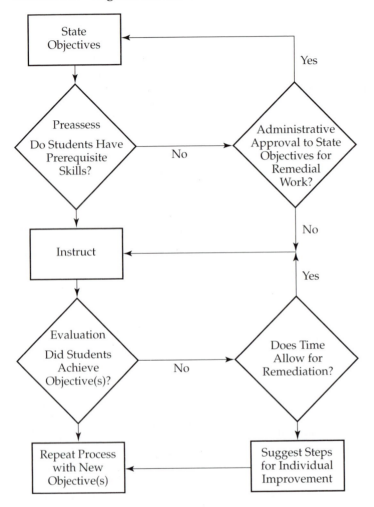

seniors, general versus advanced placement, poor or rich—should be considered. If a teacher waited until the class actually met for the first time before doing this kind of preassessment, weeks of pre-school planning time would be lost.

However, once students are actually in the classroom, it is a good idea to determine the extent to which expected prerequisite skills are present. You could simply assume that students will have the prerequisite skills. But remember that you can divide the word "assume" into ass-u-me, making an ass of you and me. In this case, if your assumption is wrong it could make for a very unpleasant year for you and your students.

Rather than making an assumption about students' mastery of prerequisite skills, a wise teacher would construct a preassessment instrument. Such an instrument would call for the recollection and application of some of the key information and skills that you consider prerequisite to beginning instruction in your class. The test should not be long nor should it be part of the students' grades. Ideally, the test will verify that the students have the prerequisite skills and, as the LIM indicates, you can move on with your instructional plans. However, the test may demonstrate that students do not have the necessary prerequisites. In this case, you have a problem and you should NOT try to solve it yourself.

Preassessment is also important if you have students with special needs, since you are likely to be asked to work with a Special Education teacher to develop an **Individualized Educational Plan** (IEP). When developing an IEP, the first question that needs to be answered is whether the student, if given alternative learning options, can reasonably be expected to achieve the stated course objectives. For example, if delivering a five-minute speech is essential to passing your course and a student has a severe speech impediment, it is not reasonable to expect the student to achieve that objective regardless of how many alternative instructional options are provided. In such cases some agreement needs to be reached concerning grading.

Your course objectives represent the minimum standards that students must reach in order to get a grade of D in the course. Some people argue, however, that the whole idea of IEPs is to modify the objectives, or develop new ones, to compensate for the student's handicap. This poses a problem. If you change the course objectives you make it possible for some students to get credit for the course without meeting its approved minimal requirements. If this is done and the student is given credit for the course, it may later be argued, in a court of law, that you provided false and misleading information on an official school transcript. Be careful. An alternative is simply to give students credit for the objectives they achieve. If the student's achievements do not meet the minimal course standards, the student could be given credit for auditing, rather than passing, the course and the administration and the school board could decide what to do about graduation requirements.

Most often, special-needs students will be able to meet the course objectives if alternative learning activities are provided. For example, visually-impaired students may need to have readers read textbook assignments to them or be provided with books with large print. They may even be provided with equipment that scans pages into a computer and enables the computer to read back the information so students can hear it. Hearing-impaired students may need to be provided with signers who can translate what you say into sign language. Accommodations such as these can be made, but they require planning. Further, while you will be aware of many instructional options, you are unlikely to be aware of all of them. Make no assumptions; ask for ideas. The idea is to help students with special needs be successful. Do all you can to this end, but do not lie to them. Do not lead them to believe they have accomplished something if they have not accomplished it.

Teachers sometimes turn to cumulative files for information about students. These files typically contain data such as test scores, attendance records, and **anecdotal comments** (undocumented statements concerning students' behavior and/or teachers' perceptions of students' abilities, attitudes, or actions). Some teachers choose not to examine such files because they feel that knowing about a student's past performance might influence their assessment of current performance. Few teachers today are willing to add anecdotal comments to a student's file because such comments might be difficult to defend in a court of law.

The Teacher's Role as a Faculty Member

As a teacher you are part of a faculty which, together, is trying to implement a curriculum. The principal is responsible for the overall implementation of that curriculum. If your preassessment reveals that a significant number of your students do not have the necessary prerequisite knowledge or skills, you should take that information to the principal and, together, decide on a course of action. You might, for example, believe that you should provide whatever remedial instruction is necessary to enable students to understand and benefit from new information. You want to start from where the students are and take them as far as they can go in the time available. That position is reasonable and the principal might agree with it.

You might, however, believe that students who get credit for your course should achieve the objectives normally associated with that course. You could point out that once the credit is on the transcript, future teachers, prospective employers, and anyone else who sees that transcript will assume that it is truthful and you want no part in providing false or misleading information for any reason. This position is also reasonable and the principal might agree with it.

Clearly, a strong case can be built for either position. However, following either course of action on your own could jeopardize your career. For example, if you arbitrarily decided to provide remedial instruction, it is not likely that you would have time to complete the rest of the planned instruction. At the end of the year your colleagues and the principal could, justifiably, claim that you did not do what you were supposed to do and that your arbitrary action weakened the whole curriculum. It could be argued that because you did not teach what you were supposed to teach, your students are now unprepared to take the next course.

On the other hand, if you decided to ignore the students' deficiencies and go forward with the planned instruction, it is likely that many students would do poorly or fail. Parents would complain to you, the principal, or school board members, and your teaching ability might well be questioned.

The wisest course of action would be to take the results of your preassessment test to the principal and discuss the options. If the principal agrees that providing remedial instruction is appropriate, and recognizes that doing so might keep you from completing the planned program, he or she can explain any lack of progress to critics. Similarly, if the principal agrees that following the existing syllabus is the appropriate thing to do, then he or she can explain that course of action to parents or other critics. The principal will, typically, know more about the curriculum and about the feelings of the faculty, the student body, and the community, than you, a new teacher. It would be wise to avail yourself of that knowledge. Further, bringing preassessment results to the principal for discussion is likely to add to your image as a professional. Not everyone thinks about preassessment or takes the time to do it.

Things to Think about Concerning Instructional Models

There is no doubt that all instructional models help teachers divide instruction into steps and analyze the steps as well as the whole. However, there are at least two other points that you should consider. First, instructional models deal with only part of the teaching–learning process, the teachers' part. The models imply that if the students do not learn, there is something wrong with the instructional system and that if the teacher tinkers enough with the system, the students will learn. That may not be so.

Second, the feedback loops indicate that if students have not achieved the objective, remedial instruction should be provided. However, if the teacher has carefully planned instruction to help students achieve a year-long sequence of objectives, little, if any, time will be available for remediation. Time is always a critical variable.

Time and achievement are two variables central to the teaching–learning process. Public schools keep time stable and allow achievement to vary. We conduct classes for X days (typically, 180–185), and then attempt to grade students on how much progress they made during that time. In doing this, we make the assumption that, like horses at the beginning of a race, all students begin at the same point. Preassessment can determine the extent to which the assumption is valid.

If achievement was held stable and time was allowed to vary, we might be able to engage in mastery learning. With enough time, we could probably help virtually all students master particular information and skills, but even then, student cooperation would be needed.

SUMMARY

Learning theories attempt to explain how people learn. Behaviorism holds that the behavior of all living things can be manipulated by controlling environmental variables. In teaching, this translates into dividing complex tasks or behaviors into smaller, simpler units, organizing the units in some logical order, and then arranging a reward system so that students are rewarded as they master each unit. Behaviorist principles are evident in our use of praise, gold stars, and grades to reward students, and it is also evident in programmed learning, particularly tutorials and drill and practice computer-assisted instruction programs.

Gestaltism holds that learning results from a complex interaction of knowledge, emotions, and environmental factors. These factors combine to help the learner see an overall pattern in a situation and this, in turn, brings about the behavior change or learning.

Field theory is an outgrowth of Gestaltism. It holds that learners perceive and interpret the world around them on the basis of their existing knowledge and experiences—their cognitive fields. In this view, what specific students learn in any given situation is largely determined by the background, skills, and intents that they bring to the situation.

Instructional models help teachers analyze the instructional process by dividing it into discrete steps. Most models include four basic steps: (1) the specification of instructional objectives, (2) preassessment of students to determine their beginning abilities relative to the objectives, (3) instructional activities intended to help students achieve the objectives, and (4) evaluation in order to determine whether students have achieved the objectives.

Preassessment is particularly important because it helps determine if students have the knowledge and skills needed to benefit from the intended instruction. Decisions about what to do if students do not have the prerequisites should be made in conjunction with the principal.

It is important to keep in mind that instructional models deal with instruction. The assumption is that if the teacher follows the steps of the model, students will learn. That assumption ignores the responsibilities of the learner. It is also important to keep in mind that instructional models do not deal with time as a variable.

The General Model of Instruction, the Goal-Referenced Instructional Model, and the Logical Instructional Model all include feedback loops. These loops call for remediation when needed, but instructional plans typically allow little, if any, time for remediation.

The ASSURE model would have teachers analyze their students before specifying instructional objectives and making instructional plans. While it is possible to make some generalizations about incoming students, teachers typically must be ready to start teaching on the first day and cannot afford to give up weeks of pre-school preparation time.

SO HOW DOES THIS AFFECT MY TEACHING?

As a professional, you need to be able to converse intelligently with your peers, to read and understand journal articles, and to raise relevant points or questions during debates about educational issues. Since learning theories and instructional models are central to many of these conversations, articles, and debates, it is useful to know something about them.

More importantly, many teachers regard the success of their students as an important measure of their own success. This does not mean that these teachers give As and Bs to all their students so that everyone feels good, nor does it mean that they condemn themselves every time a student earns a D or an F. It means, simply, that the more they can help their students succeed, the more they feel that their time and efforts have been worthwhile.

Knowing about different theories of learning and different instructional models is likely to contribute to your success as a teacher. The knowledge enables you to select and apply principles of a number of theories and models to meet varying situations. This, in turn, will help you and your students be successful.

KEY TERMS, PEOPLE, AND IDEAS

Behaviorism—Pavlov, Watson, B.F. Skinner
Gestalt Theory—Overall pattern, the whole is more than the sum of the parts
Cognitive Field—Past experiences affect interpretations of current events
Cognitive Theory—Learning is more than accumulating isolated facts
Instructional Models—Only the teaching part of the teaching–learning process
Military Model
Ockham's Razor, KISS
Systems Approach
General Model of Instruction (GMI)
Goal-Referenced Instructional Model
Logical Instructional Model (LIM)
ASSURE
Preassessment

Anecdotal Comments
Check with principal before making curricular changes
Time and Achievement as two variables (time usually held constant)

ENDNOTES

1. Morris, William, ed., *The American Heritage Dictionary* (Boston: American Heritage Pub. Co. and Houghton Mifflin Co., 1970), p. 1335.

2. Pavlov, Ivan, *Conditioned Reflexes: An Investigation of Physiological Activity of the Cerebral Cortex*, trans. G.V. Anrep (London: Oxford University Press, 1927).

3. Watson, John B., "Psychology as the Behaviorist Views It," *Psychology Review*, Vol. 20 (March 1913), pp. 158–177.

4. Watson, John B., "What the Nursery Has to Say about Instincts," in C.A. Murchinson, ed., *Psychologies of 1925* (Worcester, Mass: Clark University Press, 1926), p. 10.

5. Thorndike, Edward L., *The Psychology of Learning*, Vol. II: Educational Psychology (New York: Teachers College, 1913).

6. Skinner, B.F., *Science and Human Behavior* (New York: Macmillan, Inc., 1953).

7. Saettler, Paul, *The Evolution of American Educational Technology* (Englewood, Colo.: Libraries Unlimited, Inc., 1990), p. 84.

8. Lewin, Kurt, *Field Theory in Social Science* (New York: Harper and Row, 1951).

9. Dewey, John, "Need for a Philosophy of Education," *The New Era in Home and School* Vol. 15 (November, 1934, England), p. 212.

10. Dewey, John, *Democracy and Education* (New York: Macmillan, 1916), p. 102.

11. Piaget, Jean, *Psychology of Intelligence* (New York: Harcourt, Brace and World, 1950).

12. Dewey, John, *Democracy and Education*, pp. 89–90.

13. Ockham, William of (1285?-1349?), *Quodlibeta*, in Margaret Miner and Hugh Rawson, *Dictionary of Quotations*, 2nd. ed. (New York: Signet/Penguin Books, 1964), p. 373.

14. Levine, Daniel U., and Allan C. Ornstein, "Research on Classroom and School Effectiveness and Its Implications for Improving Big City Schools," *Urban Review* (July 1989), pp. 81–95; Allan C. Ornstein and Daniel U. Levine, "Urban School Effectiveness and Improvement," *Illinois School Research and Development* (Spring 1991), pp. 111–117.

15. Bobbitt, Franklin, "The Supervision of City Schools: Some General Principles of Management Applied to the Problems of City Schools," *Twelfth Yearbook of the National Society for the Study of Education, Part I* (Bloomington, Ill., 1913), p. 11.

16. Kibler, Robert J., Larry L. Barker, and David T. Miles, *Behavioral Objectives and Instruction* (Boston: Allyn and Bacon, 1970), p. 13.

17. Popham, James, and Eva Baker, *Systematic Instruction* (Englewood Cliffs, N.J.: Prentice-Hall, 1970), pp. 13–18.

18. Heinich, Robert, Michael Molenda, and James D. Russell, *Instructional Media*, 4th ed. (New York: Macmillan, 1993), pp. 34–37.

4

SELECTING INSTRUCTIONAL CONTENT

RATIONALE

Information about educational philosophies, about legislation and reports that have shaped our schools, and about learning theories and instructional models, is the foundation on which to build instructional plans. That information can help you grapple with the question of what you want your students to know and be able to do after instruction that they did not know or were unable to do before instruction. There may be no single right answer, but each teacher must find at least tentative answers in order to have a basis for planning instruction.

Planning for instruction presents the same paradox as the question of which came first, the chicken or the egg. Should teachers first develop a set of instructional objectives and then select the content and activities needed to help students achieve those objectives, or should they first look at the content typically included in the course and then develop objectives and select activities appropriate to that content? For all practical purposes, teachers do both. As a consequence of their general experiences in school and in the courses they took in their academic major and minor, teachers have a fairly good idea of broad instructional goals and of the goals relevant to their particular subject areas. They also know a good deal about the content in their subject areas. They pool this information to refine their instructional objectives and to plan effective instructional units.

This chapter describes some techniques that will help you clarify your instructional goals in your own mind and select and organize content that will be interesting and relevant to students. It will also help you think about providing a rationale to your students to help make them more willing partners in the teaching–learning process. With this kind of planning, students are more likely to be successful, and the more successful they are, the more successful you are.

SAMPLE OBJECTIVES

You will be able, in writing, to:

1. Describe how specific standards published by any two national subject-area councils or groups can be used to develop a cross-disciplinary instructional unit.
2. Explain the relationship between the Pygmalion and Galatea effects and illustrate each with a school-related example.
3. Select a block of content suitable for a two- to four-week instructional unit and, in no more than two pages, write a rationale for that unit using facts and cause–effect reasoning to explain to *students:* (1) why the content to be learned is an important part of the course and subject area; (2) how it will enable them to better understand and deal with the world around them; and (3) why it is of current concern to society.

BROAD GOALS

Agreement on instructional objectives is inversely proportional to the immediacy of the task. (Oh, how we educators love our jargon.) In simpler terms, everyone agrees on distant goals such as peace on Earth, good will toward men (and women), helping students become critical thinkers and problem-solvers, and preparing them to live good lives in a good society. It is when the discussion turns to what you should be doing with *your* students, in *your* classroom, that disagreements arise.

The Seven Cardinal Principles

There is no shortage of broad goals in education. Among the best known are the Seven Cardinal Principles, which were described in Chapter Two: (1) Health, (2) Command of the fundamentals, (3) Worthy home membership, (4) Vocation, (5) Citizenship, (6) Leisure, and (7) Ethical character. There is no doubt that these goals were well intended, but there is also no doubt that there were, and are, major differences of opinion about degree of emphasis and even about appropriateness. If time and resources were unlimited, perhaps teachers could focus on all these areas. However, time and resources are limited, so choices need to be made.

Five Broad Goals

Some educators have advocated focusing on the five selected broad goals:

1. Educate all the children of all the people,
2. Provide for individual differences,
3. Teach the basics,
4. Integrate knowledge, and
5. Help students learn to learn.

Each of these also has its own problems:

Educate All the Children of All the People

While this goal may sound good, it is not clear whether it means to provide *opportunities* for all students to learn or if it implies a mandate that teachers will *ensure* that all children will learn. This goal could be interpreted as putting full responsibility for the teaching–learning process on the shoulders of teachers regardless of the fact that student effort is essential for successful learning.

Provide for Individual Differences

If all students are expected to learn certain things at about the same rate, how does one meaningfully provide for individual differences? Some schools have experimented with self-pacing; having the same objectives for all students, but allowing students to work toward the achievement of those objectives at their own paces. One of the earliest such experiments was conducted in the mid-1920s in Winnetka, Illinois. A similar experiment was conducted during the mid-1960s at Nova High School in Fort Lauderdale, Florida, and the same approach was tried from 1970 to 1980 in the teacher preparation program at Illinois State University. Significantly, while each of these trial programs attracted national attention, all of them have reverted to more traditional approaches. Self-pacing poses some difficult problems with respect to professional differences, logistics, record-keeping and, most important, student motivation.

Teach the Basics

The cry of "back to the basics" is usually raised when attempts are made to broaden the curriculum. The question is, what are the basics? To the ancient Hebrews, the all-important basic was being able to read and understand the Torah, the Five Books of Moses. To the Greeks, the basics included the study of rhetoric (use of the language), dialectics (formal logic), grammar (reading, writing, and literature), mathematics, music, civic responsibilities, and participation in a systematic physical education program. The Romans adopted most of the Greek curriculum, but minimized the arts and emphasized rhetoric. During the Middle Ages (c. 500–1300) most children received no formal academic education and the curriculum at the university level focused on the trivium (grammar, dialectics, and rhetoric), and the quadrivium (arithmetic, geometry, music in the form of religious chants, and astronomy).

These subjects became known as the seven liberal arts. Clearly, each society decides for itself what the basics are and permits the list to vary as different pressures come to bear.

Integrate Knowledge

One commonly accepted goal of today's schools is to help students develop into knowledgeable, healthy, and aesthetically aware citizens. This goal was shared by the ancient Greeks, who strongly believed that most aspects of life are so interrelated as to be inseparable. This view was reflected in the Greek goal of helping individuals develop a sound mind in a sound body, and it was the basis for their two-part curriculum—rhetoric, dialectic, grammar, and music for the mind, systematic physical training for the body.

The interrelatedness of knowledge began to be lost as more knowledge became available and people began to specialize. In 1439, William Byngham founded one of the first schools of education, Godhouse College, in England.[1] Although students in the school were already teachers, Byngham started the idea of student teaching and it is also likely that he advocated that students learn subject matter as separate disciplines. Later, in 1684, Jean Baptiste de la Salle founded another school of education at Rheims, France. Baptiste de la Salle was among the first to organize subject matter to facilitate group instruction and to advocate the orderly promotion of students from one unit of subject material to another.[2] These early schools of education became known as normal schools because they set the norm or standard for good teaching practices. The idea of breaking knowledge into disciplines and dealing with each discipline separately became the norm and it continues to dominate education today. Regardless of its advantages, this approach does little to convey to students the interrelatedness of knowledge.

Help Students Learn to Learn

Another commonly accepted goal is to teach students to learn to learn so they can continue to acquire new skills, knowledge, and insights throughout their lives. Ironically, education has historically engaged more in indoctrination than in education. Throughout the Middle Ages and into the 1800s, teachers presented students with information or sets of beliefs or laws (often the Bible) and expected them to memorize all or parts of the material and to believe it without question. Intellectual curiosity and creativity have been consistently opposed by most educational systems throughout history.

The Greeks lit the lamp of learning with their spirit of inquiry. Men such as Socrates, Plato, and Aristotle believed that people could learn about themselves and the world around them by applying logic, by hypothesizing, and by observing. These learning tools virtually disappeared during the Middle Ages when the Church dominated all aspects of life, but they re-emerged during the Age of Enlightenment (1550–1760) with the work of men such as

Galileo and Sir Francis Bacon. These men believed that knowledge could be acquired by the "scientific method": (1) identifying the problem, (2) forming a hypothesis or probable solution, (3) gathering data by observing and/or experimenting, (4) interpreting the data, and (5) drawing conclusions.

Even after the Age of Enlightenment, few educators taught their students to use logic or the scientific method to verify what they were taught. It was easier to indoctrinate than to educate. Now, virtually all educators want their students to engage in reflective thinking and to use the scientific approach. The problem is deciding how much time should be spent helping students learn what is already known and how much should be spent on having them rediscover much of this information on their own.

TYLER'S RATIONALE

In 1949, **Ralph W. Tyler** (the director of research for the Eight-Year Study), wrote *Basic Principles of Curriculum and Instruction*.[3] In this work he listed four fundamental questions that he believed educators should address in establishing goals. They are:

1. What educational purposes should the school seek to attain?
2. What educational experiences can be provided that are likely to attain those purposes?
3. How can these educational experiences be effectively organized?
4. How can we determine whether these purposes are being attained?[4]

He also described three sources of ideas for educational objectives and they may turn out to be one of your greatest aids in deciding what to teach. They are:

1. Suggestions from subject specialists,
2. Studies of the learners themselves, and
3. Studies of contemporary life outside the school.[5]

If one seriously considers the sources that Tyler suggests, it becomes increasingly clear that the man had a good point. Generally speaking, people would rather be successful than unsuccessful. Every student would rather get As than Cs or Ds, and every teacher would like to help make students' lives happier and more productive. Why then are so many students and teachers less successful than they would like to be? The reason may well be that sometimes neither the teachers nor the students see the utility or relevance of the information to be taught or learned. If the utility or relevance of the information is not clear, it is difficult to be enthusiastic about teaching or learning it. Tyler's three sources can help teachers select general objectives wisely.

SUBJECT-AREA SPECIALISTS

National Groups and Councils

In an attempt to provide guiding principles for the preparation and continuing education of teachers, the **National Board for Professional Teaching Standards** developed a set of five standards or propositions that it believes characterize what experienced teachers should know and be able to do. These are:

1. Teachers are Committed to Students and Their Learning
2. Teachers Know the Subjects They Teach and How to Teach Those Subjects to Students
3. Teachers Are Responsible for Managing and Monitoring Student Learning
4. Teachers Think Systematically About Their Practice and Learn from Experience
5. Teachers are Members of Learning Communities[6]

While these provide broad direction, they provide little help in deciding what you should actually teach. Instead of looking at broad goals from the perspective of what *teachers* should do, some educators focused on what *students* should be able to do. Work in this direction was begun years ago but the most progress was made since 1989.

Educators in many subject areas formed national groups or councils and many of these organizations have developed, or are in the process of developing, sets of subject-area standards for K–12 students. Unlike the general goals proposed for teachers, the national subject-area groups have proposed specific content-area standards and have supplemented them with specifications of what students should know and be able to do.

Mathematics

For example, in 1989, the National Council of Teachers of Mathematics published *Curriculum and Evaluation Standards for School Mathematics.* Its table of contents lists the following headings:

Curriculum Standards for Grades K–4

Standard
1. Mathematics as Problem Solving
2. Mathematics as Communication
3. Mathematics as Reasoning
4. Mathematical Connections
5. Estimation

Curriculum Standards for Grades 5–8

Standard
1. Mathematics as Problem Solving
2. Mathematics as Communication
3. Mathematics as Reasoning
4. Mathematical Connections
5. Number and Number Relationships

6. Number Sense and Numeration	6. Number Systems and Number Theory
7. Concepts of Whole Number Operations	7. Computation and Estimation
8. Whole Number Computation	8. Patterns and Functions
9. Geometry and Spatial Sense	9. Algebra
10. Measurement	10. Statistics
11. Statistics and Probability	11. Probability
12. Fractions and Decimals	12. Geometry
13. Patterns and Relationships	13. Measurement

Curriculum Standards for Grades 9–12

Evaluation Standards

Standard

1. Mathematics as Problem Solving
2. Mathematics as Communication
3. Mathematics as Reasoning
4. Mathematical Connections
5. Algebra
6. Functions
7. Geometry from a Synthetic perspective
8. Geometry from an Algebraic Perspective
9. Trigonometry
10. Statistics
11. Probability
12. Discrete Mathematics
13. Conceptual Underpinnings of Calculus
14. Mathematical Structure

Standard

1. Alignment
2. Multiple Sources of Information
3. Appropriate Assessment Methods and Uses
4. Mathematical Power
5. Problem Solving
6. Communication
7. Reasoning
8. Mathematical Concepts
9. Mathematical Procedures
10. Mathematical Disposition
11. Indicators for Program Evaluation
12. Curriculum and Instructional Resources
13. Instruction
14. Evaluation Team[7]

These headings are then explained further. For example, the third standard at each level concerns Mathematics as Reasoning. The K–12 progression in this area is as follows:

Mathematics as Reasoning, K–12

In grades K–4, students should be taught to:
- draw logical conclusions about mathematics;
- use models, known facts, properties, and relationships to explain their thinking;
- justify their answers and solution processes;
- use patterns and relationships to analyze mathematical situations;
- believe that mathematics makes sense.[8]

In grades 5–8, students should be taught to:
- recognize and apply deductive and inductive reasoning;
- understand and apply reasoning processes, with special attention to spatial reasoning and reasoning with proportions and graphs;
- make and evaluate mathematical conjectures and arguments;
- validate their own thinking;
- appreciate the pervasive use and power of reasoning as a part of mathematics.[9]

In grades 9–12, students should be able to:
- make and test conjectures;
- formulate counterexamples;
- follow logical argument;
- judge the validity of arguments;
- construct simple valid arguments and, for college intending students,
- construct proofs for mathematical assertions, including indirect proofs and proofs by mathematical induction.[10]

Each of these standards is then explained in still greater detail and illustrated with examples. A similar set of standards was established for geography.

Geography
In 1994, the National Geographic Society published *Geography for Life*, a set of eighteen standards divided into six main areas. These are:

Seeing the World in Spatial Terms
1. How to use maps and other geographic representations, tools, and technologies to acquire, process, and report information from a spatial perspective.
2. How to use mental maps to organize information about people, places, and environments in a spatial context.
3. How to analyze the spatial organization of people, places, and environments on Earth's surface.

Places and Regions

4. The physical and human characteristics of places.
5. That people create regions to interpret Earth's complexity.
6. How culture and experiences influence people's perception of places and regions.

Physical Systems

7. The physical processes that shape the patterns of Earth's surface.
8. The characteristics and spatial distribution of ecosystems on Earth's surface.

Human Systems

9. The characteristics, distribution, and migration of human populations on Earth's surface.
10. The characteristics, spatial organizations, and complexity of Earth's cultural mosaics.
11. The patterns and networks of economic interdependence on Earth's surface.
12. The processes, patterns, and functions of human settlement.
13. How the forces of cooperation and conflict among people shape human control of Earth's surface.

Environment and Society

14. How human actions modify the physical environment.
15. How physical systems affect human systems.
16. The changes that occur in meaning, use, distribution, and importance of resources.

Applying Geography

17. How to apply geography to interpret the past.
18. How to apply geography to interpret the present and plan for the future.[11]

The document then goes on to provide examples of skills and learning opportunities for each area and for each grade category. For example, students in grade eight who are performing "at standard" would be able to do things such as:

- relate the content of geography to life experiences, and
- apply the principles of geography to solving social and environmental problems.[12]

Those performing "beyond standard" would be able to do things such as:

- acquire, interpret, and analyze geographic data from a variety of sources, and
- use a multistep procedure in solving problems related to geography.

Further, these standards are accompanied by practical examples of what students should be able to do. For example, when performing "beyond standard," students should be able to answer questions such as:

> *The settlement patterns and rural land use in the upper Midwest (Wisconsin, Minnesota, North and South Dakota) are considerably different than that of the Southwest (Texas, New Mexico, and Arizona). What geographical factors explain the differences between the two regions? How have such factors affected the contemporary landscape?*[13]

A sample of an extended answer is also provided.

Standards such as these can assist teachers in two ways. First, the standards give teachers in each subject area a common framework for curriculum development. In the long term this is likely to lead to greater uniformity in curricular scope and sequence nationwide. In the short term, subject-area standards can suggest practical ideas for instructional units. Second, by acquiring the standards from a variety of subject areas, teachers will be more able to see connections between their subject area and others. This will facilitate efforts at developing cross-disciplinary units and, in a larger sense, curricular integration. Information about national standards in the Arts, Civics and Government, Foreign Languages, Geography, History, Mathematics, and Science is available from the respective national organizations. Addresses and phone numbers are listed in Appendix B.

Other Faculty

In the process of developing instructional objectives, many school districts ask teachers to get together on the basis of common grade levels or common subject-area interests. Typically, district administrators also provide teachers with objectives that have already been formulated either locally or by educators elsewhere. Sometimes it is appropriate to adopt some of those objectives as they are, but more often they can be adopted after some modification.

Textbooks

Assuming that the courses you are assigned to teach have been taught before, your first instinct is likely to be to look at the texts being used. Follow your instinct. To produce marketable texts, authors must focus on what practitioners in the field consider important. They must also include the most up-to-date knowledge in the field (so look at the copyright date), must organize the information so it follows some logical order (look at the table of contents), and must present that information in terms that students find interesting and understandable (read sections of the text). With this much work already done, it makes good sense to examine the texts for ideas about objectives.

Concepts

While most texts do a good job of presenting important names, dates, events, skills, and techniques, few do as good a job identifying key concepts. As you look through texts for your course, isolate key concepts as you go. Operationally defined, a **concept** is **a group of things, either concrete or abstract, that have enough elements in common to comprise a unique set.** For example, the word "trees" represents a concept. When you think of trees you may think of conifers such as pines, cedars, and firs, or deciduous trees such as oaks, maples, and birches, but you do not think of roses or lilac bushes. All are plants, but the trees have enough characteristics in common to be members of a unique set. The same idea holds for abstractions. For example, when you think of governments, you may think of democracies, republics, dictatorships, or socialism, but you do not think of hermits or anarchy.

As you begin identifying key concepts in your subject area, focus on those most relevant to the course you are teaching and to units within that course. For example, if you were teaching General Science you might include a unit on trees. By analogy, trees is a beachball-size concept. It is large enough to contain many smaller elements.

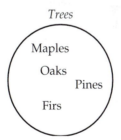

Trees

Maples

Oaks

Pines

Firs

If you were teaching a Botany course, you might want to deal with trees in greater depth and might devote an entire unit to coniferous trees. You would be substituting a baseball for the beachball.

Conifers

Pines
Firs

If you were teaching a course in advanced forestry, you might want an even narrower concept such as white pines. In this case, the ball shrinks to the size of a golf ball.

White Pines

O

If we are talking about instructional units two to four weeks in length, the broad unit on trees would have great breadth but relatively little depth whereas the unit on white pines would have great depth but little breadth. The concepts you want to focus on should be appropriate to the course you are teaching.

THE LEARNERS THEMSELVES

As the various national groups worked to develop standards for their respective subject areas, they worked from the perspective of subject-area specialists. Tyler, and common sense, suggest that the needs and interests of students must also be considered and this may pose a philosophic dilemma for some teachers. Some educators believe that there are certain things that students ought to learn whether they are interested in them at the moment or not. Others believe that unless the students are interested in the content, they will not cooperate in the teaching–learning process. The goal, of course, is to find a workable blend, but the task is not easy.

One approach that may help is to examine the key concepts and skills identified for your subject area and to think of how to adapt them to the students you will teach. This does not mean adapting them to each student because then, instead of having objectives and standards for a course, you might end up with different objectives and standards for each student. Taking individualization to this extreme would destroy the whole idea of scope and sequence inherent in school curriculums. It is possible, however, to think in broad terms about your students. Is your course designed for beginning students or for seniors? Is it a general course or an advanced placement course? Is it elective or required? Are your students typically in the lower, middle, or upper socio-economic class; inner-city, urban, suburban, or rural? Using factors such as these, you can begin thinking about how to make the content relevant to your students, i.e., how you can relate the content to the lives of your students. In doing this, it is important not to short-change your students.

Teacher Expectations—The Pygmalion/Galatea Effects

There is a significant amount of research demonstrating that teacher expectations can have a measurable impact on student achievement. In 1968, **Rob-**

ert **Rosenthal and Lenore Jacobson** conducted a series of experiments in which teachers were told that certain students were "late bloomers" and could be expected to make rapid progress in their classes. In fact, the students were selected at random, but, because the teachers expected them to do well and consciously or unconsciously treated them differently, they did make more rapid progress than their peers. The phenomenon, known as the **Pygmalion Effect,** was also demonstrated when teachers were told that certain students were slow and could be expected to make only limited progress. Again, the students were selected at random and again, the expectation became a self-fulfilling prophecy.[14]

In 1982, Jere Brophy analyzed the research concerning the Pygmalion effect and concluded that the effect did, in fact, exist but that in most cases it had minimal impact because teachers' initial expectations were fairly accurate and were usually open to change based on actual work with the students.[15] The results of the Rosenthal–Jacobson studies were reviewed in 1983 by Harris Cooper and Thomas Good[16] and in 1984 by Stephen Raudenbush.[17] These reviews confirmed the initial findings. In 1991, Rosenthal reviewed 448 studies concerning the Pygmalion effect and found that these, too, confirmed his initial findings.[18] What teachers expect of students in terms of behavior and academic performance can affect the resulting behavior and performance. It is wise, therefore, to set high standards. A simple example may illustrate the point.

If a teacher begins with the belief that students are basically lazy and unable or unwilling to do homework, that teacher is not likely to assign much homework. In fact, about 90 percent of the students in the United States spend less than one hour a night on homework.[19] By not assigning homework, or not holding students accountable for completing it, the teacher is wasting what could be a valuable learning experience. On the other hand, if the teacher begins with the belief that the students are willing to work and to apply themselves, homework would be assigned when appropriate and students would benefit.

To the extent that high expectations are established and students are helped to achieve them, students begin to have increased confidence in their own abilities. This effect is known as the **Galatea Effect.** With the Pygmalion effect, the expectations of others affect performance. With the Galatea effect, it is the person's own self-confidence that affects performance. It is a student saying to himself, "I climbed that mountain, maybe I can climb the next one." Clearly, having high expectations for students is better than having low expectations, but expectations alone will not get the job done. In order to get students to work willingly toward those high expectations, for example, to do their homework, the expectations must be relevant to the students' lives.

Central to the task of making content relevant is identifying practical applications of the concepts and skills to be learned and then explaining those applications to students. In this effort, it is not very persuasive to explain that the content will be needed for a test or to pass the course. Students may not care and they have certainly heard those arguments before. It is more persuasive to cite examples of how the concepts and skills will help students improve their performance in and out of school and/or how it can help them better understand the world around them and deal with that world effectively.

For example, literature can be made more relevant to students if teachers seek out underlying themes rather than focusing mainly on technical aspects. Herman Melville's *Moby Dick* could be read with an emphasis on analyzing the plot structure, the setting, and the use of language. On the other hand, it could be read with an emphasis on its main themes of obsession and revenge. Since it is likely that students of all races and social strata know of instances where obsession or revenge motivated actions, they can relate the cause–effect relationships in the story to their own lives. It becomes relevant to them. Shakespeare can be read in the same way. History teachers can make it a point to demonstrate how events in the past frequently have the same basic cause–effect relationships as current events.

Typically, students are willing to put forth significant effort if they see some practical payoff. It is well worth the effort to view the content through the eyes of students and, especially, through the eyes of students who tend to regard all school work as irrelevant. What would you say to those students to persuade them that the selected content can be of practical utility to them? Persuading them to participate in the teaching–learning process is more difficult than discussing content with peers, parents, or administrators, because you are asking the students to invest their time and effort. Increase their incentive by explaining practical utility.

STUDIES OF CONTEMPORARY LIFE OUTSIDE OF SCHOOL

A third area that Tyler suggested as a source of ideas for objectives is society as a whole. This source can be looked at from two perspectives. First, taxpayers pay for the educational enterprise and, through state and local school boards, exercise legal control over the schools. Teachers should ask themselves if the objectives being considered are compatible with community goals. Some communities are composed primarily of factory workers, others of farmers, and still others of white-collar workers. Regardless of type, every community wants a good education for its children, but different communities prefer to emphasize different skills and areas of knowledge. To find out if ideas for objectives are compatible with community expectations, teachers should share their ideas with parents and other community members. In addition to whatever responses are elicited, such actions do much to forge good school–

community relations. Such actions demonstrate recognition on the part of teachers that parents and other concerned citizens have parts to play in educating students and should have a voice in planning the educational program.

A word of caution. You may find out some things you do not like. For example, you may find that the community depends largely on one industry and, in order to keep that industry, water and air pollution problems are minimized or overlooked. The school board may not want environmental concerns discussed in the schools. Similarly, you might find that the community is fundamentalist with respect to religion and wants teachers to give as much, or more, emphasis to creationism as to evolution.

It is not likely that there will be serious conflicts between what you believe students should be able to do and what the local school board wants taught. If there is such a conflict, you have two choices: (1) adjust the objectives and content to the standards of the community, or (2) seek employment in a district with objectives closer to your own. It is crucial to remember that once you sign a contract, you accept the obligation of following lawful administrative mandates. You are free to work within the system to change those mandates, but if you arbitrarily change or ignore them you may be fired, regardless of your reasons.

In 1994, a teacher in South Gwinnett high school, in Snellville, Georgia, made national news by lecturing during the one minute of silence required by state law. The teacher explained his action by saying that he believed the one minute of silence conflicted with the U.S. Supreme Court ruling that school prayer was unconstitutional. Nonetheless, he was fired for failing to follow a lawful mandate.[20] He may appeal, but the point is clear. There may be serious consequences to violating your contract regardless of your reasons.

The second perspective is to view the content with respect to its relevance to current society as a whole. Students are more likely to participate in the teaching–learning process if teachers can show that the topics being studied in the classroom are of current interest in the world outside of school. One way to demonstrate this is to turn to recent editions of popular magazines such as, *Time, Newsweek, Reader's Digest, National Geographic,* and *Ebony* and look for articles that focus on some aspect of your instructional unit. The idea is to be able to point to an article in a recent issue of a widely read magazine or newspaper, and show students that people nationwide are currently talking about, making use of, or researching essentially the same things that the students will be studying. This approach helps students feel that what they are learning really is of some worth, really is relevant.

WRITING A RATIONALE

Before going too much further with the refinement of objectives and content, it is a good idea for teachers to take time to look at the general plan through the eyes of a prospective student, particularly one who might be less than wildly enthusiastic. For example, what would you say to a students who asked, "Why do we have to learn this stuff?" A good answer might fan whatever small spark of interest might be there. A poor answer is the equivalent of dousing the spark with water.

A teacher can build a strong and persuasive rationale by addressing each component of the Tyler Rationale: needs of the subject area, needs of the students, and needs of society. In writing the rationale, write as if you were talking to an individual student, perhaps the very one who asked why they had to learn "this stuff." What you are doing is analogous to selling a product. If you do a good sales job, students will be more likely to enter into the teaching–learning process as willing partners. Do a poor job and the students are likely to "tune out."

Needs of the Subject Area

The first part of the rationale should be labeled "Needs of the Subject Area," and should explain why the unit is an important part of the course and discipline. National councils of educators in most disciplines have identified skills and knowledge relevant to their respective subject areas. To the extent that the unit focuses on one or more of the skill or knowledge areas included in those recommended by a national council, it would be appropriate to explain that to students. This will let them know that it is not just you who believes that the unit's objectives and content are important; educators nationally also believe it.

Some of the content to be covered may not be included in the work by the national councils. In this case, simply ask yourself if three other subject-area specialists would be likely to agree that what you have planned is central to your subject area and appropriate for the intended students.

To make this part of the rationale as persuasive as possible, it is a good idea to include samples of interesting facts and concepts that will be in the unit. These act as hooks to capture the students' interest. The more hooks, the more likely the rationale is to interest the students. It is also a good idea to link the content and skills to be covered with content and skills already learned and with those to come.

Needs of the Student

The second part of the rationale should be labeled "Needs of the Student," and should explain to students how they can use the information and skills to better understand and deal with the world around them. Think about what you want your students to learn and how they can use that knowledge and those skills. Typically, high school students are learning how to understand and deal with other people, how to get the things they want, and how cause–effect relationships work. To the extent that you can demonstrate to students that what they will be learning will help them do any of these things, you will be providing an extra incentive for them to willingly partic- ipate in the teaching–learning process. The link can be shown in all subject areas. For example, students may wonder how studying early U.S. history can be useful. You can show them that many third-world countries and former Soviet republics are now striving for the same independence that we strove for in our colonial period. You can show them how studying Shake- speare can be useful, because his works deal with basic human emotions such as revenge, loyalty, and honor. That is what makes them classics. You can show them how studying geometry can be useful by asking them to try calculating the cost of concrete for a driveway without using geometric prin- ciples. The main point of this part of the rationale is to demonstrate to stu- dents that the content to be learned has practical value to them. The greater the practical value, the greater the incentive.

Needs of Society

The last part of the rationale should be labeled "Needs of Society," and it should demonstrate why the information and skills in the unit are of current concern to society. Showing students that magazines such as *Time, Newsweek, U.S. News and World Report, Ebony,* or *National Geographic,* have current arti- cles that relate to the unit helps establish the relevance of the information and skills to be learned to the world outside of school. Another tactic is to demonstrate how people use the skills and concepts to be learned in their day-to-day work.

SUMMARY

Philosophic differences come to the fore when discussions turn to what instructional goals should be pursued. There have been many attempts to describe broad instructional goals, with the Seven Cardinal Principals being a prime example. For better or worse, broad goals generally have little impact on what a particular teacher chooses to teach. To help make that deci- sion, Ralph W. Tyler, in 1949, suggested educators turn to three main sources: (1) subject-area specialists, (2) the learners themselves, and (3) society.

When turning to subject-area specialists, teachers often consider what is included in the texts for their courses. As teachers examine texts, they need to keep in mind both the total instructional time available, typically about 185 days, and relevant concepts. An operational definition of a concept is *a group of things, either concrete or abstract, that have enough elements in common to comprise a unique set.* This task is not easy and teachers can, and should, turn for assistance to sets of standards published by the national councils of many subject areas.

In 1989, the National Council of Teachers of Mathematics became the first national group to publish a set of standards that described what students should actually be able to do in a particular subject area, K–12. Since that time, the national councils of many other subject areas have developed similar sets of standards, most accompanied with examples of measurable outcomes. The net result is likely to be increasing curricular uniformity nationwide.

When considering the learners themselves, teachers need to keep in mind the Pygmalion and Galatea effects. Studies have shown that the expectations of teachers can have a measurable effect on the behavior and academic performance of students (the Pygmalion effect). High expectations promote high performance levels and low expectations promote low performance levels. In a similar fashion, once students have confidence in their own abilities they are willing to face challenges that they would never have considered previously (the Galatea effect). Students can be induced to meet high expectations if the expectations are relevant to their lives.

In its most basic form, relevance has to do with how students can make practical use of what they learn. If the teacher cannot explain to students how the information to be learned can help them improve their understanding of the world around them and help them deal with that world, students have little incentive to participate in the teaching–learning process. It takes effort to look at the content through the eyes of the students and to develop a rationale that is likely to persuade even a reluctant learner, but if the effort persuades even one potential drop-out to stay and learn, it is worth it.

The likelihood of developing convincing rationales increases if teachers can show that the content to be studied is also of concern to the public at large. This can be shown if teachers can find, in widely read magazines or newspapers, references to the content in question. Any links between the content to be learned and the world outside the classroom helps to establish the relevance of that content.

SO HOW DOES THIS AFFECT MY TEACHING?

To be successful in the classroom, you must help your students be successful. The emergence of national standards in many subject areas will help in identifying important skills and concepts in those areas, but the most important task is that of demonstrating to students that the content to be learned has practical utility. It would be risky to assume that your students will participate in the teaching–learning process simply because you think it would be in their best interests. Their desire to learn will be enhanced if you can provide an added inducement, and acquiring skills and knowledge that have practical utility is one of the strongest. The next step is to clearly communicate your instructional intent, and that is the focus of the next chapter.

KEY TERMS, PEOPLE, AND IDEAS

Broad Goals
Seven Cardinal Principles
Five Broad Goals
National Board for Professional Teaching Standards
Tyler's Rationale, 1949—Needs of Subject Area, Students, Society
Concepts
National Councils and Groups
Pygmalion and Galatea Effects

ENDNOTES

1. Johnson, J. A,. H. W. Collins, V. L. Dupuis, and J. N. Johansen, *Introduction to the Foundations of American Education* (Boston: Allyn and Bacon, 1979).

2. Mulhern J., *A History of Education*, 2nd ed. (New York: The Ronald Press, 1959), p. 407.

3. Tyler, Ralph W., *Basic Principles of Curriculum and Instruction* (Chicago; University of Chicago Press), 1949.

4. Tyler, p. 1.

5. Tyler, pp. 5–33.

6. *What Teachers Should Know and Be Able To Do* (Washington, D.C.: National Board for Professional Teaching Standards).

7. *Curriculum and Evaluation Standards for School Mathematics* (Reston, Vir.: The National Council of Teachers of Mathematics, Inc., 1989) (1906 Association Drive, Reston, Virginia, 22091), pp. iii–iv (ISBN 0-87353-273-2).

8. *Curriculum and Evaluation Standards for School Mathematics,* p. 29.

9. *Curriculum and Evaluation Standardsfor School Mathematics,* p. 81.

10. *Curriculum and Evaluation Standards for School Mathematics,* p. 143.

11. *Geography For Life* (Washington, D.C.: National Council for Geographic Education, Geography Standards Project, October 1994) (1600 M Street NW, Washington, D.C. 20036).

12. *Geography For Life,* p. 9.

13. *Geography For Life,* p. 11.

14. Rosenthal, Robert, and L. Jacobson, *Pygmalion in the Classroom* (New York: Holt, Rinehart, and Winston, 1968).

15. Brophy, Jere, "Research on the Self-Fulfilling Prophesy and Teacher Expectations," *Teaching and Learning Program* (Washington, D.C.: National Institute of Education, 1982).

16. Cooper, Harris M., and Thomas L. Good, *Pygmalion Grows Up: Studies in the Expectation Communication Process,* (New York: Longman, 1983).

17. Raudenbush Stephen W., "Magnitude of Teacher Expectancy Effects on Pupil IQ as a Function of the Credibility of Expectation: A Synthesis of Findings from 18 Experiments," *Journal of Educational Psychology*, Vol. 76, no. 1 (Feb. 1994), pp. 85–97.

18. Rosenthal, Robert "Teacher Expectancy Effects: A Brief Update 25 Years after the Pygmalion Experiment," *Journal of Research in Education*, Vol. 1, no. 1 (Spring, 1991), pp. 3–12.

19. Mattson, Mark T., *Factbook on Elementary, Middle, and Secondary Schools, 1993* (New York: Scholastic, 1993), p. 5.20.

20. "Silence in the Classroom," *Newsweek* (October 3, 1994), p. 48.

5

COMMUNICATING
INSTRUCTIONAL INTENT CLEARLY

RATIONALE

The time has come to synthesize the results of your consideration of different philosophies, theories, models, and sources of curricular ideas, and to put on paper your instructional objectives. As you think about objectives, consider the following information published by the U.S. Department of Education in December of 1994. A survey of 1,100 people was conducted concerning perceived problems in education and among the questions asked was, "What corrective measures might help students learn more?" In addition to recommending an emphasis on habits such as being on time and being dependable, 80 percent supported setting up *"very clear guidelines on what students should learn and teachers should teach in every major subject."*[1] Stating objectives in terms that are observable and measurable not only makes good sense educationally, it is what the public is finally learning to demand.

Teachers may have excellent ideas for instructional objectives, but unless they communicate those ideas to students clearly and concisely, the students may see little point to the instruction and "tune out." Further, if instructional objectives are communicated in terms that are observable and measurable: (1) teachers and students can work toward the same goals, (2) teachers become better able to plan instruction that will adequately prepare students to achieve the objectives, and (3) there will be few, if any, questions about whether the objective has, in fact, been achieved. This chapter will help you convert broad goals to relevant and attainable objectives, communicate those objectives to students in terms that are clear and measurable, and thereby, contribute to the success of all concerned.

SAMPLE OBJECTIVES

You will be able, in writing, to:

1. Correctly label at least 80 percent of a set of instructional objectives as: (a) lacking an observable terminal behavior, (b) lacking a minimum acceptable standard, (c) lacking both an observable behavior and a minimum acceptable standard, (d) asking for different behaviors, or (e) acceptable as written.
2. Rewrite a set of poorly written instructional objectives so that at least 80 percent of them include observable terminal behaviors (identified with an underline) and minimum acceptable standards (identified with a double underline).

WHY PRECISE GOALS ARE USEFUL

In 1921, Boyd H. Bode spoke of the need for educators to give "consideration to what constitutes a good life in the social order."[2] He was concerned that rather than having broad educational goals that would result in good people living good lives in a good society, educators might focus on simplistic, perhaps even superfluous goals, because dealing with such goals is less difficult. He was concerned that we might narrow the goals so much that we would lose sight of the original intent. That we might, for example, concern ourselves so much with teaching students to spell and describe "democracy," that we would forget about the larger goal of teaching them how to act as citizens in a democracy. He had good reason for concern, and prospective teachers should have the same concern. No one wants to see students turned into stimulus–response subjects who learn trivia. At the same time, it would be foolish to ignore the need for accountability.

Broad goals are just that, broad. To travel is a broad goal. In order to achieve this broad goal, one must be more specific, designating travel to London or to Paris. To be accountable, teachers must take broad goals, such as "to live a good life in a good society," "help students move from lower- to higher-level skills," and "become critical thinkers and problem-solvers," and express those goals in terms that are observable and measurable. As teachers, we need to be able to tell students, parents, and anyone else who is concerned, what it is that students will be able to do when they complete a particular course that they were unable to do before taking the course. We need to specify measurable outcomes.

PURPOSES AND PARTS OF PRECISE INSTRUCTIONAL OBJECTIVES

The purpose of precise instructional objectives is to explain to students, before instruction begins, exactly what will be expected of them after instruction. **Ralph Tyler** is sometimes referred to as the "father of behavioral objectives," but it was **Robert Mager** who popularized the idea that to maximize clarity and minimize misinterpretations, instructional objectives should include an observable terminal behavior, conditions (when needed), and a minimum acceptable standard of performance.[3]

Some educators claim that the specificity of precise instructional objectives (also called behavioral objectives and specific learner outcomes) leads to triviality, but that happens only if the writer of the objectives allows it to happen. It is *not* a problem inherent with the statement of such objectives. Increasing numbers of educators recognize that the approach suggested by Tyler and Mager is the surest way to tell students what is expected of them and exactly how their competence will be tested. Further, the specification of expected learner outcomes, before instruction begins, enables the teacher to more surely select instructional activities and materials that will help students acquire the needed information and skills.[4]

Observable Terminal Behaviors

Observable terminal behaviors describe, in terms that can be seen and measured, exactly what students will be expected to do at the end of instruction. Word choice is crucial. Experience has shown that words such as "know," "learn," and "understand," are less effective in describing expected behaviors than words such as "explain in writing," "underline," and "diagram." This is so because the words in the first group are not directly observable and can be interpreted in a number of ways. Consider the following examples.

You will:

1. know the differences between prose and poetry.
2. demonstrate an understanding of prose and poetry by writing the definitions of these terms and illustrating each definition with the title of an appropriate example.
3. define, in writing, the terms prose and poetry and illustrate each definition with the name of an example.

The only practical way to determine if someone knows something is to have them demonstrate the knowledge. In the first objective, the word "know" is not directly observable so students, parents, and administrators cannot be sure how the teacher expects the knowledge to be demonstrated. It could be demonstrated via an essay or objective test, by asking students to orally answer questions about it, or by having students cite examples of prose and poetry. Further, without knowing how the competence is to be demonstrated, students do not know how to best prepare themselves, and neither the teacher nor the students can ascertain when, or if, the objective is finally achieved. The lack of an observable behavior makes the first objective useless in terms of competency-based instruction. It does not clearly convey instructional intent.

The second objective is better than the first because it includes an observable behavior (by writing). Since both the teacher and the students can now describe how achievement of the objective is to be demonstrated, it becomes easier to plan instruction that will help students acquire the necessary skills, easier for students to focus their efforts on achieving the specified skills, and easier for the teacher and the students to determine when, in fact, the objective is achieved. Unfortunately, the objective is unnecessarily wordy. If the words "demonstrate an understanding of" are omitted, the intent of the objective would remain the same. Those words are superfluous and should be deleted.

The third objective is the best of the three because it includes an observable behavior, "define in writing," so everyone concerned knows what is expected, and it is concise. The more clearly students understand what is expected of them, the more likely they are to meet those expectations.

Some terms, such as "identify," "differentiate," and "solve," may appear less ambiguous than terms such as "know" and "learn," but they, too, describe purely mental activities. Teachers need to word objectives so that the results of mental activity can be observed—for example, "identify by recording on a checklist," "differentiate in writing," or "write the step-by-step procedure." Specifying the expected, overt activity sharpens the picture students have of what is expected, and this tends to reduce anxiety. With the expected behavior clear, students do not have to try to guess the teacher's intent.

Sometimes it makes sense to have students demonstrate a competence orally. While this kind of competence demonstration has its place, particularly to sample overall student competence, its disadvantage must be kept in mind. If an objective requires a student to "state orally" certain specifics, the reliability of the competence demonstration is compromised if other students hear the recitation. It would be illogical, for example, to write an objective that stated, "The student will orally state three measures of central tendency," unless provisions were made for each student to demonstrate the competence privately. If the competence were demonstrated in a classroom, the teacher would be unable to differentiate between students who understood the material and those who were merely parroting what they heard others say.

If a large proportion of the objectives will be demonstrated in writing (which is usually the case), it is advantageous to state, at the beginning of the list of objectives, that all objectives will be demonstrated in writing unless otherwise specified. This eliminates the need to include the words "in writing" in virtually every objective. Conciseness facilitates understanding.

Sometimes, teachers have a particular behavior in mind, but unintentionally specify a different behavior. Consider the following examples.

You will be able to:

4. demonstrate the ability to dissect a frog by orally describing at least three steps of the dissecting process.
5. dissect a frog following standard dissection procedures, and correctly label at least three internal organs.

Judging from the activities called for in the fourth objective, the teacher apparently started out with the intention of having students demonstrate the ability to dissect a frog. At some point, the teacher thought about having students describe the dissecting process and both behaviors ended up in the objective. It is not clear if the oral descriptions were to be in addition to, or in place of, the actual dissection. What is clear is that the only way students can demonstrate the ability to dissect a frog is to actually dissect a frog. Having students orally describe three steps in the dissecting process might be a useful activity, but it is not equivalent to actually dissecting the frog. The fifth objective communicates instructional intent more clearly.

The "terminal" part of "observable terminal," means at the end of the instructional unit. Teachers typically state about a dozen terminal objectives for a semester-long course. These objectives may be supplemented with narrower unit objectives and these, in turn, are supplemented with daily "enroute" objectives. However, the list of terminal course objectives will define the scope of your course, and will also be of greatest initial interest to students, parents, and administrators.

Conditions

The function of conditions is to clarify the student's mental picture of any constraints that will affect the demonstration of the specified competence. Conditions frequently refer to time limits or to the use of aids or special equipment, but they can refer to whatever factors are considered important to the demonstration of the behavior. For example, a physical education teacher might consider it important to specify "using a regulation baseball" in an objective concerning the hitting of line drives. Doing so would answer the question of whether a baseball or a softball is to be used. Consider the following objectives.

You will be able to:

6. describe, in writing, at least two possible advantages and two possible disadvantages associated with the use of precise instructional objectives.
7. using only notes, describe, in a paper of no more than two pages, at least two possible advantages and two possible disadvantages associated with the use of precise instructional objectives.

Objective six includes an observable terminal behavior, "describe, in writing," but students do not know if they will be expected to memorize the required information or if they can simply open their notes or a text and copy what they need. In objective seven, doubts are removed. The condition that notes may be used is stated clearly, and there is little room for misunderstanding.

While statements of conditions are usually quite helpful, and are sometimes absolutely necessary to avoid misunderstandings, some care must be taken in their use. Conditions such as "after a lecture," "as was discussed in class," or "after reading Chapter 10," usually weaken an objective because they limit the sources from which a student may draw information. How students acquire knowledge or skills should not be specified in the objective. Certainly it would not be the teacher's intention to penalize a student for acquiring information or skills outside the class, but conditions such as those just mentioned imply such a penalty. If references to specific sources must be made, those sources should be nationally available (i.e., the American Medical Association or the ASPCA). This helps avoid parochial views.

Another point to remember is that it makes little sense to try to state all conditions for all objectives. For example, the condition "with no aids," will probably be common to many objectives. To include those words in each and every objective would be repetitive and distracting. A more logical solution would be to state the conditions common to most objectives at the beginning of the list of objectives and to discuss the general nature of these conditions with students prior to instruction. It is common, for example, for a list of objectives to be preceded by a statement such as "The following objectives must be demonstrated in writing and under test conditions unless otherwise specified." Such a statement leaves little room for misinterpretation, but still enables the teacher to modify specific objectives.

As a general rule, specific conditions should be stated only when there is a possibility that doubts or misunderstandings may arise. If there are any doubts about whether conditions are needed in a particular objective, they should be included. If no conditions are initially specified in an objective, adding them at the time the competence is to be demonstrated is likely to result in strong, and justified, student resentment.

Minimum Acceptable Standards

The last element included in a precise instructional objective is a minimum acceptable standard of performance. The need for minimum acceptable standards is obvious. Unless you plan to assign a passing grade to every student who walks through your classroom door, you will need grading criteria. At the very least, you need to identify the minimal competencies that students must demonstrate to earn a grade of D, and factors such as perfect attendance and smiling a lot should not do the job. Teachers need to decide how well each of the observable behaviors must be demonstrated in order to be deemed acceptable. In making this decision, teachers should keep the Pygmalion effect in mind. If you set low standards with the hope that virtually all students will be able to achieve them, students may, indeed, meet those low standards, but their potential for doing better or more significant work will not be tapped. If you set high standards and demonstrate, by word and deed, that you believe students *can* achieve them, there is a good chance student performance will rise to meet the standards. Go for the gold.

Minimum acceptable standards can be stated in quantitative and/or qualitative terms. As the name suggests, quantitative terms specify quantities such as six out of ten, or 60 percent. Qualitative terms specify particular qualities or points that are sought. The following are examples of objectives using quantitative and/or qualitative minimum acceptable standards. You will be able to:

8. Given four sets of symptoms, diagnose, in writing, the correct disease in *at least three* of the cases.
9. Write *at least six* precise, instructional objectives, each of which includes *an observable terminal behavior, conditions,* and *a minimum acceptable standard.*
10. Explain, in writing, the proper use of the wood lathe including: (a) *the procedure for mounting material,* (b) *the proximity of the rest block to the material,* (c) *the speed of the chuck,* (d) *the proper use of the tool bit,* and (e) *at least two safety precautions.*

Objective eight utilizes only a quantitative standard (at least three). Objective nine combines a quantitative standard (at least six) with a qualitative standard (includes an observable terminal behavior, conditions, and a minimum acceptable standard). Objective ten includes a qualitative standard that describes the minimum elements necessary in a student explanation (points a–e).

Sometimes a quantitative standard can be confusing. For example, suppose that an objective called for students to solve a series of math problems with at least 80 percent accuracy. It is not clear whether students must correctly solve at least eight of ten problems or if the student could get each of the answers wrong, but still end up with 80 percent of the points because of earning partial credit for each problem. Potentially confusing points such as this one need to be anticipated and clarified.

A common misconception concerning minimum acceptable standards is that the specification of lengths of answers is, by itself, sufficient to clarify what is expected. Generally this is not so. Just as you strive to be concise, you want to encourage your students to be concise. Specifying minimum lengths works against this by requiring students to fill up *X* amount of space, regardless of how much or how little they know. Ideally, you want students to say what they have to say and stop. However, if a paper must be at least two pages in length, students will feel compelled to fill two pages even though they may only have a page and half worth of information. They did not want to write that extra half page and you will not want to read it. Why require it?

Teachers should always expect to be held to their word. With respect to objectives, this means that students may interpret your words literally and expect you to give them credit for doing exactly what you asked of them. In this sense, the objective is a contract. Consider the following objectives.

You will be able to:

11. Describe, in a paper of no more than two pages, the results of World War II.
12. Type at least two letters in one class period.

In objective 11, a student could argue that he or she should receive full credit for achieving the objective for simply writing, "The Allies won." This answer would meet the requirement of "a paper of no more than two pages," but it confuses conditions with minimum standards. The main focus should be on content, not length. To give students some idea of expected length, one could specify a maximum length such as, "in no more than two pages." This gives students some idea of expected length, but allows them to stop writing when they have said what they had to say. In addition, one must be sure to specify the content expected.

With objective 12, a student could generate an embarrassing situation by typing just two letters such as an X and a Y. If this were your student and you refused to give the student an A for the assignment, you could end up trying to explain to a parent or principal why you failed to say exactly what you meant. The argument would hinge not on the fact that the student outrageously and deliberately misinterpreted the instructional intent, it would hinge on the fact that you did not communicate clearly. The same could happen if the student turned in two messy, error-filled pages. In both cases, the quantitative limitations failed to convey the true minimum standards. Teachers need to use language clearly, precisely, and concisely, especially when communicating instructional intent.

If time or length is a consideration for achievement, it should be a minimum standard. For example, if an objective calls for students to run the 100-yard dash in 20 seconds, the specification of time is crucial. Similarly, a teacher who is teaching how to summarize can include "in less than one page" as part of a minimum standard.

Qualitative standards often imply subjective judgments. This sometimes makes it difficult to describe the particular attributes or characteristics that must be included in the behavior to meet minimal standards. For example, the following objectives become increasingly clear as additional qualitative standards are added.

You will be able to describe, in writing, the:

13. results of World War II.
14. effects of World War II on France and Germany.
15. results of World War II in terms of at least two economic developments in France and Germany.

Each succeeding objective communicates instructional intent more clearly and minimizes the chances for misunderstandings better than its predecessor. As more standards are added, the picture of the desired end product becomes more and more clear in the mind of the student. However, trying to include every possible point would make the objective so cumbersome that it would be virtually useless. For example, when evaluating papers, teachers typically consider factors such as logical organization, completeness, relevancy, neatness, and mechanics. Once it is explained to students (and specified in writing) that these factors are always considered, it is not necessary to include them in each objective. This will help keep objectives to a reasonable length.

Typically, sentences, including objectives, get longer as ideas are embellished with descriptions, examples, and sometimes other ideas. These embellishments are intended to clarify the main idea, but, if they give the reader too many things to keep in mind, they have the opposite effect. Generally, sentences or objectives longer than about 25 words tend to be difficult to comprehend. Therefore, whenever possible, objectives should be written as single sentences no longer than 25 words.

The fact that all possible qualitative standards are not included in each objective should not be taken as an abdication of the teacher's right or professional obligation to make judgments concerning overall quality, and this point should be made clear to students. The teacher should simply acknowledge the fact that many instructional objectives deal with complex concepts or human behaviors. The objectives are attempts to convey, as clearly as possible, the true instructional intent by specifying as many pertinent parameters as makes good sense. If students are expected to refer to particular ideas, points, or aspects when demonstrating a competence, those points should be identified in the objective, but terms such as "main ideas," "most important points," and "major aspects" should be used only with the understanding that the teacher is willing to accept the student's opinion regarding these matters. Opinions cannot be graded. A teacher who is not precise in describing terminal behaviors or minimal acceptable standards should not hold students accountable for the consequences of misinterpretation.

SUMMARY

To be useful in the context of accountability for teachers and students, broad goals must be translated into behaviors that can be observed and measured. Precise instructional objectives identify expected learning outcomes in terms of observable terminal behaviors, conditions, and minimum acceptable standards.

Observable behaviors are overt and include behaviors such as "write," "orally state," and "physically demonstrate." Oral demonstrations of a competence pose a problem, because in order to be sure that each student has achieved the objective, the teacher must assess each student privately. Teachers also need to be sure that each objective calls for only one behavior. Terminal behaviors are those that are demonstrated at the end of an instructional unit. Teachers generally specify terminal objectives in course syllabi and supplement those with narrower unit objectives and with daily "enroute" objectives.

Conditions may be included in a precise instructional objective, if they are needed to clarify the terminal behavior and avoid misunderstandings. Typical conditions include "under test conditions," "without aids," and "using calculators." It is common for teachers to include an observable terminal behavior and conditions in a single statement that precedes a list of objectives (for example, "The following objectives must be demonstrated in writing, and under test conditions, unless otherwise specified"). If no conditions are built into the objectives, it is unfair to impose them at the time the behavior is to be demonstrated, since students would have had no way to prepare for them. There is no place in an objective for the specification of where or how students acquire knowledge of skills. Including such conditions might result in penalizing students for using knowledge or skills that are correct, but different from those covered in class.

Minimum acceptable standards may be stated quantitatively or qualitatively. Quantitative standards specify a quantity such as 60 percent or two out of three. Qualitative standards specify the qualities or points that must be included for the behavior to be deemed acceptable. When thinking about minimum standards, it is a good idea to remember the Pygmalion effect. Teacher expectations can affect student performance. Typically, the higher the standards (within reason), the higher the performance level. Further, remember the Galatea effect. As students' self-confidence increases, so does their willingness to take on ever more demanding tasks.

Typically, teachers are more interested in the quality of student work than in the length of such work. It makes sense, therefore, to refer to maximum, rather than minimum, lengths. This gives students an idea of expected length, while at the same time making it clear that students should stop writing when they have said what they want to say.

Teachers should word objectives carefully to avoid situations in which they are forced to admit that they said one thing, but meant something else.

Teachers should say exactly what they mean. Further, to make the objective as readable and clear as possible, it should be stated as a single sentence, preferably of no more than about 25 words. Once the components of objectives are understood, teachers can move on to the task of determining if they cover a range of thinking skills. That is the focus of the next chapter.

SO HOW DOES THIS AFFECT MY TEACHING?

If you ever sat in a class and were not sure of exactly what is was that you had to do to pass that course, you know that it is not a comfortable feeling. You can help students in your classes avoid that feeling by stating precise instructional objectives. Such objectives will help you and your students focus attention and energy on the same goals. You will benefit because, once you decide what the terminal behaviors are, you are more able to select instructional activities that will appropriately prepare students. Students are helped because, by knowing exactly what is expected of them, they can continually check their own progress and assess their own mastery of the competence. Precise instructional objectives also communicate the scope of your course to parents, peers, and administrators. They constitute your statement of instructional intent and, because they are stated in observable and measurable terms, they benefit all concerned.

PRACTICE EXERCISES AND SELF-TEST

Practice Exercise 1: Identifying Weaknesses in Objectives

Some of the following objectives are stated in unacceptable form. Use the following rating scale to pinpoint the weakness(es) in each objective and check your responses with those furnished.

Rating Scale

A. Lacks an observable behavior.
B. Lacks a minimum acceptable standard.
C. Lacks both A and B.
D. Calls for two behaviors.
E. The objective is acceptable as written.

To meet the minimum acceptable standards for this course you must:

1. Know the democratic principles on which our country is founded.
2. Know the names of the U.S. senators from your home state.
3. Be an alert and an aware citizen.

4. Given a microcomputer and a diskette, correctly run a specified program.
5. Take an active role in society.
6. Demonstrate typing skill by retyping two letters in class, without errors and using block style.
7. Understand the plight of the poor people in our country.
8. Orally list at least two strengths and two weaknesses of the United Nations.
9. Demonstrate proper CPR procedures by describing each step of the process in proper sequence.
10. Demonstrate the ability to write precise instructional objectives by achieving a score of at least 70 percent on a multiple-choice test dealing with the construction of such objectives.

Practice Exercise 1—Answers: 1–C, 2–A, 3–C, 4–E, 5–C, 6–E, 7–C, 8–E, 9–D, 10–D

Practice Exercise 2: Rewriting Instructional Objectives

Rewrite each of the poorly written objectives so that it includes an observable behavior, minimum standard, and conditions. Identify the observable behavior with a single underline and the minimum acceptable standard with a double underline. Examples of acceptable rewrites are shown below, but yours may vary considerably.

You will be able to:

1. Explain, *in writing, at least two* of the democratic principles on which our country is founded
2. *Write* the names of *the U.S. senators* from your home state.
3. Select a current legislative issue, *write* a one-page letter to your U.S. senators expressing your views on that issue, and give *at least two reasons* for those views in the letter.
4. No changes needed.
5. *Write* a letter to the editor of the local paper *expressing your views* on a current local problem and include *at least two rationales* for those views.
6. No changes needed.
7. *Orally* state *at least two factors* inhibiting the elimination of poverty within our country.
8. No changes needed.
9. *Demonstrate proper CPR techniques* using a mannequin under test conditions.
10. *Recall and/or apply* information concerning the structure of precise instructional objectives well enough *to answer* correctly *at least 80 percent* of a series of multiple-choice questions concerning such objectives.

Self-test

Some of the following objectives are stated in unacceptable form. Use the following rating scale to pinpoint the weakness(es) in each objective and check your responses with those furnished.

Rating Scale

A. Lacks an observable behavior.
B. Lacks a minimum acceptable standard.
C. Lacks both A and B.
D. Calls for two behaviors.
E. The objective is acceptable as written.

You will be able to:

1. Write a critical reaction to *Moby Dick.*
2. When asked by the teacher, state orally the names of two wartime presidents.
3. Recite the Pledge of Allegiance with no errors.
4. Demonstrate a knowledge of proper tool use by selecting a saw with which to cut plywood.
5. Understand quadratic equations well enough to solve, on paper, any three that are given, without the use of aids and within thirty minutes.
6. Demonstrate easy mathematical skills with at least 80 percent accuracy.
7. Understand fully the terms volt, ohm, and alternating current.
8. Demonstrate good physical condition, in part, by running the mile in less than six minutes.
9. Understand written French.
10. Be proud to be an American 85 percent of the time.

Self-Test Answers: 1–B, 2–E, 3–E, 4–D, 5–E, 6–C, 7–A, 8–E, 9–C, 10–A

KEY TERMS, PEOPLE, AND IDEAS

Precise Instructional Objective
Ralph Tyler, Robert Mager
Observable Terminal Behavior
Conditions
Minimum Acceptable Standard

ENDNOTES

1. "Safety, Order, and 'The Basic' Top Public's Education Concerns," *Goals 2000: Community Update* (Washington, D.C.: U.S. Department of Education, December 1994, no. 19) p. 1. (For a copy of the full report at $10.00 per copy, contact Public Agenda, 6 East 39th Street, Suite 900, New York, NY 10016 (212) 686-6610.)

2. Bode, Boyd H., "Education at the Crossroads," *Progressive Education*, Vol. 8 (November 1931), p. 548.

3. Mager, Robert J., *Preparing Instructional Objectives*, rev. ed. (Palo Alto, Calif.: Fearon, 1984).

4. Kibler, Robert J., Larry L. Baker, and David T. Miles, *Behavioral Objectives and Instruction*, 2nd ed. (Boston: Allyn and Bacon, 1981); Popham W. James, *Criterion-Referenced Measurement* (Englewood Cliffs, N.J.: Prentice-Hall, 1978); and Plowman, Paul D., *Behavioral Objectives* (Chicago: Science Research Associates, 1971).

6

CLASSIFYING AND USING PRECISE INSTRUCTIONAL OBJECTIVES

RATIONALE

Do you remember when you got your first bicycle? You were probably immensely pleased and wanted to start riding immediately but, if you were like most of us, you needed some help before you were able to zip around and show Mom how you could ride with no hands. You had to progress from simple to more complex skills. Your main task as a teacher is to help your students make that same progression, to move from low-level skills and knowledge to higher-level skills and knowledge. However, you can, and should, go even further. You can help students learn to do things such as make intelligent decisions and become more self-disciplined, more tolerant, and more understanding. You can help them grow up, but it takes planning.

The previous chapter focused on how to write objectives so that the terminal behaviors were observable and measurable. This chapter focuses on how to classify instructional objectives on the basis of the kinds of thinking and action they require of students. Understanding the taxonomy of educational objectives and being able to classify them should help you write objectives that call for movement from low-level, teacher-directed activities to higher-level, self-directed activities.

One of the best-known classification schemes was developed in 1956 and is described in a book edited by **Benjamin Bloom** entitled, *Taxonomy of Educational Objectives: Handbook 1: Cognitive Domain.*[1] "Bloom's taxonomy" (as it is popularly known) is divided into three domains, and each domain is divided into levels. The cognitive domain, delineated in *Handbook 1*, concerns the acquisition and manipulation of factual information. The affective domain, delineated in *Handbook II*,[2] concerns the development of attitudes, values, and feelings. The psychomotor domain, delineated in a book entitled *A Taxonomy of the Psychomotor Domain*,[3] concerns the development of physical skills. This chapter will familiarize you with all of them. Further, the chapter will suggest ways to check the extent to which your objectives are reasonable and communicate effectively. Your written course objectives are your clearest statement concerning what you believe students should be able to do when they complete your course. This chapter will help you make that statement as powerful as possible.

SAMPLE OBJECTIVES

You will be able, in writing, to:

1. List each major level of the cognitive, affective, and psychomotor domains. (Knowledge)
2. Describe the distinguishing characteristics of each level of the cognitive domain. (Comprehension)
3. Given a series of instructional objectives, classify at least 80 percent of them as to correct domain and level and explain the main factor that would justify each proper classification. (Analysis)
4. Given an instructional topic, write one precise instructional objective at each level of each appropriate domain. (Synthesis)

THE TAXONOMY AND ITS USE

The taxonomy of educational objectives was developed to help educators classify objectives according to the skills and abilities they elicit from students. When working with the taxonomic domains and levels, keep in mind that the taxonomy is a theoretical division of skills and abilities. For example, the hierarchy of levels within each domain implies increasing complexity of thought and action, but this may not be so. Since we do not yet fully understand how the mind stores or manipulates information, we can only theorize that tasks such as memorizing basic number facts are less complex than tasks such as performing long division. The fact that it seems reasonable does not necessarily make it so. Further, the classification of any specific behavior must be made in relation to the task and the background of the individual performing that task.

Complicating the matter still further is that taxonomic divisions are more easily delineated on paper than they are in practice. Some objectives may not fit, unequivocally, into one specific level or even into one specific domain. The lines between domains and levels blend like lines between colors in a rainbow. This means that while most objectives can be clearly classified as to domain and level, the classification of others may be hazy. Fortunately, the possibility of haziness does not seriously lessen the usefulness of the taxonomy. Its power is not in its precision with respect to any one objective, but in its ability to enable teachers to see, generally, whether they have included a reasonable range of skills and abilities.

THE COGNITIVE DOMAIN

The cognitive domain deals with the acquisition and manipulation of factual information. It is divided into six major levels, each of which is divided into sublevels. When classifying objectives it is usual to do so according to major level, but to understand the major levels it is helpful to examine some of their components.

1.00 Knowledge

In the taxonomy, "Knowledge" is used as a label for the lowest level of cognitive activity. At this level, students are expected simply to have memorized and be able to recall or recognize information. Over the years, memorization has often been criticized as a trivial or unnecessary learning step. The fact is, however, that unless we commit a great deal of information to memory, we would not have time to do much of anything. Consider how much you do each day by rote memorization. You do not have to think about every movement when you tie your shoes, because you have memorized the process. You also memorized how to find your way to class, how to write your name, and how to write a check. These actions, which now require virtually no thought, took considerable concentration and time when you first learned to do them and, if you had not committed them to memory, they would still require a great deal of time and concentration. For verification, watch a three-year-old tying his or her shoelaces. The process of learning something to the point that you can use the information or skill with little or no conscious thought is called **automatization.**[4]

The range of things that can be committed to memory illustrates the complexity and richness of this level. Consider the following sublevels listed and described in Handbook I:

1.00 Knowledge
    1.10   Of Specifics
            1.11   Terminology
            1.12   Specific Facts
    1.20   Of Ways and Means of Dealing with Specifics
            1.21   Conventions
            1.22   Trends and Sequences

       1.23   Classifications and Categories
       1.24   Criteria
       1.25   Methodology
  1.30   Of the Universals and Abstractions in a Field
       1.31   Principles and Generalizations
       1.32   Theories and Structures[5]

In thinking about knowledge-level activities, it is sometimes useful to think of words that reflect those activities. Some of these words are: define, identify, label, list, and state. These words reflect the fact that information has been recalled or recognized, but they give no indication of whether the student understands what has been recalled or recognized. This is characteristic of Knowledge-level activity. Examples of Knowledge-level objectives follow. You will be able to:

1. Orally list five parts and three formats characteristic of a business letter.
2. Orally state the formula for calculating the area of rectangles.
3. Write the unit of metric measure corresponding to (not equivalent to) pounds, ounces, quarts, gallons, inches, yards, and miles (e.g., miles/ kilometers).
4. Given a map of the United States showing state boundaries, write in the name of each state.

2.00 Comprehension

The second level of the cognitive domain is Comprehension. It is the view of many educators that this is the level most emphasized in today's schools. If this is so, our level of emphasis is disappointing because the Comprehension level is low in the hierarchy of intellectual skills. This level indicates that the student can recall information, and that the information has meaning to the student. The divisions within this level are as follows:

2.00   Comprehension
       2.10   Translation—Going from one level of abstraction to another, from one symbol system to another, or from one verbal form to another.
       2.20   Interpretation—Being able to understand the interrelationships among words, symbols, or sounds well enough to describe their meaning in his or her own words.
       2.30   Extrapolation—Being able to make projections, see implications, or draw conclusions on the basis of given data.[6]

In thinking about Comprehension-level activities, it is sometimes useful to think of words that reflect those activities. Some of those words include convert, explain, describe, estimate, paraphrase, predict, and rewrite. Examples of Comprehension-level objectives follow.

You will be able, in writing and under test conditions, to:

1. Describe what is meant by the tone of a letter and cite examples of two tones.
2. Explain, in your own words, the formula for calculating the area of rectangles.
3. Translate the formula for converting degrees Fahrenheit to degrees Celsius from sentence form to mathematical statement form.
4. Using cause–effect reasoning, explain at least two probable effects of either dramatically increasing or decreasing taxes in a country.

3.00 Application

The third level of the cognitive domain is Application. As used in the taxonomy, Application means the act of using rules, principles, or generalizations in a mechanical way to complete a task.[7] It is useful to think of the student understanding a principle or rule at the Comprehension level and then using the principle or rule in a practical situation at the Application level. Some words that reflect such activities include change, calculate, convert, show, and solve. Examples of Application-level objectives follow.

You will be able, under test conditions, to:

1. Given unorganized components of a business letter and a specific business letter format, organize the components according to the specified format and type the letter without error.
2. Given the dimensions of a room and the cost of carpeting, calculate the cost of carpeting the room to within five dollars.
3. Given a series of temperatures in degrees Fahrenheit, convert, in writing, at least 80 percent of them to correct degrees Celsius.
4. Create a chart showing the percentage of personal income taken in taxes in any ten countries.

4.00 Analysis

The fourth level of the cognitive domain is Analysis. Many educators consider Analysis to be the first of the higher cognitive levels. The taxonomy includes three kinds of skills in the Analysis level.

4.00   Analysis
        4.10   Analysis of Elements
        4.20   Analysis of Relationships
        4.30   Analysis of Organizational Principles[8]

The analysis of elements requires that some whole, an idea, problem, or sample, be broken down into its constituent parts or elements. This task is done, essentially, by asking a series of yes/no questions that focus on subtle or unstated points. These questions enable you to say that particular distinguishing characteristics are, or are not, present. For example, suppose that you were trying to determine which kind of behavior modification technique was reflected in a scenario. A general question such as, "Is this an example of operant conditioning?" would not be helpful, because it leaves open the question of "How do we know?" To be useful, the questions must have the classification criteria built into them. Questions such as, "Is the subject initiating the action to change his or her behavior?" (indicative of operant conditioning), or "Does the change focus on an intrinsic reward?" (indicative of reality therapy), would be more useful. By including in the question the distinguishing characteristics of the elements being sought, we eliminate or minimize the chance of missing or misidentifying an element. We know what to look for.

The analysis of relationships focuses on the relationships between or among elements. In demonstrating this skill, the student might be asked to see if the ideas expressed in an article were consistent with one another, or to differentiate between main ideas and supporting ideas.

The analysis of organizational principles is demonstrated by describing the organization or structure of a whole. For example, it is relatively simple to explain the differences among educational philosophies. It is more difficult, however, to read an article about education and to determine the probable philosophical position of the writer. To do that, one needs to look for relationships among the ideas expressed in the article and between those and the basic principles of various educational philosophies.

Sometimes the line between Application-level and Analysis-level tasks is not clear. One of the key points of difference lies in the complexity of the task. At the Application level, the task is so clear-cut that there is little question as to which rules, principles, and procedures need to be used. The focus is on using them correctly in a new situation and without prompting. At the Analysis level, the task is more ambiguous. The elements, relationships, and organization principles sought are not so obvious and may not call clearly for the use of a particular rule or procedure.

It is important to remember that when you analyze something, you make objective observations. One test of the objectivity of the analysis is to ask whether three equally qualified experts would probably come to the same conclusion. For example, suppose that you gave three suits to three equally qualified tailors and asked them to determine which suit was best made. They would all look at things such as the quality of material, stitching, and cut, and, assuming that one suit was, in fact, better made than the others, they would all identify that suit as being best made. Analysis is a matter of identifying the true state of affairs and being able to point to the factors that make it the true state of affairs. Words that typically reflect Analysis include diagram, differentiate, relate, and separate. Examples of Analysis-level objectives follow. Note that in each objective, the student is expected to determine the true state of affairs and to document that determination with specific facts—what and why.

You will be able, in writing and under test conditions, to:

1. Explain, given a problem and two business letters written to resolve that problem, which of the two letters is better written and identify at least three elements concerning structure and/or tone to support that determination.
2. Given the relevant characteristics of a family and the costs and life expectancies of various kinds of carpeting, determine which carpeting would be most cost effective.
3. Explain what changes would have to be made in order for a cake to be properly prepared, given the elevation of a city in meters, metric measuring utensils, and a box of cake mix from a typical American store.
4. Given a standard 1040 tax form with its instructions, and a description of the family's income and expenses, determine if it would be advantageous for a family to itemize deductions, and cite at least two factors from the form and description to justify that decision.

5.00 Synthesis

The fifth level of the cognitive domain is Synthesis. In this context, Synthesis means the assembling of parts into a new and unique whole. The taxonomy describes three forms of Synthesis.

5.00	Synthesis	
	5.10	Production of a Unique Communication
	5.20	Production of a Plan, or Proposed Set of Operations
	5.30	Derivation of a Set of Abstract Relations[9]

Unique communications consists of words, sounds, shapes, colors, and actions that can be assembled to effectively convey ideas, feelings, or experiences to others. The second kind of product, a plan or a proposed set of operations, would be any new plan or set of operations that would meet specified requirements. Those requirements could be given to, or developed by, the student along with the plan or set of operations. The last kind of product is the derivation of a set of abstract relations. A typical example would be the derivation of a hypothesis.

Although students will be using knowledge and skills already mastered as the basis of their Synthesis activities, the teacher must not confuse the simple accumulation of related parts with Synthesis. For example, the task of creating a nutritious menu might be accomplished simply by selecting *X* foods from *Y* food groups. Such an activity might be appropriate at the Application level. If, on the other hand, the task is to create a one-day menu that will appeal to, and meet the nutritional needs of, a person with specified characteristics, such as a nine-year-old boy, or a high-school girl, the complexity of the task increases significantly and so does the creativity needed to accomplish it. To elicit the higher-level thinking indicative of Synthesis-level thinking, the task must require more than the application of rules and principles in a mechanical way; its main focus must be on creativity and higher-level thinking. Some words that reflect Synthesis-level thinking include compose, construct, create, develop, devise, and design.

There are a few factors that complicate the writing of Synthesis-level objectives. First, although the focus is on creativity, the product must still be evaluated. Pablo Picasso's work reflects a great deal of creativity, but suppose it was 1937 and Pablo was working on "Guernica" in your art class. ("Guernica" was Picasso's interpretation of the Spanish civil war as a surrealistic nightmare.) How would you have evaluated his work? It is likely that Pablo would have gotten an F and been sent to see the guidance counselor. If Picasso had had to work within the accepted standards of his day, his creativity would have been stifled. The dilemma is that minimum acceptable standards are needed in classroom situations, but the more detailed those standards are, the more they limit the student's creativity.

Second, it is unwise to have students respond to hypothetical situations. Logically, if you ask students to enter the world of make-believe, you must be prepared to accept their ideas of what that world is like, regardless of how outlandish or bizarre. If you ask a student to describe what the United States would be like with Newt Gingrich as President and the student says we would all turn into saints, give the student an A. In the land of make-believe, anything is possible. It is unwise to send students there and then try to grade what they say they see.

Finally, be careful not to ask students to do anything that you cannot do. For example, unless you can develop a politically and economically feasible plan to reduce the national debt, do not ask students to do so. Examples of Synthesis-level objectives follow.

You will be able, under test conditions, to:

1. Compose, for your local newspaper, an original editorial of no more than one page, in which you describe a series of changes in the local governing structure that would make it more democratic.
2. While staying within a given budget for a house, design a floor plan that provides convenience and privacy for a family with two young children and explain each of the convenience and privacy features.
3. Write a unique poem that might help young children learn the meaning of at least three units of metric measure.

4. Given a short story, create a new ending that is consistent with the original plot and characters, but which differs from the original ending in at least two significant ways.

6.00 Evaluation

    6.10   Judgments in Terms of Internal Evidence
    6.20   Judgments in Terms of External Criteria

The last and highest level of the cognitive domain is Evaluation. Evaluation is defined as the formation of a value judgment, but the most important part of the activity is not the judgment itself; it is the justification of that judgment.[10] Students will be making judgments throughout their lives. The purpose of Evaluation-level objectives is to help students learn to justify their judgments. The justification can consist of logical reasoning (such as cause–effect), references to specific facts or examples, or the use of specific criteria, but it should not reflect a lack of thought (for example, "My father believes this so I believe it too").

Do not confuse Analysis-level and Evaluation-level objectives. At the Analysis level, three equally qualified experts would be likely to arrive at the same conclusion. At the Evaluation level, each of the three might reach a different conclusion and that would be wholly acceptable, provided they could defend those conclusions with relevant, valid, and logical arguments. In a sense, you are asking for an opinion, and opinions, by themselves, cannot be judged acceptable or unacceptable. What can be judged is the quality of the defense and that is what you are after at the Evaluation level.

Some of the linked phrases that reflect Evaluation-level thinking are "state your opinion about . . . and defend that position by citing at least three relevant facts;" "Take a position for or against . . . and defend that position by using cause–effect reasoning." Examples of Evaluation-level objectives follow. Note that in each case the student is expected to make a value judgment. This is in contrast to the Analysis level, where the student was expected to determine the true state of affairs. At the Evaluation level the focus is not on determining the true state of affairs, it is on having the student develop a rational justification for a value judgment.

You will be able, in writing and under test conditions, to:

1. Explain in less than two pages which of two given business letters you believe is more effective and support your decision by citing at least three specific facts or examples.
2. State your position with respect to whether students in the United States should learn the metric system and defend your position by citing at least three factual or cause–effect arguments.

3. Explain which economic system you believe has the greatest long-term growth potential and support your belief by citing at least three factual or logical arguments that are consistent with accepted knowledge.

THE AFFECTIVE DOMAIN

Since educators typically see their primary responsibility as helping students acquire and manipulate factual information, there was quick and widespread acceptance of the *Taxonomy of Educational Objectives, Handbook I* when it was published in 1956. However, when it came to *Handbook II*, which dealt with attitudes, feelings, and values, both the development of the handbook, and its acceptance, was slower. It was not until 1964 that *Handbook II: Affective Domain* was published. There was general agreement that **affects** such as emotions, attitudes, and values exist and profoundly affect human endeavors. There was also general agreement that a typical classroom, with its many human interactions, is one of the places where attitudes and values are shaped. The question was how much, if any, instructional time and effort should be focused on building or changing feelings, attitudes, and values.

Problems to Be Considered

Consider the following points. As a teacher, you will have a great deal to do with the feelings, attitudes, and values that are developed in your classroom regardless of whether you do or do not state affective objectives. Factors as varied as the way you dress and act, and expect students to dress and act, and the way you interact with students and expect them to interact with each other, will work to shape students' feelings, attitudes, and values. For example, teachers who act dictatorially or use the language carelessly convey a different message to students than those who treat students as responsible people and take care to use the language properly. Your instructional objectives also help shape attitudes, feelings, and values. If the objectives focus primarily on low-level skills or seem irrelevant to students, attitudes in the class will be different than if the objectives focus on the attainment of high-level abilities that are clearly relevant and important to the students. Separate objectives that focus purely on attitudes, feelings, and values may not be needed.

Second, many people believe that it is the prerogative of parents or churches to develop attitudes, feelings, and values and that schools should focus on cognitive and psychomotor development. Although teachers are tacitly expected to encourage mainstream values—for example, honesty and responsibility—they may inadvertently cause a noisy conflict by espousing more complex or specific moral stances. Given the separation of church and state, and the great diversity of moral thought in the United States, it is presumptuous for anyone to stand up and shine the light of Truth on everyone else.

Third, the only way to assess the attitudes or values people have is by observing what they do or say. Teachers who decide to write objectives in the affective domain must select observable behaviors that they believe will reflect particular attitudes or values. If they happen to select inappropriate behavioral indicators, their assessment of the affect will be distorted. For example, if an objectives calls for students to be patriotic, how could that be assessed? Would it be sufficient to observe that the student stood and said the Pledge of Allegiance to the flag every day, or knew all the words to the national anthem? If not, what behavior(s) would be adequate?

Fourth, assuming that teachers could gather incontrovertible information about whether each student did or did not achieve specific affective objectives, what could be done with that information? It would be difficult, for example, to defend raising or lowering a student's test score because the student did or did not demonstrate a particular attitude and the same would be true of a final grade. In this age of accountability, teachers must be able to demonstrate that their grades were reported objectively and that they were not biased by questionable determinations of whether the student had or had not acquired certain attitudes, feelings, or values.

Finally, there is a conflict between the purpose of precise instructional objectives and the nature of objectives in the affective domain. The general purpose of precise instructional objectives is to clarify instructional intent so that teachers and students can work toward the same clear goals. Inherent in this idea is that students must know what the objectives are before instruction begins. However, knowing the affective objectives might prompt some students to demonstrate the expected behaviors only to please the teacher, and to stop demonstrating them as soon as the course ended. This *could* happen with objectives in the cognitive domain, but there at least teachers are more certain of the validity of the behaviors being observed.

Given the problems described, many teachers choose not to write objectives in the affective domain. Regardless of whether teachers write such objectives, they should understand the affective domain because it describes the progression of commitment that we all go through as our attitudes, feelings, and values develop. Therefore, we will look briefly at each of the five levels of the affective domain and see what a typical objective might look like at each level.

Levels of the Affective Domain

1.0   Receiving (Attending)
      1.1   Awareness

>   1.2   Willingness to Receive
>   1.3   Controlled or Selected Attention[11]

The lowest level of the affective domain is Receiving. At this level the student is aware of the existence of a condition or problem and is willing at least to listen attentively to what others have to say about it. The element of commitment is not present, and the behavior is somewhat analogous to "sitting on the fence." The student is aware of an issue, but has not yet made a decision about it. Words that reflect the Receiving level include asks, follows, names, replies, and uses. An objective, at this level, might be for the student to demonstrate a willingness to learn about drug abuse by contributing to an introductory discussion on the subject.

2.0   *Responding*
>   2.1   Acquiescence in Responding
>   2.2   Willingness to Respond
>   2.3   Satisfaction in Response[12]

The second level is Responding. At this level, the student is willing to go along with an idea or a value (such as being willing to follow school rules), actively volunteers to respond, and takes satisfaction in the response. The level of commitment is minimal, and the behavior is analogous to jumping off the fence, but holding on to it and being ready to jump back at any moment. Words that reflect the Responding level include answers, assists, conforms, presents, and recites. An objective, at this level, might be for the student to display an interest in solving drug-related social problems by taking a stand in classroom discussions against drug abuse.

3.0   *Valuing*
>   3.1   Acceptance of a Value
>   3.2   Preference for a Value
>   3.3   Commitment[13]

The third level is Valuing. Here the student demonstrates that an attitude has been accepted and is consistently preferred over competing attitudes or values. The commitment is clear. The student has walked away from the fence and is willing to be identified as holding the attitude or value. Words that reflect the Valuing level include completes, initiates, invites, joins, justifies, and shares. An objective, at this level, might be for the student to indicate a commitment to social reform by becoming an active member of a community service organization such as Students Against Driving Drunk. Active membership constitutes a minimum standard because each organization operationally defines the term for its own purposes.

4.0   Organization
   4.1   Conceptualization of a Value
   4.2   Organization of a Value System[14]

The fourth level is Organization. As students become more aware of values, they eventually recognize that conflicts between values do arise and must be resolved by setting priorities on values. To do so, students should use higher-level cognitive thinking, which will enable them to resolve value conflicts in a logical and defensible manner. They will then have greater confidence in their decisions. This level is a direct link between the cognitive and the affective domains. Words that reflect the Organization level include chooses, combines, compares, defends, organizes, and synthesizes. An objective at the Organization level might be for students to identify two conflicting values in their own lives and to describe how that conflict will be resolved.

5.0   Characterization
   5.1   Generalized Set
   5.2   Characterization[15]

The highest level of the affective domain is Characterization. At this level, a person has developed and internalized a value system to the extent that those values are clearly reflected in the person's behavior. When we think of a miser or a spend-thrift we are thinking of someone who has reached the characterization level. That person has reasons for holding particular values and is satisfied with those values. Since students are in the process of developing their value structures, few will reach the characterization level while in high school. Words that reflect the Characterization level include acts, displays, performs, practices, and verifies. An objective, at this level, might be for the student to demonstrate a continuing commitment to the idea of social reform by studying to be a physician who specializes in drug abuse.

THE PSYCHOMOTOR DOMAIN

The psychomotor domain is concerned with the development of motor skills and neuromuscular control. Objectives in the psychomotor domain often contain elements of the cognitive or affective domain (and vice versa), but the dominant characteristic and intent of the student's response is a physical movement. The curricular areas in which psychomotor skills receive major emphasis include typing, shorthand, home economics, industrial education, art, music, and of course, physical education. It is important to keep in mind, however, that virtually all other curricular areas depend, to one degree or another, on psychomotor skills. Speaking, gesturing, writing, and eye–hand coordination are all examples of psychomotor domain skills.

While the psychomotor domain is of primary concern to physical education teachers, all teachers need to be aware of its elements. In most school districts there is a concerted effort to minimize the extent to which students with special needs are segregated in special education rooms. This is done by including these students in regular classrooms whenever possible. If such students are placed in your classroom, you will be expected to work with a special education teacher to develop Individualized Educational Plans (IEPs) for them. Knowledge of psychomotor development will be useful in that endeavor. Further, such knowledge is useful as you watch your own children develop.

There are a number of psychomotor domain taxonomies, but the one developed by Anita J. Harrow in 1972 is one of the clearest ways of classifying the neuromuscular development stages through which students pass. As with the cognitive and affective domain taxonomies, this psychomotor domain taxonomy depicts a continuum of simple to complex achievements, and its use can greatly facilitate the conceptualization and sequencing of appropriate objectives and experiences. The levels of the psychomotor domain are listed in their entirety in Appendix C. A summary follows.

1.00 Reflex Movements

Reflex movements are involuntary actions that are typically elicited by some stimulus. Ordinarily educators are not concerned with movements at this level because they are part of the repertoire of all normal children. More complex psychomotor skills can be developed from them with little or no difficulty. Educators typically concern themselves with these movements only when a student has some impairment that limits proper execution of the movements.

2.00 Basic-Fundamental Movements

Basic-fundamental movement patterns are developed in the first year of life. The movements build on the reflex movements and consist of such behaviors as grasping, reaching, manipulating objects, crawling, creeping, and walking. Ordinarily, basic-fundamental movement patterns are learned naturally, with little or no training. Educators typically do not formulate objectives for this level unless a particular student is observed having problems in this area. Special education teachers may be required to provide appropriate activities for their students with regard to basic-fundamental movements, especially where muscular or visual impairment exists. An objective, at this level, might call for a student to skip for 20 feet.

3.00 Perceptual Abilities

Perceptual abilities focus on our awareness of the world around us and our abilities to use our bodies to interact with the world. The first of the five levels with this category is Kinesthetic discrimination—the ability to perceive one's body in relation to surrounding objects in space and to control the body and move its parts while maintaining balance.

Visual discrimination involves a number of components that are necessary for proper psychomotor execution. Visual acuity is the ability to distinguish form and fine details and to differentiate between various observed objects. Visual tracking is the ability to follow objects with coordinated eye movements. Following the movement of a ball would be an example. Third is visual memory. This is the skill to recall from memory past visual experiences or previously observed movement patterns such as dance routines or swinging a baseball bat. Figure–background differentiation is the fourth category of visual discrimination. Here the learner is able to select the dominant figure from the surrounding background. Evidence that individuals can differentiate figure and background occurs when they are able to identify the dominant object and respond to it. Ball catching and hitting thrown balls are evidence that the individual can differentiate figure and background. Consistency is the last category of visual discrimination. This is the ability to recognize shapes and forms consistently even though they may have been modified in some way.

Auditory discrimination involves the ability of the learner to receive and differentiate among various sounds and their pitch and intensity, distinguish the direction of sound and follow its movement, and recognize and reproduce post-auditory experience, such as the notes that can be used to play a song on the piano.

Tactile discrimination is the learner's ability to differentiate between different textures simply by touching. Being able to determine the slickness or smoothness of an object or surface may be essential to properly executing psychomotor movements where the body must come in contact with surfaces in the process.

Coordinated abilities incorporate behaviors that involve two or more of the perceptual abilities and movement patterns. At this level, the student is able to differentiate between the figure and the ground and to coordinate the visually perceived object with a manipulative movement. An example of an activity at this level would be to kick a moving soccer ball. Kicking the moving ball is the psychomotor evidence that there is coordinated discrimination ability. Clearly, perceptual abilities are not observable in isolation. Evidence that these abilities exist depends on the integration of various movements and cognitive skills. The following are examples of objectives written at the various levels in the perceptual abilities category:

You will be able to:

1. Without any outside assistance, walk the full distance across a balance beam and back without falling, on each of five tries (kinesthetic discrimination).
2. From an audio recording of a symphony orchestra, list the names of 80 percent of the instruments playing in any 30-second segment of the recording (audio acuity).
3. Catch 95 percent of the baseballs batted from a distance of approximately fifty yards (coordinated activities).

4.00 Physical Abilities

The physical abilities of the learner are essential to efficient execution of psychomotor movements. Physical abilities constitute the foundation for the development of skilled movements because of the demands placed on the various systems of the body during the execution of these psychomotor skills. Physical abilities are the foundation for the development of highly skilled movements. The physical abilities include endurance, strength, flexibility, and agility.

Endurance is the ability of the body to supply and utilize oxygen and to dispose of increased concentrations of lactic acid in the muscles. The lack of endurance reduces the learner's ability to perform movements efficiently over long periods of time. Development of endurance requires strenuous activity on a sustained basis.

Strength is the relative ability to exert tension against resistance. The development of strength is accomplished ordinarily through gradually increasing the extent of the resistance through the use of weights and springs. The student's own body can also be used as resistance in exercises, such as pull-ups and push-ups. Maintenance of strength requires the learner to utilize the muscles continually. Obviously, the strength required to perform various psychomotor movements depends on the nature of these movements as well as on the ability of the learner. For example, a greater amount of strength is required for wrestling than for fencing. Other activities that require a good deal of strength include football and gymnastics.

Flexibility refers to the ability to move bodily parts to the maximum limits imposed by the structure of the body's joints. Flexibility depends greatly on the extent to which muscles can be stretched during movement without resulting in injury. Hurdlers, gymnasts, and dancers are among those who are most concerned about flexibility.

Agility is the ability to move with dexterity and quickness. Agility is involved with deftness of manipulation, rapid changes of direction, and starting and stopping activities. Learning tennis, playing the piano or other musical instruments, and playing basketball are activities that require a good deal of agility. Examples of objectives at different levels of the physical abilities category include the following:

You will be able to:

1. Following the Harvard-Step Test, have your recovery period pulse count decrease to a point at or above the next highest classification level when compared with the norms (endurance).
2. Execute fifty push-ups and fifteen pull-ups correctly, with no more than a five-minute rest between the push-ups and pull-ups (strength).
3. While sitting on the ground in the hurdler's position, touch your extended foot with your fingers and hold this position for ten seconds (flexibility).
4. Complete the run-and-dodge course in less than twenty seconds (agility).

5.00 Skilled Movements

A skilled movement is the performance of a complex psychomotor task. Such movements are classified by the complexity of the skills themselves and by the proficiency with which they are demonstrated. The levels of complexity include simple adaptive, compound adaptive, and complex adaptive. Performance at each of these levels is classified as beginner, intermediate, advanced, or highly skilled.

Activities included in the skilled movement category are those that involve an adaptation of the inherent movement patterns listed in the basic-fundamental movements level. At the basic-fundamental movements level, the focus is on whether the learner can simply perform the movement. At the skilled movements level, the focus is on the extent to which the learner has mastered the skill.

In differentiating among the three categories of skilled movements, the first involves a limited amount of sensory information and only a portion of the performer's body or body parts. The second involves the extension of the body parts through the use of an implement or tool. The third incorporates total body movement, in many instances without a base of support, and necessitates the making of postural adjustments due to unexpected cues.

Mastery levels within the skilled movements category go from beginner, through intermediate and advanced, to highly skilled. At the beginner level, the learner is able to perform the skill with some degree of confidence and similarity to the movement expected. This stage is somewhat beyond the trial-and-error learning of initial attempts at learning the task. When the learner can minimize the amount of extraneous motion and execute the skill with some proficiency, the person is categorized as being at the intermediate skill level. Once the individual can perform the skilled movement efficiently and with confidence, and achieve almost the same response each time, the skill level is judged to be advanced. At this level, the student's performance is usually superior in quality when compared with similar performances of peers. Highly skilled performances are usually limited to those individuals who use their skills professionally. These people are totally involved in the use of their skills. At the highly skilled level, factors such as body structure, body function, and acuity of sensory modalities and perceptual abilities become critical. Proper execution of the skills depends heavily on each of these components. The following are examples of objectives written at different levels of the skilled movements category.

You will be able to:

1. In a five-minute test, type at a rate of 40 words per minute and make no more than five errors (simple adaptive skill).
2. From a distance of 20 feet, putt a golf ball into the cup 25 percent of the time (compound adaptive skill).
3. Properly execute the following dives with a point rating of at least 4.5: forward one and one-half, one-half gainer, and one-and-one-half forward twist (complex adaptive skill).

6.00 Nondiscursive Communication

This category of behaviors consists of nonverbal communications used to convey a message to an observer. These involve such nonverbal movements as facial expressions, postures, and complex dance choreographs. Two subcategories are included: expressive movement and interpretive movement.

Expressive movement is composed of many of the movements that are used in everyday life. The basic types of expressive movement include posture and carriage, gestures, and facial expressions. These means of expression are used to indicate the individual's emotional state. Expressive movements are not usually incorporated into typical secondary curricula. They are, however, used in modified form by learners in the area of fine arts and are included in the taxonomy for this reason.

Interpretive movements are art forms. They can either be aesthetic, where the movements are performed for the purpose of creating for the viewer an image of effortless, beautiful motion, or they can be creative movements that are designed to communicate some message to the viewer. In both cases, the performer must have a highly developed knowledge of body mechanics and well-developed physical and perceptual abilities. The following is an objective at the interpretive movements level: After selecting a piece of music, create your own movement sequence which contains recognizable rhythmic patterns, keeps time with the music, and communicates a message to the viewer on a contemporary social theme.

It should be noted that for many movements there are several components. In such cases the learner may be instructed and evaluated on either one or all of the components that make up a skill. Dividing the movements into component parts allows for more accurate evaluation and also provides the learner with more specific details that can be used to make movement corrections. Analysis of subcomponent skills is particularly useful for the highly skilled performer. However, a beginning learner may get confused if inefficient movements are analyzed in too much detail. The more advanced learners become, the more likely they are to benefit from detailed analysis.

TESTING OBJECTIVES FOR CLARITY

Once you have ascertained that your objectives are technically correct and provide for student development at a variety of levels, check to see if they communicate instructional intent clearly. One way to do this is to ask yourself if another competent person could, on the basis of the written objective alone, differentiate among students who can and cannot demonstrate the competence described.

Another way to check for clarity is to ask other people to read each objective and explain what they think they would have to do to demonstrate the competence. If their interpretation differs from yours, or if you find yourself saying, "What I really meant was . . .," the misleading objective(s) should be rewritten. This method is particularly useful if students are used as readers, since they will be more representative of the potential "consumers" than anyone else. It may be, for example, that the reading level is inappropriate for the intended students. If a fellow teacher reads the objectives, this factor may pass unnoticed. If students read the objectives, they will be quick to point out that they cannot understand what was written and intended.

USING PRECISE INSTRUCTIONAL OBJECTIVES

Once teachers have: (1) gleaned ideas for instructional objectives by considering ideas from subject-area specialists, students, and society; (2) converted those ideas into precise instructional objectives, and (3) classified the objectives into domains and levels to ensure that students will develop a range of skills and abilities, the next step is to get administrative approval to use them. School administrators are responsible for ensuring the implementation of an approved curriculum. For this to happen, the objectives of various courses must complement one another. Administrators can help see that they do, but only to the extent that they are aware of each teacher's objectives. It is prudent, therefore, to get administrative approval for course objectives and for any major changes in course objectives. This minimizes the chance of jeopardizing the success of the overall curriculum.

SUMMARY

The classification of objectives into domains and into levels within those domains enables educators to determine if those objectives include a desirable range of skills and abilities. The three domains include the cognitive, affective, and psychomotor, and the levels within them are considered to be cumulative. The domains and their levels are summarized below.

Cognitive Domain—Bloom, Benjamin S., 1956

1.00	Knowledge	Simple recall. No understanding necessary.
2.00	Comprehension	Lowest level of understanding—demonstrated by translation, interpretation, and extrapolation.
3.00	Application	Utilization of rules, principles, and procedures in a mechanical way.
4.00	Analysis	Identification of components within a whole, recognition of relationships among those components, and recognition of the organization of the whole.
5.00	Synthesis	Combination of parts into a new and unique whole.
6.00	Evaluation	Making, defending, and supporting value judgments.[16]

Affective Domain—Krathwohl, David R., 1964

1.00	Receiving	Sensitization to the existence of certain phenomena and the willingness to direct attention to them. No commitment.
2.00	Responding	Sufficiently committed to seek out and discuss examples and to gain satisfaction from association with the value or attitude. Minimal commitment.
3.00	Valuing	Behavior is motivated not by the desire to comply or obey, but by the individual's realization that some attitude or value has become important to him or her.
4.00	Organization	The resolution of value conflicts and the beginning of the organization of a value system hierarchy.

5.00   Characterization   Values are internalized and are reflected in the person's lifestyle.[17]

Psychomotor Domain—Harrow, Anita J., 1972

1.00	Reflex movements	Movements or actions elicited in response to some stimulus, but without conscious volition on the part of the learner.
2.00	Basic-fundamental movements	Actions such as reaching, crawling, and walking that are inherent motor patterns based on the reflex movements of the learner and that emerge without training.
3.00	Perceptual abilities	Recognition of, and discrimination among, various perceptual modalities such as kinesthetic, visual, auditory, and tactile modes and coordinated abilities such as eye–hand coordination.
4.00	Physical abilities	Functional characteristics of organic vigor (endurance, strength, flexibility, and agility) which, when developed, provide the learner with a sound, efficiently functioning instrument (his or her body) to be used when making skilled movements.
5.00	Skilled movements	Development of increasing degrees of skill or mastery of movement patterns learned at earlier stages of development.
6.00	Nondiscursive communication	Use of movement such as facial expressions, postures, gestures, and modern dance choreographs, to communicate.[18]

Affective domain objectives are typically less precise and more time-consuming to write than objectives in the other domains. This is so, in part, because it is necessary to decide on an observable behavior that reflects the target affect. Determining which behavior is, in fact, an accurate reflection of an attitude, feeling, or value is difficult. Even if appropriate behaviors could be identified, dealing with affective objectives in terms of grading poses other problems.

After instructional objectives are written, they should be classified and, if necessary, adjusted to ensure that a range of skills and abilities is developed. Ideally, the objectives will move students from teacher-directed, lower-level skills to student-directed, higher-level skills. The objectives should be checked for clarity by having others, particularly students, read and interpret them and, finally, the objectives should be approved by the administration to ensure that they fit into the overall curriculum. The following checklist might help in verifying the adequacy of objectives:

1. Is the objective a single sentence, preferably of twenty-five words or less?
2. What is the single observable behavior? Underline it.
3. Is the behavior to be demonstrated under controlled conditions so there will be no question about who did the work? (No group work or homework assignments.)
4. What is the minimum acceptable standard? Circle it.
5. Is the standard reasonable in light of the ability level of the students?
6. Could a parent or someone else who is not a specialist in the subject evaluate achievement of the objective as well as the teacher could?
7. If there is a series of objectives, are they arranged from the lowest to the highest level?
8. Describe two ways achievement of the objective will help students better understand or deal with the world outside of school.
9. How does the objective help the student integrate knowledge or learn to learn?

SO HOW DOES THIS AFFECT MY TEACHING?

Your success as a teacher depends, to a large extent, on the success of your students. Like everyone else, students willingly invest their time and efforts only in those activities that they believe are relevant to their lives. To the extent that you can show students how achieving the course objectives can be of practical help to them in dealing with their world, and can show them how they will be moving from low-level, teacher-directed activities to higher-level, student-directed activities, they will be willing participants in the teaching–learning process. Taking the time to classify instructional objectives will help ensure that students will progress from lower- to higher-level skills and will develop a range of abilities. Further, having a set of well-developed objectives and a plan by which they can be achieved will give you a greater sense of confidence when you meet your students. This sense of confidence will be communicated to, and eventually shared by, the students.

PRACTICE EXERCISES

Practice Exercise 1: The Domains

Classify each objective as belonging to the cognitive (C), affective (A), or psychomotor (P) domain.

____ 1. Explain, in writing, which of two possible solutions to the problem of social unrest is more likely to eliminate the problem and cite two facts in support.

____ 2. Recite the Emancipation Proclamation from memory with no more than two errors.

____ 3. Thread a movie projector so that, when the projector is turned on, the film will not flicker.

____ 4. Show increased interest in band music by attending eight out of the ten concerts offered during the year.

____ 5. Given ten quadratic equations, solve correctly, on paper, at least eight.

____ 6. Demonstrate concern for the democratic principles of free enterprise by orally stating these concerns.

____ 7. Show a growing interest in art by participating extensively in discussions about art forms.

____ 8. Transfer bacteria from a culture to a petri dish in a manner that produces properly spread colonies and no contamination.

____ 9. Write an original short story that has appropriate sentence structure and organization and that meets the requirements of heightened action.

____ 10. Given a series of paintings, explain, in writing, which one you believe is best and cite two elements of the painting in support.

Practice Exercise 1 Answers: 1–C, 2–C, 3–P, 4–A, 5–C, 6–A, 7–A, 8–P, 9–C, 10–C

Practice Exercise 2: Cognitive Domain

Classify each objective into its level in the cognitive domain. Check your responses against the answers provided. Resolve discrepancies, if any, by further study, analysis, or consultation with your instructor or peers. When in doubt, classify the objective at the highest level implied.

Levels of the Cognitive Domain

| K. Knowledge | AP. Application | S. Synthesis |
| C. Comprehension | A. Analysis | E. Evaluation |

____ 1. Given three garments of varying prices, choose the garment you consider to be the best buy and cite at least two written reasons for the decision, based on the construction of the garment.

____ 2. List, in writing, at least five factors that led up to the Spanish-American War.

____ 3. Given a new list of possible reasons for World War I and World War II, classify them, in writing, under World War 1 or World War II with no errors.

____ 4. State, in writing, four common ingredients in pastry.

____ 5. Given the necessary material, compare, in writing, the state welfare program in Illinois to that in California on at least five points.

____ 6. Explain, in writing, using at least five examples, why many Blacks moved to the North at the end of the Civil War.

____ 7. Given comprehensive material on the waste of natural resources, write an original legislative bill calling for conservation of a natural resource.

____ 8. Write a unique legal, ethical, practical plan to increase student participation in school activities.

____ 9. On a ten-minute written quiz on ceramics, explain three ways of hand-building a pot.

____ 10. Given two sculptures, choose the one that you judge to be better and defend that choice by citing, in writing, at least three points of superiority in the selected piece.

____ 11. Given the names of two Cubist painters, contrast and compare the styles of each painter in a one-page paper citing at least four similarities and three differences.

____ 12. Solve 90 percent of the two-digit multiplication problems on a written math test.

____ 13. Calculate and write down how much 1 gram of N HCI will have to be diluted to prepare 500 ml of 0.5N solution.

____ 14. Given a list of tasks that must be done during an eight-hour period, create a written work plan that organizes the tasks so that the time will be used efficiently to complete them.

____ 15. Use Robert's Rules of Order to conduct a class election without any violations of procedure.

Practice Exercise 2 Answers: 1–E, 2–K, 3–A, 4–K, 5–A, 6–C, 7–S, 8–S, 9–C, 10–E, 11–A, 12–AP, 13–AP, 14–S, 15–AP

Practice Exercise 3: Psychomotor Domain

Classify each objective into its level in the psychomotor domain. Check your responses against the answers provided. Resolve any discrepancies by further study, analysis, or consultation with your instructor or peers.

Levels of the Psychomotor Domain

R. Reflex movements	PH. Physical abilities
B. Basic-fundamental movements	S. Skilled movements
P. Perceptual abilities	N. Nondiscursive communication

You will be able to:

____ 1. Given bacteria cultures, petri plates, wire loop, and Bunsen burner, transfer bacteria from the culture tubes to the petri dishes using proper streaking techniques and preventing contamination.

____ 2. Type 40 words per minute in a three-minute timed test with no errors.

____ 3. Drive an automobile in heavy traffic, properly executing a right turn, a left turn, a lane change, a stop, and a parallel park.

____ 4. Draw at least 25 Old-English letters demonstrating correct proportion and style.

____ 5. Dance the waltz in proper time.

____ 6. Given a series of ten pictures, point to the dominant figure (as opposed to background figures) in at least eight instances.

____ 7. Without any outside assistance, demonstrate a unique dance routine that is coordinated with at least four minutes of music and that communicates the theme of "war."

____ 8. Show an increase in grip strength of five pounds after two weeks of training.
____ 9. Swim 1,000 yards in less than 19 minutes and have a heart rate of no more than 120 beats per minute after one minute of rest.
____ 10. While battling against a complete defensive team, hit a pitched baseball safely three out of ten times.

Practice Exercise 3 Answers:　1–S, 2–S, 3–S, 4–S, 5–S, 6–P, 7–N, 8–PH, 9–PH, 10–S

KEY TERMS, PEOPLE, AND IDEAS

Taxonomy of educational objectives
Cognitive domain, Benjamin Bloom, 1956—Acquisition and manipulation of information
Automatization—Saves time by reducing need for conscious thought about frequently done tasks
Affective domain, David Krathwohl, 1964—Feelings, attitudes, values
Psychomotor domain, Anita Harrow, 1972—Psychomotor development

ENDNOTES

1. Bloom, Benjamin S. et al., eds., *Taxonomy of Educational Objectives: The Classification of Educational Goals, Handbook I: Cognitive Domain* (New York: Longman, Inc., 1956).

2. Krathwohl, David R. et al., *Taxonomy of Educational Objectives: The Classification of Educational Goals, Handbook II: Affective Domain,* (New York: Longman, Inc., 1964).

3. Harrow, Anita J., *A Taxonomy of the Psychomotor Domain* (New York: Longman, Inc., 1972).

4. Shiffrin, Richard M., and Walter Schneider, "Controlled and Automatic Human Information Processing: Perceptual Learning, Automatic Attending, and a General Theory," *Psychological Review,* Vol. 84 (March 1977), pp. 127–190.

5. Bloom, *Handbook I,* pp. 62–78.

6. Bloom, *Handbook I,* pp. 89–96.

7. Bloom, *Handbook I,* pp. 120–123.

8. Bloom, *Handbook I,* pp. 144–148.

9. Bloom, *Handbook I,* pp. 162–172.

10. Bloom, *Handbook I,* pp. 185–187.

11. Krathwohl, *Handbook II,* pp. 98–115.

12. Krathwohl, *Handbook II,* pp. 118–134.

13. Krathwohl, *Handbook II,* pp. 139–151.

14. Krathwohl, *Handbook II,* pp. 154–163.

15. Krathwohl, *Handbook II,* pp. 165–174.

16. Bloom, *Handbook I.* Reprinted by permission.

17. Krathwohl, *Handbook II.* Reprinted by permission.

18. Harrow, *Taxonomy of the Psychomotor Domain.* Reprinted by permission.

7

WHOLE-CLASS INSTRUCTIONAL ACTIVITIES

RATIONALE

Stating objectives in observable and measurable terms will tend to make students, and others, see you as competent and professional. Having projected this image, and with the objectives clear, the next step is to engage students in a variety of learning activities that will help them achieve those objectives. These activities must be varied for at least two reasons. First, no single instructional activity can help students develop an adequate range of cognitive, affective, and psychomotor abilities. Second, regardless of how well an activity is done, continual repetition will eventually make it boring.

This chapter will focus first on some generic teaching skills—skills that are useful across subject-area and grade-level lines. Then, attention will shift to how to select and use whole-class instructional activities to capture and maintain student interest, enliven your classes, and help students achieve the stated objectives. With the right activities, students will look forward to your class and are more likely to be successful.

SAMPLE OBJECTIVES

You will be able, in writing, to:

1. Define terms such as set induction, higher-order questioning, practice, and closure, and cite an example of each that is relevant to your subject area. (Knowledge)
2. Explain at least two procedures likely to increase the effectiveness of three given whole-class instructional activities such as informal lectures or general discussions. (Comprehension)

3. Given a precise instructional objective, select a sequence of three relevant, whole-class activities and cite at least two factors likely to make those activities, in that sequence, at least as good as sequences of other activities. (Application)
4. Watch video tapes of parts of two lessons in which the teachers are using the same instructional technique (lecture, discussion, etc.) and determine which teacher is using the technique more properly. Cite specific examples from the tape to support your analysis. (Analysis)

GENERIC SKILLS

Good teaching results from a combination of skills, knowledge, and attitudes that cannot be precisely described. It is an excellent example of the whole being greater than the sum of the parts. Nevertheless, teacher education is based on the principle that, to the extent that teaching is a science, it can be systematically analyzed and improved. As a result of that on-going analysis, certain instructional procedures have been identified as being useful in a variety of instructional settings, so we will examine those first. It is important to keep in mind that the list of skills is *not* all-inclusive nor does use of the skills guarantee student learning. Consistent use of these procedures is, however, likely to enhance student learning.

Set Induction

Set induction refers to establishing a particular mindset, an anticipation of what is to come, at the beginning of a lesson. It gets students ready to learn. Ideally, what you do during the first minute or two of the lesson will actively involve the students and lead logically into the rest of the lesson. For example, if you were a history teacher and the class was about to begin a unit on transportation, you could begin by telling students to open their textbooks to page 101 and read the first few paragraphs. Ho-hum. On the other hand, you could hold up a gold-painted railroad spike and ask how that might be relevant to the unit. It is likely that some, if not all, students will remember hearing about how a gold spike was used to complete the transcontinental railroad, and they will be eager to demonstrate their knowledge. A favorable set will have been induced and all it required was a little forethought and planning.

Communicating the Objective

Once student interest in the lesson has been stimulated, the next step is to communicate the lesson's objective. While it is true that most lessons build on one another, and that some carry over from day to day, it will facilitate the teacher's planning and students' learning if the instructional objective for each lesson is made clear. This enroute objective (so called because it is used enroute to the terminal objective) can be communicated by writing it on the board or by orally explaining it, but in any case, a moment or two should be taken to ask a student to paraphrase the objective. This will help to ensure that students understand what they are supposed to be able to do at the end of the lesson. It is essential that students see the objective as being relevant to their lives. Some teachers advocate writing the objective on the chalkboard and leaving it there for the entire period to help students focus their attention.

Stimulus Variation

Most people learn about the world around them via their senses of sight, sound, taste, touch, and smell. Educators focus, almost entirely, on just two of these senses, sight and sound. For example, if students learn about Hawaiian luaus, they typically do so by reading, hearing, and/or seeing pictures of them. They could, however, plan and conduct one. Actual participation would entail all the senses and would likely result in a long-remembered experience.

Not all subjects lend themselves to learning via taste, touch, or smell, but even the use of gestures, voice inflections, and visual aids can help. There is room for variety in instructional activities in all subjects. If instructional objectives include the range of abilities that they should, achievement of them will *require* a variety of instructional activities and materials. Variety is "the spice of life," and instruction should be "spiced up" with a variety of activities. However, teachers must be certain to select activities that directly contribute to the achievement of specific instructional objectives. The objectives should drive the activities.

Review/Repetition

The purpose of review is to literally give students another view of the material. The most effective method is to have the students themselves provide the main points. This is so because if some students failed to understand a point when it was presented by the teacher, they might very well fail to understand it again if the teacher presents it in the same way during review. If students present main points, they are likely to do so in a somewhat different way than the teacher and their phrasing or examples might help other students understand more fully.

There are at least three ways of handling review or repetition. **Simple repetition** takes place when the teacher asks a student to paraphrase a main point after it has been discussed, but before the teacher moves on to the next point. **Spaced repetition** takes place periodically throughout a lesson, typically at the end of important blocks of information. **Massed repetition** takes place at the end of the lesson and is typically thought of as review. It is here that student involvement is most useful.

Practice

Once skills or techniques are introduced, the best way to develop proficiency with them is through practice—if you want to swim well, get in the water and practice. **Analogous practice** is similar, but not identical, to the terminal behavior. For example, students in a beginning swimming class would be engaging in analogous practice if they practiced correct breathing techniques standing by the pool and making appropriate arm and head movements. They would be engaging in **equivalent practice** if they were in the water and actually practicing their breathing technique while swimming. **Guided practice** is typically used in initial practice sessions so the teacher can give students frequent corrective feedback concerning their efforts and help them avoid making mistakes. **Independent practice** is useful once students have somewhat mastered basic skills and are unlikely to make serious mistakes.

Closure

Just as every lesson has a beginning, every lesson has an end. There is a big difference however, between a planned ending and having the bell ring mid-sentence. There are two major purposes of closure. The first is to give students a sense of accomplishment—a feeling that they took a step in the right direction, that they accomplished something more than just attending one more class. The second purpose is to relate the information just learned to previous experiences, previously learned information, and/or information yet to be learned or events likely to happen. This bridge building helps students make a meaningful whole out of what might otherwise be isolated pieces of information.

WHOLE-GROUP INSTRUCTION

Whole-group instruction takes place when all students engage in a teacher-directed, academically oriented activity such as an informal lecture or a guided discussion. The fact that the teacher typically uses such activities to provide students with planned and organized information leads to the identification of many such activities as direct instruction activities. Research by **Rosenshine,**[1] **Evertson** et. al.,[2] **Jones and Jones,**[3] **Ornstein and Levine,**[4] and others indicates that students taught via direct instruction tend to score more highly on standardized achievement tests than students taught by other methods. This is particularly true with low-achieving students and with low-level objectives. Many teachers also like whole-group direct instruction because it allows them to control the selection and pace of instructional activities, thus simplifying classroom management.

With whole-group direct instruction so commonly used, some educators identified sets of generic skills that characterized direct instruction and could serve as a paradigm for planning such lessons. The generic skills, and the models that include them, are highly consistent with the Essentialist point of view.

The Madeline Hunter Method

In 1984, **Madeline Hunter** described a lesson planning structure called Instructional Theory in Practice (ITIP). Among other things, this structure identified a set of generic skills that provided a paradigm for planning systematic and effective direct-instruction lessons. This set of skills came to be called the Hunter Method and includes the following skills:

1. Anticipatory Set—Stimulate interest and focus attention.
2. Objective and Purpose—Explain to students what they should be able to do by the end of the lesson and why it is important to them.
3. Instructional Input—Select instructional activities that will help students achieve the stated objective.
4. Modeling—Show students how the information is used or skills are performed. Use many examples.
5. Checking for Understanding—Sample student understanding before they practice.
6. Guided Practice—Monitor initial practice carefully to help students avoid or overcome errors.
7. Independent Practice—Practice with minimal teacher supervision.[5]

In 1987, Barack Rosenshine also identified generic skills that characterized direct or explicit instruction. Those steps were as follows:

1. Begin each lesson with a short statement of goals.
2. Briefly review previous material.
3. Present new material in small steps, which have students practice after each step.
4. Give clear and detailed instructions and explanations.
5. Provide a high level of active practice for all students.
6. Guide students during initial practice.
7. Ask many questions, check for student understanding, and get answers from all students.
8. Provide systematic feedback and correction.

9. Obtain a student success rate of 80 percent or higher during initial practice.
10. Provide explicit instructions for exercises and, where possible, monitor and help students.
11. Provide for spaced review.[6]

Both sets of skills call for the teacher to focus clearly on an academic objective, communicate the objective to students, provide extensive content coverage, and actively engage students. Both sets of skills are useful in planning and teaching direct-instruction lessons. Effective teaching, however, is a complex whole and it is not likely that any single set of skills or steps will be best for all teachers in all circumstances. Teachers need to make informed choices about objectives, content, and methods, and the more information they have, the more informed those choices can be.

What follows are descriptions of various instructional techniques that typically fall under the whole-class, direct-instruction heading. These techniques are most appropriate when objectives call for students to acquire information or understand concepts.

Formal and Informal Lectures

Lecturing has fallen into some disrepute, partly because too many lectures were poorly done by too many teachers. A good lecture, one that is well planned and delivered smoothly and with conviction, can be an exciting learning experience, and will be perceived as such by students. The line between such a lecture and an artistic performance is very fine indeed, and the extensive use of lectures should be reserved for teachers with the personality and ability to do such work. It is possible for almost any teacher to plan and orchestrate a lecture that is cohesive and polished and that will capture the interest of all but the most reluctant students. However, the time spent planning such a lecture precludes all but an occasional use of this method by most teachers.

Rather than striving for the perfect "formal" lecture, that is, a lecture in which students do little except listen to a virtuoso performance, most teachers do better to concentrate on identifying those points, skills, and procedures that will enable them to deliver "informal" lectures, providing for student participation rather than passive student reception. This approach has the advantages of being well within the capabilities of most teachers, involving students, and, therefore, being more effective. From this point on, the term *lecture* refers to the informal lecture.

Purposes of Lectures

Lectures are used appropriately to: (1) quickly and concisely present a great deal of new and integrated information, (2) clarify relationships among general points or between specific causes and effects, (3) explain procedures, and (4) point out inferences, inductions, deductions, and assumptions. Some of this information could be provided on handouts, but lectures allow you to add emphasis by voice inflection, to make instant modifications on the basis of student reactions, and allow for spontaneous student responses and questions, thus making it possible to clarify points as they are raised by the students.

Planning Lectures
There are a number of appropriate lecture-planning procedures, but perhaps the most common is to construct a word or phrase outline. As the first step in this process, the teacher writes down the specific instructional objective students will be able to achieve after listening to and participating in the lecture. The kinds of objectives for which lectures are most appropriate are generally those at the low cognitive levels. For example:

1. Explain in writing at least two economic causes of World War I.
2. In no more than one page, define ethnocentrism and illustrate it with at least two examples.

Objectives such as these are appropriate to lectures because their terminal behaviors are not time consuming (and thus do not detract too much time from the lecture) and they do not require much, if any, student practice. Students can be expected to achieve such objectives simply by virtue of having been exposed to the information.

The lesson's objective should serve as the standard against which all prospective elements of the lecture are measured. Elements that clearly contribute to student achievement of the objective should find their way into the word or phrase outline, whereas those that contribute little or nothing should be discarded. This procedure assures cohesiveness and facilitates evaluation of the lecture's effectiveness.

Word or Phrase Outlines.   The outline may consist of short sentences, phrases, or even single words. In fact, many teachers have found that they can lecture most effectively if they reduce their notes to a minimum using single words or short phrases. Voluminous notes, either in the form of lengthy outlines on sheets of paper or many brief items on index cards, tend to inhibit rather than help. Faced with detailed notes, many beginning teachers tend to refer to the notes more often than necessary, simply because they are there. In some cases, the referrals become so frequent that the lecturer is, in effect, reading the notes. Further, voluminous notes tend to tie the lecturer to the podium, increase the probability of losing one's place, and decrease opportunities to make eye contact with students. Still further, if you make frequent referrals to notes, you create the impression of not knowing your content. Extensive notes, in most cases, simply do not add to the smoothness and polish of a final delivery. Outlines can frequently be shortened by simply eliminating the word "the" and by using phrases rather than sentences.

The lecture outline should serve to spark memory, not be a source of new information. It should contain the key phrases, facts, figures, names, and dates that are at the heart of the material. The outline should organize the material into logical blocks and subdivide these blocks into manageable sizes to facilitate student learning. When first beginning to plan lectures, it is a good idea to write down the approximate time each part of the lecture should take.

Another part of planning concerns checking the content for its suitability for the students' level. It is easy to make notes without realizing that students may not be familiar with certain terms, especially those that are technical or complex. If such terms are used, they should be starred or underlined to remind you to define and explain them.

Instructional Aids.   Plan on using appropriate instructional aids. Almost any lecture will hold students' attention longer if pictures, maps, graphs, cartoons, or similar support materials are used. The time to consider such aids is when the lecture is being planned.

Teaching Students How to Take Notes.   There are two parties in an informal lecture, the lecturer and the students. Teachers can increase their effectiveness by helping students learn how to take notes. For example, the teacher can hand out a list of instructions such as the following:

1. Notes for each day should start on a separate page, carry the date and title of the lecture and, if the lecturer is a guest, his or her name.
2. A consistent outline format should be used, such as the following:
   I. Major topic (Outline Format)
      A. Subheading (Logical Organization of Content)
         1. Explanations (sequential steps, causes and effects, etc.)
            a. Further explanations
               (1) proper indentation—easy reference. Sentences of more than one line should begin under first word of first line (as shown here).
3. Notes tend to be more useful if students write down only major points rather than trying to copy the lecture virtually word for word.
4. Students should look for techniques such as restating, rephrasing, and listing points on the board or overhead projector as clues that these are major points.
5. Contextual clues such as "There are *three* main facts here" are often used at the beginning of a series of points and can facilitate the outlining of information.

6. The development of a personal shorthand system for abbreviating frequently used words and phrases can save considerable time.
7. There are advantages to writing neatly enough so that rewriting the notes is not necessary. Students can read and study neatly written notes in less time than it takes to recopy them. Some students, however, find that the act of recopying or rephrasing notes assists in learning. Tell students about both approaches and let them decide which is best for them.
8. Space may be allowed, as the notes are being taken, to add personal thoughts, comments, questions, and reactions.
9. Some students, particularly visually handicapped students, may benefit from taping lectures.

Some educators advocate teaching students the double-column, Cornell System, of taking notes. Using this system, students leave a 2 ½" margin on the left of their note paper. This space is used to write in key words or to formulate questions answered in the notes. Both procedures are likely to help students learn and remember key ideas.[7]

Delivering the Lecture

Capture Interest.   Even after considerable effort has been made to prepare a lecture well, it may still be ineffective because of weak delivery or style. As with any other instructional procedure, lectures are enhanced by the stimulation of student interest *at the very beginning.* This initial interest arousal is enhanced by involving students as directly as possible and should "tune them in" to what the lecture is about. You need to induce a favorable anticipatory set. There is some evidence that teachers who can initiate lessons well can elicit more learning than teachers who do not concentrate on the initial stages of a presentation.[8]

Language usage can also contribute to or detract from the effectiveness of a lecture. Using language of appropriate complexity and formality is an art worth practicing. The Elder Sophists made their living teaching little other than the appropriate use of language. If new words are to be introduced, clearly identify and define them so students will understand their meanings in the context in which they are used. Using complex language early in the lecture may cause students to "tune out" because they feel the lecture is going to be "over their heads." If this happens, it is difficult to recapture their interest.

Explain Organization of Material.   Good lecturers explain to students how the lecture is organized. Common organizations include cause–effect relationships, chronological order, easy-to-difficult, concrete-to-abstract, or rule-example-rule. Explaining to students how the information they will be hearing is organized will help them orient their thinking and organize their notes.

Use Instructional Aids.   The effectiveness of a lecture is increased by visually reinforcing verbal information. If students *see* important facts, figures, names, and dates as well as *hear* them, the probability of their being remembered increases. Further, varying the stimulus can, in itself, be a device helpful in refocusing the attention of students whose interest may be wavering. Among the most common visual aids are posters, chalkboards, overhead projectors, and document cameras. These devices are easy to use and provide sufficient latitude for creative utilization.

Gestures.   Just as the use of formal visual aids adds to the interest of a lecture, so do physical movements. Appropriate gestures can help punctuate sentences and emphasize important points. Moving from behind the desk or podium and walking about can provide visual stimulation, but all these movements must stop short of being distracting.

Voice—Modulation and Rate.   The way in which the voice is used also influences effectiveness. Voice inflections, for example, can place emphasis on particular points and can dramatize quotations and asides. By varying the pitch and volume of the voice, lecturers add the variety necessary to capture the interest of the students. Rate, too, is important. The average rate of speech is 100–150 words per minute. In everyday conversations, we can comprehend spoken information at the rate of about 250–300 words per minute,[9] but lectures are not everyday conversations. If you want students to be able to take notes and to listen to what you are saying, as opposed to simply hearing it, slow down to about 120 words per minute.

All teachers *can* improve their lecture delivery techniques. For example, audio and video tape recorders can be used to help detect problem speech patterns and distracting physical movements. By taping segments of a lesson and dividing the number of words spoken by the number of minutes elapsed, you can calculate the words per minute. Listening to an audio tape or watching a video tape of yourself will also reveal tendencies to speak in a monotone, mispronounce particular words, use personal pronouns, or insert words such as "you know" "um,"or "uh." We tend not to realize our own idiosyncrasies until we listen to ourselves and analyze what we hear.

Use Lots of Examples.   The use of numerous and relevant examples has been shown to facilitate student understanding of content. Generous use of examples, analogies, and illustrations will help to keep student interest high and produce more learning. It is also a good idea to ask students for examples.

Involve Students.   When students are actively involved, their interest is higher, and the teacher can assess their responses to determine the extent to which they understand. Student participation is best encouraged by careful planning. Sets of key questions can be prepared and asked at appropriate places in the lecture. The experienced teacher is constantly aware of nonverbal cues and student behaviors such as blank stares, the slow shaking of a head to indicate disagreement, or a raised hand. Prompt attention to these cues can help students stay on track. Having students reiterate points, by answering questions, will often clarify important points for students who are still struggling with a new idea.

Summarize.   A good lecture concludes with a summary and review of the main points. While this activity can be done orally, it may be helpful to students if visual aids are used for reinforcement. Visual reinforcement helps to emphasize important points and it gives students a chance to double-check notes, fill in points they may have missed, and correct errors.

Summary

In summary, the lecture is one of the most often used instructional procedures. Lectures have the advantage of enabling a teacher to present a large body of information in a relatively short period of time, and they are relatively easy to direct and control. Possible disadvantages are that lectures can: (1) encourage passive, rather than active, student participation, (2) inhibit much of the student–teacher interaction needed for proper evaluation of the instructional process, (3) foster unquestioning acceptance of presented material, (4) fail to capitalize on student curiosity or creativity, and (5) tend to center more on the content than on what students are to do with the content. Each of these problems is avoidable.

Questioning

The judicious use of questions can be the basis for valuable instructional experiences. The main purposes of questioning are to: (1) find out how well students understand a particular block of information, (2) shift student attention from one point to another, (3) increase retention of important points by isolating and emphasizing them, (4) point students in the right direction before starting assignments, and (5) elicit high-order thinking on the part of students. Questions can be asked that call for analysis, synthesis, and evaluation. All higher-order questions provide practice for students in formulating and orally communicating specific answers to specific questions.

The "Overhead" Questioning Technique
Using the following steps of the "overhead" questioning technique may prove helpful in increasing the effectiveness of questioning:

1. *State the question clearly and precisely.* A question such as, "What about microcomputers?", for example, gives the student little direction for an answer. It is necessary to ask a follow-up question to clarify the first question. It would be better to ask, "How does a microcomputer differ from a large computer?" or "How could a microcomputer be used in this class?"
2. *Pause after asking the question and allow it to "hang overhead."* When you ask questions in a classroom, you generally want all students to think about the answer. To encourage this, ask the question clearly and then pause before calling on someone. Let the question "hang" over everyone's head. The pause gives students a chance to think about the question and encourages all students to do so, since they do not know who is to answer.

    One researcher found that teachers typically allow only one second after asking a question before expecting a response. The researcher also found that when the "**wait-time**" was increased to three or four seconds, more students tend to provide more appropriate responses.[10] Even three or four seconds may be too short a time. Many students have learned that if they just sit quietly, many teachers will get so uncomfortable with the silence that they will answer their own questions. If a student does not volunteer an answer, call on someone.
3. *Call on students at random.* Since it is desirable for all students to think about the questions, do not follow any pattern when calling on students. Any pattern, be it a seating arrangement, an alphabetical arrangement, or any other kind of sequence, has the effect of reducing attention on the part of those students who feel they will not be called on.
4. *Provide immediate feedback to students.* Indicate the appropriateness of students' answers. If an answer is not wholly correct, try to use the part that is correct or state the question to which the given answer would have been appropriate. Cues or hints can be used to help students answer appropriately, but care must be taken. If the hints are too obvious, students may feel embarrassed and be reluctant to answer in the future. Do nothing that might embarrass a student and do all that you can to help each student succeed.

Categorizing Questions

The nature of questions should be varied to ensure differing types of responses. One way to check on variety is to compare the kinds of responses expected with the levels of the cognitive domain. The following examples may be helpful in placing questions into appropriate categories.

1. *Knowledge (simple recall).* "What are the three basic parts of a precise instructional objective?"
2. *Comprehension (basic understanding).* "What is meant by the term *in loco parentis*?"

3. *Application (basic use)*. "Traveling at 60 miles per hour, how long would it take to travel the approximately 300 miles from Chicago to St. Louis?"
4. *Analysis (pulling an idea apart)*. "What words or phrases, if any, are used in this article that cause it to be biased?"
5. *Synthesis (putting together something new)*. "Assuming that the basic objectives of this course stay the same, suggest one or two alternative ways students might be helped to achieve those objectives."
6. *Evaluation (making and defending a judgment)*. "Which of these three lesson plans would you most prefer to follow and why?"

Another way to categorize questions is according to their essential function.

1. *Lower-order questions*. A lower-order question may be defined as any question that has served its purpose as soon as an acceptable answer is given. Typically, such questions come from the first three levels of the cognitive domain, although virtually any question that can be answered with one or two words can be considered a lower-order question.
2. *Higher-order questions*. A higher-order question requires students to analyze, synthesize, or evaluate. Answers to higher-order questions usually include cause–effect reasoning and/or the citation of relevant facts in support of an initial response.
3. *Probing questions*. A probing question is asked to encourage students to go beyond initial responses, to explain themselves further. An example of a probing question might be, "Good, you are right so far, now can you give us an illustration?" By asking students to provide examples, illustrations, and rationales, you can frequently determine the depth of their understanding more accurately than by using lower-order questions alone. Probing questions often begin with "why."
4. *Cueing questions*. As the name suggests, cueing questions are used to provide cues or hints to help students arrive at the correct answer. Avoid making the cues too obvious. You do not want to embarrass students, you want to help them be successful.
5. *Open-ended questions*. An open-ended question has no definite right or wrong answer. For example, if your purpose is to encourage students to go beyond the recollection or explanation of previously acquired information and to hypothesize, project, and infer, it might be appropriate to ask what they think about the probability of extraterrestrial life forms. Such questions are particularly useful at the beginning of a discussion.
6. *Convergent questions*. Convergent questions are arranged in a series and are designed to "converge" on a particular point or idea. For example, questions such as "Are there fewer or more farmers now than twenty years ago?" and "How do farm subsidies affect consumer prices?" could be used to help students focus attention on the issue of government farm

subsidies. Convergent questions may be used to induce a principle or deduce an answer.

7. *Divergent questions.* Divergent questions are asked to draw students' attention away from one point and to stimulate thinking about different, but related points. Divergent questions are particularly useful in inspiring student discovery of analogous situations. "What present-day parallels do we have, if any, to the Athenian agora?" is an example of an analysis-level question being used to stimulate divergent thinking.

Encouraging Participation

Encouraging students to ask questions is a skill that can be developed. Aside from asking reasonable questions, as opposed to questions about trivial points, perhaps the most important things teachers can do with respect to questioning is to make it clear that asking thoughtful questions does not indicate ignorance, it indicates a willingness to learn. In all cases, teachers should respond to students' questions thoroughly, courteously, and in a friendly manner. They should also indicate the importance of students' questions by comments such as "That was a good question because...." Finally, the teacher must *never* humiliate or embarrass a student who gives a wrong answer. To encourage student participation, treat students as you want to be treated.

Demonstrations

Demonstrations have the unique advantage of enabling students to observe the demonstrator doing something instead of simply talking about it. It is a form of modeling. A correctly conducted demonstration, whether of some laboratory procedure, physical skill, or other action, is usually a stimulating instructional experience simply because it is being done "live." A typical objective calling for a demonstration would be: "Following Red Cross guidelines, apply an arm splint to a subject within three minutes."

Planning Demonstrations

To make demonstrations effective, the teacher must sometimes break down complex procedures into separate components and decide what components can be adequately demonstrated in the time available. For example, it is not likely that a home economics teacher would have time to demonstrate how to assemble ingredients for a cake, use alternative ingredients when one or more of those called for is not available, blend the ingredients, bake the cake, frost it, and discuss pitfalls, all within a typical classroom period. The task would need to be divided.

Having decided what can adequately be demonstrated in the time allowed, the next step is to plan each component. Depending on the nature of the demonstration, initial steps may include an overview description of the skill, process, or procedure. If machinery or equipment of any kind is to be used, safety aspects *must* be stressed. In fact, if your course exposes students to particular hazards, school rules typically require that safety precautions be prominently posted in the room at all times and be followed meticulously.

An outline of main points may be written on the chalkboard for quick reference, or students may be given handouts containing this information. Detailed descriptions should not be unnecessary. New terms, labels, and relationships should be dealt with before the demonstration begins and should be clearly pointed out and explained as they are encountered during the demonstration. It is also wise to test all the equipment to be used to be sure it functions properly.

Conducting the Demonstration

Before the demonstration is begun, be sure that all students can see and hear clearly. This is important, so do not make assumptions, check. If small instruments or fine manipulations are called for, schools so equipped often use a closed-circuit TV camera or video tape equipment. Many classrooms, in which large numbers of demonstrations take place, are equipped with mirrors above demonstration tables.

Effective demonstrations blend verbal skills with accompanying psychomotor skills. Gifted demonstrators are able to use the full range of questioning skills, drawing students' attention to crucial steps and to the way each step is carried out. Exaggerated movements should be avoided, because they might confuse or mislead students when they practice the movements themselves.

If students are watching a demonstration in order to learn how to do something themselves, they should be allowed to practice as soon after the demonstration as possible. Student questions should be answered, but the sooner students practice the skills or procedures they just saw, the fewer mistakes they are likely to make.

If the practice session is to result in some product (as opposed to resulting in the improvement of some process), examples of satisfactory and unsatisfactory products should be made available, so students can compare and contrast their own products with the models. The use of models is a good idea for all assignments, because it helps students be successful. Opportunities for creative responses in the development of a product should be encouraged as long as established standards are maintained.

As students practice the skill or procedure, the teacher should provide individual corrective feedback and encourage students to assess their own performances. This is particularly important when dealing with students with special needs. Allowances should be made for individual differences.

For example, if the instructions begin, "Using your right hand," left-handed students are likely to find the movement awkward. Student's idiosyncrasies should cause concern only if they are likely to inhibit future performance.

If a demonstration involves valuable or potentially dangerous material or equipment, the teacher must carefully compare the cost and/or dangers involved with the expected benefits. If material or equipment is too valuable or too dangerous, it would be wise to choose a different procedure.

Guest Speakers

The chief purpose of inviting guest speakers into a classroom is to help students achieve specific objectives by giving them access to people with expertise in a particular area or who have views different from those already explored in class. The presence of a guest speaker also establishes direct contact between the classroom and the "real" world.

Planning for Speakers

To maximize the usefulness of a guest speaker, students should be involved in the process of selecting the speaker. When the class identifies a particular area in which a speaker can provide a unique contribution, a list of potential speakers should be compiled. The names of the prospective speakers should then be cleared with the principal or other appropriate administrator, and permission obtained to invite them to speak to the class. Administrators may be able to suggest individuals who are willing to speak to classes and who have been well received in the past. They can also help you avoid trouble.

When talking with prospective speakers, it is a good idea to let them know the age and grade level of the students, the topic being studied, how much the students already know about the topic, and what type of unique contribution he or she might make. Assuming that the speaker can come when needed, it is a good idea to discuss the general format of the presentation, suggest that time be allowed for questions and answers, and ask if a tape recording may be made. It is also useful to provide the speaker with a list of questions to which students have been unable to find satisfactory answers.

Conducting the Activity

On the appointed day, have a student meet the speaker at the entrance to the school and act as escort to the classroom. The teacher should formally introduce the speaker to the class. After the presentation is complete, it is the teacher's responsibility to tie loose strands together and bring about closure. Points may have been made that will require further study, and aspects of the content presented may need to be related to previously learned material and to the instructional objective underlying the presentation. If students do not suggest writing a thank-you note, the teacher should remind them of the need to do so and make sure that one is written, carefully checked, and sent.

Field Trips

The logical extension of bringing part of the world into the classroom is taking the class into the "real" world. Field trips are useful because they give students firsthand experience available in no other way. It is not likely, for example, that many students would get to see the printing of a newspaper unless they saw it on a school field trip. Similarly, many students are first introduced to art museums, concerts, and professional plays via field trips.

Planning Field Trips

Field trips should be related directly to specific instructional objectives and these objectives should be used as a springboard to produce specific questions to be answered by students while they are on the field trip or on their return. During a trip, many activities and new experiences will be competing for the students' attention, and the questions will help focus their attention on the most important activities and experiences.

Student involvement during each step of planning a field trip helps generate interest and make the trip more worthwhile. For example, while some students are building questions that focus attention on important points, others may gather information about the facilities at the site of the field trip. This latter group may wish to write for information on the availability of guided tours, admission costs, dates and times the facility is open, specific clothing requirements, and the availability of food. Still another group may obtain information about transportation. Even though the teacher could probably make all the arrangements, students should help. In doing so, they will learn such things as whether school district regulations allow classes to use school buses for field trips and, if so, whether this use is dependent on the buses being returned before they are needed to transport students home from school at the end of the day; whether the distance is such that students will have to leave particularly early or get back after school hours; how to charter a bus if necessary; and the importance of school insurance policies that cover field trips and their ramifications for the use of private automobiles.

Financing Field Trips

If chartered transportation is needed, it must be paid for, and this may be an inhibiting factor. Depending on the student population, it may be unfair to expect parents to contribute enough money to cover both the incidental expenses of their children and the transportation costs. This poses a dilemma. If students are asked to raise the needed funds, regardless of what they might learn about business operations during the fund raising, time for that activity will come at the expense of study time. To the extent that we want students to do well academically, we should do all in our power to free them to study. If the needed funds can be provided by parents or the PTA, there is no problem. If funds become a problem, a different activity should be considered. If money is collected, it is important to give each student a receipt and to keep a copy, and to keep accurate and public records. Some schools have adopted specific procedures concerning the handling of money and if such procedures exist at your school, follow them explicitly.

Permission Slips

Most schools require that the parents or guardians of students going on a field trip sign permission slips. These slips are not legal documents meant to protect schools and teachers from a lawsuit; they are simply devices to assure school administrators that parents know where the students will be going that day and approve of the trip. The teachers can extend the utility of permission slips by including on them details parents would wish to know, such as departure and arrival times, whether students are to bring food with them or purchase it, and special clothing requirements.

Other Considerations

All these considerations may be influenced by board and administrative policies concerning absences from other classes, providing for students who are unwilling or unable to go, securing enough qualified chaperones, and dealing with special cases such as financially or physically handicapped students or students with particular religious or dietary restrictions. There may also be regulations concerning taking along a first-aid kit or extra cash. Students should be asked to demonstrate that they know where the bus will be waiting for the group should they get separated, and what time it is scheduled to leave the field trip site. It should be made clear to students that their behavior will reflect on the school as a whole. They can either tarnish or polish the school's reputation and its relationships with the community. Be sure that all students are together before leaving the field trip site. It is considered good practice to return with as many students as you had when you left and, preferably, the same ones.

Follow-up Procedures

Proper follow-up activities are particularly important with respect to field trips. Unlike other instructional activities, field trips involve other faculty by keeping students from attending their classes. If the field trip does not yield worthwhile results, the sponsoring teacher may find it difficult to secure permission for other trips. This possibility, coupled with financial problems, has caused some boards of education to require very strong rationales for field trips. When the field trip has focused on specific objectives and students are given adequate preparation, follow-up discussions and evaluations are easy. General and ambiguous reactions to the trip, while perhaps of passing interest, are not the main concern. The experience should be evaluated on the extent to which it helped students achieve the stated objective(s).

School–community relations tend to improve as interaction between the two increases. Guest speakers and field trips provide interaction and thus help to improve school–community relations.

General Discussions

The purpose of general discussion is to give students practice in on-the-spot thinking, clear oral expression, and asking and responding to questions. Such discussions are also useful for assessing the diversification of views and exploring ideas.

Preparation
The teacher's initial step should be to gather and make available to students appropriate background information, materials, and sources. The success of a discussion depends on the degree to which students are informed and prepared. This preparation can be done as homework and will be facilitated if students are given a series of key points to look for or think about. It is a good idea for the teacher to prepare a list of key questions for use in stimulating or changing the direction of the discussion. These questions can guide discussions along those lines most likely to contribute to student achievement of the instructional objectives.

Since one of the aims in discussions is to encourage student-to-student communication, it can be helpful to arrange desks or chairs in such a way that students can comfortably see each other. Circular, semicircular, or horseshoe arrangements are useful.

Procedures
The teacher should explain certain ground rules: all comments and questions will be impersonal; ideas, not the people who suggest them, will be the focus of the discussion; common courtesies such as not interrupting, raising a hand to be recognized, and not monopolizing the time will be observed. If there are consistent violations of the rules, students may wish to establish a process for helping their peers who are lax in proper participation procedures.

Potential Problems
Sometimes teachers unconsciously allow one or two students to monopolize the discussions. This can be avoided by asking for the comments and opinions of those students who do not volunteer, but care should be taken not to

force such participation. If students feel threatened, their participation will decrease rather than increase. Asking for opinions rather than for specific facts is a good way to encourage participation without posing a threat.

Digressions can be a problem in any discussion. Some digressions may have meaning and relevance for students, but you must decide if the digression is important enough in its own right to allow it to continue. The point of the discussion is to help students achieve a particular objective. Digressions that are frequent or long may jeopardize the achievement of the particular objective and, by extension, the timely completion of the unit as a whole.

Exploratory Discussions

A central purpose of exploratory discussions is to stimulate student thinking and interaction. General discussions have a similar purpose, but there is a difference between the two. General discussions typically focus on academic or emotionally neutral topics. Exploratory discussions can focus on controversial issues (such as premarital sex, use of illegal drugs, and abortion) and thus provide opportunities for students to discuss such issues without fear of censure. Such discussions help make students aware of the other students' views and can thus help them become more tolerant of differing viewpoints.

Procedures

In conducting an exploratory discussion, the teacher must define the topic clearly and make sure that students understand that there will be no negative criticism of other students' views during the discussion. This does not preclude disagreement and alternative views, but if a tone of ridicule emerges, students will become reluctant to voice further opinions, thus defeating the purpose of the discussion. While the later scrutinizing of a general class feeling is not threatening to individuals and can cause little harm, the scrutinizing of a particular student's opinion or comment may cause negative attention to be focused on that student. This may result in an unintended and undesirable reaction. Typically, divergent and probing questioning will predominate throughout the discussion.

One of the problems of exploratory discussions is that they are often explorations into the affective domain, and it is sometimes not clear just what was gained by students. Students themselves may feel that little was accomplished. To minimize these difficulties, the teacher can synthesize the various contributions and use them as a basis for further instructional experiences that are more precisely defined. There may be few concrete accomplishments directly attributable to an exploratory discussion, but it is likely that some students will be enlightened by the variety of opinions held by their peers and will gain new insights.

Exploratory discussions may also be used in conjunction with a resource person knowledgeable in the area to be studied. The function of such a person would be to present new ideas and opinions to which students could respond.

Brainstorming

The purpose of brainstorming is to generate a wide variety of creative ideas concerning a problem in a short period of time. To conduct a brainstorming session, the teacher acts as a facilitator whose primary responsibility is to see that proper procedures are followed.

Procedures

After the problem is identified, the facilitator explains that the point of the brainstorming session is to acquire as many creative ideas as possible as quickly as possible. Everyone is encouraged to contribute any idea, regardless of how strange it may seem. The facilitator makes it clear that no idea or contribution is to be discussed, evaluated, or criticized during the brainstorming session and that each idea suggested will be added to a written list of ideas.

The effectiveness of brainstorming sessions depends on rapid pace, short duration, and close adherence to the rule that no idea or contribution during the brainstorming is to be discussed. At the end of the session, the students will have a number of suggestions written down relating to the central topic. The facilitator then helps the students divide the ideas into general categories and move into an exploratory discussion in which the various ideas are discussed. If such discussion is allowed to interrupt the brainstorming session itself, the necessary free-wheeling atmosphere is inhibited.

Guided or Directed Discussions

A directed discussion is appropriate if students are to be guided through a series of questions to the discovery of some principle, formula, relationship, or other specific preselected result. In guided discussions, students are given practice in inductive or deductive step-by-step thinking. **Inductive reasoning** goes from the specific to the general. Students are led to conclusions about a set of things by the examination of only a few members of that set. People in China typically have two arms and two legs, as do people in France, the United States, and South Africa. It is reasonable to assume, therefore, that all people typically have two arms and two legs. **Deductive reasoning** goes from the general to the specific. A common form of deductive reasoning is **syllogistic reasoning.** A syllogism consists of a major premise assumed to be true of a whole class of things; a minor premise that identifies an entity as a member of that class; and a conclusion that is inescapable if the major and minor premises are true. For example:

Major Premise—All men are mortal.
Minor Premise—Socrates is a man.
Conclusion—Socrates is mortal.

There is some danger in using directed discussions, because the teacher has already determined what the students are to discover. If students become too frustrated in the chain of logic leading to the discovery, they may react with the attitude, "Why didn't you just say so in the first place?" and the value of the experience will be lost. Many teachers who use this technique feel that using it for only ten- or fifteen-minute blocks of time works best. Once the conclusion is reached or the principle is discovered, it makes sense to switch to another instructional experience to make use of that conclusion or principle. It has also been found helpful to begin guided discussions with a statement such as, "There is an underlying point here" or "Let's see if we can reach a conclusion concerning. . . ." Statements such as these help set the stage for the guided discussion and minimize the possibility of students' seeing the experience as guesswork.

An analogy might be made between a guided discussion and a computer-assisted instruction program. In both, the most likely student responses to questions must be anticipated and appropriate questions (or instructions) planned. Both are designed to provide reinforcement for correct answers and both are built around a series of sequential steps. The important difference is that, in a guided discussion, the teacher can monitor the interaction very closely and modify the remaining questions to capitalize on some unexpected student response.

If used cogently, guided discussions can provide a rich instructional experience. Students enjoy discovering and solving, and once they have "discovered" a principle, they remember it longer than if it is simply explained to them.

Reflective Discussions

Reflective discussions are used to assist students in developing analytical skills, arriving at alternative explanations, finding solutions to selected problems, and classifying ideas into major categories. These skills relate directly to objectives at the higher cognitive levels (i.e., analysis, synthesis, and evaluation). A typical objective for a reflective discussion might be, "You will explain orally how some aspect of daily life would differ if we lived under a socialistic government."

Preparation.   A good way to begin a reflective discussion is for the teacher to define a particular problem relative to the instructional objective, then devise a series of open-ended questions to encourage a variety of responses. Additional specific questions will be generated and asked spontaneously during the discussion.

To help maximize the benefit of reflective discussions, one student can be delegated to list the identified main points of each response on the chalkboard. To supplement this listing, the teacher can elicit from the class appropriate headings for clusters of responses that have points in common. In this way, as students are given practice in classifying ideas and in analysis skills, a basis is provided for predicting and hypothesizing solutions to the original problem.

Potential Problems.   Unlike guided discussions, which can often be conducted at a rapid rate since the teacher has prior knowledge of the result, reflective discussions should be conducted at a relatively slow pace and include periods of silence. Time must be allowed for students to consider alternate possibilities and to think about the ramifications of those possibilities. Many teachers feel that the slowness of reflective discussions is a serious drawback and that the time they require can be used in more valuable ways. Other teachers feel the "thinking" time required is one of the strongest attributes of reflective discussions and use the discussions frequently. In deciding how often to use them, the teacher must weigh these factors and balance time used against the opportunities for divergent responses, large-scale student participation, practice in classification, and reflection. At their roots, these are all matters of philosophic position.

Evaluation of Discussions

Discussions are time-consuming instructional procedures in relation to content gained by students, especially in comparison with experiences such as reading assignments or lectures. The advantage most forms of discussion have over these other activities, however, is that they capitalize on student curiosity and creativity, encourage participation, and allow for development of higher-level thought processes.

Discussions, like all instructional procedures, must be evaluated to determine effectiveness. The best way to judge a discussion is to determine if students can achieve the instructional objective for which the discussion was chosen as the learning activity.

Teachers sometimes find it useful to note which students do or do not contribute to discussions and what types of contributions are made by individuals. It is sometimes found, for instance, that even though students did not participate vocally in a discussion, they were involved mentally and developed analytical skills. Nonparticipation may indicate that the student needs special, individualized help, but it may also mean that these students are simply thinking about what is being said. By comparing evaluation results with patterns of participation, it may be possible to determine which students need the maximum amount of encouragement to participate, since participation, in their cases, might aid learning.

The quality of students' responses is a valid indicator of the effectiveness of discussions. When students make comments indicative of muddled thinking or misconceptions, the teacher has at least two choices. The teacher could ask the student to explain the factual basis for the response. The risk here is that there may be no factual basis and the student will be embarrassed and get very defensive. Another approach is to point out that while some people share that particular view, there is considerable evidence that supports a different view. Sometimes, students make extreme points purely for effect, to impress their peers or to elicit special attention from the teacher. If it becomes clear that a student is engaging in "artificial" participation, attempting to take care of the problem during the ongoing discussion is likely to produce denials or challenges by the concerned student and should be avoided. A private conference is usually more fruitful.

Effective evaluation of discussions takes thought, but the potential for improvement makes the effort worthwhile. The more discussions are used and evaluated, the more polished the teacher will become in their use.

Contests

Competitiveness is at the heart of our democratic way of life and it is reflected in school in activities as varied as sports, elections for school councils, and competition for college admission. You can bring some of the excitement of competition into your classroom by having occasional contests.

The simplest way to do this is for the teacher to assign all students a block of content to study and for the teacher to prepare a list of questions going from simple to complex. The following day, divide the class into half either randomly or by some variable such as sex or height. Then, have each "team" sit together and follow a quiz-show format. Ask a question of the first member of Team One. If that person answers correctly, the team earns two points. If the person cannot answer or answers incorrectly, but someone else on the team can answer correctly, the team earns one point. If no one on Team One can answer the question, but someone on Team Two can answer correctly, Team Two earns two points. The first person on Team Two is then asked a question and the process is repeated. This procedure is repeated until all students on each team have had a chance at a question.

To stimulate a sense of teamwork, a different format, one that links whole-group with small-group activities, can be used. For example, students could be divided into groups of four to six students each. Fewer students in a group tend to make the competition unwieldy because of the number of groups that result. Larger groups tend to reduce the amount of teamwork that takes place among members. With the teams known beforehand, all students are given a block of content to study. If this format is followed, the questions prepared by the teacher can be more complex than with the first format. This is so because it is likely that members of each team will work together to some extent and will come to class well prepared. The following day, the quiz-show format can be used, but each team is allowed to earn points only on the questions answered correctly by the team. Play-offs between the teams having the greatest number of points are also possible.

In using contests it is crucial that the questions asked by the teacher be seen as fair. This means that a good deal of thought needs to go into the development of the questions. The earliest questions should be at the Knowledge or Comprehension level and should be designed not only to sample student knowledge, but also to enable students to earn points quickly. Once each team has amassed some points, its members will have a stake in the activity and this will increase interest and participation. This interest and participation is then likely to continue even when the questions become more challenging. Variations of these formats include: (1) specifying a maximum amount of time to be allowed for each question, (2) having teams construct and pose questions to each other, and (3) having students submit questions to the teacher, who then selects questions from among those submitted. With option three, it is a good idea to have an understanding with the students that if there are not enough suitable questions submitted, teacher-developed questions may be used.

SUMMARY

There are a number of generic skills that are useful in many instructional settings. Among those skills are set induction, communicating the objective, stimulus variation, review/repetition, practice, and closure. As useful as these skills are, it is crucial to remember that good teaching is more complex than simply sequencing a set of skills and using them mindlessly.

You will be responsible for the progress of your class as a whole and a good deal of your time is likely to be used in whole-group, direct, instruction. Research indicates that if instruction is predominately teacher-directed and academically oriented, students are likely to achieve higher scores on achievement tests than if instruction is predominately student-directed. Madeline Hunter and Barack Rosenshine identified sequences of skills typical of direct instruction. Those sequences begin with inducing a favorable mindset and communicating the objective, include the use of a variety of instructional activities, and conclude with a review, practice, and closure.

Lectures are used mostly as a way to convey information quickly and concisely. Formal and informal lectures differ in that informal lectures provide for student involvement. In planning a lecture, the teacher should prepare a word or phrase outline and appropriate visual aids. Students should be taught to take notes in an outline or double-column format. While delivering the lecture, speak at about 120 words per minute, maintain eye contact with the students, use a great many examples, and make use of visual aids. Conclude by asking students for main points.

Another commonly used whole-group technique is questioning. When using the "overhead" questioning technique, ask a question of the whole group, allow it to "hang over everyone's head" for at least four or five seconds, and then ask for an answer. Call on students randomly to increase attentiveness and participation. Questions can be categorized according to the levels in the Cognitive domain, or according to function. Some of the function types include probing, cueing, open-ended, convergent, and divergent.

Demonstrations have the advantage of enabling students to see something being done as opposed to being able only to hear about it being done. Teachers should practice the demonstration beforehand, arrange students so they can see clearly, explain all safety precautions, explain each step as it is being done, and have students practice the skill or procedure as soon after the demonstration as possible.

Guest speakers and field trips have the advantage of exposing students to the "real world." Both activities should be cleared with the principal. Field trips have two drawbacks that need careful consideration. First, taking students out of school interferes with the instructional plans of other teachers who have those students in class. Enough such disruptions can threaten the integrity of the entire curriculum. Second, if funding for a trip is required, expecting students to raise that money detracts from the time they should spend studying. Fundraising activities for any purpose are, therefore, highly questionable.

Discussions can help students acquire new information, but they are particularly useful in giving students practice in voicing ideas and defending points of view. Regardless of the type of discussion, it is a good idea to ensure that students are prepared by making specific assignments prior to the discussion. Friendly competition can be utilized in the classroom by pitting teams of students against one another in contests that follow quiz-show formats.

SO HOW DOES THIS AFFECT MY TEACHING?

As a teacher, you will be given five or six classes of 20 to 30 students each and expected to help all the students learn. At the beginning of the year, when you are trying to establish a good teaching–learning environment and help students build their knowledge base, much of your time will be spent dealing with the students as a single group. To the extent that the whole-group activities are well planned and well conducted, students will feel that their time is being well spent, their respect for you will increase, and so too will their willingness to participate in the teaching–learning process. Knowing how to sequence and use some of the generic skills associated with direct instruction will help make your whole-group instruction more effective.

In the discussion of Madeline Hunter and Barack Rosenshine, a sequence of generic instructional skills, such as set induction, communicating the objective, and practice, was described. There is evidence that use of those sequences of skills results in consistent, well-structured lessons, and in student learning. Further, that model is consistent with calls for greater standardization in the schools, more accountability, higher standards, and with the whole idea of a curriculum.

However, the other side of the story is that there are also advantages to diversity. New ideas and new techniques come from experimentation and risk taking. The questions you need to wrestle with are how much risk you are willing to take, and what it is that you are risking. It is one thing to experiment in a lab. There, if things go wrong, (and assuming that the lab is not blown up), the researchers dispose of the bad stuff and start over. They lose the cost of their materials. When you experiment in a classroom, if things go wrong, irreplaceable instructional time will be lost. So, keeping in mind that your foremost responsibility is to the students in your class, you decide where to draw the line between standardization or diversity. Your decision depends largely on your philosophical viewpoint.

KEY TERMS, PEOPLE, AND IDEAS

Generic skills, useful in many instructional settings
    Set induction
    Communication of the objective
    Stimulus variation
    Review/Repetition
        Simple, spaced, massed repetition
    Practice
        Analogous, Equivalent
        Guided, Independent
    Closure
Direct Instruction (Madeline Hunter, Barack Rosenshine, Alan Ornstein)
    Formal and informal lectures
    Word or phrase outline
    Cornell System
    Overhead questioning technique
    Wait-time
    Probing, cueing, convergent and divergent questions
    Demonstrations
    Guest speakers
    Field trips, permission slips
    Discussions
        General

Exploratory
Brainstorming
Guided/Directed
Reflective
Inductive reasoning
Deductive reasoning
Syllogistic reasoning
Contests

ENDNOTES

1. Rosenshine, Barack V., "Content, Time and Direct Instruction," in Penelope L. Peterson and Herbert J. Walberg, eds., *Research on Teaching: Concepts, Findings, and Implications* (Berkeley, Calif.: McCutchen, 1979), pp. 28–56; also Rosenshine, Barack V., "Explicit Teaching," in David Berliner and B.V. Rosenshine, eds., *Talks to Teachers: A Festschrift for Nate Gage* (New York: Random House, 1987), pp. 75–92.

2. Evertson, Carolyn, C. Anderson, L. Anderson, and J. Brophy, "Relationship Between Classroom Behaviors and Student Outcomes in Junior High Mathematics and English Classes," *American Educational Research Journal*, Vol. 17 (Spring 1980), pp. 43–60.

3. Jones, Vernon F., and Louise S. Jones, *Comprehensive Classroom Management: Motivating and Managing Students*, 3rd ed. (Boston: Allyn and Bacon, 1990).

4. Ornstein, Allan C., and Daniel U. Levine, "School Effectiveness and Reform," *Clearing House* (November–December 1990), pp. 115–118.

5. Hunter, Madeline, "Knowing, Teaching, and Supervising," in Philip L. Hosford ed., *Using What We Know About Teaching* (Alexandria, Vir.: Association for Supervision and Curriculum Development, 1984), pp. 175–176.

6. Rosenshine, Barack V. "Explicit Teaching and Teacher Training," *Journal of Teacher Education*, (May-June, 1987), p. 34.

7. Pauk, Walter, *A User's Guide to College: Making Notes and Taking Tests* (Providence, RI.: Jamestown Pub., 1988), p. 7.

8. Schuck, Robert F., "The Effect of Set Induction upon Pupil Achievement, Retention and Assessment of Effective Teaching in a Unit on Respiration in the BSCS Curricula," *Educational Leadership Research Supplement 2*, no. 5 (May 1969), pp. 785–793.

9. Heinich, Robert, Michael Molenda, and James D. Russell, *Instructional Media and the New Technologies of Instruction*, 4th. ed. (New York: Macmillan, 1993), p. 181.

10. Rowe, Mary B., "Wait-time and Reward as Instructional Variables," *Journal of Research in Science Teaching* (February 1974), pp. 81–97.

8

SMALL-GROUP AND INDIVIDUALIZED INSTRUCTIONAL ACTIVITIES

RATIONALE

People are always competing, either against themselves or against others, and for things as varied as money, power, goods, services, titles, and a "better" life for themselves and/or for their children. Our schools, with their emphasis on whole-group instruction, do much to further the spirit of competition, because each student is typically competing with all others for recognition and grades. However, if we are to produce citizens who are able not only to compete among themselves, but also to work together in joint ventures, perhaps we ought to do more to further the spirit of cooperation. This chapter will focus on small-group and individualized activities. The more teachers know about different instructional procedures—such as large-group, small-group, and individualized—the more they will be able to vary instructional procedures and thus help students develop a wide range of skills and understandings. Further, if teachers select wisely, student interest will be maintained and their probability of success will increase. This chapter will help.

SAMPLE OBJECTIVES

You will be able, in writing, to:

1. Explain what concepts are central to cooperative learning strategies such as STAD and TGT, and how the steps of those strategies attend to those concepts. (Comprehension)
2. Describe each of the five steps of the "scientific method." (Comprehension)

3. Identify an "ill-structured" problem suitable for a problem-based learning project in your subject area, and explain at least three kinds of information students would need, outside of your subject area, in order to complete the project. (Analysis)
4. Construct a self-instructional package that could be used for enrichment by students in your subject area. (Synthesis)

SMALL-GROUP ACTIVITIES

Small-group and individualized activities usually follow whole-class activities. Whole-group activities are most often used early in each instructional unit, because they effectively help students acquire the facts, figures, names, dates, sequences, and other components that make up a well-developed knowledge-base. However, the acquisition of such a knowledge-base does not automatically lead to the development of higher-level skills such as analysis, synthesis, evaluation, or skilled movements. Students need to be given opportunities to combine pieces of information into meaningful wholes, voice and defend positions, and critically analyze what they see, hear, and do. It is here that small-group and individualized activities are most useful.

Small-group activities, because of the more direct and continuous involvement of individuals and because of the increased opportunities to check ideas against those of others, facilitate achievement of complex tasks. This is particularly so when those tasks require the use of skills and knowledge that cut across subject-area lines because students can divide the workload and capitalize on each other's strengths. Further, teachers can use small-group activities to make students more responsible for their own learning. This happens when students identify problems of particular interest to themselves and plan how to work to solve those problems with little or no teacher direction. The opportunity to maximize the relevance of instruction to the needs and interests of students reaches its epitome in individualized activities.

Proportions of Whole- versus Small-Group Activities

A point of continuing discussion is the proportion of time that should be devoted to whole-group versus small-group instruction. Some teachers argue that most instructional time should be devoted to whole-group, direct instruction because (1) students must have a common and strong knowledge-base on which to build, and large-group direct instruction is the most efficient way to build that knowledge-base, and (2) large-group direct instruction tends to minimize classroom management problems. Other teachers argue that most of the time should be devoted to small-group or individualized activities because (1) students learn best by doing, and (2) "less is more"; students who cover less content, but who spend more time considering and working with it, will acquire longer lasting knowledge. Given the fact that teachers typically work with 120–180 students every day, it is likely that large-group instruction will continue to predominate, but it should not exclude small-group and individualized activities. We want to produce citizens who can cooperate, as well as compete, with each other.

Determining Group Make-up

Putting students in groups of four seems to result in the greatest productivity. Larger groups tend to be unwieldy and to subdivide on their own, and pairing students typically results in too many groups. Some teachers favor **heterogeneous** grouping, the assigning of one or more high, middle, and low achievers to each group. Variations of heterogeneous grouping include grouping students randomly or in alphabetical order. The advantage of heterogeneous grouping is that it tends to maximize social development because students learn to work with people with widely varying abilities. The disadvantage is that the brighter students may simply do most of the work, rather than helping the slower students.

Other teachers favor **homogeneous** grouping, the assigning of students to groups on the basis of common ability levels, interests, or friendships. The advantage of homogeneous grouping is that people tend to congregate, and work best, with others who have abilities and interests similar to their own. The commonalties provide a motivating force and also enable students to get to work more quickly. The disadvantages are that such grouping amounts to segregation, and that because of their commonalties, students in such groups tend to digress more than students in heterogeneous groups.

Clarifying Overall Purpose

Regardless of how groups are formed, it is the teacher's responsibility to ensure that all students understand how their work will benefit them individually and contribute to their achievement of course objectives. Before groups are formed, the teacher should explain the need for each person to do his or her part if the group, and the class as a whole, is to accomplish its task. It is a good idea to discuss the potential problem of having one or two group members do less than their share of the work. Students can be asked to suggest procedures for minimizing the problem and for dealing with it if it occurs. A written operating plan clarifying who is to do what by when helps to minimize the problem. Ultimately, it is the teacher's responsibility to monitor, and grade, each individual's work.

Concluding

When small-group activities are completed, results should be shared with the entire class. This enables all students to benefit from the work of each small group and it also provides the teacher with an opportunity to publicly commend the members of the groups for their efforts. Panel discussions and debates are among the activities that provide opportunities for the dissemination of group results. Descriptions of small-group strategies follow.

Panel Discussions

The purpose of a panel discussion is to enable a small group of students to delve deeply into an area of interest and then to act as a source of information for the rest of the class. To arrange a panel discussion, the teacher appoints panels of three to five students. Each group takes responsibility for selecting a chairperson, dividing research responsibilities, and setting up a time schedule. The teacher intervenes only if the responsibilities assigned to, or assumed by, some students are inappropriate for their ability levels. For some students, it may be necessary for the teacher to provide specific advice, references, and sources. There will be little benefit to those students however, if the teacher or other panel members do most of the work.

When the panel is ready to act as an authority, the chairperson or other moderator may follow several courses of action. One approach is for the moderator or chairperson to explain briefly what the panel is prepared to discuss with the class, introduce the panel members, and identify their individual areas of special interest, and begin accepting questions from the class.

In another approach, the moderator or chairperson briefly introduces the topic to be discussed and then introduces each of the panel members, allowing each about five minutes to discuss or explain his or her particular area of interest. The moderator or chairperson then summarizes the findings and opens the panel to questions and comments from the class. This procedure has the benefit of providing the rest of the students with information on which to base questions.

In both approaches, the moderator or chairperson ensures that all panel members participate on an equal basis and that sufficient time is left for a final summation. Time is also allowed for the teacher to bring the panel discussion to a close near the end of the class period and to establish the relationship of the discussion to the instructional objective.

Debates

Debates are similar to panel discussions in that small groups of students work together gathering information. The difference between the two is that with debates, the purpose of each group is to present facts, ideas, and values relevant to a particular view of a controversial issue. In conducting debates, each panel is given a certain amount of time to present its case and to answer questions about it. When all panels have made their presentations and answered questions, the class, as a whole, can discuss the issue and try to reach consensus.

Role Playing/Skits

Role playing is useful for dramatizing particular social problems and for increasing student empathy for the feelings, viewpoints, and problems of other members of society (affective domain objectives). Students might be asked, for example, to play the role of a pro-choice or pro-life activist, and to cite at least three arguments they might use to persuade others to join their cause.

To use role playing successfully, the teacher must make certain that all students understand that they will be playing specific roles, acting the way they believe their assigned characters would actually behave. A ground rule should be that the role playing will be stopped if students step out of their roles or begin to get too emotionally involved.

Once the ground rule is understood, the teacher identifies a situation in which two or more people interact and the specific roles and "positions" of the participants. After this is done, students should be asked to volunteer to play each of the roles. No one should be forced to participate.

Participants should then be allowed to confer briefly about how they intend to act out the situation (not to rehearse) and should then act it out. Usually two or three minutes is sufficient for students to decide how they intend to present the situation and another ten minutes for the actual presentation.

Before any discussion of the presentation takes place, it is sometimes worthwhile to have a second set of students confer and act out the same situation. After the second presentation, students can compare and contrast pertinent points. No effort should be made to evaluate the students' performances. The focus of the discussion should be on the differing perceptions of the roles by the participants and nonparticipants, on an attempt to understand the probable feelings and beliefs of the person(s) in the real situation, and on an examination of personal rationales for values held.

It should be noted that there is some risk associated with the use of role playing. If students play their roles too convincingly, other students may suspect that they are not acting at all; that they are saying and doing what they personally believe. If this happens the seeds of dissension may be sown and tentative relationships that might have flowered between or among students may be stunted. These subtle, but significant, risks may well outweigh any potential gains.

COOPERATIVE LEARNING

All small-group activities foster cooperative learning, but some strategies are more likely to be effective than others. **Robert Slavin,** at Johns Hopkins University, has done extensive research on different cooperative or, as he refers to them, Student Team Learning, strategies. He maintains that three concepts are central to effective Student Team Learning: (1) team rewards, (2) individual accountability, and (3) equal opportunities for success. He was also instrumental in developing four main cooperative learning strategies: (1) Student Teams—Achievement Divisions, STAD; (2) Teams-Games-Tournament, TGT; (3) Team-Assisted Individualization, TAI; and (4) Cooperative Integrated Reading and Composition, CIRC. The STAD and TGT strategies are adaptable to most subjects and grade levels, while the TAI and CIRC strategies work best, respectively, in grades 3–6 and in reading and writing.[1] All of the strategies are intended for use after whole-group instruction, to extend knowledge and provide opportunities for teamwork.

Student Teams—Achievement Divisions (STADs)

When using the STAD strategy, Slavin recommends putting students in teams of four and mixing membership on each team with respect to ability levels, sex, and ethnicity.

> *Students then work together within their teams to make sure that all team members have mastered the lesson. Finally, all students take individual quizzes on the material, at which time, they may not help one another.*
>
> *Students' quiz scores are compared with their own past averages, and points are awarded based on the degree to which students meet or exceed their earlier performance. These points are then summed to form team scores, and teams that meet their criteria may earn certificates or other rewards. The whole cycle of activities, from teacher presentation to team practice and quiz, usually takes three to five class periods.[2]*

The STAD strategy incorporates Slavin's three main concepts. Students are accountable for their own learning because they take quizzes individually. In order for the team to earn rewards they must help each other succeed and, since "team scores are based on students' improvement over their own past records, there is equal opportunity for all groups to be successful."[3]

Teams-Games-Tournaments (TGT)

> *The TGT strategy uses the same teacher presentations and teamwork that STAD does, but replaces the weekly quizzes with weekly tournaments in which students compete with members of other teams to contribute points*

to their team scores. Students compete at three-person "tournament tables" against others with similar past records in mathematics [or other subject areas]. A "bumping" procedure, which consists of changing students' table assignments weekly based on their performance in each tournament, keeps the competition fair. The winner at each tournament table brings six points to his or her team, regardless of which table it is; this means that low achievers (competing with other low achievers) and high achievers (competing with other high achievers) have equal opportunity for success. As in STAD, high-performing teams earn certificates or other forms of rewards."[4]

PROBLEM-BASED LEARNING

Problem-based learning is, perhaps, the single best way to introduce students to the complexities of "real-life" problems. Central to using problem-based learning is student familiarity with the "scientific method."

The Scientific Method

Although **Sir Francis Bacon** (1561–1626) did not invent the steps that came to be called the **"scientific method,"** he was one of the earliest thinkers to recommend induction and experimentation as the basis of the scientific method. He made his recommendation in 1620, in a book entitled, *Novum Organum,* (New Organon, referring to Aristotle's book on logic, the *Organon*).[5] The procedure he recommended has been reduced to the following steps:

1. Identify the problem.
2. Formulate a hypothesis (a probable solution or explanation).
3. Gather, evaluate, and categorize available data.
4. Reach some conclusion (either reject or support the hypothesis on the basis of the evidence acquired).
5. Take some action appropriate to the results.

Using Problem-Based Learning

Rather than simply describing the procedural steps of problem-based learning, those steps will be illustrated via a problem-based learning exercise that was completed by students at the **Illinois Math and Science Academy (IMSA).** The IMSA is a state-funded, residential, magnet school that selects top students from the state of Illinois and provides them with a three-year high-school experience focusing on math and science, delivered via an innovative curriculum. The project was entitled *Jane's Baby* and it was the privilege of this author to be present when W. J. Stepien demonstrated the steps involved, in brief form, at a workshop.

Preparation

Before starting his demonstration, Stepien explained how he and his colleagues prepared for the project. The first step was to decide on an ill-structured problem. They wanted students, on first seeing the problem, to be able to apply the general knowledge and reasoning skills they had accumulated to date. However, they also wanted students to see that "real-life" problems are typically far less well-defined than classroom assignments and that they typically cannot be solved by turning to large amounts of well-organized information. One of the problems they selected involved an anencephalic fetus.

After selecting the problem, the IMSA faculty thought it through on their own and identified some of the issues that students would be likely to encounter. They then identified the kinds of resources students were likely to need in their investigations and verified that those resources were available. Some materials could be made available in the classroom, but part of the power of problem-based learning is that students find out that they need to look for answers outside the classroom. If resources are scarce, teachers should consider putting some of them on reserve in the school library or in other central locations. If students are going to use resource people, the teacher needs to talk with them to make sure that they are willing to work with the students. If so, the teacher must then explain that they are not to simply tell students the answers, they are to help students understand what questions need to be answered and to guide them toward the appropriate information. Only then can the students be referred to these human resources. In this case, since students might well seek advice from a doctor, a teacher talked with a doctor who agreed to work with students if they asked. It should be noted that teachers typically spend more time preparing a good problem-solving project than preparing any other kind of instructional activity.

Procedure

Students were given the following scenario:

> *You are the head of pediatrics at a large city hospital. Jane Barton is one of your patients. Doctor, what will you do in the case of Jane's baby?*
>
> *Jane Barton is pregnant. She first came to see you about two weeks ago after she and her husband received the results of tests ordered by her family doctor. The tests indicate that Jane and Ralph's baby is anencephalic. The couple is concerned about the fetus and wonder what to do if Jane cannot deliver a normal, healthy infant.*[6]

A medical report of the situation was attached to the scenario. (For further details concerning the *Jane's Baby* project and others like it, contact Dr. William Stepien, Illinois Math and Science Academy, 1500 West Sullivan Road, Aurora, IL 60506–1000.)

Identifying the Problem.   After reading the scenario and the medical report, students were asked if a problem existed and, if so, what it was. Students agreed that two problems existed: (1) what to tell the Bartons and how to assist them, and (2) there were many things they needed to learn about.

Stating a Hypothesis.   As the first step in stating hypotheses, students were asked to list, in three columns on the chalkboard, what they knew about the problem, what they needed to know, and what they should do. Part of their work is shown in Table 8.1.

Students concluded that, in this situation, they could not state hypotheses until they had more information. This, in itself, was a major step because it brought home the ill-structured nature of many "real world" problems.

Gathering, Evaluating, and Categorizing Data.   Since a major purpose of problem-based learning is getting students to gather, interpret, and evaluate information on their own, it would be self-defeating for the teacher to act as a major source of information. A better role is that of resource person, one who helps point students to the sources of information, rather than as a supplier of data. This is in contrast, for example, to guided discussions in which the teacher not only provides information, but also directs students to predetermined outcomes. In this case, students found it necessary to get and consider information about how long anencephalic infants typically lived; what kinds of procedures would be covered by insurance; what state and/or federal laws said about abortion, organ transplants, and the use of fetal tissue for research; religion; and ethical and moral issues.

As they gathered data, the students established, modified, strengthened, and discarded hypotheses. It frequently happened that new information generated the need for still more information, so students had to continually engage in analysis and synthesis. To aid them in their work, they were given problem logs. Part of one such log is shown in Figure 8.1.

Reaching a Conclusion.   In a typical classroom assignment, once the data are gathered and analyzed, students are ready to conclude that the evidence warrants either the support or rejection of the hypothesis. In the minds of many, any conclusion reached by the students is less important than the practice they got in applying the scientific method to a problem. In the case of *Jane's Baby*, a number of possible conclusions were considered.

Taking Some Action.   As the final step, students take some action. In a typical classroom assignment, students might demonstrate the objective by writing a letter to someone arguing for a change in policies or practices. In the case of Jane's Baby, students, in their roles as doctors, had fifteen-minute "consultations" with Mr. and Mrs. Barton (played by volunteers from the community

TABLE 8.1 Jane's Baby

What do we know?	What do we need to know?	What should we do?
Jane Barton is pregnant.	What is the medical description of anencephaly?	Order another test to confirm the diagnosis.
Jane is married.	What is Jane's general health?	Discuss the condition of the fetus with the Bartons before too long.
Medical tests indicate that her baby is anencephalic.	Does she have children?	Have technology ready to help the baby at birth.
Jane and Ralph feel that their baby might not be normal.	What test did she have? How accurate is it?	Use the tissue/organs of the fetus in some way.
Jane has been referred by another doctor.	Is abortion possible in this case?	
Anencephalic babies don't live very long.	What is the law on abortion in our state?	
It has something to do with the brain.	How do Jane and Ralph feel about abortion?	
	Are there alternatives to abortion is this case?	
	How long do anencephalic babies live?	
	What is their "quality of life"?	

Stepien, William J., Shelagh A. Gallagher, and David Workman, "Problem-Based Learning for Traditional and Interdisciplinary Classroom," *Journal for the Education of the Gifted,* Vol. 16, no. 4 (Summer 1993), pp. 338–357.

and faculty). In these "consultations," students became aware of two other aspects of the problem: (1) who actually had to make decisions, and (2) the communication skills needed to help the patients understand the problem and the risks involved in each possible solution.

Advantages/Disadvantages

The chief advantages of problem-based learning are that it helps students (1) learn how to deal, systematically, with ill-structured problems—problems that involve a number of interrelated factors; and (2) recognize that some problems, and perhaps most "real-life" problems, have multiple answers, none of which may be clearly right or wrong. Few other instruc-

FIGURE 8.1   Problem Log for Jane's Baby*

Log Exercise

1. Based on your current understanding of Jane's situation, write a statement of the problem you face.

2. Provide a medical description of anencephaly. (Provide your own drawing to clarify your verbal description.) Specifically,

    a. What causes anencephaly?

    b. What is the prognosis for an infant born with anencephaly?

    c. Describe the nature of cranial abnormalities in an anencephalic infant.

    d. What brain functions are missing in an anencephalic infant? What functions are present?

3. Describe the ethical dilemma(s) you and the Bartons face in this situation.

4. Now that you have investigated this problem, what is your advice to the Bartons?

Stepien, William J., Shelagh A. Gallagher, and David Workman, "Problem-Based Learning for Traditional and Interdisciplinary Classroom," *Journal for the Education of the Gifted*, Vol. 16, no. 4 (Summer 1993), pp. 338–357.

tional procedures call for students to deal, simultaneously, with factual data and with ethical and moral values.

The chief disadvantage is the amount of preparation time required. When teachers spend hours preparing materials for lectures, discussions, or contests, they can often use those materials the following year with relatively few changes. However, in problem-based learning, each class of students should be given a new problem. If this is not done, students in a current class might very easily get needed information from students who dealt with the problem earlier and thus short-circuit the learning process. Developing new projects, however, is a time-consuming task. In the long-term, teachers can capitalize on the power of problem-based learning and minimize preparation time by developing a sequence of problems. This enables the teacher to use a different problem each year for four or five years. Another option is to try to arrange for resources as they are needed, but if the project stalls because of a lack of appropriate resources, the teacher will have wasted a lot of student time and enthusiasm. Stepiens has written an informative article concerning ways to engage students by having them take on the roles of scientists, doctors, artists, and historians. It is entitled "Problem-Based Learning: As Authentic as It Gets,"[7] and anyone interested in actually using problem-based learning, as opposed to simply talking about it, is likely to find the article highly useful.

OUT-OF-CLASS ASSIGNMENTS/HOMEWORK

There are at least four purposes served by out-of-class assignments, or homework. These include:

1. *Helping students acquire new information.* When teachers assign a section of a book to be read as a basis for a future discussion, or ask students to view a particular TV program or video tape, they are asking students to acquire new information. This information can be dealt with during class time, but it is acquired outside of class.
2. *Providing practice in particular skills.* Some skills, such as word processing, solving mathematical problems, and golf swings, can be polished by repeated practice (well, maybe all but the golf swings). It would be a poor use of class time to provide extended periods for such practice, but students can practice out of class.
3. *Giving students practice in long-term planning.* Some assignments, such as term papers and projects requiring correspondence, require a good deal of student planning. The fact that students must plan ahead to achieve the objective is, in itself, a valuable experience. Some teachers see such value in it that they consider it, alone, to be sufficient justification for such assignments.
4. *Providing for student creativity and particular student needs.* In-class activities generally force students to be one of a group and leave little opportunity for them to demonstrate skills unique to them as individuals or to engage in instructional activities they feel are of particular interest to them personally. By working with individuals in planning out-of-class assignments, teachers can do much to make school relevant and interesting.

Despite the strengths of these advantages, there is considerable controversy about out-of-class assignments. Proponents point out that the chief responsibility of students should be to study, and that many valuable educational activities cannot be completed solely within the four walls of a classroom or within usual class meeting times. Opponents argue that many students have neither the time nor the environment in which to do the work. They also point out that once students leave the classroom there is no assurance that they will be the ones actually doing the assignment; that friends, relatives, or parents may do the actual work. They also point out that they can typically count on little, if any, parental support in encouraging students to complete homework.

For whatever reasons, U.S. students typically do very little homework. Consider the information in Table 8.2.

Ironically, there is little doubt that students who complete meaningful out-of-class assignments benefit from them. The following steps will help make such assignments effective.

TABLE 8.2   Time Spent on Homework Each Night*

	Percent of 13-year-olds	Percent of 17-year-olds
No homework assigned	18	20
Did not do assignment	4	15
Spent less than 1 hour	38	28
Spent 1–2 hours	30	27
Spent more than 2 hours	10	10

*U.S. Department of Education, National Center for Education Statistics, National Assessment of Educational Progress, *The Reading Report Card, 1971–88,* by Educational Testing Service, in Mattson, Mark T., *Factbook on Elementary, Middle, and Secondary Schools, 1993,* (New York: Scholastic, 1993), 9.5.20.

Make sure that students understand exactly what they are to do and how the assignment will be graded. To minimize misunderstandings, it is a good idea to give all assignments in writing. For frequently assigned work such as reading assignments or answering specific questions, assignments can be written on the chalkboard, preferably in an area of the board reserved for this purpose. Students quickly learn to check the board for new assignments, and they can copy them down at any time during the period. If the assignment is unique or not clear-cut, it is better to provide each student with a handout that details the assignment and the grading criteria. Students should know what qualities are associated with each grade, D through A. Further clarification should be provided by soliciting and answering questions about the assignment.

If the assignment is long-term in nature, a due date should be established, with point penalties detailed for work turned in after that date. Students should be encouraged to bring in drafts of partially completed work for periodic appraisal. If the assignment is individualized, the teacher should make sure there is agreement on exactly what is to be done, by when, and what the final product is to be. The teacher can facilitate student accomplishment of out-of-class assignments by making sure that required instructional materials are available. Needed books, magazines, video tapes, and other materials should be placed on reserve in the library.

All assignments should be carefully evaluated and promptly returned to students with notations concerning strengths and weaknesses. All teachers, regardless of subject area, are responsible for helping students improve their writing. Therefore, all teachers should point out errors in spelling, punctuation, and grammar in all student work. The careful grading and prompt return of assignments will assure students that their work is important and is being used to help them succeed. Further, the prompt grading of assignments helps the teacher detect students' problems and evaluate the effectiveness of instruction. While it may not be practical to return students' work the day after it is received, it should be returned before students are again asked to make use of the skills and knowledge they practiced. They need the benefit of your feedback to avoid making mistakes a second time. To make it more likely that assignments of three or more pages can be returned promptly, it is useful to schedule due dates at the end of the week. This gives the teacher the weekend to grade the papers.

Some teachers, fearing that students will not complete homework assignments at home, allocate class time to work on assignments. While it might be reasonable to have students start assignments during class time, particularly if the assignment involves procedures or concepts that might be difficult for students to understand, it also has a major drawback. If teachers complain, on one hand, that there is never enough instructional time to accomplish what needs to be accomplished, it is difficult to justify using very much, if any, of that time having students do things that they should be doing at home. A reasonable rule of thumb is that homework should be done at home.

INDIVIDUALIZATION

It is likely that even Og, the caveman, realized that individual differences exist, and Plato described how societies could become virtually utopian if they recognized and accommodated individual differences. Schools, however, have always had difficulty implementing the idea. The **Winnetka Plan** was put into practice in 1919 by Carelton Washburne (1890–1968), Superintendent of Schools in Winnetka, Illinois. In the Winnetka Plan, teachers agreed on a set of objectives and then developed self-instructional materials that enabled each student to progress at his or her own rate. Students self-tested themselves prior to being tested by the teacher and moving on to new objectives.[8] In the same year, a similar plan, the **Dalton Plan,** was put into practice by Helen Parkhurst (1887–1973), at an ungraded school for crippled children in Dalton, Massachusetts. It was adopted by a high school in Dalton in 1920.[9]

Neither the Winnetka nor the Dalton plan gained wide acceptance, largely because students were willing to accept the freedom made possible by the individualization and self-pacing, but they were unwilling to accept the responsibility that had to go along with it. Unwilling may be a bit too harsh. It must be remembered that schools have been, and continue to be, highly structured places. Students are not typically given a great many choices and virtually none with respect to when to do certain tasks. Having become accustomed to supervision and guidance by teachers, and the need to meet deadlines, it is not surprising that students put off and/or failed to complete work when freed of the supervision, guidance, and deadlines.

In 1971, educators at Illinois State University experimented with a large-scale, self-paced, competency-based teacher education program called the **Professional Sequence.** As did the Winnetka and Dalton plans, the Professional Sequence seemed like a good idea. Students would complete a series of required and optional self-instructional packages and would demonstrate competencies via written tests, lesson plans, and actual teaching in microteaching and high school classroom settings. Although the ISU educators were familiar with the self-discipline problem inherent in the Winnetka and Dalton plans, they believed that it would not be a problem at the university level. The juniors and seniors in their program would be motivated not only by the prospect of graduation, but by the prospect of teacher certification. They were wrong. Aside from older and married students, an unacceptably large percentage of the students failed to complete the program in a timely manner. It was stopped in 1980 and the program returned to the more traditional format of scheduled classes.

Individualization, like peace on Earth and good will toward men (and women), is an excellent idea, but it seems impractical in the context of mass education and limited time. Nonetheless, there are ways to implement the idea in a limited way.

Self-Instructional Packages

Self-instructional packages are a form of out-of-class assignments that enable teachers to maximize the individualization of instruction. Self-instructional packages are built around specific instructional objectives and include a carefully sequenced set of learning activities that students can complete at their own rates. Such packages are ideal for enrichment activities and for Individualized Educational Plans. They typically include the following parts:

1. A brief rationale that explains how the information and/or skills to be learned can be used by the student.
2. One or more precise instructional objectives.
3. A preassessment instrument to help the student identify areas of strength and weakness.
4. Either all the information the student needs to achieve the objective, or references to specific sources of information.
5. Practice exercises.
6. Specific grading criteria if the objective calls for a paper or similar product, or directions of when and where to take a test if the objective is to be evaluated in that way.

Assuming that effective self-instructional packages are constructed, teachers need to use them with care. In particular, the teacher needs to talk with the prospective user and get his or her agreement to do the work by a certain time. This face-to-face discussion, and the student's willing commitment do to the work, should set the stage for a successful learning experience and for helping the student move toward independence.

Contracts/Portfolios

Another way to individualize instruction to the maximum extent is to use contracts. To do this, the teacher and the student agree on a particular task to be done, a specific timetable, and specific D through A grading criteria. To help ensure that the student makes timely progress, the timetable should include periodic progress checks.

One major advantage to contracts is that students can play the major role in selecting the project, establishing the timetable, and developing the grading scale. They can take a major role in planning their own learning and in making it relevant to their own lives. The major disadvantage is that students, typically, have had very little practice in planning their own learning. Teachers have always selected the topics to be studied and spelled out learning activities. When they are given the opportunity to do these things with little teacher direction, students are lost. They often do not know how or where to begin, and some will be so forthright as to say, "Please, just tell me what to do and I'll do it." Helping students learn to assume increasing control over their own learning and lives should be one of the overall objectives of all teachers, but it does take time and patience.

One increasingly common use for contracts is in the development of student portfolios—compilations of products representing the student's best efforts academically and creatively. Since students play a major role in establishing the terms of learning contracts, they frequently have a greater commitment to perfecting the product. These products, then, can reflect best efforts.

The down-side of contracts and portfolios is that, because they are highly individualized, the more they are used, the more difficult it becomes to maintain a coherent curriculum with recognizable breadth and depth. Everything has a cost.

SUMMARY

Small-group activities usually increase student involvement and interaction. Since the results of small-group work are shared with the entire class, all students benefit from the in-depth work of separate groups.

Students can be assigned to small groups heterogeneously, to maximize the interaction among students with differing abilities or interests, or homogeneously, to capitalize on common ability levels or interests. In either case, groups of about four students tends to maximize productivity.

Panel discussions and debates are particularly useful for enabling the class as a whole to benefit from the in-depth work of groups of students. Regardless of how students are assigned to panels or teams, procedures for dealing with students who may not do their share of the work should be discussed. Ultimately, it is the teacher's responsibility to evaluate and grade each student.

Role playing can be an effective technique in helping students increase their awareness of the attitudes and feelings of others. A potential problem in role playing is that students may act out their own feelings or attitudes or that other students may believe that this is happening. If this happens, long-lasting ill feelings may be generated.

Four cooperative learning strategies were investigated and developed by Robert Slavin. Common to all four are the concepts of team rewards, individual accountability, and equal opportunities for success. Two of the strategies, Student Teams—Achievement Divisions (STAD), and Teams-Games-Tournament (TGT), are particularly useful in grades 6–12.

Problem-based learning is an excellent way to introduce students to the complexities of "real-life" problems. Teachers prepare extensively by identifying an ill-structured problem, exploring the kinds of issues that students are likely to encounter, making sure that appropriate human and other resources are available, and developing enroute tasks to be accomplished by certain times. Students then follow the "scientific method" in attempting to solve the problem. Problem-solving learning almost always cuts across subject-area lines and, if done properly, requires students to balance factual information with ethical and moral values.

Out-of-class assignments can help students learn. Assignments should be written on the board or given in the form of a hand-out. It is crucial that students understand exactly what they are to do and exactly how the assignment will be graded. Homework should be returned to students before they are called on to use the skills or knowledge a second time, and feedback concerning content and mechanics should be provided for all assignments.

Self-instructional packages and contracts enable teachers to maximize the individualization of instruction. Self-instructional packages are typically prepared by the teacher and given to students for purposes of enrichment or as part of Individualized Educational Plans. Experiences, such as those with the Winnetka and Dalton plans, demonstrate that students often lack the self-discipline to use self-instructional material without close supervision.

Contracts are agreements between a teacher and students concerning exactly what is to be done, by when, and exactly how the product will be evaluated. Since the student plays the major role in planning and carrying out a contract, the result often reflects that student's best efforts. For this reason, the products of contracts are often included in portfolios of the student's work.

SO HOW DOES THIS AFFECT MY TEACHING?

It is likely that one of the reasons you chose teaching as a career is that you believe you can help students learn, and you will, in fact, be able to do that. After you agonize over just what it is that you want students to learn and, more important, what you want them to be able to do, you need to help them become competent. Whole-group activities will help them acquire a common and strong knowledge-base, but it, like so many other aspects of modern life, will emphasize competition. Students also need to learn how to work cooperatively.

Small-group activities give students the chance to work cooperatively with others and to understand the actions and points of view of people whose abilities and values may differ from their own. These abilities are essential, if our society is to function smoothly, and perhaps some of our current problems reflect the fact that such abilities have traditionally been considered secondary to academic achievement in our schools. Academic achievement is important, crucially so, but its attainment does not have to exclude helping students learn to understand and work with others. You can, and should, foster this second goal by using small-group activities.

KEY TERMS, PEOPLE, AND IDEAS

Small-Group Activities
> Heterogeneous
> Homogeneous

Cooperative Learning, Robert Slavin
> Student Teams—Achievement Divisions (STAD)
> Teams-Games-Tournaments (TGT)
> Problem-Based Learning

Ill-structured Problems
> Scientific Method, Sir Francis Bacon
> Panel Discussions/Debates
> Role-Playing

Out-of-Class Assignments/Homework
> Winnetka Plan, Dalton Plan

Self-Instructional Packages
> Contracts/Portfolios

ENDNOTES

1. Slavin, Robert E., *Cooperative Learning: Theory, Research, and Practice* (Englewood Cliffs, N.J.: Prentice-Hall, 1990), p. 3.

2. Slavin, pp. 3–4,

3. Slavin, p. 4.

4. Slavin, p. 4.

5. Hellemans, Alexander, and Bryan Bunch, *The Timetables of Science* (New York: Simon and Schuster. 1988), p. 130.

6. Stepien, William J., Shelagh A. Gallagher, and David Workman "Problem-Based Learning for Traditional and Interdisciplinary Classroom," *Journal for the Education of the Gifted*, Vol. 16, no. 4 (Summer 1993), pp. 338–357.

7. Stepien, William, and Shelagh Gallagher, "Problem-Based Learning: As Authentic as It Gets," *Educational Leadership*, Vol. 50, no. 7 (April 1993), pp. 25–28.

8. Washburne, Carleton W., and Sidney P. Marland, *Winnetka: The History and Significance of an Educational Experiment* (Englewood Cliffs: N.J.: Prentice-Hall, 1963).

9. Parkhurst, Helen H., *Education on the Dalton Plan* (London: G. Bell and Sons, 1922).

9

SELECTING AND USING INSTRUCTIONAL MEDIA

RATIONALE

For many educators, it is somehow unsettling to realize that in a technologically advanced country such as ours, instruction is carried out much as it was 2,400 years ago in the days of Socrates, Plato, and Aristotle. While there is nothing wrong with telling, asking, and discussing, there are other tools that teachers can use to supplement and, in some cases, to replace these basic instructional activities. Some of the tools, such as computer simulations and interactive CDs, make it possible to give students experiences that were impossible or impractical just a few years ago.

There is an ancient proverb that says, "A picture is worth a thousand words." One wonders what the "exchange rate" would be for a time-lapse motion picture that enables students to watch a rosebud as it unfolds into full bloom or a film that gives students an idea of the drama and mindless passions aroused by one of Hitler's torchlight parades. How does one calculate an "exchange rate" when a student experiences an accident in an auto simulator rather than in a real car? Without the use of mediated instruction, many valuable and interesting learning experiences would be either impossible or impractical, and the students' education would be that much poorer.

Since virtually all teachers find themselves using mediated instruction at one time or another, this chapter is devoted to describing the utilization steps, strengths, and weaknesses of various kinds of mediated instruction. The more tools you can use to enhance and enrich learning experiences, the more successful your students are likely to be, and the more successful they are, the more successful you will be.

SAMPLE OBJECTIVES

You will be able, in writing, to:

1. Define and exemplify terms such as technology, hardware, software, IBM compatible, word processors, spreadsheet, and database. (Knowledge).
2. Describe six steps that lead to effective utilization of instructional media. (Comprehension).
3. After writing a precise instructional objective, describe two sequences of instructional activities, including the use of mediated instruction, that could help students achieve the objective, and explain one advantage of each sequence. (Synthesis).
4. Describe and exemplify three factors that hinder the expansion of CAI. (Comprehension).

DEFINITION OF TECHNOLOGY

When people talk about technology in education, they generally have in mind devices such as overhead projectors, document cameras, video cassette recorders, and computers. The term, however, stems from the Greek *tekhne,* which meant a blending of science and art. The dictionary definition of "technology" is: "a. The application of science, especially to industrial and commercial objectives. b. The entire body of methods and materials used to achieve such objectives."[1] Behaviorists were the first to demonstrate that their approach was scientifically based. Their work with stimulus–response learning provided strong evidence that the idea of dividing complex tasks into smaller, less complex tasks, and using an appropriate reward structure, was an effective learning strategy. Cognitive strategists operate on more theoretical ground in trying to relate learning to cognitive processes that are still not well understood.

To the extent that teachers communicate expected learning outcomes in terms that are observable and measurable, they are following behaviorist principles. They have determined what the student should be able to do at the end of the course and their plans reflect their best thinking about how to divide the complex behaviors expected, so that students can master them efficiently. To this extent, teachers use a technological approach, whether they do or do not use technological devices. With this beginning point, we can turn our attention to the selection and use of a variety of teaching aids.

GENERAL UTILIZATION FACTORS

Mediated instruction, by definition, includes any instruction that makes use of some device (mechanical or otherwise) to facilitate learning. Although there is tremendous variety in the forms of mediated instruction available, some utilization procedures apply to all forms. Among these are the following.

Select mediated instruction for specific instructional objectives. To be most effective, mediated instruction should be an integral part of the instructional procedures. Its use should not be an afterthought. Further, in many schools it is necessary to reserve equipment well in advance. Planning on your part is crucial. If mediated instruction is used on the spur of the moment, without relationship to specific objectives, students will realize that it is being used as a time-filler or diversion. The clear message the teacher will be sending is, "I did not have anything else planned, so let's do this."

Become familiar with the material or device prior to using it with students. Depending on the form of mediated instruction being considered, the teacher should read it, view it, handle it, and otherwise use it prior to exposing students to it. This will not only provide assurance that the instructional aid is exactly what was expected, but it will also enable the teacher to estimate how much time to allow for correct use, pinpoint specific strengths and weaknesses, and thus better prepare students. When mechanical devices are involved, the teacher will become more proficient in the operation of the device and thus avoid the distraction (and embarrassment) that accompanies the misuse of equipment.

Prepare the students. If students are to derive the full benefit of mediated instruction, if they are to know what to look for, they should be given some idea of its general content or purpose beforehand. Usually a brief description is sufficient to orient students, but it may be useful to provide guide questions for students to answer. This helps to further focus student attention on important points.

Use the mediated instruction correctly. There is little value in attempting to use mediated instruction if there is insufficient time for its proper use or if other conditions are not appropriate. Common sense will provide good guidance in the use of most mediated instruction. For example, if a device has a volume control, remember that it controls only the machine's volume, not the students'. If students are noisy, raising the volume on the device will not necessarily cause them to quiet down. In fact, it may have just the opposite effect. They may talk louder, so they can hear each other more easily.

For visual aids, lighting may be a problem. In most classrooms, there is sufficient light for most activities, but in some rooms it may be difficult or impossible to darken the room enough to effectively use devices such as film projectors and opaque projectors. In others, glare from windows may be a problem. It is a good idea to see if lighting will be a problem before reserving the equipment.

Conduct follow-up activities. Follow-up activities provide an opportunity to clarify confusing points, answer questions, discuss interesting points, and integrate the new information with previous learning. Follow-up activities also allow the teacher to point out subtle points that may have been missed, to correct misconceptions, and tie up loose ends.

Evaluate the mediated instruction. After using any form of mediated instruction, it is helpful to write a short evaluation of how effectively it helped students achieve the specified objectives. As these evaluations accumulate, they can be used to help select the most appropriate and effective form of mediated instruction for each type of objective.

READING MATERIALS

Textbooks

In 1454, **Johann Gutenberg** (c. 1398–1468) used movable metal type to print the *Bible of 42 lines,* so called because each of the 1,282 pages had 42 lines.[2] In 1658, **Johann Comenius** (1592–1670) published *Orbus pictus* (The World in Pictures). It was the world's first illustrated textbook specifically written for children. Since that time, educators have made increasing use of books as instructional aids. Today, books are the most common instructional aid available and they can also be one of the most powerful. Textbooks have a number of sometimes forgotten advantages. For example, they can provide students with a common body of information arranged in a logical order. This facilitates discussions and can help students see cause–effect relationships. Most high school texts also include chapter summaries, questions to be answered, and associated learning activities that provide guides for studying the information. Considering that most textbooks can be used repeatedly and that most contain pictures, charts, graphs, and/or maps, they are relatively inexpensive. Finally, textbooks can be adapted to individual needs and interests and to self-pacing.

As with any instructional tool, textbooks can be misused, and most of the disadvantages associated with them stem from such misuses. Perhaps the greatest misuse is to allow them to dictate what is taught. To be marketable, textbooks must contain accurate, up-to-date information deemed important to educators nationwide. However, this does not mean that the information is, by itself, automatically relevant to your students or to your objectives. Further, unless there is a school rule to the contrary, it is not necessary to cover the entire book or to devote equal time to each chapter or unit. The course objectives, written with consideration of the needs and abilities of your students, should dictate the direction and pace of instruction. A textbook is a foundation, a beginning point. Teachers should build on the content of the textbook to help make the content relevant to students.

A good first step in using a textbook is to review it. Although you will know most, if not all, of the material, the author's approach may be unique.

After reviewing the book, you will be able to make students aware of the author's perspective and of new information developed since the book was published. There might also be unintentional biases that should be discussed.

The next steps are to explain to students why that particular text is being used and to give them an overview of it. Taking time to do these things, like taking time to go over the course syllabus, lets students know that you recognize that they are real live people who appreciate knowing "the big picture." Most students can also benefit from a short review on using a textbook. A survey of the table of contents, with comments concerning what will be emphasized; a discussion of the author's perspective; an explanation of how the index is organized; and a survey of a representative chapter will help make students aware that you are trying to help them be successful.

When surveying the representative chapter, point out that it is helpful to convert the chapter title and headings into questions and then to read to find the answers. It is also helpful, before reading the chapter, to look at the chapter summary and the questions at the end of the chapter. Paying attention to words in boldface and italics, to captions, and to pictures, maps, and charts, often makes it easier to understand major points. Having students write answers to questions posed by the teacher or the author is another way to focus student attention on important points in each chapter.

AUDIO AIDS

Radios, Record, Tape, and CD Players

Radios, record, audio tape, and compact disk (CD) players all utilize a single sensory input, sound. With the advent of films, television, and videotapes, purely auditory devices are being used less frequently, but they still have their place. Radios, for example, because they are less expensive and cumbersome than televisions, are a convenient means for getting up-to-the-minute news reports for class analysis. Records, audio tape, and CD players make it possible to conveniently listen to plays, operas, concerts, and speeches, while tape recorders make it possible to record broadcast material, guest speakers (with their permission), class debates, and other activities for later use and analysis. These forms of mediated instruction are also used extensively as audio models for students. Audio tape recorders provide an added dimension by enabling students to record, and then listen to, their own voices for diagnostic or developmental purposes.

One problem with the use of audio-only aids is that they lack a visual attention point. Students, used to watching a teacher, a TV, or computer monitor screen, may literally not know what to look at while listening to an audio-only aid. Unless part of the reason for using such an aid is to help students learn to listen, it may be helpful to provide visual focal points, such as pictures or maps, that relate to what the students are listening to.

Research in the area of listening is enlightening. For example, one study (Brown, 1969) revealed that approximately 45 percent of the average adult's working day is spent listening and that this figure rises to 60 percent for elementary school students and to 90 percent for high school and college students. Unfortunately, the same study showed that even if students are concentrating on what they hear, they retain only about 50 percent and within two months will be able to recall less than half of that.[3] In a more recent study (Strother, 1987), it was estimated that about 45 percent of all classroom communication time is spent listening.[4] With so much time spent listening, students might well profit from instruction and practice in effective listening. Radios, record, audio tape, and CD players can provide that practice.*

Telephones

Telephones represent yet another purely auditory form of mediated instruction. Although the telephone was invented in 1876, and the radio in 1895, the telephone's nineteen-year advantage has not been reflected in its greater use by educators. This is unfortunate, because the telephone companies have much to offer and they are generally quite willing to work with educators.

One use of telephones is **teleconferencing.** Many phones have a conference mode that makes two-way communication possible between a whole class and a speaker at some distant point. Teleconferencing is more convenient than asking a speaker to come to a class, but has many of the advantages of actually having the speaker there. All students can listen at the same time, ask questions, and receive answers.

Although student preparation is important with all forms of mediated instruction, it is particularly important with teleconferencing, because phone charges are calculated according to the time the telephone line is in use. Adequate preparation includes letting the speaker know, in advance, the objective of the teleconference and some of the key information students are seeking. Preparation of the students would include formulating specific questions to ask the speaker.

In 1971, the American Telephone & Telegraph Company developed a device called a **Variable Speech Control** (VSC). The purpose of the VSC is to change the rate at which speech can be understood by omitting pauses and

---

*Some sources of audio aids are Educational Corp. of America/Rand McNally, P.O. Box 7600, Chicago, IL 60680; and National Public Radio, 2025 M Street, N.W., Washington, D.C. 20036.

shortening vowel sounds. The practical applications of the device include enabling blind people to listen to, and comprehend, spoken words nearly as quickly as sighted people can read and comprehend written words, and enabling teachers and students to make greater use of taped materials by allowing them to listen to recorded tapes in shorter periods of time. "Research has shown that learning time can be cut (as much as 50 percent and an average of 32 percent) and comprehension increased (as much as 9.3 percent and an average of 4.2 percent) by using compressed and variable-speed audio tapes."[5]

VISUAL AIDS

Still and Motion Pictures

Still pictures, whether in the form of paintings, magazine clippings, photographs, slides, or filmstrips, have unique properties that make them extremely valuable as instructional aids. Among these properties are their abilities to (1) convey abstractions powerfully without depending on verbal descriptions, (2) focus attention on a characteristic situation or on a particular step in a process, and (3) allow students to study an image at length, to refer back to it conveniently, and to make side-by-side comparisons.

Pictures, from sources such as magazines, travel bureaus, and commercial concerns, are one of the easiest to acquire and least expensive forms of mediated instruction. The instructional value of pictures will be increased if they are selected for use in particular instructional units. Complex or "busy" pictures may cause some students to miss important points. Pictures in color usually attract and hold attention better than those in black-and-white, and all pictures must be large enough to be seen easily. Ensuring that the picture does not present a biased view (unless such a view is intended) is important.

Different photography techniques can provide unique pictures in either still or motion form. Chief among these techniques are **time-lapse** (showing events in condensed time), **micro** (pictures taken through a microscope), **long-range** (magnifying distant objects), **X-ray** (looking below the object's surface to show internal structures), **infrared** (showing heat patterns), and **slow-motion** (slowing events down). Students may watch as a flower unfolds into full bloom or as a single cell divides. They can see the Earth as astronauts see it or gain an understanding of the phenomenon of nuclear fission. **Animation** is a technique in which a sequence of still pictures, when seen in quick succession (typically 24 frames per second), gives the impression of movement because each picture is drawn so that it differs from the one before it by only a small incremental change.

If a picture seems particularly useful, you may want to save it for repeated use. In such cases, it is a good idea to protect the picture by mounting it on poster board and laminating it. Two sources of pictures are Encyl-clopedia Brittanica and Educational Insights.*

Opaque Projectors

Sometimes a picture is of particular benefit, but is too small to be seen by the entire class at one time. In such instances, an opaque projector may be useful. The "opaque" will project and enlarge any flat picture, whether it is a single sheet or a page bound in a book. Further, most opaque projectors have a built-in light arrow that can be used to draw students' attention to particular points on the projected image. Some teachers use the "opaque" to project images on chalkboards, so they can be traced.

Opaque projectors use a large and powerful bulb as a light source. This bulb generates so much heat that "opaques" have a built-in, heat-absorbing glass plate between the bulb and the projection stage. In spite of this, thin materials sometimes curl or scorch. Proper use includes checking to see that the heat-absorbing glass plate is in place and frequently checking the material being projected.

Another problem associated with opaque projectors is that unless the room is dark, students may not be able to see the projection. If the room is dark enough to see the projection, students will be unable to take notes and, in some cases, supervision may become a problem. For these reasons, opaque projectors are best used for very limited lengths of time.

Slides and Filmstrips

Slides and filmstrips have all the advantages of pictures and the added advantage of increased realism. Because slides are actual photographs and are shown via a bright light source, colors appear more brilliant and scenes appear more real than in printed pictures. In addition, it is much easier to store a set of slides than a set of large, mounted pictures.

A more significant advantage associated with slides is the opportunity they provide for teachers to create their own instructional aids. Many teachers make it a point to take along a camera and slide film (rather than print film) when vacationing or traveling. As a consequence, these teachers are able to build up an impressive set of slides that are useful in stimulating and maintaining student interest. Many teachers have also initiated class projects wherein students organize a slide program complete with an accompanying tape recording. Such projects have the dual advantages of being useful, interesting learning activities, and increasing the teacher's store of instructional aids.

*Encyclopedia Brittanica Educational Corp., 310 S. Michigan Ave., Chicago, IL 60604; and Educational Insights, 19560 Rancho Way, Domingues Hill, CA 90220.

A filmstrip is essentially a series of connected slides. Most filmstrips are prepared commercially and many have brief captions printed on each frame. Some filmstrip projectors are sprocketless, thus prolonging filmstrip life. Typically, as the filmstrip is advanced, the caption is read by the teacher or by students and the frame is discussed. Some filmstrips have recorded captions that are played back via a tape recorder. Sources of slides and filmstrips are Educational Images and Audio Visual Narrative Arts, Inc.*

Bulletin Boards

Bulletin boards are ideally suited for the display of visual materials such as pictures, cartoons, postcards, newspaper clippings, outstanding papers, and student-made **collages** (an artistic composition of objects pasted over a surface) and **montages** (a pictorial composition made from many pictures or designs closely arranged or superimposed on each other). Bulletin boards promote learning best when they concern a single idea or topic. They should be neat and uncluttered, make use of bright colors and attention-getting materials such as colored yarn and plastics, and they should be pictorially, rather than verbally, oriented. The instructional value of bulletin boards is usually increased if viewer participation is encouraged. Ways to do this include manipulative devices and questions with answers covered by flaps.

A bulletin board's instructional value lasts a relatively short time, in some cases not more than a few days. Having gone to the trouble of constructing an exceptional bulletin board, there is no reason to take it down as long as students continue to find it useful. However, once students stop paying attention to the display or the class moves on to some other topic, the bulletin board should be replaced.

Teachers can, and should, encourage groups of students to put up new bulletin boards throughout the year. This helps increase student interest in the associated units and is likely to result in increased learning as students do the research and creative work needed to produce an attractive and interesting display. The teacher can provide advice and assistance in the form of suggesting sources for, and providing, actual materials.

Maps and Globes, Charts and Graphs

Maps, globes, charts, and graphs are grouped together because these forms of mediated instruction are heavily emphasized in the new national standards in mathematics, history, and geography. Students may have had little

*Educational Images, P.O. Box 367, Lyons Falls, NY 13368; and Audio Visual Narrative Arts, Inc., Box 9, Pleasantville, NY 10570.

practice in interpreting maps, globes, charts, and graphs, so specific instruction in these skills may be needed.

Maps and globes are used to show portions of the Earth's surface in a less than life-sized scale. Cartographers construct maps and globes to emphasize political, geographic, and climatic divisions, and have developed different map projections. It is helpful to draw students' attention to the particular projection being used and to discuss the way it distorts the real size and shape of particular geographic features. Without an understanding of projection, students may have misconceptions about maps.

Students' attention should be drawn to the legend of the map or globe. It is here that the cartographer explains the meanings of the symbols used, gives the scale to which features are drawn, and provides additional information such as the meanings of particular colors.

The teacher should study maps and globes before using them. In today's world, political boundaries and the names of cities and countries change more often than one might suspect, so it is common for maps and globes to be out of date. When this happens, students' attention should be drawn to the inaccuracy and correct information provided.

Charts differ from graphs and diagrams in that they may include a wider variety of pictorial forms. The most common kinds of charts are flow charts (showing sequential steps), process charts (showing some process from start to finish), and time charts (showing developments over a period of time). The instructional value of charts is maximized when time is taken to be sure that students can read and interpret the data.

Graphs and diagrams generally have only simple lines or bars. Graphs are used primarily to condense and convey numerical data into visual, iconic, form. The most common kinds of graphs are circle and pie graphs (used to show the relationship of parts to the whole), bar graphs (used to show comparative data such as the changes in unemployment from year to year), and line graphs (used to plot profiles of patterns).

Although students should be given special instruction in the use of maps, globes, charts, and graphs, teachers should use the least complicated aid that will serve the immediate purpose. Trying to select an aid that can be used in a variety of lessons will be a false economy if students have difficulty interpreting the aid or are confused by it. Sources for maps, charts, and graphs include the National Geographic Society and United Scientific Company.*

Chalkboards

Chalkboards are available in almost every classroom and most teachers use them frequently to display instructions, diagrams, examples, and other infor-

*National Geographic Society, Educational Services, Washington, D.C. 20090-8019; and United Scientific Co., 70 Lincoln St., Boston, MA 02111.

mation that is subject to frequent change. Board work also gives students the chance to demonstrate their abilities and allows active student participation.

There are a number of ways the teacher can use chalkboards to make them more valuable to students. Printing is often easier for students to read than cursive writing and characters at least two inches high can be read easily from a distance of about 30 feet (the length of an average classroom). It is difficult for students to understand teachers who face the board and talk at the same time, so when you write on the board, stop talking. As a point of information, having your back to students for more than a minute or two is unwise. If an accident occurs while you are writing on the board for an extended time, it might be argued that you are partly to blame since you failed to provide adequate supervision.

The use of templates to facilitate the drawing of frequently used shapes saves time and results in greater consistency. An inexpensive template can be made by simply tracing a design and punching holes along the traced lines. Tapping a dusty chalk eraser along the template while it is held to the board will create a dotted outline. Pictures can also be traced on the board from projected images.

When using the chalkboard, avoid cluttering. Once an item on the board has served its purpose, it should be erased so students will not be distracted by it. It is a good idea, however, to reserve one area of the board for announcements and homework and to leave that information on the board throughout the period. Some teachers also leave the objective(s) for the lesson on the board. Certain types of colored chalk (those containing oil) are intended for use on paper, not on chalkboards. If that kind of chalk is used on a chalkboard, it may stain the board permanently.

Overhead Projectors

Of the types of projectors available to teachers, overhead projectors are the most commonly used. Overhead projectors project images drawn, written, or printed on transparent film (usually acetate). They are often used instead of the chalkboard because they allow a teacher to write so that everyone can see and, at the same time, continue monitoring what is going on in the room and maintain eye contact with students. Another advantage is that the overhead projector can be used without darkening the room. This facilitates notetaking and student interaction.

Using an overhead projector requires only a sheet of clear plastic to protect the glass projection plate from stains, and grease pencil, china marker, crayon, or special felt-tipped pen. Grease pencils, crayons, and china markers contain a wax-based material that blocks light. What is drawn or written with them will show as black regardless of their color. Color makes projections more eye-catching and interesting and can be easily achieved using special felt-tipped pens filled with a water-based, non-beading, transparent ink. The ink can be removed with a damp paper towel or by holding the sheet under running water.

Some overheads come equipped with a roll of acetate. The teacher writes on the acetate and then simply rolls up the used surface to expose an unused portion. This temporarily eliminates the need to erase. Teachers can simply write or draw on blank transparencies, but preparing transparencies before-hand results in more professional looking projections that are easier for stu-dents to read. Further, such transparencies subtly communicate to students the fact that you took the time to prepare appropriate materials.

Transparencies are easy to make. Use a word processor or presentation pro-gram, such as Microsoft's *PowerPoint*™, for the creative work. Then, instead of using a laser printer to print the work on paper, print it on a blank trans-parency specifically designed for that purpose. This same special transparency can be used in a copier so a written, typed, or traced page, or a page from a book or magazine, can also be made into a transparency. A word of caution. If an ordinary transparency is run through a laser printer or copier it is likely to melt and ruin the equipment (along with your whole day). Use only trans-parency material specifically designed for use in laser printers and copiers.

Readability is important.

Characters about this size project clearly.

Crowding, either horizontally or vertically, makes the transparency hard to read. Allow more than the usual amount of space between lines and between words in large type, and print no more than twenty lines on a transparency.

Overlays are sheets of acetate laid over a base transparency. A typical overlay sequence might consist of a base transparency showing an outline map of the United States. Over this, the teacher might place a transparency showing major river systems. A third overlay might depict major cities so students could see their proximity to rivers, and a fourth transparency might be used to show railroad development.

It is often possible to acquire commercially prepared transparencies and overlays made by experts who have a wealth of materials with which to work. Such transparencies are usually more polished than teacher-made materials, but they cost more.*

Most overhead projectors have a thermostatically controlled switch that permits the fan to continue operating until the interior of the projector is cool. If the machine does not stop when turned off, do not pull the plug. It will stop automatically when it has cooled down.

---

*Transparencies may be obtained from Denoyer-Geppert Science Co., 5225 Ravens-wood Ave., Chicago, IL 60640; Hammond Inc., 515 Valley St., Maplewood, NJ 07040; Rand McNally, P.O. Box 7600, Chicago IL 60680; and United Transparencies, 435 Main St., Johnson City, NY 13790.

Document Cameras

Document cameras combine the best features of opaque and overhead projectors. As do opaque projectors, document cameras project the image of any document, transparent or not, in its original color(s). The advantage of the document camera is that the room does not have to be darkened.

Real Things

Real things, such as specimens, can be used to help students learn. Depending on what is being taught, teachers and students may display models, mock-ups, pets, coin collections, insects, or dozens of other objects. The list is as limitless and as varied as there are real things in the world that may be displayed without danger or great expense. Modified representations of real things, such as cut-away or "exploded" models, are also helpful. In the latter, the whole is broken into segments and each segment is held apart from the others, while the pieces maintain the same relative positions as in the unexploded model. Other good teaching tools are models that students can assemble and disassemble, and **dioramas** (three-dimensional scenes that students construct).

AUDIO-VISUAL COMBINATIONS

Multimedia Kits

As more educators adopt the systems approach to education, more are finding multimedia kits helpful. Multimedia kits are compilations of instructional materials that include a variety of mediated instruction forms. These materials are designed to help students achieve specific instructional objectives by exposing them to different types of closely integrated educational experiences.

A typical multimedia kit may contain booklets, filmstrips, audio tapes, and artifacts. All the components are selected with a single purpose in mind—to generate and maintain students' interest in a particular topic or subject while, at the same time, providing them with as much pertinent information as possible.

Multimedia kits can be used well with groups, but they can also be useful as self-instructional aids that students use at their own convenience and at their own rates. As with most other forms of mediated instruction, multimedia kits may be prepared by teachers themselves or purchased ready made.*

*Sources of multimedia kits include Agency for Instructional Technology, Box A, Bloomington, IN 47402-1020; IBM Corp., Multimedia & Educational Division, 4111 Northside Parkway, Atlanta, GA 30327; and The Discovery Channel, Interactive Multimedia Division, 7700 Wisconsin Road, Suite 900, Bethesda, MD 20814-3522.

Film, Television, and Video Tapes

Films, television, and video tapes provide students with more of a "you are there" feeling than do most other forms of mediated instruction. They also enable students to view demonstrations (both scientific and social), experiments, natural phenomena, and other events that would be too difficult, dangerous, or even impossible to view otherwise (for instance, moon walks and erupting volcanoes).

Proper preparation of students and good planning in the use of films and video tapes can enhance learning. Providing questions to be answered or study guides, and explaining new words, will help. Further, films and tapes can be stopped at crucial points in order to focus students' attention on a particular point, and they do not need to be shown from start to finish. These are tools; it is up to the teacher to use them wisely.

Most schools, universities, and libraries maintain film and/or tape libraries and most media center people and librarians are willing to help familiarize teachers with their holdings and to help in ordering or reserving materials. There are many sources for these materials.*

Television is effective in a variety of ways. The ability to use programs as they are being broadcast depends on whether the class meets when the program is being broadcast. Such programs can be video taped for later viewing, but an agreement following the Copyright Act of 1976 requires that such taped material be used within ten days of taping and again if needed, but must be erased within 45 days.[6]

Educational television, or ETV, programming is often of particular value to teachers. The Public Broadcasting Service (PBS), for example, often carries instructional programming aimed at high school and college audiences. Some PBS programs, such as "Sesame Street," "Masterpiece Theatre," and "Nova," have won awards for their high quality. The Discovery channel and The Learning Channel (TLC) are other sources of programs suitable to a wide variety of subject areas.

One of the newer applications of broadcast television is "**Channel One,**" a creation of **Whittle Communications.** With "Channel One," schools are given the equipment needed to receive the satellite transmissions and record

---

*Ambrose Video Publishing Co., 1290 Ave. of the Americas, New York, NY 10104; American Media Inc., 1454 30th St., Des Moines, IA 50265; Coronet/MTI Film and Video, 108 Wilmot Road, Deerfield, IL 60015; Filmmakers Library, 124 East 40th St., New York, NY 10016; International Historic Films, P.O. Box 29035, Chicago, IL. 60604; National Video Clearinghouse, Inc., 100 Lafayette Drive, Syosset, NY 11791; and PBS Video (Public Broadcast Service), 1320 Braddock Place, Alexandria, VA 22314. Perhaps the single best source of information about films, filmstrips, video tapes, and other forms of audiovisual materials is the National Information Center for Educational Media (NICEM), P.O. Box 40130, Albuquerque, NM 87196.

and play back the program. In exchange, students watch a daily twelve-minute news program that includes two minutes of commercial advertising.[7] "CNN Newsroom" is a program similar to "Channel One."

Another way to use television is for **distance learning.** In this application, students at different sites are able to see and hear each other. Students get the benefit of interacting with other students, speakers, or teachers in distant places without the need to travel. The idea is excellent and it opens up new possibilities for teaching and learning.[8]

Closed-circuit television is still another way to use the medium. In closed-circuit television, only TV sets connected directly to a transmitter, or adapted to receive the 2,500 MHz (megahertz) wavelength reserved for closed-circuit television, can receive the programs. Closed-circuit television is most often used on an "in-house" basis to televise meetings and debates, demonstrations and experiments, and even regular classes. Because it is an in-house operation, students can participate in the actual program development and televising, thus adding yet another dimension to their educational experience.

Video tape recorders and players are replacing film projectors and becoming a major instructional tool. Schools are acquiring VCR equipment, not only for taping and saving lectures, demonstrations, and theatrical presentations, but also for use in everyday teaching situations. They enable teachers and students to see themselves as others see them. Coaches, for instance, have found VCR equipment invaluable for instant feedback of student psychomotor skills, and teachers tape their own lessons in order to analyze their strengths and weaknesses.

CD-WORM, or compact disk-write once read many times, is an emerging technology that enables users to create their own compact disks. Since the disk cannot be erased, its utility is somewhat limited.

PROGRAMMED INSTRUCTION

Programmed instruction is one of the clearest examples of the behaviorist teaching strategy. Teachers have long wished for a way to ensure that students mastered one point before moving on to the next, and in 1925, **Sidney L. Pressey** demonstrated a "teaching machine," which helped ensure that this happened. Pressey's machine was more of a testing machine than a teaching machine. It presented the learner with a question and a choice of four answers. The student answered the question by pressing one of four keys, but the next question was revealed only if the answer was correct. Pressey's device not only kept a record of student's answers, but also could function as a reinforcer by keeping track of points earned.[9]

Programmed instruction did not gain wide attention until 1954, when B.F. Skinner published an article entitled, "The Science of Learning and the

Art of Teaching."[10] In this article, Skinner explained how the principles of operant conditioning were relevant to the teaching–learning process.

In programming material, the author takes information and breaks it into a series of small, carefully sequenced, steps. As students move from step to step, they receive immediate feedback concerning their learning progress. One of the major differences between programmed and traditional texts is that with programmed materials, students are actively participating in the learning process (they must construct or select responses), whereas with traditional texts, students are passive readers. A second difference is that the formation of misconceptions is reduced (or eliminated entirely) because the sequential nature of the program carefully relates each new piece of information to the one immediately preceding it.

There are two basic strategies for all programmed materials, whether they are presented via programmed texts, teaching machines, or computers. **Linear programming** is most closely associated with the work of **B. F. Skinner.**[11] In linear programs, each student goes through an **identical series of small instructional blocks or "frames,"** usually less than six sentences in length. Students' attention is drawn to key information by the **use of cues** such as **bold face** type, *italics*, or underlining, and the student is then presented with a question calling for the key information. The student constructs or selects a response and, in a programmed text, turns a page or uncovers an "answer area" and sees if the answer is correct. If a "teaching machine" is used, the student cannot move on until the right answer is selected. This ensures that the last thing the student sees with respect to that question is the correct answer. Linear programs are designed to ensure a **high success rate.** If designed properly, students should be able to answer at least 90 percent of the questions on the first try.[12]

Nonlinear (branching, or intrinsic) programming is associated most closely with **Norman A. Crowder.**[13] In nonlinear programs, students are presented with **larger blocks of information,** sometimes as long as a page. As in linear programs, each block is followed by a question, but in branching programs there is **no use of cues** to ensure a correct answer. Each of the possible answers is keyed to additional information. The author anticipates wrong responses so, when students select a **wrong answer,** they are referred to pages or parts of the program containing **remedial information.** They are then referred back to the original question or to new information. When students answer correctly, they move on to the next block of new information. Since the path that any one student takes through the program is dependent on his or her answers to individual questions, it is possible for every student to take a different path. While the paths and rates of progress may differ, all students acquire the same basic information.

One characteristic of all programmed materials is that they must, by their very nature, eliminate student creativity. All acceptable responses are programmed and divergent thinking is, in terms of the program, incorrect thinking. There are some who believe that for the basic content that makes up much of our needed knowledge-base, programmed materials will eventually replace traditional kinds of instruction. They believe that it is in the integration and application of knowledge that human teachers are most needed.

COMPUTER-ASSISTED INSTRUCTION (CAI)

The first large-scale computer, the Electronic Numerical Integrator and Computer (**ENIAC**),was put into operation in 1946. Its main function was to help scientists and engineers work on problems related to military needs. The first commercially available computer, the UNIVersal Automatic Computer 1 (**UNIVAC 1**), was introduced in 1951.

Advantages of CAI

Educators were not far behind the scientists, engineers, and businessmen with respect to computer use. Although not designed as such, it soon became clear that the interaction possible with computers could make them powerful instructional tools. In 1963, **Patrick Suppes** implemented large-scale CAI projects in schools in East Palo Alto, California, and in McComb, Mississippi. The Computer Curriculum Corporation (CCC) was formed shortly thereafter to market the materials.[14] These efforts were followed in the early 1970s with large time-sharing projects such as the **PLATO** (Programmed Logic for Automated Teaching Operations) project at the University of Illinois, and the **TICCIT** (Time-Shared Interactive Computer-Controlled Information Television) project at Brigham Young University. The time-sharing in these projects consisted of having the CAI programs in a large mainframe computer with hundreds of computer terminals connected to it via telecommunication lines. Since most of the time in CAI is spent waiting for the student to read and respond to computer output, the mainframes could provide virtually instantaneous feedback to all the students connected to them.

CAI held many promises. For example, students would be able to work at their own rates. Overworked teachers would be able to devote more of their time to helping those students who most needed their help, and students would be more actively engaged in learning since they had the "teacher's" full attention. Further, other forms of mediated instruction, such as books, video tapes, and television, are one-way communicators. Information goes from them to students. Computers are two-way communicators. Information, questions, and other stimuli go from them to students, but then the students provide input that shapes the next output from the computer.

This interaction makes it possible for computers to approximate some of the individualization typically associated with tutoring.

For all its advantages, the delivery of CAI via time-shared systems depended on linking distant terminals, via telecommunication lines, to central computers, and this was costly. In 1977, Tandy/Radio Shack introduced the TRS-80, Model 1; Apple Computer introduced the Apple II; and Commodore, Ltd. introduced the Commodore Personal Electronic Transactor (PET). These were the first fully-assembled, commercially available microcomputers and they solved the problem of telecommunication costs. For all intents and purposes, microcomputers launched the "computer revolution" by making the power of computers available to virtually everyone.

By 1981, about 42.7 percent of all high schools used microcomputers. By 1990, the figure was about 98.8.[15] Hundreds of research studies have been conducted comparing the effectiveness of CAI versus "traditional" instruction. Almost universally, these studies show that while instructional time is typically reduced, there is no significant difference in achievement scores.[16] These studies also show that elementary students are more likely than secondary students to profit from CAI.[17]

Most educators are now well aware of the existence of CAI and many have the opportunity to select software (the actual programs, usually on a disk). They make their choices from among the following categories of programs.

Drill and Practice Programs

As the name implies, drill and practice programs provide drill and practice over skills and knowledge already learned and, due to their purpose, most focus on low-level skills. These programs can help students because: (1) each student is able to progress at his or her own rate, (2) such programs often automatically adjust the complexity of the content to the abilities of the student, (3) students receive immediate feedback concerning the appropriateness of each response, and (4) the interaction is fast so the learner is directly involved with the work (on task) all the time. There is some evidence that students gain the most from the use of drill and practice programs during the first 15 minutes of use. After that, the fast interaction seems to tire students, resulting in diminishing returns.[18]

Tutorial Programs

As the name implies, tutorial programs function like a tutor presenting new (primary) information. These programs can help students because they provide information, ask a question about the content and, depending on the student's response, either go on to the next block of new information or branch to remedial information designed to clarify misconceptions. The branching in most tutorial programs is relatively limited, with students typically choosing from among three or four answers to each question. The sophistication and cost of the program is largely dependent on the extent of the branching.

Tutorial programs are most useful for remediation or enrichment. Remediation is called for when a student either misses a lesson or does not understand a lesson. If an appropriate tutorial program is available, it may provide the additional help such a student needs to progress. Enrichment is called for when a student already possesses the skills and knowledge to be taught to the class as a whole. Such a student should be encouraged to acquire new skills or knowledge and for this, the use of a tutorial program might be appropriate.

Usually, tutorial programs are *not* the best tool for teaching a whole class a particular skill or piece of information. When a teacher is presenting new information to a whole group, often a student will ask a question or make a comment that will help clarify things for other students. That kind of interaction is missing from CAI. For the most part, people teach people at least as well as machines teach people. Therefore, for whole-class instruction, teachers would be wise to do the job themselves.

Simulation Programs

Simulation programs present approximations of real-life situations. A student may simulate a pioneer traveling the Oregon Trail, the ruler of a country, or a chemist with a laboratory full of dangerous chemicals, but in all cases, the student is safe and in charge. Simulation programs can help students because they remove the danger or inconvenience of the real-life situations, but still require the student to make a decision about what to do next and to deal with the consequences of that decision. Without a computer, it would not be possible for each student to make his or her own decision and to have the next event be consistent with his or her choice. Since recognition of cause–effect relationships is essential to the maturation process, simulation programs can be said to help students mature.

Simulation programs also help students integrate knowledge and learn from mistakes. These features combine to make simulation programs among the most valuable that students can use. By enabling students to engage in activities that would be impossible, impractical, or too dangerous to engage in otherwise, simulation programs provide learning opportunities that are unique and invaluable.

Simulation programs are the most time-consuming to write because the programmer must provide sequences of choices consistent with each decision by each student. To enable each student to experience the cumulative consequences of each of his or her choices, the programmer must develop extensive branches and this can require thousands of hours of programming time.

Despite the fact that good simulation programs seem to put the learner in full control of the direction of the program, that control is an illusion. All programs, regardless of how extensive their branching may be, are closed systems. The student can only select choices from among those presented by the programmer so, although it might appear otherwise, there is no room for creativity on the part of the student. There is only one end result of each possible path, and it has already been written by the programmer.

Some simulations programs are designed for use in classrooms with only a single computer. The *Decisions Decisions* series developed by Tom Snyder Productions is an excellent example. These programs are designed so that small groups of students act as units. The students learn relevant content, such as how a revolution might affect rebels, merchants, and government officials, prior to using the computer. When they go to the computer, it is to simulate the actions that the group decided were best in a given situation. The computer reacts and presents the group with new choices, but before they can decide what to do next, the group typically needs to gather new information and to confer. While they are doing these things, another group of students uses the computer. Such programs are an excellent way to capitalize on the power of computer simulations, while simultaneously providing opportunities for cooperative learning.[19]

There is one down-side to simulations. Because they are so effective in capturing and maintaining students' interest, it is difficult to use them within regular class periods. Students get involved and want to see the consequences of their decisions and to follow their plans through to the end. Typical class periods often make this impossible, so conventional divisions in the school day actually hinder the most effective use of simulation programs.

Gaming Programs

Gaming programs capitalize on fast action, graphics, and, all too often, violence. These programs typically have little relation to instructional objectives and their use in the classroom can rarely be justified. One possible justification might be to help beginning students gain confidence in their ability to use computers.

Developments in CAI

When microcomputers became popular in the early 1980s, thousands of instructional programs were put on the market. Most of those programs were (and most new programs still are) **stand-alone** programs. They "stand alone" in that they focus on isolated skills or information. They are not designed to relate to other programs or to units of study. This makes it difficult for teachers to integrate them into instructional plans.

Some vendors responded to this problem by marketing sequences of programs that built on each other (for example, programs that deal, sequentially, with nouns, pronouns, and other parts of speech) or had some common element, typically a record-keeping system that kept track of students' achievements as they went from program to program. These **computer-managed instruction** (CMI) programs are somewhat easier to build into a curriculum, because they can help students develop a sequence of skills. Further, because they typically keep track of the student's performance through more than one program, they enable the teacher to see if any performance pattern is evident that might point to particular areas of strength or weakness. These programs are also easier for teachers to learn to use than stand-alone programs because all programs in the series use the same commands.

The most complete form of CMI is the **integrated computer curriculum.** An integrated computer curriculum is one in which some subject area such as math or reading is dealt with through a series of grade levels such as 4–6 or 6–12. Some programs deal with two or more subject areas as well as two or more grade levels. The most sophisticated of these integrated computer curriculums include a series of precise instructional objectives, a variety of program types (tutorial, drill and practice, and simulation) to help each student achieve the objectives, and a sophisticated record-keeping system that tracks each student. Two of the largest companies that market such integrated computer curriculums are the Computer Curriculum Corporation, and WICAT (World Institute of Computer Assisted Teaching).

Interactive Video

Another CAI development is interactive video. This technology links the interactive capability of computers with material stored on videotape or disks. Instead of calling up just words or still pictures, the computer can start a videotape or disk player and make use of action materials such as a segment of a political speech or an actual demonstration. This technology mates two sophisticated learning tools, computers and television. Interactive video provides somewhat less intense interaction than regular CAI because students spend part of their time watching the video portion of the program. The ability to build into the program full-motion events, however, more than compensates for the decrease in interaction.

In 1992, about 2,000 high schools, or 14 percent, had interactive videodisk players. By 1994, the number had grown to about 4,500 or 27 percent.[20]

Networking

Networking refers to linking one computer with others. If the network links computers in a relatively small geographic area, such as a school or suburban school district, it is referred to as a **local area network or LAN**. The largest network is the worldwide **INTERNET**. Via INTERNET, you and your students can access libraries, art galleries, and databases throughout the world and can share ideas via **electronic mail (e-mail)** with people worldwide. The INTERNET gives new meaning to the idea of distance learning.[21] As of 1993, it is estimated that 300,000 people were taking courses for credit via distance learning, and the number is growing quickly.[22] In 1992 about 1,700 high schools, or about 10 percent, had networks. By 1994, the number had grown to about 6,600 or 39 percent.[23]

The idea of networking and all that it entails, particularly e-mail and user groups, poses some interesting questions for educators. For example, it is now possible for teachers to make things such as syllabi, assignments, study questions, and one-on-one conversations, available to students via LANs or Internet. There is a question, however, of whether teachers really want to be available to students 24 hours a day, seven days a week. Further, there is a question of whether it is equitable to make some things, even one-on-one conversations, available to students who have ready access to computers, while putting those same things out of the reach of students who do not have ready access to computers.

CD-ROM and CD-I

A CD-ROM (Compact Disk-Read Only Memory) contains a large amount of digitized information. For example, whole encyclopedias, complete with text, pictures, and sound, can be recorded on CD-ROMs and easily accessed by students. Using an encyclopedia on CD-ROM, for example, students can gain information about a topic, be referred to further information related to that topic, and then, without moving from their chairs and with just a few keystrokes, get that related information. In 1992 about 2,500 high schools, or about 15 percent, had CD-ROMs. In 1994, the number was about 6,700 or 40 percent.[24]

A CD-I (Compact Disk-Interactive) contains visual and audio data typically found on a CD-ROM, with computer-assisted instruction programming. It will provide for more flexibility than traditional CD-ROMs and more realism than traditional CAI.

Disadvantages of CAI

Individualization in a Group Instruction Setting

At the same time that CAI opens up new possibilities for individualizing instruction and for having students achieve objectives that were impractical or impossible before CAI, it also poses some serious problems. Perhaps the most fundamental of these problems is that most schools are set up to provide instruction to groups, not to individuals. For example, while most teachers try to work with individuals as much as possible, the main thrust of their planning, teaching, and evaluating is geared to working with groups. Computers, however, like pens, pencils, and hand-held calculators, are tools best used by individuals as they work at their own rates. Computers simply do not fit very well into a system set up for group instruction.

This basic problem generates other problems. For example, lesson planning is complicated because teachers plan lessons for whole classes. If some students are directed to engage in activities other than those planned for the class, the teacher must have separate plans for those students. The plans might not be as extensive as complete lesson plans but if, for example, some students are going to be working at computers, the teacher should be able to explain to a parent or to a principal how the computer work will help those students achieve specific course objectives. Many teachers find that they do not have enough time or energy to make additional plans, so they avoid activities that require them. To the extent that computers cause teachers extra work, many teachers are reluctant to use them.

Aside from the problem of extra planning, a related problem is that while students are using computers they are missing all or part of the planned lesson. When it is time to use the information they missed, those students who were using the computers will, in effect, be penalized. It is unfair to ask students to use information or skills presented while they were directed to engage in some other activity. To be fair, some adjustment would have to be made in evaluating these students and this, again, would mean more work for the teacher.

Inadequate Teacher Preparation

Another problem hindering the use of CAI in schools is the fact that relatively few prospective teachers receive adequate instruction in how and when to use CAI effectively. In too many teacher education programs, students spend more time talking about computers than they do actually using them to acquire skills or knowledge. Most prospective teachers have moved into the computer age by learning how to use a word processor and, while this application is useful, it does little to help prospective teachers learn about CAI.

Differing Expectations

Most teachers go into teaching to work with students and each intends to do the best possible job. It is not likely, however, that many teachers envision their students spending a great deal of time sitting in front of a computer monitor that is approximately 18 inches in front of their noses and interacting with a computer program that is providing stimuli visually via the monitor and aurally via headphones. In this situation, the teacher is not needed. This reduced or non-role differs significantly from the role teachers expect to play and from the role that administrators and parents expect them to play. Even though students may be learning, the teacher may be seen as not teaching.

Hardware and Software Problems

Computers have few moving parts so, with reasonable care, they last a long time. However, about every three years hardware advances, particularly advances in the speed and power of central processing units (CPU), make it possible for software writers to develop more powerful programs that make use of the new hardware. The older hardware and software becomes obsolete. Few schools can afford to replace their computers with new ones every three years.

Further complicating matters are incompatible operating systems. A **disk operating system (DOS)**is the program that tells the computer how to access and use the programs stored on the hard and floppy disks. When microcomputers first became available, each company (Tandy/Radio Shack, Apple, and Commodore) wrote its own DOS. For example, Tandy/Radio Shack used the Tandy/Radio Shack Disk Operating System (TRSDOS), and Apple used the Apple Disk Operating System (Apple DOS).

When IBM entered the microcomputer market in 1981, it contracted with a company named Microsoft to write the DOS for the new IBM personal computers (PCs), and the result was the **Microsoft Disk Operating System (MS-DOS).** As the microcomputer market expanded, other companies began producing computers and, in order to capitalize on the power of IBM in the business world, they made their computers IBM compatible—they made them to operate with MS-DOS. Windows 95™ is Microsoft's newest operating system.

Today, most software comes in versions designed for either IBM compatible or Apple Macintosh computers, but there are programs that enable IBM compatibles and Macintoshes to exchange information. Further, vendors produce parallel versions of programs such as Microsoft's *Word*®, and *Excel*®, to run on IBM compatibles and Macintoshes, and this helps reduce conversion problems. Nonetheless, the problems with hardware and software obsolescence and incompatibility hinder the more rapid expansion of CAI.

Still further, many older buildings lack appropriate wiring and appropriate work space for CAI. Problems such as these are expensive to correct.

APPLICATION PROGRAMS

Unlike CAI programs, which help students learn or practice skills or information, usually for specific subject areas, application programs are tools used to do particular kinds of tasks. There are four major types.

Word Processors

Word processors are to typewriters what typewriters were to pens and pencils. They facilitate the transfer of ideas from your head to paper. Teachers use word processors, such as Microsoft's *Word®* and Novell's *Word Perfect®*, to generate all kinds of documents including syllabi, handouts, and tests. Students use them to develop writing skills and complete written assignments.

The use of word processors can save users countless hours of typing and retyping, and they make it more likely that users will correct their own work, but there is one troublesome point. Prior to word processors, students did their original thinking and writing at home. Class time was used to analyze what they had written. When word processors are used in schools, time that had been used for analysis must now be used for doing the original writing. The advantages of having students work at word processors must be weighed against the loss of instructional time.

Spreadsheets

Spreadsheets are programs used to keep track of, and manipulate, data arranged in rows and columns. Programs such as *Excel®* and *Lotus 1 , 2, 3®*, and derivatives of them, greatly simplify grade keeping. Once teachers enter column headings for students' names and for work to be graded, all that remains is to enter the scores for each assignment or test. Built-in functions enable the program to calculate the average of each column of scores; the total points earned by each student; the number of points needed for an A, B, C, and D; and the number of scores falling in each category. As each new set of scores is entered, all of this data is automatically updated.

Databases

Databases such as *Access®* and *Paradox®* enable teachers to build, maintain, and easily manipulate banks of data such as test items and portfolios of student work. There are also professionally developed databases containing demographic, geographic, and other data. A prospective teacher's knowledge of, and ability to use, such tools will be a plus during a job interview.

Presentation Tools

Programs such as *Powerpoint®* and *Freelance®* facilitate the production of professional-looking transparencies and handouts. If the appropriate hardware is available, documents generated with such programs can be displayed on a large-screen monitor in addition to being displayed on the computer's regular monitor.

Scanners

Scanner or optical character readers "read" the words on a page and save them in a computer's memory, just as if they had been entered from a keyboard. The file created can be saved as a word processing file or simply as data. The capability of scanners enables teachers to take any typed or printed page and convert it to a computer file. There is no longer a need to enter printed data via a keyboard.

Voice Synthesizers

Voice synthesizers can be used in conjunction with scanners to facilitate learning for the visually handicapped. One or more pages can be scanned into a computer's memory and then a voice synthesizer can be used to orally read the material. Students who have difficulty reading can listen.

SUMMARY

Two reasons instructional media are used are to: (1) help vary the stimuli by which students learn, thus helping to capture and maintain interest, and (2) expose students to stimuli and experiences that might not otherwise be available, safe, or practical. Regardless of the kind of media being considered, there are certain steps that a teacher can take to help ensure that the media are selected and used properly. These steps include:

1. selecting media that will help students achieve specific instructional objectives
2. becoming familiar with the content of the material or the operation of the device before using it with students
3. preparing the students so they can focus on specific elements or ideas
4. maximizing the utility of the media by properly adjusting volume, brightness, size, or clarity
5. conducting follow-up activities in order to clarify confusing points and to bring about closure
6. evaluating the experience to determine to what extent it contributed to students' achievement of the specified objective.

Many forms of mediated instruction are available to teachers, including textbooks, films and filmstrips, overhead transparencies, maps and charts, bulletin boards, real things, audio and video tapes, television, and computers. Although each form of media has specific advantages and disadvantages, only computers have the advantage of being two-way communicators. The ability to respond to the input of individual students makes computers among the most powerful instructional tools that a teacher can use.

The expansion of computer utilization in the schools makes it possible for teachers to help students acquire skills that are highly relevant to our increasingly technological society. Two of these skills are the ability to use computers for word processing and to search large databases for specific information. Computers are also used to provide different forms of computer-assisted instruction, including drill and practice, tutorials, and simulations.

The use of CAI is hampered by the fact that schools are currently set up to provide group instruction, whereas computers are best used by individuals. This basic conflict generates problems for teachers with respect to planning, teaching, and evaluating. Other problems concern hardware and software incompatibility.

SO HOW DOES THIS AFFECT MY TEACHING?

You cannot build a house with just a hammer or just a saw. You need a variety of tools, and the same is true of teaching and learning. No single procedure or tool can be used to help students achieve the variety of skills and knowledge that should be called for in your instructional objectives. There is a rich variety of tools available and the only factor limiting the use of most of them is the desire and/or creativity of the teacher. You can just lecture or lecture and discuss, but tools are readily available with which you can do much more. The most successful teachers use them.

Computers present serious challenges and great possibilities. Few schools are designed, and relatively few teachers are prepared, to capitalize on the potential of computer technology. Taken to its extreme, CAI could enable students to stay at home and learn much of what they now learn in school settings. The socialization factor would be missing, but its importance is a matter of philosophic position. What is most important is that you recognize that variety is important in capturing and maintaining student interest and that as you use new tools and teach students how to use them, you are helping to expand possibilities for them. Not only will the appropriate use of instructional tools help students achieve the objectives of the course, it will also make them aware of tools that they might use in other contexts. Use media. It will help you and your students be successful. At the same time, think about the truly revolutionary changes that computers can make in the way students are educated. Are you, for example, prepared to respond, on your own time and via e-mail, to each and every student who wants to ask a question or debate a point? Think about it. Just because a thing can be done does not, necessarily, mean that it is wise to do it.

KEY TERMS, PEOPLE, AND IDEAS

Technology
Mediated Instruction
Audio Aids
    Radios, Record, Tape and CD Players
    Telephones, Teleconferencing, Variable Speech Control
Visual Aids
    Opaque, Slide, and Filmstrip Projectors
    Bulletin boards
    Overhead projectors, transparencies, overlays
    Document cameras
Audio-Visual
    Multimedia kits
    ETV, Whittle Communications, Channel One
    Distance learning
    Closed-circuit television
    Video tape recorders and players
Programmed Instruction
    Sidney Pressey, teaching machine
    B.F. Skinner, Linear programs—identical small steps, cues, high success
      rate
    Norman Crowder, Branching programs—larger blocks of information,
      no cues, remediation, different paths
Computer-Assisted Instruction (CAI)
    Computer-Managed Instruction (CMI)
    Patrick Suppes, Computer Curriculum Corporation
    Time-sharing, PLATO, TICCIT
    Microcomputers, 1979
    CAI types: Drill and Practice, Tutorial, Simulation, Games
    Stand-alone, computer managed, and integrated curriculum programs
    Interactive video
    Networking, LAN, INTERNET, e-mail
    Disk Operating System (DOS), Central Processing Unit (CPU)
Application Programs
    Word Processors
    Spreadsheets
    Databases
    Presentation tools
CD-ROM
CD-I
Scanners
Voice Synthesizers

ENDNOTES

1. The *American Heritage Dictionary*, 2nd ed. (Boston: Houghton Mifflin Co., 1985), p. 1248.

2. "Gutenberg, Johann," *Encyclopedia Britannica*, 1960 ed., p. 12.

3. Brown, James W., Richard B. Lewis, and Fred F. Harcleroad, *A.V. Instruction—Media and Methods*, 3rd ed. (New York: McGraw-Hill, 1969), p. 327.

4. Strother, Deborah B., "On Listening," *Phi Delta Kappan*, Vol. 68, no. 8 (April 1987), pp. 625–628.

5. Olsen, Linda, "Technology Humanized—The Rate Controlled Tape Recorder," *Media and Methods* (January, 1979), p. 67; and Short, Sarah H., "The Use of Rate-Controlled Speech to Save Time and Increase Learning in Self-Paced Instruction," *NSPI Journal* (May 1978), pp. 13–14, as seen in Heinich, Robert, Michael Molenda, and James D. Russell, *Instructional Media*, 4th ed. (New York: Macmillan, 1993), p. 181.

6. Heinich , Robert, Michael Molenda, and James D. Russell, *Instructional Media*, 4th ed. (New York: Macmillan, 1993), pp. 436–437.

7. Yeager, Elizabeth Anne; and Eric A. Pandiscio, *Newcasts in the Classroom*, *Educational Leadership*, Vol. 50, no. 8 (May 1993), pp. 52–53.

8. Rutherford, LeAnn H., and Sheryl Grana "Fully Activating Interactive TV: Creating a Blended Family," *T.H.E. (Technological Horizons in Education) Journal*, Vol. 22, no. 3 (October 1994), pp. 86–90.

9. Pressey, Sidney L., "A Machine for Automatic Teaching of Drill Material," *School and Society*, Vol. 25, no. 645 (May 7, 1927), pp. 549–592.

10. Skinner, B. F., "The Science of Learning and the Art of Teaching," *The Harvard Educational Review*, Vol. 24 (Spring 1954), pp. 86–97.

11. Skinner B. F., *The Technology of Teaching* (Englewood Cliffs, N.J.: Prentice-Hall, 1968).

12. Saettler, Paul, *The Evolution of American Educational Technology* (Englewood, Colo.: Libraries Unlimited, 1990), pp. 295–296.

13. Crowder, Norman A., "Automatic Tutoring by Means of Intrinsic Programming," in Gatanter, Eugene, ed., *Automatic Teaching: The State of the Art* (New York: John Wiley, 1959), pp. 109–110.

14. Niemiec, Richard P., and Herbert J. Walberg, "From Teaching Machines to Microcomputers: Some Milestones in the History of Computer-Based Instruction," *Journal of Research on Computing in Education*, Vol. 21, no. 3 (Spring 1989), p. 272.

15. *The World Almanac Book and Book of Facts*, 1994 (Mahwah, N.J.: Funk and Wagnalls, 1993), p. 196.

16. Kulik James A., R. L. Bangert, and G. W. Williams, "Effects of Computer-Based Teaching on Secondary School Students," *Journal of Educational Psychology*, Vol. 75, no. 1 (1983), pp. 19–26.

17. Niemiec, Richard., G. Samson, T. Weinstein, and H. Walberg, "The Effectiveness of Computer-based Intruction at the Elementary School Level: A Quantitative Synthesis," *AEDS Journal*, no. 3 (1985), pp. 19–37.

18. Poulson, Gloria, and Elizabeth Macken, *Evaluation Studies of CCC Elementary School Curriculums, 1975–1977* (Palo Alto, Calif.: Computer Curriculum Corp., 1978), p. 2.

19. For information about the *Decisions Decisions* series, contact Tom Snyder Productions, 90 Sherman Street, Cambridge, Mass. 02140 (1–800–342–0236).

20. *The World Almanac Book and Book of Facts,* 1995, p. 221.

21. For further information on the most recent work concerning computers in schools it is recommended that the reader turn to periodicals such as *Electronic Learning* (P.O. Box 2041, Mahopac, N.Y. 10541), *The Computing Teacher* (1787 Agate St, Eugene, Ore. 97403), and *T.H.E. Journal Technical Horizons in Education,* 2626 S. Pullman, Santa Ana, Calif. 92705-0126); and/or write for information to corporations such as Computer Curriculum Corporation, (P.O. Box 10080, 700 Hansen Way, Palo Alto, Calif. 94304-1016); Education Systems Corporation (6170 Cornerstone Court East, San Diego, Calif. 92121); and MECC (3490 Lexington Avenue North, St. Paul, Minn. 55126).

22. Weiss, Jiri, "Distance Learning: Bridging the Gap with Technology," *Syllabus,* Vol. 8, no. 2 (October 1994), p. 38.

23. *The World Almanac Book and Book of Facts,* 1995, p. 221.

24. *The World Almanac Book and Book of Facts,* 1995, p. 221.

10

PLANNING A COURSE SYLLABUS AND INSTRUCTIONAL UNITS

RATIONALE

Philosophies, objectives, content, learning activities, and instructional media do little good until they are brought together to form a coherent plan that will maximize learning. If you intend to simply follow the textbook, you will not need to do much planning. However, if you want to help your students develop a wide range of cognitive and psychomotor abilities, and help them become more self-sufficient problem solvers, planning is necessary. Just as planning a route for a car trip helps you get to your destination expeditiously, instructional plans help you and your students achieve instructional objectives expeditiously.

The chapter explains the logic and procedures for developing course syllabi and instructional units. A syllabus and unit plans help teachers logically sequence content and activities so that students acquire and use increasingly complex skills and knowledge. Such plans also enable teachers to use time wisely and to anticipate, and thus minimize or avoid, problems. As with all endeavors, planning does not guarantee success, but it does make success more likely.

SAMPLE OBJECTIVES

You will be able, in writing, to:

1. Take a position for or against detailed course syllabi and, in no more than two pages, use relevant facts and/or cause-effect reasoning to defend your position. (Evaluation)

2. Construct a syllabus for a one-semester course in your subject area and include: (a) precise instructional objectives including at least three from the higher levels of the cognitive or psychomotor domains, (b) grading criteria and policies, and (c) a tentative content outline and calendar showing test and due dates. (Synthesis)
3. Describe and exemplify at least four components of a "Herbartian" unit. (Comprehension)
4. Construct an instructional unit for a given length of time in your teaching field, and include: (a) a rationale, (b) precise instructional objectives including a least one from the higher levels of the cognitive or psychomotor domains, (c) appropriate content and learning activities, and (d) two ways to evaluate student progress. (Synthesis)

THE TIME FACTOR

Most school districts have calendars based on about 180 days of instruction. That converts to about 36 weeks and it is all the time you will have to accomplish whatever you hope to accomplish. There is talk of increasing the length of the school day and of increasing the length of the school year, but until additional funds are available, little expansion is likely to take place.

While 180 days may seem like a reasonably long time, you will find that it is too little time to do all you would like, and too much time to treat as a single block. To solve this problem, many teachers think in terms of instructional units lasting two to four weeks and they develop terminal objectives for each of nine to eighteen units. If you look in the tables of contents in typical texts you will find that they are already divided into units of three to five chapters similar to the following example from a popular United States history text.

Unit 1   The making of Americans
   Ch. 1   What Europeans found: the American surprise
     2   An assortment of colonies.
     3   New ways in a New World
Unit 2   Forming a new nation 1763–1800
   Ch. 4   The road to revolution and victory
     5   From confederation to nation
     6   The United States begins
     .
     .
     .
Unit 12   The United States looks ahead
   Ch. 34   A new world of competition
     35   Changing leaders in Washington
     36   New directions[1]

As you begin to think about your own instructional goals, think in terms of the full year, in terms of units, and in terms of observable and measurable objectives.

THE COURSE SYLLABUS

You have probably heard stories of young children who, on a car trip, continually ask "Are we there yet?" A likely reason for their questions is that no one sat down with them and showed them, on a map, where they were starting from, the route to be taken, and where they would end up. Since they had no sense of the whole journey and no landmarks to look for, they had no way to assess their progress. In many high school classrooms, students are in a similar situation. They do not have a clear idea of where they are headed or how they will get there. Your class can be different. You can provide a road map complete with route, landmarks, and final destination. It is called a syllabus, and what follows is one way to construct one.

Identifying Data

The syllabus should begin with the name of the course (and number, if appropriate), the semester and/or year, your name, and the school's telephone number. Some teachers also include the room number and their home phone number with a request to only call prior to a certain time such as 9:00 p.m. The idea here is that you want students and parents to come to you first if they have questions or problems related to your course. Make it easy for them do so. As a point of information, once students understand that you have included your home phone number to help them, very few misuse the information.

Overview/Rationale

The next component is a brief overview of the course. The intent is to concisely describe each of the units that will be studied and to explain to the students the relevance, to them, of these units and of the course as a whole. Do not assume just because you want, or are required, to teach particular content to students, that they are interested in learning it. Build the overview/rationale carefully. If students are persuaded at the outset of the course that they can gain useful information and skills, they will be more willing participants in the teaching–learning process.

Objectives

This section contains the dozen or so precise instructional objectives that make up the minimal competencies for the course. The objectives, written with consideration of the needs of the subject area, students, and society, should do three main things. First, they should bring the rationale to life by specifying, in terms that are observable and measurable, how students will demonstrate the competent use of specific skills and knowledge. Second, their sequence should demonstrate that students will be developing a strong base of knowledge and skills and will then use that knowledge and those skills to deal with increasingly complex, real-life problems and issues.

Finally, the objectives should clearly answer the question, "What do I need to do to pass this course?" The answer is "achieve all of the objectives." Students and parents often mistakenly see a set of objectives as ceilings rather than floors. To avoid this, consider preceding the objectives with a statement such as, "The following objectives must be demonstrated, in writing and under test conditions (unless otherwise specified), in order to earn a passing grade in this class." This may seem intimidating, but it effectively communicates the minimum acceptable standards for the class and can avoid a great deal of ill will later on.

Grading Criteria

Most students are concerned about grades. They want to know if they might be given surprise quizzes, if there will be mid-term and final exams and, if so, if they have to take them (this might be covered by school policy). They also want to know if grades will be based on the traditional scale where the lowest A is 90 percent of the possible points, the lowest B is 80 percent, the lowest C is 70 percent, etc., or some other scale. Further, they want to know if extra credit points are possible and, if so, how they might be earned, and about any other factors that might affect their grades. Thinking about the grading criteria as you plan the syllabus gives you time to check school rules, to find out what other teachers in the building do, and to construct criteria that are fair and workable. More will be said concerning grading in Chapters 12 and 13.

Tentative Content Outline and Calendar

Next, take out a copy of the school calendar and, in the left margin, write in the week number of each week in the semester or year. This will make it easier to think about time allocations. Then, arrange the objectives in the order they will be dealt with during the semester or year and, with calendar in hand, start estimating how much time you believe it will take for students to achieve each of the objectives. Typically, you will be able to group the objectives into broad units and then start allocating time for each unit (about two weeks for Unit 1, four weeks for Unit 2, etc.). These tentative allocations represent your best guess of the time needed for each unit. When you get done you may find that you do not have enough time for the last unit or that you have too much time. You then go back and make adjustments. It is also wise to include tentative homework and other assignments.

In doing this planning, consider scheduling tests for the beginning of a week. This makes it possible for you to review for the test with students toward the end of the preceding week and for students to study during the weekend. Scheduling due dates for papers and other assignments at the end of a week gives you the weekend to grade them and get them back to students at the beginning of the following week. Since you will be working from the school calendar, you will be able to plan around holidays and school events.

Main Advantage

The main advantage of detailed planning is that it provides security and stability. Students will know what to expect and when to expect it. If they wish to do so they can work ahead to avoid conflicts with assignments in other class or with other activities. They will also be able to bring drafts of their work in to you for feedback and have time to make needed changes. Educators often talk of having students become more active participants in their own learning. Giving students a detailed syllabus, with test and due dates specified well in advance, makes students more responsible for allowing themselves enough time to prepare for those tests and to meet those deadlines. As a bonus, students will not have to worry about surprise assignments or major tests. Further, if parents have access to a detailed syllabus, it makes it easier for them to work with the student, and with the teacher, to help ensure the student's success.

Main Disadvantage

There is a disadvantage to detailed planning; it limits your freedom to pursue interesting, but unanticipated, discussions or projects. It seems that security and freedom are inversely proportional. If you want more of one, you must have less of the other. However, the whole idea of planning is to provide structure, to provide a road map to reach a set of goals expeditiously. The choice to stray from the syllabus is always there, just as is the choice to take some of those interesting side roads on a trip. However, if you take enough side trips on your way to you final destination, you will run out of time or money before reaching that destination. In school, straying from the syllabus means using time originally allocated to achieving the objectives that you determined were relevant to your subject area, your students, and society as a whole, and that were approved by the administration.

Unless a major flaw in your planning suddenly becomes apparent or some dramatic event necessitates a change in plans, it is wise to stay with the syllabus for the semester or year. Then, if changes are wanted or needed, they can be made the following semester or year. Doing this helps keep everyone on track and makes it easier for the administration to back you if the need arises. You will be following the approved plan. Failure to follow the syllabus is likely to result in a great deal of student resentment, especially among those students who made plans based on it.

Most teachers who take the time to construct a course syllabus intend to follow it, but most also realize that no plan is perfect so they give themselves some flexibility. They slightly overestimate the time allocated for each unit. Beginning teachers tend to plan on the basis of how much time they think they will need to cover the material. However, they often forget to consider the time it will take students to learn the material and do something useful with it. If a day or two is built into each unit for synthesizing discussions or other activities, additional time is available if things go a bit slower than anticipated, and time for in-depth discussions or other activities is available if all goes according to the original plan.

Summary Sheet

On the last page of the syllabus it is a good idea to provide a summary of dates when assignments are due and tests are scheduled. It is also a good idea to provide a column listing the points possible for each assignment and test and an adjacent column in which students can write the number of points they actually earned for each assignment or test. This makes it possible for students to maintain a running record of the points they earned and makes it difficult for any student to claim that they had no idea of how well or poorly they were doing in the class.

As a point of information, in 1994, two students at a university in New York sued their instructor and the university claiming, in part, that the instructor "never gave the class a syllabus that outlined coverage, testing, and grading." The students also claimed that the way the course was taught differed greatly from the description of the course in the course catalog. The charges brought by the students included breach of contract, educational malpractice, and violation of New York's statute concerning unfair and deceptive business practices. On May 5, 1994, the judge ruled in favor of the students.[2] The university involved is appealing the decision, but whether the decision is upheld or reversed, the message for all teachers is clear. Avoid problems by thinking carefully about each element of the syllabus—the rationale, objectives, grading criteria, rules concerning making up missed work or tests, needed materials, and the tentative content outline and calendar. The syllabus should not be a straitjacket, but neither should it be a potato sack. Sections of an abbreviated syllabus are shown at the end of this chapter in Figure 10.1.

THE FIRST DAY

On the first day of school both you and your students will be apprehensive. You will not know them and they will not know you, but you have the advantage. You will have planned for this day, you will have set the stage. As the students walk into your room they should see eye-catching, interesting bulletin boards appropriate to the first unit. Instructional aids such as maps, charts, reference books, tools, or models should be visible. The room should look like a place in which students will be learning a particular subject. You should be dressed professionally. All of these things will help convey a purposeful and businesslike atmosphere before you even say hello.

After greeting the students and checking the role, distribute the syllabus and take time to discuss it. Such a discussion gives students "the big picture." It also gives you the opportunity to show them how the objectives are relevant to their lives whether or not they go on to college, and how the planned activities will help them achieve the objectives. Students should be asked if they see ways to make the course more relevant. They are not likely to make many suggestions, but the fact that input was solicited will make an impression. It will tell students that you consider them adult enough to think seriously about the work ahead. If students are convinced that they will be gaining useful skills and knowledge and that you believe they are capable of achieving the objectives, the hardest part of your task is done. The students will be more likely to be successful and their success will be a measure of your own success—everyone benefits.

Teachers often bemoan the fact that parents do not seem interested in the education of their children. While this is probably true for some parents, it is also true that most parents do not have a very clear idea of what their children are studying. How much of your high school course work did you discuss with your parents? If you are interested in stimulating parental involvement, mail a copy of the syllabus to each student's parents along with a cover letter explaining what the parents can do to help their son or daughter be successful. Invite them to call or come to school if they have questions or concerns. These steps represent part of the "extra mile," the extent to which you are willing to go to help students succeed. Your concern will be noticed and will be well received.

Once you have the syllabus tentatively planned, and well before you meet your students for the first time, it is wise to plan each block or unit of instruction. We will, therefore, next look at unit planning.

HERBARTIAN UNITS

The idea of unit planning is not new. **Johann Herbart** (1776–1841), a German educator, believed that the teaching–learning process was amenable to analysis and improvement. He explained four steps that he believed would facilitate learning, regardless of the duration of instruction, and would facilitate analysis of the teaching–learning process.

1. *Clearness*—Breaking objects or ideas into elements and having the learner focus on each detail or fact in isolation, absorbing as much information as possible.
2. *Association*—Helping learners, once they gained sufficient knowledge about the object or idea, to relate it to objects or ideas already known. To build generalizations and abstractions.
3. *System*—Helping the learner see interrelationships and how parts fit together to make a meaningful whole.
4. *Method*—Testing ideas against reality.[3]

Herbart's ideas were brought to the United States and, in the mid-1890s, the National Herbart Society was formed with **Frank McMurray** and **Charles DeGarmo** being two of its principle proponents. Over the years, Herbart's four steps were transformed into the following five steps.

1. *Preparation*—Developing an appropriate learning environment by gathering and organizing appropriate materials and by helping students recall ideas that were learned earlier and that relate to the new information.
2. *Presentation*—Communicating the skills and information as clearly as possible and with the abundant use of examples relevant to the students.
3. *Association*—Helping students clarify their thinking by bringing out similarities and differences between old and new ideas.
4. *Generalization*—Helping students broaden their understanding of ideas by bringing out the interrelationships and applicability of ideas in various contexts.
5. *Application*—Providing opportunities for students to use the information and skills that they learned. Knowledge not used is knowledge lost.

These steps are the essence of the Herbartian Unit. Their underlying premise is that instruction is most successful when it builds on what students already know and provides a way for students to put what they have learned to practical use. What follows is a way to build a foundation for an instructional unit.

THE TYLER RATIONALE IN ACTION— WAIMON KNOWLEDGE STRUCTURES

Ralph Tyler's identification of three main sources of instructional objectives has a modern counterpart with respect to unit planning. **Morton D. Waimon**

(Professor of Education at Illinois State University) used Tyler's three sources of objectives to develop the idea of a knowledge structure. A knowledge structure is an outline of major and minor concepts. For purposes of this discussion, a concept is a group of things, either concrete or abstract, that have enough elements in common to make up a unique set. In the case of a knowledge structure, Roman numeral I focuses on the needs of the subject area and consists of the most basic and powerful concept of the unit. Think of this concept as the umbrella that will cover all the other concepts in the unit. It is a concept that experts in the subject area would agree to be true and to be central to the whole unit. This does not mean, however, that there is only one possible central concept for a given unit. There may be many. You simply need to decide on one that "works for you." For example, a high school Earth science teacher might teach a unit about the formation of the Earth's crust. Roman numeral I for this knowledge structure might be:

I. The Earth's surface is affected by many dynamic forces and processes, such as internal heat, solar radiation, meteorite impact, and human activity, all of which continually change its appearance.

In a more advanced class, such as a college-level geology class, the teacher might focus an entire unit on just the effects of the Earth's internal heat upon surface formations, so Roman numeral I for that knowledge structure might be:

I. The heat trapped in the Earth' s core and mantle when the Earth was formed is now thought to be the primary cause of volcanoes and the movement of tectonic plates.

Under the major concept, the teacher would list a number of minor concepts that expand on, but do not duplicate, the information in the major concept. In the Earth science knowledge structure about the formation of the Earth's crust, the minor concepts might be:

A. Internal heat affects the surface by causing volcanism, plate tectonics, mountain building, and earthquakes.
B. Solar radiation, acting on the atmosphere and surface of the Earth, causes erosion by wind, water, and ice.
C. Human activities, particularly the expansion of agriculture and urban areas and the retrieval of natural resources, have accelerated many changes in the Earth's surface.

The function of the first major concept and its associated minor concepts is to present the substance of the unit: the basic facts and information. Most of this information will be available in textbooks, although the wise teacher will check texts at levels more advanced than the one being used for the course. The focus of the next two major concepts is different.

Herbart, Dewey, and countless other educators have emphasized that students are more likely to learn, remember, and be able to use information if its utility is made clear. That is the function of the second major concept. Here, the teacher focuses on the needs of the students, on how individuals can use the information. Going back to the example about the Earth's crust, a second major concept might be:

II.   Individuals can do relatively little to alter the natural factors that shape the land but, via conservation efforts, they can help to preserve or improve landforms, and by increasing their understanding of the formation of landforms they can better understand the interactions between the land and the people.

This concept flows logically from the last minor concept (I. C) because it builds on the link between people and landforms. It also focuses attention on the fact that information about landforms can be put to practical use. Minor concepts that expand on this second major concept might be:

A.   Homes that are built or landscaped to capitalize on natural features are generally more comfortable and less costly to live in than homes not so built or landscaped.
B.   Farmers who practice conservation tillage tend to preserve the topsoil on their property while decreasing their expenditures for fuel and chemicals.
C.   By better understanding the relationship between the kind of land on which people live and how those people live, we may gain a better understanding of the interactions among the peoples of the world.

Having established the intellectual basis for the unit and having begun to address ways in which individuals can make use of the information, the next task is to establish the fact that this topic is relevant to current concerns of society as a whole. One way of developing this concept is to check recent periodicals for articles relating to the topic of the knowledge structure. Citing such articles to students will help establish the relevance of their studies. A major concept that addresses this need for the unit on landforms might be:

III.   Advancements in technology have enabled us to make significant changes in the Earth's topography and therefore we need to consider the long-term and global effects that these changes might produce.

Again, the major concept follows logically from the last minor concept by linking interactions among people of the world with changes in the Earth's topography made by relatively few people. Minor concepts that expand on this major concept might be:

A. High levels of emissions from factories and motor vehicles are posing problems ranging from an increase in average temperatures worldwide (due to the "greenhouse" effect) to the accelerated erosion of priceless artifacts.
B. Harnessing natural power sources, such as wind, water, nuclear energy, and the Sun, will result in the conservation of fossil fuels and the preservation of the land surrounding them.
C. Large-scale earthmoving projects, such as dam building or changing the direction of rivers, can affect people thousands of miles from the site of the project, so their needs, too, should be taken into consideration before the project is begun.

There is no law that says a knowledge structure must have three, and only three, major concepts or that each major concept must be followed by three, and only three, minor concepts. The format seems to fit the need fairly well, but it can be modified to better meet specific needs. The key point to keep in mind is that with a knowledge structure, the major concepts address the academic, personal, and social significance of the unit. These concepts can serve as a strong and integrated framework for a unit plan.

COMPONENTS OF A UNIT PLAN

A unit plan usually begins with a rationale that concisely explains why and how the unit is relevant to the course, the students, and society. The rationale is typically followed by half a dozen or so precise instructional objectives, the actual content needed to achieve the objectives, learning activities appropriate to the content and the objectives, optional learning activities, and a list of needed materials. A unit plan typically ends with a plan for evaluation. A unit plan represents a teacher's most complete idea of what students will accomplish in a given block of time and how it will be accomplished.

The construction of a unit plan takes time, but the benefits are great. First, by looking at each instructional unit, the teacher can ensure that students are provided with a sequence of activities that is likely to help them move from low-level, teacher-directed activities to higher-level, student-directed activities. The activities can also be designed to help students integrate knowledge from other subject areas. Further, once the teacher does the necessary gathering and organizing of information and materials, that work will be useful in future years. Occasional updating may be needed, but the teacher will not have to start from scratch each time the unit is taught. It pays, therefore, to do the job well the first time.

Overview/Introduction/Rationale

This component is similar to the overview/rationale for the course, but it deals with only a two- to four-week block of time. Its main purpose is to concisely tell students what the unit will be about, to give them the "big picture," and reasons to want to learn. A brief explanation of the major concepts from the knowledge structure might be useful. Understandably, students are likely to be most interested in the practical utility of what they will learn. Therefore, time should be specifically allocated to explaining to students how they will be able to put what they learn to practical use and to show how the content is relevant to today's world.

Objectives

The second part of a unit plan should be a list of three to six precise instructional objectives that will move students to increasingly higher levels of the Cognitive and/or Psychomotor domains. It should be remembered that we are talking about terminal objectives here, the objectives to be demonstrated at the end of the unit. Daily, or enroute, objectives are part of daily lesson plans. Check to see that higher-level objectives are included. Whenever practical, students should be called on to use their new knowledge and/or skills to accomplish a real-life task, not just to pass a test.

Content

The bulk of the unit consists of the actual information to be presented. This information, in outline form, should go beyond the information in the students' text. It should be detailed and specific, and it should correlate with the objectives of the unit. Time should be taken to sift through a good deal of material, and particularly original sources, so that the most important and/or interesting content can be selected. During this sifting, teachers frequently discover relationships among facts and concepts that they had not seen previously.

Taking the time to acquire content from a number of different sources has advantages. First, multiple sources act as an accuracy check, ensuring that names, dates, facts, figures, and relationships are correct. Second, they both provide and stimulate you to think of relevant examples and anecdotes. Finally, this kind of preparation will increase your self-confidence because it will increase your command of the subject matter. This confidence will be seen by your students. They will see you as being well prepared and ready and able to help them learn and succeed.

There are many sources to which teachers can turn for unit plan ideas. One excellent source is compilations called resource units. Many public schools, state departments of education, and university instructional materials centers maintain resource units on a wide variety of topics. These compilations often contain instructional objectives, rationales, and subject-matter outlines, suggestions for learning activities, optional experiences, instructional aids, bibliographies, and even sample tests. The wealth of material available in most resource units can tempt teachers to build their own units solely from this material, but resource unit material should be supplemented not only with the most current material available but also with whatever other material is needed to meet the specific objectives.

Other logical sources for unit plan ideas include college texts and notes, personal experiences, libraries, and on-line databases. Many sources in the school library will have relatively low reading levels, so teachers can skim them and extract relevant information fairly quickly. The librarian may have suggestions for other possible aids. National councils, such as those listed in Appendix B, are also useful. There is less chance for errors or misinterpretations to occur if original work is cited, so cite original sources whenever possible and let students do their own interpreting.

The subject-matter outline for the unit should cover all the information students will need to achieve the objectives. The outline should be complete enough to be used without the need for supplemental sources (which may not be available when needed) or "remembered" material (which may be forgotten when needed). A helpful rule to follow is that, if the content will help students learn or remember something, put it in the outline. This includes facts, figures, definitions, diagrams, explanations, examples, and anecdotes.

The primary advantage of building a comprehensive subject-matter outline is that it eliminates the need to do last-minute research or to search for appropriate examples. Everything needed is built into the unit while there is time to be selective and thorough. A second advantage is that the teacher will become more familiar with the "big picture." Knowing the exact nature of the material to be presented in the future, the teacher can refer to points yet to be made (thus cueing the students) and can more readily refer to points previously made (thus appropriately reinforcing prior learning).

Instructional Activities

Each learning activity should be selected on the basis of how well it will help students achieve the instructional objectives. It is a good idea to give serious thought to how you will begin each lesson. If your set induction is interesting and actively involves the students, you will have done much to stimulate students' desire to cooperate and learn. The objectives themselves will suggest appropriate experiences. For example, a low-level objective such as "Describe, in writing, at least two examples of natural landforms" could be facilitated by use of a film or video tape. Activities for a higher-level objective such as "Given a series of facts and fallacies concerning pollution, you will underline each of the facts" might be a guided practice session accompanied by student discussion.

When selecting learning activities, effective teachers consider the types of practice that students will need as preparation for the achievement of the instructional objectives. For the objective cited earlier concerning facts and fallacies about pollution, a teacher may wish to plan one activity that would provide analogous practice (such as listing fallacies on the board and briefly discussing why they are fallacies) and another activity that would provide equivalent practice (such as examining articles containing both facts and fallacies about pollution and identifying the specific facts and fallacies).

As prospective teachers go through college they typically swear to themselves that when they get into their own classroom, they will not spend much time, if any, lecturing or guiding tightly structured discussions. Of course, when they get into their own rooms, these are the very techniques they most frequently employ. You, however, know how to do things differently. You know about problem-based learning, cooperative learning strategies, and contests, about having students use information, about instructional media, and about variety being the spice of life. Here is where you can put all those good intentions and that relevant knowledge to work.

Instructional Aids

The long-range planning exemplified by unit plans enables the teacher to order films, books, video tapes, models, and other instructional aids early enough to assure availability when needed. Good planning will allow sufficient time to preview material, test equipment, and make alternate plans if necessary.

Evaluation

The final step in planning a unit is to construct the instrument(s) needed to determine whether the objectives have been achieved. Some objectives may be evaluated by paper-and-pencil tests and, despite the protests of those who want "authentic" evaluations, paper-and-pencil tests are both educationally sound and effective. They should not, however, be the only instruments used. For example, skill tests or actual products may be called for. If so, checklists of criteria should be constructed. Whenever possible, it is a good idea to look for ways students can demonstrate competencies by doing things directly and clearly related to out-of-class (real-life) problems. There are three things guaranteed to entice students to want to learn: relevance,

relevance, and relevance. Linking evaluation to practical utilization of knowledge and skills helps demonstrate relevance.

TOPICAL OUTLINES

Topical outlines usually arrange information so that each section logically follows the one before it. If the unit about the Earth's surface were arranged topically, the major points might look like this:

I.   The Earth's surface is affected by many dynamic forces and processes, such as internal heat, solar radiation, meteorite impact, and human activity, all of which continually change its appearance.
II. Heat from the Earth's hot core is a major cause of surface formations, not only because that heat causes volcanoes, but because the heat keeps the rock supporting the crustal plates molten, enabling them to drift into, over, and under one another, forming mountains and causing earthquakes.
III. Solar radiation powers the water cycle and the air circulation process, two of the major causes of erosion of the Earth's surface.
IV. The impact of large meteorites is relatively rare due to the Earth's thick atmosphere, which, via friction, destroys most things falling through it. When such impacts do occur they can cause massive cratering and destruction.

The topical outline could easily be continued, but one point should be clear. While the outline does permit the logical presentation of information, it does not address the basic question of the utility of the information. If that utility is not clear, students may view the information as irrelevant to their lives and see little reason to learn it. Take the time to demonstrate to students how the knowledge can be of practical use.

ORGANIZING THE PARTS OF A UNIT: AN ABBREVIATED MODEL

The preceding unit plan components can be arranged in many ways. A simple outline form is one way, as exemplified in the abbreviated model in Figure 10.2, at the end of the chapter. A full model is included as Appendix E.

Another procedure for organizing unit plans is to write out separate lesson plans for each of the objectives. Since the objectives, subject matter, learning activities, and materials have already been selected (or, in the case of learning activities, at least seriously considered), the writing of separate lesson plans is greatly facilitated. The advantage to such an organizational pattern is that little preparation is needed once the unit is under way. The disadvantage is that the lesson plans may impose too rigid a structure on the progress of the class, discouraging deviations from the plans even when such deviations would be worthwhile.

Still another way of organizing unit plans is by introductory, developmental, and concluding blocks of subject matter and experiences. The teacher may decide, for example, to use certain subject matter and certain learning activities to stimulate interest in the unit. Other blocks of subject matter and other experiences may be designated for use in developing understanding and general instruction, while still others may be earmarked for concluding activities such as summarization and reinforcement.

OPTIONAL ACTIVITIES

Optional activities are included in a unit plan to provide ways for students to go beyond the planned day-to-day activities and/or to provide activities for students with special needs. Activities such as constructing a bulletin board, model, or diorama, participating in a panel discussion, or engaging in an independent study project have potential for extending learning and for individualizing learning activities.

Perhaps the most common optional activities involve carefully selected special readings. While gathering and selecting content for units, you will encounter numerous sources of information written at differing levels of difficulty and representing various points of view. By building a file of short, annotated bibliography cards of such sources, you will have a ready-made pool of sources to which students with varying abilities can be directed. Slower students can be given material written at a lower level so they do not fall behind, while brighter students can be directed to more challenging material, such as college-level texts, trade books, reports, and interviews. The key is to gear optional activities to the specific abilities of the students in the class.

Finally, the optional activities section is an excellent place to place experimental experiences. Since you are likely to generate some innovative and creative instructional possibilities while planning units, these untried experiences may be listed in the optional activities section and attempted on a voluntary basis by students. If the activities prove fruitful, they may become part of the regular instructional activities. An abbreviated unit plan is included, for your examination, as Figure 10.3 at the end of the chapter.

PLANNING FOR EVALUATION AND FUTURE USE

The final step in planning a unit is to construct the instrument(s) needed to determine whether the objectives have been achieved. The objectives of the unit dictate the types of evaluation instruments needed. At the same time that the evaluations are constructed it is a good idea to construct answer keys and/or appropriate models. If skill tests are to be used, appropriate checklists should be constructed.

Good unit plans include objectives that require students to synthesize a number of subsidiary skills in the process of achieving the terminal objectives. Such objectives enable the teacher to develop evaluation procedures that enable students to clearly see the applicability of the content. Objective and essay tests have important roles, but it is desirable to supplement them with other forms of evaluation whenever possible. More will be said concerning evaluation in Chapters 12 and 13.

After the unit plan has been constructed and the components are in polished form and suitably organized, it is useful to make an expanded title page. It should include:

title of the unit;

the name of the course for which the unit was written (such as American History or Home Economics I);

the type of student and grade level for which the unit was designed (such as general—freshmen, or college preparatory—juniors);

a brief overview of the unit (four or five lines describing the main points covered);

a brief statement describing the unit preceding or following the unit (to help place the unit in a logical sequence); and

a close estimation of the time frame needed for the unit.

This information will save time when instructional programs are being planned for future classes and the use of a previously written unit is being considered. Such concise data also facilitate the sharing of unit plans among teachers if such arrangements can be made.

SUMMARY

To quote Alfred North Whitehead once again, "Lack of time is the rock upon which the fairest educational schemes are wrecked."[4] Teachers will typically have about 180 days in which to accomplish all of their goals. Therefore, when planning instruction, it is best to do so with a calendar in hand.

A course syllabus is beneficial to the teacher and to the students. Planning the syllabus requires the teacher to think in terms of the total time available and how to best use that time. Time for each instructional unit can be allocated, test dates and due dates for papers can be tentatively set, and grading criteria can be laid out. Then, before anyone else sees the document, the teacher can review it, make adjustments as needed, and end up with a plan that is clear and workable.

Typically a syllabus will include identifying data such as the name of the course, the year, the name of the instructor, and the school's phone number. Sometimes instructors add other data such as their home phone number (with instructions to call only before a certain time). Following the identifying data, the next segment of a syllabus is typically an overview/rationale. The purpose of this segment is to give students a general idea of the scope and sequence of the course content and to explain how the skills and information to be learned will be relevant and useful to them.

The next segment, the objectives, lists the dozen or so terminal objectives that must be achieved if the student is to get a passing grade in the course. It should be emphasized that the course objectives represent a performance floor, not a ceiling. This segment is typically followed by grading criteria and procedures so students will know exactly how points can be earned and how final grades will be calculated.

The next, and longest, segment consists of a tentative content outline and calendar. It is in this section that students will see how the whole semester or year is laid out in terms of when particular blocks of content will be covered, when tests are scheduled, and when papers and other assignments are due. It should be the intention of the teacher to follow the syllabus, but it is also the teacher's responsibility to use common sense. A syllabus or any other plan is just that, a plan. The idea is to follow the plan as closely as possible and, unless there is an exceptionally good reason to do otherwise, to leave major changes until the next semester or year. A page at the end of the syllabus summarizing test dates and due dates for assignments, as well as columns showing the points possible for each test and assignment and an adjacent column for students to write in the points they actually earned, is also helpful to students.

A knowledge structure consists of a series of major and minor concepts. The first major concept focuses on the needs of the subject area and provides the academic basis for the unit. This underlying and powerful concept is like an umbrella, which covers all other concepts in the unit. The second major concept focuses on the utility of the information to students. Here the teacher develops concepts that could make a difference in the lives of the students. This section should not be confused with the rationale. The knowledge structure deals with concepts whereas the rationale deals with reasons. The third major concept focuses on the relevance of the information to society as a whole. Here the teacher would develop concepts that focus on the impact the information has on the decisions made by society as a whole, by the government, or by governmental agencies. Following each of the three major concepts are three minor concepts that expand on, but do not duplicate, the major concept. Ideally, the third of these minor concepts builds a bridge to the major concept that follows.

The teacher can promote student interest and participation in the unit by taking the time to build a rationale. The rationale should take the form of a monologue to a student and should present facts and ideas that the targeted student would be likely to find interesting and persuasive. The rationale is, in essence, the teacher's best attempt to persuade students that the unit will be worth their time and effort.

Once this conceptualization has been completed, the teacher can prepare an instructional unit. A typical unit plan has a title page indicating the title of the unit, an estimation of time required for the unit, the name of the course for which the unit was designed, and the academic grade level for which the unit was designed. The next page typically consists of a brief overview that describes the concepts and facts to be presented and a brief description of preceding and following units (to place the unit in the overall structure of the course). Next, the teacher includes a rationale to explain, from the viewpoint of the student, what benefits will be gained (this will probably be the same rationale that the teacher put together while developing the knowledge structure). Following this is a list of the precise instructional objectives of the unit. These objectives should reflect a variety of cognitive or psychomotor levels.

The bulk of the unit will consist of the facts, definitions, examples, explanations, and anecdotes, in outline format, that students will need to achieve the objectives. These should be gleaned from a variety of sources, including the text for the course, college texts, and similar resources. Most teachers continually update the content sections of unit plans, so they find it useful to cite the sources of their information. These sources should be cited either in a bibliography intended for student use or in a bibliography intended for the teacher's use.

The next section of the unit plan typically consists of the learning activities. These might be organized in a general outline, in separate lesson plans, in broad categories such as introductory, developmental, and concluding, or (in keeping with the knowledge structure) in terms of database development, utility, and social significance. The unit should also include appropriate instructional media.

The next section should include optional activities. These should take the form of either remedial activities intended for students who are having difficulty with the regular instruction or enrichment activities intended for students who are more advanced than the bulk of the students. The enrichment activities can help the student move ahead of the class, perhaps into a new unit or into a unit that the rest of the class will not have time for (vertical growth) or help them learn more about the content of the unit being worked on (horizontal growth).

The last section of the unit consists of the evaluation instruments that will be used to determine the extent to which the objectives have been achieved. Those instruments should include the actual answer keys, model answers, or checklists that will be used.

SO HOW DOES THIS AFFECT MY TEACHING?

If someone told you that you had to drive from Chicago to San Francisco, it is likely that you would want to look at a map. You would want an overview of the trip and you would want to plan routes and travel times. When students walk into your room they know that they will be studying a particular subject area, but they, too, would like an overview of the "trip." They want to know what the final destination is and how they will reach that destination. The syllabus, with its objectives, grading criteria, and tentative content outline and calendar, provides that overview. Further, the syllabus puts all of the relevant information into the hands of the students at the very beginning of the course so students can do some planning on their own. They can work ahead, bring work in for feedback, and help themselves be successful. Planning a syllabus takes time and effort on your part, but it gives the students a road map that can help them stay on the route to success.

Unit plans help you at least as much as they help students. Just as a well-planned syllabus adds to your confidence that appropriate time has been allocated for the achievement of the course objectives, well-planned units add to your confidence that each instructional block is relevant to your subject area, your students, and to society as a whole. Further, since you will have built into the units a variety of learning activities, you will be reasonably sure that student interest will be stimulated and maintained. Perhaps most important of all, although your students will never know how much time you put into the plans, students will notice that the semester or year is progressing smoothly with a succession of interesting and relevant activities. It will become clear that you cared enough to do your homework, to do what you could to help ensure that students will be successful. Students are not fools; they typically respond well to those who try to help them.

KEY TERMS, PEOPLE, AND IDEAS

Limited time, about 180 school days

Course syllabus—overall plan including objectives, grading criteria, and tentative content outline and calendar

Johann Herbart—Preparation, Presentation, Association, Generalization, and Application

Knowledge Structures—Needs of the subject area, students, and society

Unit Plans—Objectives, content, teaching–learning activities, optional activities, and evaluation procedures for a two- to four-week block of instruction

FIGURE 10.1   **Sections of a Possible Syllabus for a Secondary Education
Methods Class**

SECONDARY EDUCATION, C&I 216
Spring, 199_, 4 semester hours
Instructor: Michael A. Lorber, Ph.D.

Phone Numbers			Office Hours: DeGarmo 212
Office:	DeGarmo 212	438–2839	Mon. & Wed.: 1:15—3:30
Dept. of C&I:	DeGarmo 232	438–5425	
FAX Number		438–8659	Other Times by Appointment
Home (Before 9:00 p.m.)			(I encourage you to come in to discuss
E-Mail: malorber@ilstu.edu			drafts of your work and any concerns.)

Overview

This course focuses on four major units: planning, teaching, evaluating, and
classroom management. The planning unit includes an examination of major
educational philosophies and learning theories, the development of educational goals in the United States, and writing instructional plans. The unit on
teaching focuses on selecting and using a variety of instructional procedures
and tools to stimulate and maintain student interest and higher-level
thought. The unit on evaluation focuses on learning how to write and use
objective and subjective tests, how to develop other evaluation procedures,
how to interpret and communicate performance results, and teacher evaluation. The unit on classroom management focuses on the purposes of classroom management, philosophical issues, specific techniques, and legal
issues. Students will practice planning, teaching, and evaluating in
microteaching and actual classroom settings.

Course Objectives

To earn grade of D in this course you must:
A. Recall and apply information concerning educational philosophies, the
goals of education, learning theories, instructional models, and the
structure and classification of objectives well enough to answer correctly
at least 60 percent of a series of multiple-choice questions concerning
these topics.
B. Demonstrate the ability to construct mini-units that match textbook content with goals that have intellectual, personal, and societal significance
for students in their future outside of school by:
1. Writing a rationale that, in no more than two pages, uses facts, examples, and cause–effect reasoning to explain to *students* (a) why the
content to be learned is an important segment of a course or subject
area, (b) how it will enable them to better understand and deal with
the world around them and, (c) why it is of current concern to society.

2. Writing instructional objectives that (a) contain an observable, terminal behavior and minimum acceptable standards of performance, (b) reflect each major level of the cognitive domain, (c) show a logical progression through an instructional unit, and (d) have clear out-of-class applicability.

3. Writing, for each of three sequential, 20-minute lessons and three sequential 55-minute lessons, a plan no longer than a page and a half that includes (a) a precise instructional objective at the Comprehension level or higher, (b) the content necessary for students to achieve the objective, (c) a variety of learning activities that explain the steps to be followed in teaching the lesson and which across the lesson incorporate both large- and small-group activities as well as a range of mediated instruction, and (d) the needed materials other than those normally found in a classroom.

C. Recall and apply information concerning the selection and use of instructional procedures and materials well enough to answer correctly at least 60 percent of a series of multiple-choice questions concerning these topics.

D. Teach three 20-minute lessons in a microteaching setting and three 55-minute lessons in a high school classroom, following the approved plans.

E. Analyze instruction holistically and with respect to specific skills by accurately describing, on a *Teaching Skills Analysis Form*, the strengths and weaknesses of specific activities and teaching skills for each lesson taught and observed.

F. Demonstrate the ability to systematically and objectively evaluate the extent to which students have achieved stated objectives by:

1. Recalling and applying information concerning the principles of (a) measurement and evaluation, (b) characteristics of teacher-made tests, (c) calculating, interpreting, and reporting grades, and (d) teacher evaluation, well enough to answer correctly at least 60 percent of a series of multiple-choice questions concerning these topics.

2. Constructing a multiple-choice test that: (a) samples the content included in an instructional unit, (b) consists of six questions, each with four choices, (c) includes two analysis-level questions, and (d) meets the criteria for questions as described in typical measurement and evaluation texts.

3. Constructing a one-item essay test that: (a) samples the content included in an instructional unit, (b) asks a question at the analysis or synthesis level, (c) includes content-based, D–A grading criteria, and (d) includes a model answer.

G. Demonstrate the ability to use word processing, spreadsheet, and database programs.

H. Recall and apply information concerning classroom management goals and procedures, Maslow's Hierarchy of Needs, behavior modification techniques, and legal aspects of classroom management, well enough to answer correctly at least 60 percent of a series of multiple-choice questions concerning these topics.

Grading Criteria

A. Grades will be based on the number of points accumulated on unannounced quizzes, multiple-choice tests, written work such as objectives, lesson plans, and analyses, and actual teaching. The lowest grade on a 100-point test or paper will be dropped.*
B. Dependability and effort will be graded by giving each student ten points for dependability and promptness, but deducting ten points for each unexcused absence and five points for each tardiness.
C. Five extra points can be earned for written work that is turned in, for the first time, free of spelling, grammatical, structural, typographical, and format errors. Five points will be deducted if there are three or four errors, and ten points will be deducted if there are more than four errors.
D. Ten points per calendar day will be deducted for work turned in after class time on the due date.
E. Specific requirements and grading criteria for each assignment, along with the general format to be followed, are in the *Supplemental Materials.*
F. Final grade categories will be determined by multiplying the maximum points possible, excluding Extra Credit points, by the following percentages: Lowest A = 90%, Lowest B = 80%, Lowest C = 70%, Lowest D = 60%.

Tentative Content Outline and Schedule

Week 1—Introduction, Educational Philosophies and History
A. Discuss syllabus
B. Educational philosophies—Greeks, Perennialism, Essentialism, Progressivism, Existentialism
C. Broad goals—Why the schools are as they are
D. Assignments:
   1. Study Ch. 1–4 in the text.
   2. View *Productivity and the Self-Fulfilling Prophesy: The Pygmalion Effect.* This 30-minute tape is on reserve in the Media Resource Center, 6th Floor, Milner Library.

Week 2—Learning Theories, Instructional Models, and Rationales
A. Learning theories—Behaviorism, Field Theory, Cognitive, Constructionism
B. Structure and use of unit plans, content outlines, and knowledge structures
C. Tyler's Rationale—Needs of the subject area, students, and society

D. Instructional models—GMI, Goal-Referenced Instructional Model, LIM, ASSURE
E. The structure, advantages, and disadvantages of precise instructional objectives
F. Assignments:
   1. Write a rationale for the three-lesson microteaching mini-unit. Specific format requirements, grading criteria, and an example for this assignment are in the "Unit Plan/Rationale" section of the *Supplemental Materials*. See last page of syllabus for due date.
   2. Study Ch. 5 and 6.
   3. Complete *The Structure of Precise Instructional Objectives via CAI*, and *The Cognitive Domain via CAI*. These computer-assisted instruction (CAI) programs take about 20 minutes each to complete and are available in the College of Education Microcomputer Lab, DeGarmo 309.
   4. Write one objective at each of the six major levels of the cognitive domain. Specific format requirements, grading criteria, and an example for this assignment are in the "Cognitive objectives" section of the *Supplemental Materials*. See last page of syllabus for due date.

Week 3—Writing and Classifying Precise Instructional Objectives
A. Classifying objectives via *The Taxonomy of Educational Objectives*
B. Objectives for students with special needs
C. Adapting objectives/content for different populations
D. Cognitive objectives due
E. Review for Test One
F. Assignment: Study for Test One—Ch. 1–6, notes, CAI material, and videotaped material. See last page of syllabus for test date.

.
.
.

Week 14—Principles of Classroom Management and Maslow's Hierarchy
A. Test Three—Bring two sharpened, No. 2 pencils with erasers
B. Principles and goals of classroom management
C. Maslow's Hierarchy of Needs

Week 15—Behavior Modification
A. Behavior modification—operant conditioning and reality therapy
B. Legal Issues
C. Review for Test Four—Ch. 12 and notes

Week 16—Current Issues
A. Test Four—Bring two sharpened, No. 2 pencils with erasers
B. Current Issues (Where the jobs are, Inclusion)
C. Complete departmental form for evaluating instructors

Summary of Important Dates and Points
NOTE: Students are encouraged to turn work in BEFORE the due date.

				Possible	*Got*
Week	2	Jan.	26	Rationale (Due Thursday, by 1:00)	100	
Week	3	Feb.	01	Six cognitive objectives	100	
	4		06	Test 1—Goals, Theories, Objectives	100	
Week	6		20	Test 2—Instr. Procedures and Media	100	
Week	6		23	Microteaching lesson plans (Due Thur., by 1:00)		
				Concept 1	100	
				Concept 2	100	
				Analysis Level	100	
Week	10	Mar	20, 22, 24, 27, 29, 31 Microteaching		
			31	TSAFs—Due after microteaching (25 x 3)	75	
Week	12	Apr.	06	Three LSFE lesson plans—due date is flexible		
				Plan 1	100	
				Plan 2	100	
				Plan 3	100	
				Six-item objective test (Due Thur. by 1:00)	100	
				One-item essay test (Due Thur. by 1:00)	50	
Week	14		17	Test 3—Measurement and Evaluation	100	
Week	16	May	01	Test 4—Classroom Management	100	
				Typed course/instructor evaluation		
			Quizzes 25, 25, 25, __, __	75	
			Attendance	10	
			Subtotal of points	1510	
			Drop lowest grade*	−100	
			TOTAL POINTS	1410	
			Extra Credit	+ 50	

*If a test is missed, that grade is the one that must be dropped. Quizzes may not be made up.

FIGURE 10.2   Sample Knowledge Structure, Written by Kenneth D. Lovett, September 1988

FORMING THE EARTH'S CRUST

I.   The Earth's surface is affected by many dynamic forces and processes, such as internal heat, solar radiation, meteorite impact, and human activity, all of which continually change its appearance.
     A.   Internal heat affects the surface by causing volcanism, plate tectonics, mountain building, and earthquakes.
     B.   Solar radiation, acting on the atmosphere and surface of the Earth, causes erosion by wind, water, and ice.
     C.   Human activities, particularly the expansion of agriculture and urban areas and the retrieval of natural resources, have accelerated many changes in the Earth's surface.
II. Individuals can do relatively little to alter the natural factors that shape the land but, via conservation efforts, they can help to preserve or improve landforms, and by increasing their understanding of the formation of landforms they can better understand the interactions between the land and the people.
     A.   Homes that are built or landscaped to capitalize on natural features are generally more comfortable and less costly to live in than homes not so built or landscaped.
     B.   Farmers who practice conservation tillage tend to preserve the topsoil on their property while decreasing their expenditures for fuel and herbicides.
     C.   By better understanding the relationship between the kind of land on which people live and how those people live, we may gain a better understanding of the interactions among the peoples of the world.
III. Advancements in technology have enabled us to make significant changes in the Earth's topography and, therefore, we need to consider the long-term and global effects these changes might produce.
     A.   High levels of emissions from factories and motor vehicles are posing problems ranging from an increase in average temperatures worldwide (due to the "greenhouse" effect) to the accelerated erosion of priceless artifacts.
     B.   Harnessing natural power sources, such as wind, water, nuclear energy, and the Sun, will result in the conservation of fossil fuels and the preservation of the land surrounding them.
     C.   Large-scale earth-moving projects, such as damming or changing the direction of rivers, can affect people thousands of miles from the site of the project, so their needs, too, should be taken into consideration before the project is begun.

FIGURE 10.3   Abbreviated Unit Plan, Written by Kenneth D. Lovett, September 1988

SHAPING THE EARTH'S SURFACE

I. Overview
    This unit will explore the natural and manmade processes and forces that shape the Earth's surface as seen today.
II. Rationale
    Ever wonder why there are no mountains in the Midwest or why there are volcanoes in Hawaii and on the west coast but none on the east coast? These are just some of the topics to be discussed in this unit.
III. Objectives: Upon successful completion of this unit, the student will be able to:
    A. List the major physical features of the Earth's surface, how they were formed, and what effect these features have on mankind. (Comprehension)
    B. Describe at least three ways in which modern technology has influenced the ongoing changes of the Earth's surface. (Comprehension)
    C. Take a position for or against strict laws protecting the environment and defend your position by citing relevant facts and/or using cause–effect arguments. (Evaluation)
IV. Subject Matter
    A. Dynamic forces of the Earth
        1. Plate tectonics has been continually changing the surface of the Earth for millions of years.
            a. Evidence supporting this phenomenon
                (1) Mid-oceanic ridge
                (2) Fossil remains
                (3) Matching continental coastlines
            b. Physical features created by this process
                (1) Deep ocean trenches
                (2) Continental margin mountain ranges
        2. Volcanism and mountain building processes are continually increasing the elevation of the surface of the Earth
            a. Volcanic activity can result in two types of eruptions
                (1) Explosive
                (2) Nonexplosive
            b. The type of eruption determines the shape of the resulting cone
                (1) Cinder cone
                (2) Shield
                (3) Composite

    B.   Human influences on the Earth's surface
       1.   Changes brought on by agricultural processes
          a.   Removal of natural vegetation
          b.   Increase of erosion processes
       2.   Changes brought on by urban expansion
          a.   Alteration of land by construction
          b.   Changes in wind patterns due to high-rise buildings
V.   Materials and Experiences
    A.   Dynamic forces of the Earth
       1.   Materials
          a.   Overhead and slide projectors
          b.   Transparencies of tectonic forces and plates
          c.   Slides of different types of volcanoes and mountains
       2.   Experiences
          a.   Use lecture and discussion to communicate content
          b.   Use overhead projector and transparencies to explain concepts
          c.   Use photographs and slides to provide illustrations

ENDNOTES

    1. Boorstin, Daniel J., and Brooks Mather Kelly, *A History of The United States* (Lexington, Mass.: Ginn and Co., 1981), pp. vii–viii.

    2. Zirkel, Perry A., "Courtside: Students as Consumers," *Phi Delta Kappan,* Vol. 76, no. 2 (October 1994), pp. 168–171.

    3. Herbart, Johann F., *Texbook of Psychology* (New York: Appleton, 1894).

    4. Whitehead, Alfred North, *Essays in Science and Philosophy* (New York: Philosophical Library, 1947), p. 176.

11

PLANNING DAILY LESSONS

RATIONALE

Lesson plans are useful because they enable teachers to take the overall instructional strategy exemplified in a unit plan and divide it into segments that can be completed (conveniently and logically) in single class periods. Further, lesson plans help ensure that teachers include in their lesson all that they intended to include, and that students leave the room with a sense of accomplishment. This chapter will help you learn about some of the basic components of lesson plans, the steps for writing lesson plans, and some of the arguments against lesson plans. Despite the arguments of dissenters, being able to construct and follow good lesson plans will take you a long way toward helping your students, and thus yourself, be successful.

SAMPLE OBJECTIVES

You will be able, in writing, to:

1. List at least three components of a lesson plan. (Knowledge)
2. Given a precise instructional objective, describe at least two instructional activities that are logically associated with the objective and explain how these activities will help students achieve the stated objective. (Application)
3. Take a position for or against requiring student teachers to construct daily lesson plans and, in no more than two pages, defend that position by citing relevant facts and using cause–effect reasoning. (Evaluation)
4. Construct, for each of three sequential lessons of a given time length, a plan no longer than two pages that includes: (a) a precise instructional objective at the comprehension level or higher, (b) the content necessary

for students to achieve the objective, (c) a variety of instructional activities that explain the steps to be followed in teaching the lesson and which, across the lessons, incorporate both large- and small-group activities as well as a range of mediated instruction, and (d) the needed materials other than those normally found in a classroom. (Synthesis)

LESSON PLAN COMPONENTS

A lesson typically consists of an instructional objective, a block of content sufficient to enable students to achieve that objective, instructional activities that detail the activities in which students will engage to learn the content, the instructional materials needed to facilitate learning, and sources.

Objectives

The main source of objectives for daily lesson plans should be the list of objectives generated for the course or unit. Since these terminal objectives typically represent fairly complex behaviors, it is likely that each will need to be divided into a series of less complex, **enroute,** objectives. These will be the day-to-day objectives that help students develop, in some logical order, the needed skills and knowledge.

To be most effective, enroute objectives should be written so that students can clearly see some out-of-class applicability. One way to do this is to focus on concepts and skills rather than on isolated facts, incidents, or literary works. For example, rather than focusing on Herman Melville's *Moby Dick* as a novel in and of itself, focus on *Moby Dick* as an example of stories that deal with obsession and revenge. Not many students are likely to encounter a white whale in or out of class, but most will encounter feelings of obsession or revenge. A sea-going story written in 1851 can, with the right emphasis, be highly relevant to students today.

When developing enroute objectives it is important to think in terms of the time available for each class period. When people complete a task, whether it is shoveling a driveway, mowing a lawn, dusting a house, or baking a cake, they derive a sense of accomplishment by completing the task. Students are people. If you write enroute objectives so that they can be completed in a single class period, students will be able to walk out of the room feeling that they accomplished something, that they took a small but definite step toward reaching the final goal. That is a good feeling for students to have and it is within your power to provide it. Students come to your class day by day. Plan lessons that can be accomplished day by day.

Sometimes lessons do carry over to a second day. While this is usually less desirable that completing each lesson in a single class period, it is not a fatal flaw. Plans can be made to work in a two-, three-, or even four-day time frame. However, it should be noted that stopping properly in mid-lesson is easier said than done. Under ideal circumstances, lessons include closure, a summary, review, and at least a sampling of student competence. This kind of lesson provides students with a feeling of accomplishment and serves as an impetus to further learning. Some elements of the ideal lesson will have to be omitted or at least modified if the lesson is carried over to a second day.

In order to break a lesson into segments of two or more days, the teacher needs to build into the lesson plan a series of possible stopping points. This is almost the same as writing a series of mini-lesson plans, but if it is done, and if the teacher keeps close track of the time, it is possible to summarize, review, and lay the groundwork for the next day's work.

Keeping track of time is important in all lessons. If the teacher goes off on some tangent and then realizes, at the end of the period, that there are still a few points that need to be covered, he or she may end up trying to make those last points after the class should be over and half the students are out the door. Conversely, teachers who end up with extra time at the end of a lesson will need to deal with the classroom management problems that typically occur when students are not actively engaged in meaningful activities. More will be said about how to estimate time in the learning activities section.

When writing objectives, keep in mind that it is likely to be impractical to have students individually demonstrate the expected skills or knowledge. To do so in most cases, each student would have to write something, and this would consume too much time if done every day. An alternative is to have the objective call for an oral demonstration. This enables you to randomly call on students to explain a major point or to demonstrate all or part of a skill. While you cannot be sure that the performance of the randomly chosen students accurately reflects the abilities of all other students, it is a reasonable and practical way to sample competence at the end of most lessons.

Content

The content section of a lesson plan should include all the information students need to achieve the objective. This means that all of the needed names, dates, facts, figures, definitions, explanations, cause–effect relationships, and even examples, should be there. There are at least three reasons for making the content section so complete.

First, people often temporarily forget information, even if they know it well. For example, you may have had the experience of being asked for a name or a phone number, not being able to recall it the time, but then having it spring to mind hours later. It is almost as though your mind continued searching for the name or phone number past the time you needed it and called you back when it found it. When that happens socially it is simply a bit embarrassing and frustrating. If it happens to you in your classroom, it could be highly embarrassing. If you have the needed information in the lesson plan, a quick glance at the plan solves the problem.

Second, you are likely to have more than one section of a class. What may happen is that in your first section you will cover all the information you intended to cover. However, in later sections, since you will remember having covered certain points, you may not cover them "again." The problem would become apparent when students in the earlier sections were able to use certain information or skills and students in later sections were unable to do so. Having all the content in the plan and following the plan with each section will help avoid this problem.

A third problem concerns substitute teachers. If all goes well, you and your family will remain healthy. Even so, it may become necessary for you to miss a day or two of school and a substitute teacher will be called in. Typically, the substitute teacher will be reasonably competent and both willing and able to follow well-made lesson plans. Therefore, well-made lesson plans can help avoid the loss of instructional time.

What has just been said concerning completeness should not be misinterpreted. You should not, for example, try to write into a lesson plan every single thing that will be covered. You are not writing a script, you are listing highlights to help ensure that crucial points are not forgotten or unintentionally omitted.

To make the content most useful it should be arranged in a word or phrase outline and organized, with appropriate headings, to help students learn. The idea is to construct the plan so that you can conduct the lesson smoothly. A word or phrase outline makes it easy to glance down to check a fact or to see that nothing is being omitted. If the plan is too detailed you will end up looking at it so much that students will begin to wonder if you know what you are talking about or if you are just reading material from the plan. This would be unfortunate, because you will know what you are talking about. There is no reason to jeopardize the confidence that students have in you by trying to find information in an overly detailed or poorly organized lesson plan.

The actual form of the plan will depend on the teaching–learning activities selected. A lecture, for example, is facilitated best by a word or phrase outline of factual information. A discussion moves most smoothly if the plan consists of key statements, examples, and pivotal questions with possible answers. Activities such as demonstrations or experiments can progress smoothly if the content consists of procedural steps and descriptions, whereas art lessons might require limited verbal but extensive visual content, such as slides or pictures. Regardless of the form of the content, it should still contain the minimum data students need to achieve the objective.

Some instructional objectives require that students demonstrate a skill that is not dependent on specific content. For example, suppose the objective calls for students to write a precise instructional objective at each level of the Cognitive domain so that each objective builds logically on its predecessor. Aside from the technical information about the structure of precise instructional objectives, the content of the objectives could concern any subject area.

Trying to concoct hypothetical content, other than for use as examples, would be pointless. In lessons of this kind, providing the basic factual information and guidelines for practice may be all that is needed.

Instructional Activities

This is the section of the lesson plan where you mentally walk through the lesson, planning and allocating time for each step. The time allocation for each step should be written in the left margin or in a column specifically left for that purpose. It is likely that you will make changes in the plan as you develop it and as you consider the advantages and disadvantages of specific activities. As you make changes, remember to change the time allocations and to keep track of the total length of time planned and available.

In a lesson, the first thing most teachers must do is to check attendance and report absences. In most states, you are legally responsible for students assigned to your class unless you report that they are absent. This should take no more than a minute. A seating chart may be helpful. Some teachers then allow another minute or two for announcements and/or the collection of homework.

The lesson actually begins with a set induction that lasts a minute or two. A good set induction does more than get the students' attention. A shout or slamming a book on a desk top can do that. A good set induction stimulates interest, actively involves the students, and provides a lead into the lesson but, again, it lasts only a minute or two.

The next step is to communicate the objective. Some teachers simply explain what students will be able to do at the end of the lesson. Others find it useful to write the objective on the board and to leave it there throughout the period. In either case, the objective should be stated in terms of what students will be able to do, as opposed to what the teacher wants (therefore, do *not* say, "At the end of the period I want you to be able to...." Instead say, "At the end of the period you will be able to..."). It is also a good idea to have one or two students paraphrase the objective. This helps ensure that students understand what is intended. The communication of the objective, and the provision of any needed feedback, should take only a minute or two.

From this point on, the range of activities is limited only by your own creativity. Here is where you choose to lecture or to use small-group activities, to have a discussion or to use video tape or, perhaps, CAI. The activities should facilitate student achievement of the lesson's objective and should include a closure to build bridges to previously learned content and to content yet to come. The evaluation should at least sample the extent to which students have achieved the objective.

As each activity is listed, record the estimated time for it in the time column. Since these are estimates, try to avoid blocks of less than three or four minutes (except for the taking of attendance, set induction, and communication of the objective). Be sure to add up the minutes to see that all the available time is accounted for. Beginning teachers tend to overestimate the time needed for various activities and thus end up trying to improvise in order to use up excess time. A safer course of action is to include a separate sheet of additional content that is relevant to the objective and can be used to fill unexpected free time. It is better to have too much material than not enough.

Evaluation

In the description of instructional activities, one activity should be student demonstration of the stated competence. Because of limited time, oral explanations are often more practical than having each student write or do something. Ultimately each student will need to apply the skills and knowledge to achieve the terminal objectives. The evaluation component should contain space for the teacher to write comments concerning student achievement of the objective, the reaction of the class to particular activities, and possible ways in which the lesson could be improved.

Closure

A lesson should not end because the end-of-period bell rings. It should end because the teacher and students have completed the planned activities. The last of these activities should include linking the information and/or skills just learned to previously learned information and/or experiences and to information and experiences yet to come. This is consistent with the thinking of the field theorists and of educators such as Dewey and Herbart. By linking information to known information, students can make better sense of the whole, and by linking information to information yet to come, you help prepare students to learn more.

Materials

It is a good idea to use instructional aids. They help stimulate interest and provide a change of pace. In this section of the lesson plan, list only those materials that will be needed but are not usually in the classroom. For example, do not use time or space to list things such as a chalkboard or an overhead projector if these materials are standard equipment in the room. However, if you need a second overhead projector, a specific video tape, a VCR player, or a large-screen monitor, listing them will remind you to make sure they will be available when needed. Since not all lessons require special materials or equipment, it is not necessary to include this component in every lesson.

Sources

Hopefully, you will be teaching for a long time and, logically, you may well want to use a unit or lesson more than once. You will find it easier to modify, extend, or update material if you document, in standard footnote or endnote format, the sources of your information as you build them into the original plans. Think about the times you wrote term papers, included a particular fact or quote, and then wasted hours trying to find its source because you forgot to document it as you used it. Avoid the problem. Document as you go. Using at least two current sources helps ensure that the information is accurate.

It should be noted that despite the best made plans, a lesson may still not be successful. You can do your part and even more, but you cannot do the students' part. If they choose not to cooperate, the best plans in the world will be ineffective. However, students are not fools. They want to be successful, so the surest way to encourage their participation is to show them how the skills and knowledge to be learned will be of practical utility to them, how the skills and knowledge can help them deal with life and problems outside of school. Relevance, relevance, relevance = success, success, success.

Miscellaneous Components

Since lesson plans reflect the needs of the teachers who write them, not all plans have the same components. Virtually all plans include the components described previously, but other components can be added. For example, the date, title of course and/or subject, grade level, and title of the unit can be added, and sections for homework assignments and special announcements can also be added.

Length

As a student teacher and as a certified teacher, planning may pose a problem. On one hand, you will want plans that are complete enough to function as useful guides. On the other hand, logic and experience will tell you that you that (1) you will not have time to generate three- or four-page plans for each lesson, and (2) long plans are more cumbersome to use than shorter plans. A good rule of thumb is to keep the entire plan to less than two pages.

ARGUMENTS AGAINST LESSON PLANNING

Although the reasons for lesson planning are strong, there are still some who argue against such plans. They point out that:

1. Lesson plans are largely unnecessary since most teachers already know what and how they are going to teach.
2. Once teachers go to the trouble to write a lesson plan, they tend to follow that plan closely, rather than feeling free to capitalize on immediate student interests.
3. Planning lessons takes an inordinate amount of time, and this time could be better spent doing content-area research or gathering instructional material.
4. The presence of a lesson plan can cause complications when a teacher chooses to deviate from the plan and an administrator expects the plan to be followed.
5. Once a series of lesson plans is written, if any lesson goes much more quickly or slowly than was anticipated, subsequent plans must be modified or scrapped, thus wasting time and effort.

If you have the choice of constructing lesson plans or planning as you go, consider the following points. First, classroom management problems are most likely to arise when students have nothing meaningful to do. A well-planned lesson helps ensure that students will be engaged in meaningful activities throughout the class period.

Second, many shcool systems and individual principals require teachers to prepare lesson plans, and some go so far as to require that those plans be approved before they are implemented. This requirement was not made lightly. It was made to help ensure that lessons go well and that students are engaged in meaningful activities directly related to approved objectives.

Third, and perhaps most important, when teachers are well prepared they feel more at ease and confident. This confidence comes more easily after years of experience, but even student teachers can, and will, feel confident if they can make sound lesson plans and check them with their cooperating teacher. The confidence they gain will be noticed by their students and will help the students have confidence in them.

SAMPLE LESSON PLANS

Having examined typical lesson plan components, we will look next at how they might be combined into a lesson plan. The sample plans cover a variety of subject areas and include a variety of formats. All are workable and useful, but they are only samples. Other structural formats are possible for the plans and other learning activities might be equally effective in helping students achieve the same objectives. The comments in parentheses are included to help explain the various components. They would not be included in an actual lesson plan.

SAMPLE 1: Concept Lesson

UNIT: Input, Output, and Storage Devices

CONCEPT: Input Devices

OBJECTIVE: You will be able to orally describe how two computer input devices operate to enter data into a computer. (Comprehension)

CONTENT
Input devices and modes include at least the following:

1. **Punched cards** (virtually obsolete).   Either a beam of light activating a photoelectric cell or a metal brush is used to detect the presence or absence of a hole at each predetermined spot on a card. This information is converted into electrical impulses.
2. **Punched paper tape** (virtually obsolete)   Analogous to a continuous punched card; however, the metal brush cannot be used because of the weakness of the paper tape.
3. **Magnetic tape.**   Spaces on a strip of magnetic tape are magnetized or demagnetized and then "read" by a device sensitive to magnetic fields.
4. **Magnetic ink.**   Characters are printed in ink containing a magnetic substance. When the characters are "read" they are compared with precoded characters. When a match occurs, the computer recognizes the character and converts its value into a series of electrical impulses. Used extensively on checks.
5. **Optical Character Readers (Scanners).**   Can convert characters printed on a page to digital form for transfer to a computer file. From there the data can be handled as if it had been entered from a keyboard. Tests and student work can be scanned into word processing programs and modified as needed.
6. **Universal Product Code Readers.**   Can read the bar codes printed on virtually all products and convert them to digital form for use in pricing and inventory control programs.
7. **Optical Scanners.**   Marks made in pencil at small, but specific, spots on a sheet of paper are "read" via reflected light and converted to a series of electrical impulses. Optical scanners are used extensively to machine-score tests.
8. **Scientific Instruments.**   Most instruments now used by scientists are either monitored or controlled by computers that accept data either in digital or analog form.
9. **Touch Screens.** By touching a screen at a given location the user intercepts infrared beams. The computer reads the point of interception and uses that data to continue the program.
10. **Profile scanners.**   Uses a TV-like device to convey images to a computer for comparison against a series of precoded images. When matches occur the data are acted on. Used to guide some missiles, to enable robots to move about freely, and for crude personnel identification.

INSTRUCTIONAL ACTIVITIES

Min.
1   1. Take attendance.
2   2. Begin by showing students a mark-sensing form and asking if anyone knows how information gets from it into a computer. Briefly discuss responses and,

if no one knows, explain that a beam of light is reflected off the shiny graphite marks at specific locations and is converted into electrical signals to the computer. (It is not likely that many students would know how information is taken from a mark-sensing form, so their interest might well be stimulated and their answers would provide active involvement. Another idea would be to show students a blank check and one that had cleared the bank and ask them about the difference in the number of magnetic ink characters at the bottom of the check.)

1   3. Explain the objective and ask one or two students to paraphrase it to verify understanding. Provide additional explanations as needed.

2   4. Ask students to list devices used to enter data and list them on board as mentioned. (To the extent that students can list devices they will be actively involved, and they may also list some devices that the teacher had not included.)

5   5. Ask students to explain operation of listed devices. If they are not sure how devices work, provide needed information. When the explanations are complete, erase board. (Students might not be able to explain the operation of the devices they name, but some might be able to do so. Giving them the opportunity to demonstrate their knowledge will help build their self-esteem. If students name a device with which the teacher is unfamiliar, the teacher should acknowledge the fact and tell the class that he or she will find out how that device works. Be sure then that this is done and that the information is shared with the class. This can be a useful experience since it demonstrates to students that teachers, too, continually learn.)

1   6. Show Transparency A listing the input devices included in content section and check off those discussed.

20 7. Use Trans. 1–10 to explain each remaining device in the content section. (The operation of each device should be described on a separate transparency. This will make it easy to discuss only those not already discussed.)

5   8. After operation of each device has been explained, turn off overhead and review by asking students to recall main points. Provide corrective feedback as needed and praise all reasonable responses. (A student-driven review is usually more helpful for students since they will hear each major point explained by a peer rather than explained again by the teacher.)

5   9. Ask students to list all of the ways that information is, or could be, fed into a computer in the school.

3 10. Close by explaining that new input devices are continually being developed to meet new needs, but that in all cases, it is necessary to convert information into electrical signals so that they can be processed by computers.

6 11. To evaluate, ask volunteers to name a computer input device and explain how it enters data into a computer. Get at least six devices listed. Provide corrective feedback as needed and praise all reasonable answers. (The length of this lesson, as planned, would be about 50 minutes. The times allocated for each activity are only estimates. Students' questions or comments may take more or less time than planned. Nevertheless, it is a good idea for beginning teachers to estimate the length of time for each component to help avoid grossly miscalculating the time required for the lesson.)

50

MATERIALS: Overhead projector and transparencies. (List only those materials that are not ordinarily in the classroom. Do not list materials such as chalkboards or chalk unless there is a specific reason to do so.)

SAMPLE 2: Concept Lesson to Be
Carried Over to the Next Day

UNIT: Romantic Literature

CONCEPT: Characteristics of Romanticism

OBJECTIVE: You will be able to orally explain at least two characteristics of Romanticism. (Comprehension)

CONTENT
1. Definition: Romanticism is a way of looking at life and at oneself with a state of mind centered around emotions.
2. Major characteristics of Romanticism
   A. A return to "nature" (clean air, water, walks in the woods)
   B. Sympathy for rural life and its activities (dealing with nature and a few friends)
   C. Sentimental contemplation
   D. Predominance of imagination over reason (good will toward all, peace on earth)
   E. Idealization of the past (the "good old days," or the "Golden Age of...")
   F. Concern for all that is aesthetically beautiful in the ideal sense
   G. Praising of childhood (with its innocence and enthusiasm)
   H. Idealization of women (soft, caring, nurturing, feminine)
   I. A wish to explore the personal inner world of dreams and desires (soul searching)

INSTRUCTIONAL ACTIVITIES

Min.
1   1. Take attendance.
1   2. Begin by showing students pictures of a jackhammer and a sunset and asking what thoughts each picture brings to mind. Briefly discuss answers.
2   3. Ask two students to paraphrase the objective written on the board. Provide feedback as needed.
5   4. Explain, exemplify, and discuss the term "Romanticism."
6   5. Show five-minute segment of an original *Star Trek* episode featuring emotionless Mr. Spock.
15   6. Lead discussion of value of emotions and introduce various points listed in content section if they are not brought out by students. Use overhead to list the points as they are made.
10   7. Divide class into groups of four or five students and tell them to prepare a three-minute skit for presentation the following day. Assign some groups to prepare skits portraying people as they normally are, and other groups to pre-

pare skits portraying people as very machine-like and emotionless. Allow time for skit preparation to begin.

3   8. Review by asking students for the major characteristics of Romanticism.

3   9. Close by explaining that the next day, the three-minute skits will be presented and the feelings they arouse will be discussed as a way of further exploring the idea of Romanticism.

4   10. To evaluate, ask students to cite and exemplify characteristics of Romanticism.

50

MATERIALS: Star Trek video tape featuring Mr. Spock, VCR player, large-screen monitor

---

The next plans are for a sequence of three 20-minute micro lessons. The first two plans are for concept lessons intended to help students understand a concept. The third is for an analysis lesson intended to enable students to engage in higher-order thinking and to use the information they learned.

SAMPLE 3: Concept Lesson One
(20-Minute Micro Lesson)

UNIT: Organizing the Elements of a News Story

CONCEPT: The Lead

OBJECTIVE: You will be able to orally describe the function of any of the five Ws, (who, what, when, where, and why) that are typically in a news story lead. (Comprehension)

CONTENT

1. The first paragraph of a news story is called the lead.
2. The lead tells *who* did it, *what* happened, *when* and *where* it happened, and perhaps *why* it happened.
3. Good reporters find answers to each of these questions, determine the most important fact (key thought) answered by these questions, and build lead around this key fact.
   A. *Who?* Should be answered first when a person is the most important or interesting factor in the story.
   B. *What?* Should be answered first when what happened is the most important or interesting factor in the story.
   C. *When?* Should be answered first when the time of the occurrence is the most important/interesting factor in the story.
   D. *Where?* Should be answered first when the place of occurrence is the most important/interesting factor in the story.

   E. *Why?* Should be answered first when the reason for the action will attract the attention of the greatest number of readers.

4. All essential facts should be included in the first paragraph.

INSTRUCTIONAL ACTIVITIES

Min.

1　1. Begin by showing two sentences on the overhead projector and asking students which one they think is the more interesting and why. Briefly discuss responses.

1　2. Explain the objective and ask a student to paraphrase it.

4　3. Using Trans. A, define and discuss the elements used to build a news story lead.

2　4. Use Trans. B. to show two news leads. Ask students to identify differences and similarities between them.

5　5. Distribute handout that explains when each of the five Ws should be used as the first key item in the lead. Discuss each of the general rules and provide examples using Trans. C–F.

3　6. Review by asking students to provide one hypothetical example for each of the five key-thought leads discussed. An example of a "where" key thought lead is: The Jefferson High School Gymnasium will be the site for the boys' basketball final playoff next March.

1　7. Close by returning to the first Trans. used in lesson and discussing the reasons why one of the two examples is clearly a more effective lead for a news story.

3　8. Evaluate by asking students, at random, to describe the function of one of the five Ws.

20

MATERIALS:　Transparencies and handout

SAMPLE 4: Concept Lesson Two
(20-Minute Micro Lesson)

UNIT:　Organizing the Elements of a News Story

CONCEPT:　The Body

OBJECTIVE:　You will be able to orally describe at least two characteristics of a well-organized news story.

CONTENT

1. Organizing the body of a straight news story requires that the reporter weigh each factual element related to a story and determine its news value to the story.

2. The lead is the most newsworthy idea in the story and should, therefore, be explained first. The paragraphs immediately following the lead should amplify and expand on the key thought in the lead.

3. The paragraphs following the appropriate explanation of the key thought should include other details and facts arranged in order of descending importance.

4. Having the broadest, most important part of the story at the top, with facts of lesser importance beneath, is called the inverted pyramid style.
5. Each paragraph should contain information about a single detail or fact.
6. Paragraphs should be organized so that specific information is presented first and secondary detail (amplification) is presented later.

INSTRUCTIONAL ACTIVITIES

Min.

2   1. Read short news story to the class and then ask students to choose which of four symbols drawn on the chalkboard best represents the organization of the information contained in the story. Briefly discuss responses.

1   2. Ask two students to paraphrase the lesson's objective written on the board.

3   3. Using Trans. A, discuss the characteristics of a well-written inverted pyramid news story.

4   4. Distribute handout that diagrams the inverted pyramid approach to organizing the elements of a news story. Discuss the order of descending news value in each paragraph.

4   5. Show Trans. B–E of short news stories with paragraphs in random order. For practice, ask students to place paragraphs into descending order of importance.

2   6. Review by asking students to list, in order, the characteristics of a well-written inverted pyramid news story.

2   7. Close by explaining that the organization of the elements in a news story is a natural extension of logic (once you gather the facts, determine the relative importance of each fact).

2   8. Evaluate by asking students, at random, to describe elements of a well-organized news story.

20

MATERIALS: Transparencies, handout

The next sample differs from the previous samples in two important ways. First, the lesson is intended to immediately follow the preceding lesson (Sample 4) and second, it is an analysis lesson. Note the difference in the structure of the content section. Each question includes the distinguishing characteristic or quality being sought and each can be answered either yes or no. However, these questions are *not* those that are asked in class. These questions are those that you would ask yourself if you were making the analysis. The idea of the analysis lesson is to use cueing questions, when needed, to help students arrive at the questions in the content section. In this case, you are trying to lead students to discover, on their own, the key questions that they should ask themselves in order to organize the key elements of a news story.

It is important to keep in mind the fact that students should do the analyzing. It is easy to deprive students of the opportunity to think for themselves by telling them too much during an analysis lesson. The point of the lesson is not to show students how easily you can make the analysis. The point is to help them learn which questions to ask themselves so that they will know how to make similar analyses on their own. Therefore, do not lecture, review, or tell. Ask cueing questions that lead students to discover important points for themselves. This helps students learn to learn.

SAMPLE 5: Analysis Lesson
(20-Minute Micro Lesson)

UNIT: Organizing Elements of a News Story

SKILL: Analyzing the Elements of the Inverted Pyramid Style News Story

OBJECTIVE: Given two news stories, determine which is the better example of the inverted pyramid style and cite examples from both stories to support the decision. (Analysis)

CONTENT

1. Does the lead clearly and concisely answer the questions asked by the five Ws (who, what, when, where, and why)?
2. Does the lead accurately focus on the key thought (the most important or interesting fact) answered by the five Ws?
3. Is the key thought amplified and further explained in the paragraph(s) following the lead?
4. Are the secondary facts/details of the story organized in order of descending importance?
5. Does each paragraph focus on, or contain information about, a single detail or fact?
6. Could the story stand on its own if the final two or three paragraphs were deleted?

INSTRUCTIONAL ACTIVITIES

Min.

2   1. Begin by showing two news stories (Trans. A & B) and asking students which would be better to submit to the news editor of the local newspaper. Discuss students' reasons for choosing one over the other and write some of the reasons on the board. (Story A is clearly a better example of the inverted pyramid style.)

1   2. Explain the objective and ask a student to paraphrase it.

4   3. Show Trans. B and ask students how the elements might be changed to conform to an inverted pyramid style. Provide cues leading to the questions in the content section, as needed.

4   4. Show Trans. C & D and have students explain which of the two is better and why. Provide as little assistance as possible.

4   5. Show Trans. E & F and have students explain which of the two is better and why.
4   6. Evaluate by showing students Trans. G & H and having students explain which of the two is better and why.
1   7. Close by pointing out that the key to writing cogent news stories is first understanding the reasoning for organizing the elements in the inverted pyramid style.

20

MATERIALS: Two overhead projectors and transparencies

DIFFERENT FORMATS

All of the sample plans shown thus far follow the same outline format. There are other formats that work as well. The following is an example of part of a plan that uses a different format.

Hour or Grade: 9:00   No. of Students: 25   Activity: Soccer   Date:_____

Instructional Objective	Facilties and Equipment
Psychomotor: Dribble the soccer ball around 3 cones placed 10 feet apart using the proper form.	Half a gym
Affective: Demonstrate cooperation by controlling your own ball so that it does not interfere with others' practice.	6–8 Soccer balls 8 cones
Cognitive: Orally identify the importance of dribbling around a defender and pushing the ball down the field.	

Min.	Learning Activities, Teaching Strategies, Management Tasks	Content Emphasis
3	*Warm-ups*	*Point of Emphasis*
	Formation: Students will spread out in two lines. One student will be asked to lead exercises.	Make sure ankles are nice and loose because you are going to use them a lot.
	Exercises: Student leader will be asked to lead class in three exercises that will work parts of the body that are used in the game of soccer (legs, ankles, & arms).	Make sure you feel a pull in the back of your legs.

Min.	Learning Activities, Teaching Strategies, Management Tasks	Content Emphasis
3	*Set Induction* Formation: A semi-circle will be formed around the instructor (no matter how many students). *Method of Presentation:* Direct *Objective:* To help the student learn a basic soccer skill—dribbling. *Transition:* Tell students to go to a soccer ball that is already positioned on the floor.	*Value of Skill* Touching the ball in any direction Moving the ball Being prepared to cut to the left or right Hooking it backward in order to evade a defender Starting or stopping
5	*Pacing: Drill #1* *Content Information* Making friends with the soccer ball *Method of Presentation* Direct with teacher demonstration *Management Tasks* *Organization* Students are in a group of an unlimited number spread throughout half the gym. *Equipment* 1. Students obtain equipment by squads. 2. 1 ball for each player *Directions* Students should take the ball for a walk, jog, or run. *Transition* Have students stop practicing to receive instructions for the next progression of the skill.	*Rules* Keep look-out for other students so there are no collisions. No bouncing, kicking, or any other activity that does not pertain to the specified drill. *Analysis of Skill* Use the inside of the foot (between the big toe and heel). Follow through Weight forward *Points of emphasis* Touch the ball gently Push the ball Relax the foot *Common errors* Using the wrong part of the foot Kicking the ball instead of using an easy push *Cues* Start the ball! Stop the ball! Control! Nice and easy!

Courtesy of Dr. William Sparks and the Teacher Education faculty in the Department of Health, Physical Education, Recreation, and Dance, Illinois State University.

SUMMARY

Appropriate preparation is one of the most important components of effective teaching. Lesson plans demonstrate that planning. The following checklist includes the components that will help make a lesson plan a useful document.

I. Objective
   A. Clearly specifies an observable terminal behavior and a minimum acceptable standard.
   B. Can be classified at a specific and appropriate cognitive or psychomotor level.
   C. If an analysis-level objective, it specifies what is to be analyzed.
   D. Is relevant to students and has some practical or long-term usefulness.
II. Content
   A. Contains accurate information and, where appropriate, examples and anecdotes.
   B. Goes beyond what is in the students' text and beyond the superficial.
   C. Is complete enough to enable students to achieve the objective and for a reasonably competent substitute teacher to teach the lesson.
   D. Arranged in a word or phrase outline format.
   E. Enough content for the length of the lesson (and a bit more).
III. Learning activities provide for
   A. An appropriate set induction and the communication of the objective
   B. Stimulus variation with respect to modes of presentation (lecture, discussion, etc.) and the appropriate use of media
   C. Practice—analogous and/or equivalent
   D. Review—main points provided by students, not the teacher
   E. Closure—builds bridges to content learned earlier and to content or experiences yet to come
   F. Evaluation—should parallel objective(s)
IV. Materials: Includes all materials needed for the lesson except those normally in the classroom.

SO HOW DOES THIS AFFECT MY TEACHING?

Knowing what you are trying to accomplish and how you intend to accomplish it gives you a sense of confidence. In most cases you will be able to follow your plans as written, and students will not only engage in a sequence of activities that are logically linked and make sense to them, they will also leave the room with a feeling of accomplishment. As long as students feel they are making progress toward a goal that is relevant to them, they will cooperate in the teaching–learning process and, if they do that, both you and they will be successful.

A short-term advantage to lesson plans is that as a student teacher or a beginning teacher, if you bring well-constructed plans to your cooperating teacher or principal you will demonstrate your intention to act profession-ally. Since these are the people who will be evaluating you, getting their input and acting on it can help improve your teaching and your ratings.

12

PREPARING AND ADMINISTERING TESTS

RATIONALE

The main reason teachers evaluate students is to determine the extent to which those students have achieved specific instructional objectives. This information helps students identify areas of strength and weakness and gives them a basis for comparing their abilities to those of other students. The information also provides a basis on which teachers can assess the effectiveness of particular instructional procedures and materials. Further, the data are used by students, parents, other teachers, admissions officers, and employers to make decisions about educational and vocational options. For all of these reasons, evaluation that is as accurate and unbiased as possible is needed.

This chapter begins with an examination of some of the basic principles and terminology related to measurement and evaluation. Its main focus is on ways to prepare objective and subjective tests, administer such tests, and use alternate forms of evaluation. Since the grades students get are the most frequent cause for student and parent concern, this chapter, and the following chapter that focuses of calculating and interpreting grades, should be of particular interest to you.

SAMPLE OBJECTIVES

You will be able, in writing, to:

1. Define terms such as measurement, evaluation, reliability, validity, objective and subjective as they apply to measurement and evaluation. (Comprehension)

2. Explain how criterion-referenced and norm-referenced evaluation differ and cite at least one example of how each could be used in your subject area. (Comprehension)
3. Construct a multiple-choice test that: (1) samples the content included in an instructional unit, (2) consists of six questions, each with four choices, (3) includes two analysis-level questions, and (4) meets the criteria for questions as described in typical texts that deal with measurement and evaluation. (Synthesis)
4. Construct a one-item essay test that: (1) samples the content included in an instructional unit, (2) asks a question at the analysis or synthesis level, (3) includes content-based, D–A grading criteria, and (4) includes a model answer. (Synthesis)
5. Develop an evaluation procedure that assesses student achievement with other than an objective or essay test, and includes the specific criteria by which grades of A–F could be objectively determined. (Synthesis)

BASIC TERMINOLOGY

Test

In this discussion, the word test means to sample student abilities. It is essential to recognize that even under ideal circumstances, tests are not perfect instruments and that at any given time, students may have health or emotional problems that will keep them from doing as well as they might. Although we might be able to carry out grade calculations to 20 decimal places, we are still dealing with samples of abilities, not absolute measures. With different questions, or even the same questions but a different day, the sample results might be very different.

Measurement

There is a difference between measurement and evaluation. Measurement has to do with quantifying something by assigning numbers to it. We measure height and weight, but even here, the measures are not exact. Given the fact that educators are trying to assess a complex mix of skills and knowledge, it should not be surprising that the tests, papers, and projects that make up our measurement tools are relatively imprecise. This means that we must engage in evaluation as well as measurement.

Evaluation

Evaluation means making a value judgment. To be as accurate as possible, a value judgment should be based, in part, on whatever measurement data are available, but it should go beyond that data to include assessments about such factors as the student's ability to write and speak effectively, to organize ideas clearly, and similar qualities that defy simple quantification. Evaluations are more holistic assessments than are measurements.

Validity

Neither measurement nor evaluation makes much sense unless we measure and evaluate the right thing. Validity refers to how accurately an instrument measures whatever it is supposed to measure. There are at least three kinds of validity to consider.

Content or face validity reflects the extent to which a test covers what was taught—not what the syllabus or objectives called for, but what was actually taught (hopefully, there will be a perfect match). Teachers sometimes construct tests that seem to cover the content taught but, in fact, do not. For example, if the instruction focused on developing understandings of trends and issues, the test should give students the opportunity to demonstrate their understanding of those trends and issues. If the test focused on specific names and dates, or the grammatical correctness of responses, its content validity would be low.

Predictive validity measures how well performance on one test or task reflects probable performance on other tests or task. For example, the ACT and SAT college entrance exams are given because they provide some insight into the probable success of students in college. Performance on the test is used to predict performance in college. Preassessment tests sometimes have high predictive validity.

Construct validity has to do with the ability of a test to assess psychological constructs such as honesty or tolerance. Teachers do not usually deal with construct validity, but it is useful to know the term because some standardized tests, such as those used by many government agencies and large companies, assess psychological constructs.

Reliability

Reliability refers to how consistently an instrument measures whatever it measures. It refers to the test results, not to the instrument itself. To the extent that the results are reliable, the relative positions of scores will remain the same on repeated administrations of the test or on the administration of an equivalent form of the test. Students who score high on one form will score high on an equivalent form. If the results are not reliable, students who score high on one form may score low on an equivalent form. If you took a senior-level trigonometry test and administered it to a group of freshmen in an English class, the scores would probably be low. They would be just as low if you then administered an equivalent form of the test. The content validity of these tests would be zero, because they did not test what was taught. The reliability, however, would be high because the relative positions of the grades on each form of the test would likely stay the same.

The degree to which a test is reliable is expressed as a decimal known as a reliability coefficient. These coefficients range from the highest degree of reliability (1.00) to the lowest (.00). It is also possible for a test to have a negative reliability coefficient, possibly as low as −1.00. This would indicate that those students who scored highest on one measure scored lowest on the other. Reliability coefficients of .65 and higher are desirable.

Generally, longer tests are more reliable than shorter tests. For example, commercially available tests, such as college entrance exams and standardized achievement tests, frequently have hundreds of items and require hours to complete. Their length contributes to their reliability, because so many questions are asked that it is unlikely that the test will miss large areas of relevant skills or knowledge possessed by the student. If the student took an equivalent form of the test, the same skills and abilities would be assessed and the score would be close to the previous score unless new skills or abilities were acquired between the test administrations.

Because long tests are very time-consuming, teacher-made tests usually do not consist of hundreds of items. A test of about fifty items is long enough to yield reliable results and is not too long for students to complete within a class period. When planning a multiple-choice test, teachers should allow about thirty seconds for each four-choice item. A fifty-item test should take about twenty-five minutes to complete. Since time is needed to take attendance, make announcements, and distribute and collect the test, more time is needed. In order to allow students as much time as possible to recall and apply their skills and knowledge, a full class period should be used for a major test.

The same factors that make longer tests more reliable than shorter ones apply to semester grades. Teachers who use a variety of performance samples including tests, papers, and projects to assess students' abilities can justifiably have more confidence in the reliability of their grades than can teachers who rely on a mid-term and final exam plus a paper or two.

A word needs to be said here concerning grading on the basis of improvement. Some teachers believe that it is appropriate to grade students on the amount of progress that they, personally, made, regardless of whether stated objectives were actually achieved. An example might be for a physical education teacher, at the beginning of the semester, to ask students to run the 50-yard dash or to do push-ups, and to tell them that their final grade will depend on the extent of their improvement. Most students will quickly see that it is to their advantage to do poorly at the outset so that at the end of the semester, it will seem as though they made large gains. The reliability of this measurement technique is not high.

Criterion-Referenced Evaluation

Criterion-referencing means that the grade reflects performance relative to some preset standard. A passing grade means that the standard has been met; a failing grade means that the standard has not been met. For example, the minimum acceptable standard of a precise instructional objective spells out what constitutes a D-level demonstration of a particular ability, assuming that D represents the lowest passing grade. A driving test is an example of a criterion-referenced test. As long as you pass, it does not matter if you get the lowest passing grade or 100 percent.

Since the scores on a criterion-referenced test are either pass or fail, all the items should be about equally difficult. Differences in difficulty levels would be necessary if a spread among scores were needed, but none is. Students either pass or fail the test and, if the instruction was successful, many more students will pass than will fail. Beyond knowing if a score was above or below the minimum passing grade, the exact score does not matter.

The most common applications of criterion-referencing are those in which cut-off scores are established for such things as competence tests and entrance tests. A certain score must be obtained in order to move on or to be considered for admission. Most other forms of evaluation are norm-referenced.

Mastery Learning

Mastery learning is a way of using a criterion-reference point. That point is a specified level of mastery. In its "pure" form, mastery learning requires that instead of holding time stable and allowing achievement to vary within the fixed time span, achievement is held stable and time is extended until the student reaches the desired level of mastery. There are, obviously, practical difficulties in implementing mastery learning in its "pure" form. However, teachers can use the idea of mastery in the traditional time-stable, achievement-varies framework.

In the normal course of affairs, students do an assignment, it's graded, returned, and everyone moves on to the next topic. To the extent that time allows, you can help students improve their levels of mastery and, at the same time, you can make it possible for them to improve their grades. You can do this by letting them redo the assignment and averaging the original grade with the grade on the redone work. While this process does not guarantee mastery, it has a number of advantages.

The most obvious advantage is that if students redo the work, taking advantage of the feedback you provided on the original work, their degree of mastery will increase. Secondly, the averaged grade will be higher than the original grade (if, for some reason it is not, let the student keep the original grade), so the student's semester average will be higher than it might otherwise have been. Finally, and most important, you are giving the students the opportunity to put forth additional effort to help themselves. If, at the end of the semester, some students are not doing well, and if those students did not take advantage of opportunities to redo work, they will find it difficult to blame anyone but themselves for their grades. The opportunity to redo work helps make students more accountable for their own actions. It is a good idea, even if your workload does not permit its use for all assignments.

Norm-Referenced Evaluation

Norm-referencing means that the grade reflects performance relative to the performance of some norming group. A norming group is a group of people who have some relevant characteristic in common, such as grade level or age. The students in a class constitute a small norming group, whereas all high school seniors who take a college entrance examination constitute a large norming group.

Since our society is basically competitive, teachers need data that allows them to rank-order students according to abilities. It is not enough to separate students according to those who can and cannot do something. Finer distinctions are needed, and norm-referenced evaluation provides them. To rank-order students in terms of demonstrated abilities, the teacher must create test items of varying difficulty levels so that differing ability levels can be assessed.

Although norm-referenced tests require items of varying levels of difficulty, they do not require trick questions or questions that deal with trivial points. Most students prefer to do well, rather than poorly, on tests and are willing to study to do so. Their desire to do well will be lessened if the instruction focuses on important skills and ideas but the test includes questions that focus on relatively unimportant points. Students can make a serious attempt to learn important skills and information, but they cannot learn every possible bit of information. What follows are some principles that can help teachers develop effective tests.

BASIC PRINCIPLES OF MEASUREMENT AND EVALUATION

Obtain Enough Samples

Students need feedback in order to identify strengths and weaknesses and the more feedback you provide, the more students are able to correct mistakes and achieve the objectives. On the other hand, it is not practical to test every day and, even if it were, too much testing sends the wrong message to students. It tells them that grades, per se, are all-important. A balance is needed.

Students should not have to go more than a week without feedback concerning their progress. This feedback may take the form of grades on a formal test or paper, comments written on homework assignments, or comments made to individuals during class discussions. The behaviors called for in the objectives dictate the kinds of activities in which students will need to engage and the most appropriate forms of feedback about progress. Since the purpose of the feedback is to help students form or shape their abilities in order to demonstrate specific objectives, evaluations carried out during instruction are known as **formative evaluations.** Evaluation carried out at the end of the instructional unit is called **summative evaluation**—it sums up the skills and knowledge included in the unit.

Obtain Different Kinds of Samples

At the end of each grading period and at the end of each semester or year teachers are required to give each student a grade—a single letter to represent the achievements of weeks and weeks of work. That grade should reflect the student's achievements as accurately as possible. Some of the achievements might be assessed via objective tests such as multiple-choice or matching tests. Other objectives will require students to use skills and knowledge in more creative and holistic ways. To assess achievement of these objectives, teachers use essay tests, papers, and projects of one kind or another. The point is that the accurate assessment of students' achievements requires the use of a variety of assessment techniques.

Another reason to vary assessment techniques is that students respond to assessment instruments in different ways. For example, some students take objective tests well while others "freeze up" on such tests. Some students write well, while others are more adept at demonstrating their knowledge orally. Still others are better at completing projects that require the utilization of knowledge, such as constructing a tape–slide sequence or manipulating a hypothetical stock portfolio. If only one or two assessment techniques are used, the real extent to which students have mastered skills and knowledge may be masked by their reaction to the assessment mode itself. A variety of assessment techniques is needed.

Drop the Lowest Grade

There is another advantage to frequent assessments. They make it possible to drop a low grade. Tests only sample skills or knowledge and these samples can be flawed by factors such as less-than-perfect test items or a student's health when the test was taken. If you have ten or more samples of each student's skills and knowledge, you can afford to drop the lowest grade. Dropping the lowest grade will not seriously distort a student's achievement pattern, but it will help minimize the effects of a low score, regardless of the reason for that score. Knowing that the lowest grade will be dropped acts as an incentive for students to continue working, despite the low grade. They know that their averages can always be improved and, just as important, they know that even though you did not have to do it, you did something extra to help them succeed.

Assess Student Effort

The issue of student effort is one that troubles many teachers. On one hand, it is necessary to have students' grades reflect their actual achievements. On the other hand, it does not make good sense for teachers to ignore honest effort of the part of students even if it does not translate into adequate achievement levels. One way to reflect effort and attitude is to report them in supplementary comments. This may help students' morale, but it will not help their grade.

Another approach is to provide a way for students to earn points by demonstrating effort. For this technique to work, students must be able to demonstrate extra effort as opposed to additional content-area work or greater ability. The difference is significant. Students who are not doing well in your class are not likely to be able to do additional content-area work or demonstrate greater ability. The reason they are not doing well in the first place is because they are having difficulty with the content and tasks already required. Make it possible for them to earn extra credit by doing things they can do.

One way to do this is to award extra points, perhaps five, for every paper that is turned in with no spelling, punctuation, or grammatical errors. These errors most often reflect carelessness rather than lack of ability, so students could earn the extra points by simply taking the time to proofread their work carefully. Whatever extra credit work is available must, in fairness, be available to all students. Do not inadvertently structure it so that only the better students can take advantage of it.

In order to keep achievement and effort points separate, the points for effort should *not* be added to the grade for the paper. They should be reflected by a separate notation on the paper. If a student got 75 points out of 100 for achievement and the full five points for effort, the grade on the paper should appear as 75/100 +5. Use a separate column in the grade book to keep track of the extra points each student accumulates. Since all students have the same opportunity to acquire the extra credit points and the awarding of those points is objective, the total number of points each one earns is a fair measure of effort demonstrated.

Use Quizzes

For purposes of this discussion, quizzes are short tests, usually consisting of one to ten questions, which students complete in less than ten minutes. In an ideal world, all of your students would come to class every day prepared for the work at hand. Since we do not live in an ideal world, it is possible that some of your students will choose to attend to other matters rather than preparing for your class. You do not have to like this situation, but you do have to recognize it and deal with it.

One way to encourage students to prepare for your class is to build into your syllabus, and announce on the first day of class, that a short quiz will be administered at the beginning of each class period. The point value of each quiz will be small, perhaps just five or ten points, but the fact that students know they will be taking the quiz may act as an incentive for them to prepare.

Some teachers prefer to use surprise quizzes. The possible use of such quizzes should be included in the syllabus. During the discussion of the syllabus, students can be told that the surprise quizzes are a kind of Damoclean sword. Since the possibility of a surprise quiz is always there, it is wisest for them to come to class prepared every day.

Whether announced or surprise quizzes are used, you can increase their incentive value by dropping the lowest quiz grade and/or by allowing the sum of the quiz points to substitute for a low grade on a test or paper. Your interest is not so much in the quiz grades themselves as it is in encouraging students to come to class prepared.

PAPER-AND-PENCIL TESTS

Paper-and-pencil tests are not the only kind of assessment instruments that teachers should use, but they will probably be the most common. There are three basic reasons for this. First, paper-and-pencil tests present the same task to all students under the same test conditions. This means that the test results provide a reasonable basis for sampling and comparing student progress and/or ability with respect to the relevant skills and knowledge. Second, paper-and-pencil tests generate products (students' responses) that are easily stored. This means that the tests and the results can be kept readily accessible for analysis or review either to improve the test or to explain to students or parents how a grade was determined. Third, paper-and-pencil tests can be used equally well to broadly sample students' knowledge or to probe deeply into particular areas.

OBJECTIVE TESTS

Questions that require true-false, multiple-choice, matching, or completion answers are called forced-choice or "objective" tests. They are forced-choice because students are forced to select or construct responses from a given or very limited range of options. They are "objective" only in the sense that there is no need to make value judgments about the answers. They are clearly either right or wrong. There are, however, many value judgments made during the construction of objective tests. For example, it is the teacher who decides which questions to ask, how many questions to ask, and what vocabulary to use. These judgments are largely value or subjective judgments.

Objective tests are popular for a number of reasons. First, such tests are intended to sample broadly, but not deeply. Rather than asking one or two questions, which might be the "wrong" questions for some students, objective tests ask many questions about different aspects of the topic, thus sampling students' knowledge more broadly. The typical analogy is to compare objective tests with digging post holes in a field. You dig a lot of holes, but none are very deep. By contrast, essay tests are analogous to digging wells. Very few, but very deep. Further, objective tests are easy to score and they lend themselves well to item analyses, so teachers can continually improve items and develop a test bank of valid and reliable questions.

Objectives tests encourage students to focus on, and organize, pieces of information rather than focusing on the whole. This could result in students' knowing isolated facts but having little idea of the relationship of those facts to each other or to the whole. This problem can be minimized or avoided by writing questions that require students to use information rather than simply recall it. For example, rather than asking a series of questions that require the recollection of the amount of cholesterol in various foods, ask a question in which students look at two recipes and determine which one contains the least cholesterol. Here they use information in a practical way, rather than simply recalling it.

General Rules

What follow are some general rules that can guide the construction of good objective test items.

A. *Keep the objective clearly in mind.* For example, a terminal objective might call for students to recall and apply information concerning educational philosophies, the goals of education, learning theories, instructional models, and the structure and classification of objectives well enough to answer correctly at least 60 percent of a series of multiple-choice questions concerning these topics. If so, be sure all questions relate directly to one or another parts of the objective.

B. *Keep the language simple.* Unless the purpose of the test is to survey the extent of students' vocabularies, there is no point in using words that are unfamiliar to students or in phrasing questions so they are difficult to understand. Students will be justifiably angry and frustrated if they get answers wrong because they did not understand what was being asked, rather than because they did not know the right answer. Compare the following two examples:

> 1a. The physical relationship between most petroleum products and most purely aqueous solutions is generally such that physical interaction and diffusion of the two is severely limited.   (A) True, (B) False.
> 1b. As a general rule, oil and water do not mix.   (A)True, (B) False.

It should be noted that it *is* appropriate to expect students to become familiar with the jargon associated with particular subject areas. It would be unfortunate, for example, if a chemistry student kept visualizing little furry creatures every time the instructor mentioned the word mole (a unit of measurement in chemistry). However, there is a difference between using appropriate jargon and using overly complex or unfamiliar words and phrases. Ask questions as simply and concisely as possible to help ensure valid and reliable test results.

C. *Ask students to apply, rather than to simply recall, information.* If students can apply the information they learned, it is likely that they have committed it to memory. It does not follow, however, that because students have memorized information they can also apply it. This being the case, it is better to write questions at the Application level than at the Knowledge level. Consider the following examples:

> 2a. The area of a rectangle is found by multiplying the length by the width.
>   (A) True, (B) False.
> 2b. A room 10 feet wide and 12 feet long has an area of 22 square feet.
>   (A) True, (B) False.

The computation involved in example 2b is not difficult, yet it enables students to apply what they learned and thus emphasizes learning for the sake of practical application rather than learning for the sake of passing tests.

D. *Make sure that each item is independent.* Check questions to be sure that one question does not provide a clue to some other question or that the answer to one question is not crucial to the answer of another. Both situations decrease the reliability of the test results. For example,

> 3. The number of square feet in a room 12 feet long and 12 feet wide is:
>   A.   24.
>   B.   48.

    C. 98.
    <u>D</u>. 144.
    E. 240.
4. At $10.00 per square *yard,* what would it cost to carpet the room described in question three?
    <u>A</u>. $160
    B. $240
    C. $480
    D. $980
    E. $1,440

Given these two questions, any student who missed question three would almost certainly miss question four. Other than having the student miss two items instead of just one, nothing was gained by linking the questions. It would have been more advantageous if questions three and four had been combined, for example, "How much would it cost to carpet a room 14' x 12' if carpeting costs $10 a square yard?" The extra space could be used for a separate and distinct item.

E. *Do not establish or follow a pattern for correct responses.* Regardless of how clever an answer pattern is, some student will eventually discover it and compromise the test results. The problems involved with detecting compromised tests and doing something about them are far greater than any possible advantage to patterning responses.

F. *Do not include trick or trivial questions.* Sometimes teachers are tempted to ask questions that require extended effort for correct interpretation or that deal with unimportant points. This temptation may stem from being unable to build items as quickly as one would like, or from a desire to ensure a wide spread among test scores.

When used, trick or trivial questions not only reduce the validity and reliability of tests, but they may have a powerful negative effect if they antagonize students.

G. *Be sure that there is only one correct or clearly best answer.* When you go over the test with students, they are likely to have questions. You will be able to satisfy most students if you are able to go through items and explain why each wrong answer is, in fact, wrong. However, whether an answer is right or wrong should never come down to your saying, "Because I said so," or "Because that is what it says in the text." You should be able to cite more than one source for specific facts and you should give students the option of bringing in other sources if they believe those sources justify their answer.

H. *Avoid trivia.* A test uses valuable instructional time, so use that time to emphasize crucial points. Consider the following:

    5a. The first microcomputer was the:
        <u>A</u>.   Altair 8800.

  B.   Apple.
  C.   Radio Shack Model I.
  D.   Commodore PET.
  E.   IBM PC.
5b. The "computer revolution" began when the first fully assembled micro-
     computers became commercially available in the:
  A.   early 1960s.
  B.   late 1960s.
  C.   early 1970s.
  <u>D.</u>   late 1970s.
  E.   early 1980s.

For most students, knowing that the Altair 8800 was an assemble-it-
yourself microcomputer available in 1975, is of less long-term value than
knowing that the "computer revolution" began in the late 1970s, when
microcomputers first became commercially available. Ask questions that
have long-term value.

Multiple-Choice Items

Multiple-choice items are particularly useful because they can sample cognitive skills ranging from simple recall through analysis. The following
examples illustrate several levels of cognition.

Knowledge

The purpose of Knowledge-level questions is to have students recall information, but be sure that the information to be recalled is worth remember-
ing. If students are asked to recall information that they perceive as relevant
and useful, they are more likely to take the teacher and the course seriously.
Consider the following.

6. Which of the following domains described in "Bloom's" taxonomy is most
    concerned with the acquisition and manipulation of factual information?
  <u>A.</u> Cognitive
  B. Intellectual
  C. Affective
  D. Empirical
  E. Psychomotor

Comprehension

The purpose of Comprehension-level questions is to have students translate
from one symbol system to another, to interpret (put into their own words),
or to extrapolate (go beyond the data given). Consider the following.

7. "Milton! Thou shouldst be living at this hour; England hath need of thee;
    she is a fen of stagnant waters"—Wordsworth.

The metaphor, "She is a fen of stagnant waters," indicates that Words-worth felt England was:
A. largely swampy land.
B. in a state of turmoil and unrest.
C. making no progress.
D. in a generally corrupt condition.

Application

The purpose of Application-level questions is to have students apply skills and knowledge to problems and situations that are new to them. Consider the following:

8. The scores on a test were 95, 90, 90, 85, 70, 60, and 0. What is the mode?
   A. 47.5
   B. 70
   C. 81.66
   D. 85
   E. 90

Whenever possible, anticipate the mistakes the student might make. In example eight, 47.5 is the mean of the highest and lowest scores, 70 is the mean, 81.66 is the mean of the middle three scores, and 85 is the median. The advantage of creating options in this way is that you can use the students' wrong answers to diagnose the source of their difficulty.

Analysis

The purpose of Analysis-level questions is to have the student engage in higher-order thinking. This can be done by having the student examine a whole, looking for its constituent elements, for relationships between and among elements, or for organizational patterns. Depending on the objective, the "whole" could be a poem, a musical excerpt, an editorial, a hypothetical situation, a picture, or even a rock sample, but it is necessary that students be given something to examine that requires careful analysis. Further, to help ensure that Analysis-level thinking is taking place, it is useful to have the student identify the true state of affairs and why it is the true state of affairs. Consider the following:

9. John came down with the flu three weeks ago from an outbreak at school. He got over it about a week ago, but now his brother Tim has come down with the same viral infection. John would like to visit Tim but is not sure if he should. John should be told:
   A. not to spend too much time with Tim because his own immune system could be exhausted from fighting the virus the first time.
   B. not to visit Tim because his own cells will have stopped producing interferon by now.

C. to visit Tim because his own helper T-cells will remember how to fight the virus properly.

D. to visit Tim because his own red blood cells will remember how to produce a specific kind of interferon that combats the virus.

10. The Education for All Handicapped Children Act of 1975 (Public Law 94–142) requires that all handicapped children be educated and that they be educated in the least restrictive environment. Which of the following was the most critical assumption made by the drafters of the legislation?

A. That all students would be willing to be in the "least restrictive environment" in order to be in compliance with the law

B. That regular classroom teachers could provide for the needs of handicapped students about as well as could the special education teachers

C. That sufficient funds would be available since special education students frequently need special materials

D. That special education teachers were not doing a very good job with their students so the students should be placed in regular classrooms whenever possible

Principles for Writing Multiple-Choice Items

A. *Put as much of the item as possible into the stem.* The stem of a multiple-choice question is the part that asks the question or states the problem. Typically, students read the stem once or twice, but they read the options many more times. You can reduce their reading time, thus allowing more thinking time, if you put most of the reading material in the stem. Further, if the stem does its job properly, it gives the student an idea of what is sought before reading the options. Consider the following.

11a. The term "junk" food:

A. refers to a food that has few essential nutrients but high caloric value.

B. refers to a food that has neither essential nutrients nor caloric value.

C. refers to a food that has both high nutritive value and high caloric value.

D. refers to a food that has both high nutritive value and low caloric value.

11b. The term "junk" food refers to foods that are _____ in nutrients _____ in calories.

A. low/but high

B. low/and low

C. high/and high

D. high/but low

In example 11a, the options contain repetitive words, which not only take students time to read, but might also confuse them. Rather than writing options that contain repetitive words, build those words into the stem where they will only have to be read once.

In example 11b, the options are shorter than the stem (which is, itself, a good guide), the stem clearly and concisely asks the question, and it provides sufficient data to help the student start thinking about the correct answer.

B. *Make options plausible.* When testing, you are not trying to trick students, you are trying to differentiate between those who know and those who are pretending to know. You want all options to look reasonable to someone who is unsure of the information. In example eight, you saw how to anticipate the kinds of mistakes students might make and build options on that basis. This can help create plausible options.

You must also take care that students cannot safely ignore options because they are so clearly wrong. Going back to example 11b, you can see that option D is clearly a wrong choice and will be ignored by students. Something that is high in nutrients and low in calories is not likely to be considered "junk" food. Writing options such as this wastes your time and the students' time.

C. *Beware of grammatical clues.* Sometimes teachers point to right answers with inadvertent grammatical clues. For example, the word "an" is almost always followed by a word beginning with a vowel. The word "a" is almost always followed by a word beginning with a consonant. A student who knows this basic rule may be able to use it to identify correct choices or to eliminate incorrect choices. You can avoid the problem by using "a(n)" rather than "a" or "an." Another grammatical clue is the inappropriate use of singular and plural forms of words.

D. *Length may be a clue.* In trying to add enough information to make the right answer right, teachers tend to make that option longer than the others. This, itself, may be a clue to students who are just guessing. Check to be sure that all options are about the same length.

E. *Avoid "always" and "never."* It is safest to operate on the premise that there is likely to be an exception to every rule. This being the case, there is little reason to use "always" or "never." Students are generally safe ignoring options that specify "always" or "never," and they know it. Those words constitute an unintentional clue.

F. *Use "all of the above," and "none of the above" with care.* The use of "all of the above," is weak because as soon as students see any two correct answers they know that "all of the above" must be the correct choice. The use of "none of the above" is sometimes useful to see if students have confidence in their knowledge. For instance, in example eight the correct answer (E), could have been replaced with "none of the above." Students who knew what the mode was, would recognize that it was not listed. Students who were unsure would likely go back and select one of the wrong choices.

G. *Focus on the rule rather than the exception to the rule.* When students study for a test they try to learn the true state of affairs, what is, rather than what is not. When writing questions, write them so they call for the true state of affairs, rather than for the exception. Consider the following:

12a. Which of the following are <u>NOT</u> parts of a central processing unit?
    <u>A</u>.   RAM units
    B.   Resistors
    C.   And/or gates
    D.   Transistors
12b. Which of the following is part of a central processing unit?
    A.   RAM
    B.   A monitor
    <u>C</u>.   And/or gates
    D.   A keyboard or other input device

If it is necessary to use a negative, be sure to call attention to it by capitalizing and underlining it. Students will be looking for what is, rather than the exception. Help them notice the change in focus or, better yet, reword the question so the negative is eliminated.

H. *Check for correct spelling and punctuation.* Proofread each question and its choices to make them as easy to read as possible and to eliminate errors. Any time that you make a spelling or grammatical error, students are likely to notice and, during a test, that distraction wastes time for the students.

If the stem is part of a statement that will be completed by one of the choices, it should end with a colon. In this case, each choice should begin with a lowercase letter and end with a period because the stem, plus the choice, will form a complete sentence. See examples 3, 5a, 5b, 7, 9, and 11a.

If the stem is a complete question, it should end with a question mark (for example, "Which of the following best describes a CPU?"). In this case, the choices would begin with capital letters but would not end with periods unless they were complete sentences. See examples 6, 10, 12a, and 12b.

I. *Make "visual packages."* Your intent should be to help students do as well as possible on the test. You can make things a bit easier for students if each question and its options makes up an easy-to-read "visual package." After writing the stem, skip a line between it and the choices. This makes it easier for students to separate those components. List choices one under the other on separate lines. This takes more space than listing them, separated by commas, on one or two lines, but it makes it easier for students to consider them. Then, be sure to keep entire questions (stem and choices) together on a single page. If there is not room on a page for the stem and all the choices, move the entire question to the following page. This will eliminate the need for students to flip back and forth and will reduce the chance of students' missing an option altogether.

True/False Questions

True/false questions are often singled out as prime examples of the superficiality of objective testing, and they often stand justly accused. Superficiality, however, is not an inherent weakness. True/false questions can be written at the Comprehension, Application, and even Analysis levels. Consider the following.

Knowledge
13. Most high school teachers who use computers for their own preparation work use the computer for word processing.   (A) True, (B) False

Comprehension
14. The statement $X + Y - Z$ is the equivalent of $Z - Y + X$.   (A) True, (B) False

Application
15. A man earning $250 a week would earn $13,000 a year if he worked every week.   (A) True, (B) False

Analysis
16. If every teacher were given his or her own computer, the most difficult problems currently limiting wider use of computer-assisted instruction would be solved.   (A) True, (B) False

Any superficiality in true/false questions is there because the teacher failed to use the tool properly. However, it is true that students who have no idea of the correct answer still have a one-in-two chance of guessing correctly. Their chance of guessing correctly drops to one-in-four on multiple-choice questions with four questions, and to one-in-five when the questions have five options. Given the 50:50 chance of guessing correctly on true/false test questions, many teachers prefer to use multiple-choice questions. If you do choose to write true/false questions, the following points may help.

1. *Be sure that every item is wholly true or wholly false.* Consider the following.
   17. Most high school teachers who use computers for their own preparation work use the computer for word processing and database management. (A) True, (B) False

While it is true that most high school teachers who use computers for their own preparation work use them as word processors, it is not true that they also commonly use them for database management. The fact that the statement is partly true and partly false could result in unnecessary arguments.

2. *Whenever possible, avoid such terms as "generally" and "usually."* These terms, while not as obvious giveaways as "always" and "never," are still open to varying interpretations.

Matching Items

Matching items are used most easily to measure low-level cognitive skills such as recall and comprehension. A typical matching test might ask students to link people with events or dates. Variations include asking students to match terms with numbers on a diagram or to match labels for a chart, graph, or map in which such labels have been replaced by letters or numbers. Guidelines for the construction of matching items follow.

1. *Keep the number of items to be matched short.* If students are required to search through more than ten or so items as they respond to each question, they will spend valuable time just searching. Their time would be better spent responding to another series of items in another question.
2. *Make sure that all items concern one topic.* Unless all items are concerned with one topic, students can simply eliminate some options as being irrelevant to some questions. This reduces the reliability of the test.
3. *Include more possible answers than questions or stipulate that some answers may be used more than once or not at all.* These steps will minimize the possibility of students arriving at the right answer via the process of elimination.
4. *Arrange the options in some logical order such as chronological or alphabetical.* This will make it easier for students to search through the options and will help avoid providing unintentional clues.

Completion Items

Completion items depend almost entirely on the student's ability to recall a key word or phrase. This poses two problems. First, most secondary school teachers are after more than rote memorization. Second, teachers recognize that many people, particularly while in stressful situations such as a test, have difficulty recalling specific words, names, or dates. For these reasons completion items are not used as frequently as other kinds of test items. Here are some points to keep in mind if completion items are written.

1. *Write items that can be completed with a single word or a short phrase.* There is a difference between a completion item and an essay exam. When students are required to fill in more than a word or two, the grading of the item is complicated and it ceases to be a completion item.

2. *Be sure that only one word or phrase can correctly complete the sentence.* In a phrase such as, "The first World War began in _____." either a date or the name of a country could be correct. Guard against this by trying different words or phrases to see if there are correct alternatives. Revise each item until only the word or phrase sought can be used correctly.
3. *Put the blanks near the ends of the sentences so the student is guided toward the correct response.*
4. *Make all the blanks the same length.* Sometimes unintentional clues are provided when teachers try to make the size of the blanks correspond to the size of the word or phrase to be inserted. The items should be clear enough to make this kind of clue unnecessary. Make all blanks the same size—usually five or six spaces.
5. *Do not put more than two blanks in any item.* The more blanks in the item, the greater the chance the student will be unable to determine just what is sought.

Preparing Tests and Students

Regardless of the type of objective test used, there are some things that teachers can do to help students succeed. First, divide the test into discreet sections and order the sections, and the questions in them, so they reflect the order in which the information was originally presented or learned. This makes it easier to verify that the test reflects the major topics covered and that the number of questions per section is proportional to the amount of time spent on that topic in class. People tend to remember sequences better than isolated facts, so if the test questions follow the same sequence as the original instruction, students will find it easier to remember specifics than if questions about those specifics appear randomly throughout the test.

Second, schedule major tests for a Monday and conduct a formal review session, with the test in hand, on the preceding Friday. The review session helps the students focus on the ideas and information that will be tested. They should be told how many sections and questions are on the test, what each section will cover, how many questions will be in each section, and the type of questions that will be included (multiple-choice, true/false, etc.). They should also be told how many points the test will be worth, how much time they will have for the test, and that they should bring sharpened pencils with erasers, and work to do if they complete the test early. Giving students this information will help reduce their anxiety. There are fewer unknowns.

In going over the information included in each section, teachers should proofread the test again to be certain that there are no questions on the test that have not been covered in class or in assigned readings. Students may also raise questions that did not occur to them during the course of instruction so these, too, can be answered.

Scheduling tests for the beginning of a week, and reviewing at the end of the previous week, works to the advantage of students because it gives them the weekend to study. All of these steps will help students succeed.

SUBJECTIVE (ESSAY) TESTS

Essay tests are useful in assessing students' abilities to synthesize and evaluate because they call on students to gather, organize, interpret, and evaluate data, draw conclusions, make inferences, and express their thoughts coherently. However, essay tests are inherently biased in favor of those students who can write quickly, neatly, and effectively. They also take considerably longer to grade than objective tests. Since teachers often deal with about one hundred students per day, it should not be surprising if more objective, than essay, tests are given. Nonetheless, you are likely to use essay tests at some point and the following principles will help make those tests effective instruments.

Principles for Constructing Essay Tests and Reviewing

1. *Be definite about what is expected from students.* As questions are formulated, keep in mind the types of thought processes in which students are to engage, and the types of points that should be included in their responses. Consider the following.

   18. Discuss the effects of World War II.
   19. In your opinion, what was reflected by the Republican wins in the House and Senate in 1994?

   Example 18 provides so little direction that students would not be able to formulate precise answers. Some students might concentrate on military effects, others on social effects, others on technological effects. The structure of the question is too broad. Depending on the teacher's intent, some students would find they had included some of the appropriate information while others would find they had not—even though all might have been able to formulate acceptable answers had they known more precisely what the teacher expected.

   Example 19 presents an even worse problem: it asks for an opinion. Opinions may differ from one another, but that does not make some right and others wrong, regardless of what may have been covered in class or in outside readings. Teachers who ask for opinions should be prepared to award every answer full credit. For example, a perfectly acceptable answer to question 20 might be, "Not much."

2. *Describe the task clearly.* Provide sufficient direction so that if students have the necessary information they will be able to formulate acceptable answers. Compare the preceding two examples with the following example.

20. Outbreaks of the flu are an all too common occurrence in schools, offices, and other places where large numbers of people, in close quarters, come into daily contact. Assuming the environment is reasonably sanitary, explain what factors, other than those listed above, are necessary for a virus to infect a sizable portion of the population. Also explain how a virus of this sort infects individuals, being sure to describe, in order (if there is any), which defenses the host organism will use against the virus and why those defenses will be used.

Here, the teacher is quite clear about what is expected and has described the task clearly. A student who possesses the requisite information should have little difficulty. A student who does not have that information will find it difficult to write anything that makes much sense.

3. *Specify grading criteria.* Specifying grading criteria is a good idea. To do this, make a list of the important, points that would have to be included for the answer to earn a grade of D. These are the points that you expect all students to know. Then, increasingly sophisticated criteria should be listed, ending with the points that only the best students would include in their answers (the A criteria). A partial set of grading criteria for question 20 might include the following.

1. To qualify for a grade of *D,* the student must explain:
   A. That full-scale outbreaks are possible only if a large portion of the population has never been exposed to the virus.
   B. That an individual's first line of defense is the skin and mucous membranes.
   C. At least one secondary line of defense such as phagocytes, helper T-cells, and interferon an individual will use against the virus. Use terminology correctly.
2. To qualify for a grade of *C,* the student must explain the above information and also include the following:
   A. The virus must be displaying a lytic life cycle to be contagious.
   B. A correct description of two defenses, after that of the skin and mucous membranes, an individual could use to fight a virus, but not necessarily getting them in the right order.
3. To qualify for a grade of *B,* the student must explain the above information and also include the following:
   A. The reason a large part of the population has or has not been exposed to or vaccinated against the virus.
   B. A detailed description of the phagocyte and antibody defense mechanisms in correct order of activation with an explanation of why each defense is used.
4. To qualify for a grade of *A,* the student must explain the above information and also include the following:
   A. A detailed description of the interferon defense mechanism in correct order of activation and a correct explanation of why the defense is used.

    B.   A correct identity of the part of the virus' life cycle the defenses attack.

4. *Write out a sample A-quality answer.* This step is helpful two ways. First, by writing out the response yourself, you get some idea of how long it takes to do the job. You can then use that information, together with your knowledge of the writing abilities of your students (gathered, perhaps, during a preassessment test) to estimate how much time it will take students to answer the question. Second, your answer can serve as a model answer against which each student response can be compared. This will help increase the reliability of your grading. Do this for five or six questions, each similar in complexity to example 20.

5. *Review.* Reviewing for objective tests makes good sense and so does reviewing for essay tests, but the techniques differ. When reviewing for objective tests you go over the general content in each section of the test. When reviewing for essay tests, give the students copies of the five or six questions you developed and explain that on the day of the test, you will select two or three questions to be answered. You will have a good idea of how many questions you can expect students to answer because you took the time to write out A-level responses yourself. Consider the advantages of handing out the questions.

    First, since students do not know which questions they will be called on to answer, those who intend to be successful will study all the questions. This, in itself, is beneficial since it increases the likelihood of students understanding not only isolated facts, but also how those facts relate to one another with respect to five or six central issues or points.

    Second, although students do *not* get copies of the grading criteria, you have the grading criteria in hand so you can go over the main idea in each question. This enables students to identify areas where their knowledge is weak so they have a better idea of where to focus additional study time.

    Third, during the test, students will be expected to first mentally gather and organize data and to then express the relationships among the data clearly, concisely, and in writing, in order to demonstrate their in-depth understanding of some complex whole. This is not an easy task nor is it one for which students have had much practice. Giving them the questions ahead of time allows them, if they wish to do so, to work together and practice the skill. Even though these cooperative efforts are beneficial, they do not happen all that often. You can increase the likelihood of their taking place if you give students the test questions. Keep in mind that the test grades are less important than the learning that should take place as students prepare for the test.

6. *Make sure that students have sufficient time and materials to do the job.* One of the unique strengths of essay tests is the opportunity they provide for

students to analyze relationships among points within a topic or problem and to formulate responses by synthesizing the information they possess. Even when students have the questions beforehand, when they take the test they still need to recall information, organize their thoughts, perhaps outline their answer, and then write it legibly. If students are unduly pressed for time, their responses may not be as true a reflection of their abilities as they might otherwise have been. Writing out model answers and then adding to the time it took you to write out those answers provides a way of estimating how many questions you can reasonably expect students to answer in a given period.

Many teachers find it easier to read responses that are written in ink on lined paper. Responses written in ink is easier to read than those written in pencil because the graphite in the pencil "lead" creates more of a glare, especially under electric light. The lined paper helps ensure that lines of text are reasonably straight. The fact that students cannot erase is offset by the fact that they can cross out. Further, it is a good idea to insist that students identify the number of the question they are answering. This helps avoid misunderstandings later.

7. *Compare each response with a model answer.* There is a tendency, after grading a few responses, to begin comparing those read later with those read previously. This tendency can be offset by making frequent reference to the model answer(s) that were prepared in order to estimate the time students would need to write their answers.

8. *Grade all responses to each question then go back and grade all responses to the next question.* This procedure solves two problems. First, it reduces the halo effect, the probability that if a student did an outstanding job on the first question, the grader will evaluate that student's next answer more favorably than if the first answer was wrong or mediocre. The reverse can also happen where a poor first answer causes the grader to be more critical of the student's second answer. Grading all responses to each question avoids the problem.

   Second, grading all responses to each question before moving on to the next question enables the grader to see if a significant number of students (perhaps more than one third) missed the same point(s) or misinterpreted something in the same way. The omission or difference will conflict obviously with the grading criteria. If this happens, the most likely explanation is that something was said in class, or appeared in what students read, that was misleading. In this case you would want to adjust the grading since it would not be fair to deduct points for something that might be, at least partially, your fault.

9. *Avoid mixing essay items and objective test items on the same test.* The intellectual operations required to synthesize a response to an essay item are significantly different from those required to select a response to an

objective test item. This mental "shifting of gears" takes time. Of greater importance is the fact that students have no way to adequately judge how much time to spend on each part of such tests. If you want to help students do as well as possible, administer objective and essay tests on different days.

ADMINISTERING TESTS

1. *Help keep the honest students honest.* Tests are stressful situations and, while most people are honest, given enough stress, some may be tempted to cheat in order to pass. If cheating occurs it poses major problems. How can you be sure that student A was, in fact, cheating from student B? Did student B deliberately allow student A to see the answers? If cheating did occur, what should be done? It is a mess and it makes sense to do what you can to avoid the problem.

   When possible, arrange chair in rows so that there is an empty row of chairs between the rows of students. When students are sitting directly behind one another is it more difficult for them to see another person's answers than if they are sitting side by side.

   Actively proctor the test. Rather than grading papers from a previous class or doing other work, keep an eye on the students. Whenever a student looks up, he or she should see your smiling face. Knowing that you are watching will, by itself, help deter cheating.

2. *Number each test and have students record the number on their answer sheet.* This procedure helps ensure that all copies of the tests are returned in their entirety. This, in turn, makes it possible for the teacher to administer the same test to other students and still be reasonably sure that the test is not "out." Further, it is easier to store answer sheets than entire tests. Some teachers go so far as to tell students that points will be deducted if they make any marks on the test, thus further ensuring that the tests can be used with other students.

3. *Do not answer questions after the test has started.* If you recall, when you took your SAT or ACT exam certain procedures were followed to help ensure that all students took the test under as nearly alike conditions as possible. It is a good idea to follow the same procedures when you administer your own tests.

   Before the test starts, ask if students have any last minute questions that arose while they were studying. If they do, answer them even in the unlikely case where one or two might be virtually the same as questions on the test. However, announce that once the test starts no questions concerning the test will be answered. Students are to interpret and answer each question as best they can.

There are sound reasons for following this procedure. If individual students have questions and you go to them and privately provide additional information, you will be acting unfairly to all the other students. They, too, might benefit from the additional information. However, trying to avoid this unfairness by interrupting the test and calling everyone's attention to the points in question poses its own problems.

Interrupting students during a test destroys their train of thought. This, itself, might cause students to forget an important point and/or put down a wrong answer. Further, enough interruptions could seriously detract from the time students have to think about each question.

A wiser course of action is to take time to go over the test carefully before using it during the review and to go over it again, in your mind, as you review. If any questions need to be revised or any points clarified, you can attend to them prior to duplicating the test. If the test has already been duplicated, any needed corrections or information could be written on the chalkboard and gone over prior to the test. Once the test starts, allow students to work on it without distractions or interruptions.

ALTERNATIVE EVALUATION PROCEDURES

While pencil-and-paper tests are likely to remain essential tools in measuring and evaluating student progress, they are not the only useful tools. The ultimate measure of the skill and knowledge acquired by students is their ability to use those skills and that knowledge in practical applications. The problem is in structuring these applications so that we are able to validly and reliably assess students' abilities. The following principles may help.

1. *Specify standards clearly.* You are the teacher and you must assign grades. Therefore, it is your responsibility to think about, and clearly communicate to students, the minimal acceptable standards for every objective. People who prefer to deal in generalities and long-terms benefits have difficulty doing this, but the fact remains that at the end of the grading period, you must assign grades. Students will be more successful if they clearly understand what is expected of them. Consider the following objectives. Each involves a student construction, but in each case the product is less important than the cognitive skills necessary for its construction.

   You will be able to:

   A. Write a mailable one-page letter to a company or politician in which some problem is delineated, a desired course of action is outlined, and supporting rationales for that action are given. ("Mailable" is a business term used to denote a letter that is free from errors in spelling, grammar, punctuation, usage, etc., and ready for signature and mailing.)

B. Given a spreadsheet program, use its various operations and functions to build a grading program that will calculate the mean and median of sets of scores as they are input and continually update the total points earned by each student. Write a brief explanation of the sequence of the steps and of what takes place at each step.

C. Construct a poster approximately 2' x 3' designed to sway people's opinion for or against some controversial issue and describe, in less than three pages, how each element (such as color, message, design, and figure placement) helps make the poster a powerful communicator.

The elements included as part of the minimum acceptable standards for these objectives spell out the criteria to be used in assessing achievement. To achieve each objective, students must use higher-order thinking skills and, unless students demonstrate these skills, they cannot meet all the criteria. For example, suppose a student wrote the following letter in response to the first objective.

Dear Sir:

I recently purchased a new Doohicky, and it does not work right. Neither the store I purchased it from nor your factory representative accepted responsibility for the Doohicky's malfunction, and now I'm tired of fooling with it and want a refund. Unless I get the refund within two weeks, I will turn the issue over to my attorney.

Sincerely yours,

This letter contains all the elements suggested in the objective, but its lack of specifics and its tone leave much to be desired. What can be done?

2. *Whenever possible, provide a model.* Models are helpful from a number of standpoints. Regardless of how explicitly written criteria are, seeing an actual product will help students more clearly understand what is expected. This understanding is further clarified if both good and bad models are provided, and explanations of why they are good and bad are included. By using written models, audio tapes, video tapes, and/or three-dimensional products, you can provide models for virtually every kind of behavior or product students are expected to produce.

3. *Provide a checklist.* A checklist is an elaboration of the stated minimum acceptable standards. It will be impossible, in most cases, to specify all important steps or criteria in every objective, but in the case of those

objectives calling for the construction of some product, regardless of whether the product is a paper or a paperweight, a checklist can help students. In the case of the sample letter, for example, students could have been given a checklist for writing letters of complaint that included such items as, "Did you specify where and when you bought the product?" and "Did you explain exactly what your problem was?"

Checklists can function as both instructional and evaluation aids. As instructional aids, checklists provide students with a logical sequence of steps or points that, if followed or included, lead to the development of an acceptable product. As evaluation aids, checklists provide students (and evaluators) with a list of the specific points being sought in the final product. Since checklists can be much more detailed than the standards included in instructional objectives, they can be particularly helpful to students. Example of checklists for a problem-based learning experience can be seen in Chapter 8, Figures 8.1 and 8.2.

SUMMARY

Teachers use measurement and evaluation techniques in order to determine the extent to which students have achieved specific objectives. The information acquired also enables teachers to assess the effectiveness of instructional activities and materials, and it enables students to compare their abilities against specific criteria and against the abilities of peers.

Since tests only sample skills or knowledge, teachers can have greater confidence in the semester grades they record if those grades are based on a fair sampling of student achievement. The more grades that are averaged, the more likely the average will reflect the students' abilities. Further, with ten or more grades on tests and paper, the lowest grade can be dropped without seriously affecting reliability, thus giving students an incentive to continue working even though they may have done poorly on one test or paper.

Variety is also important in measurement and evaluation because students have different abilities. Some may take objective tests well, others may do better on essay tests, and still others may demonstrate their abilities best by completing projects. Varying assessment methods increases opportunities for students to demonstrate their skills and knowledge, thus increasing their opportunities to be successful.

Teachers should check the validity of their tests. Face or content validity reflects the extent to which the test assesses what was taught. Predictive validity reflects the extent to which performance on one test can be used to accurately predict performance on some other test or task. Construct validity concerns the extent to which a test measures psychological constructs such as honesty or tolerance.

Dealing with student effort is often difficult. One effective technique is to find ways in which students can demonstrate effort as opposed to ability in the subject area. One way is to award extra points to papers that have no spelling, punctuation, or grammatical mistakes and to accumulate those extra credit points in a separate column in the grade book. At the end of the marking period, an examination of the extra credit column will help show how much effort the student demonstrated during that period.

Test reliability refers to the consistency with which the test measures whatever it measures. Reliability tends to increase with the number of items because as the number of items increases so does the extent of knowledge being sampled. The more adequate the sampling, the more likely it is that students will do equally as well if tested with an equivalent form of the test. Reliability coefficients extend from 1.00 for perfect correlation, to .00 for no correlation, and to −1.00 for perfect negative correlation.

Criterion-referenced tests are those in which students either meet or fail to meet certain criteria. If the criteria are met, the student passes; if not, the student fails. Criterion referencing can be used to establish cut-off points for admission to programs or schools and for similar purposes, but most often teachers need norm-referenced tests.

Norm referencing means that a student's performance is assessed in relation to the performance of students in some norming group. A norming group consists of members that have some relevant characteristic in common, such as age or grade level.

The most common type of evaluation instrument is the paper-and-pencil test. These tests present the same task, under the same conditions, to all students and result in a product that can be easily examined and analyzed. Objective tests are used to sample abilities through analysis-level thinking, with respect to a fairly large topic. About thirty seconds should be allowed for each four-choice multiple-choice item, so about fifty items can be used per test.

Essay tests are used to sample higher-level abilities, such as the abilities to analyze, synthesize, and evaluate. Since different thought processes are involved with each kind of test, students will do best if objective and essay questions do not appear on the same test.

Assessments that require the integration of many skills and pieces of information are most useful because they emphasize the application of what is learned. Before any test is administered, the teacher should conduct a formal review with the test in hand. The teacher should go over each part of the test explaining what topics are covered, what content is sampled, and how many items are in each part of the test. When reviewing for essay tests, the teacher should give the students the actual questions to be asked and should go over, but not hand out to students, the associated criteria. Students should be told that they will be asked to answer two or three specific questions.

Objective tests

I. Advantages

    A. Provide a broad sampling of students' knowledge
    B. Present the same problems and the same alternatives to each student
    C. Minimize the chance of student bluffing
    D. Permit rapid scoring with little or no need for subjective decisions
    E. Permit items to be improved on the basis of item analysis
    F. Permit increased reliability through item improvement

II. Disadvantages

    A. Cannot be used to assess abilities to synthesize or create
    B. Increase the probability of guessing
    C. Require a relatively long time to construct items

III. Utilization Factors

    A. Construction and administration

        1. Keep the language simple.
        2. Ask students to apply rather than simply recall information.
        3. Make sure that each item is independent.
        4. Do not establish or follow a pattern for correct responses.
        5. Do not include trick or trivial questions.
        6. Do not answer questions after the test has started.

    B. Multiple-choice items

        1. Put as much of the item as possible into the stem.
        2. Make all options reasonable.
        3. Make all options about the same length.
        4. Do not provide unintentional clues.
        5. Avoid the use of all-inclusive or all-exclusive terms (always/never).

    C. True/false items

        1. Avoid when possible since chance of guessing correctly is one in two.
        2. Be sure that each item is wholly true or wholly false.
        3. Be sure that items are not dependent on insignificant facts.
        4. Avoid the use of negatives and, if used, call attention to them by underlining and/or capitalizing the negative word.

    D. Matching items

        1. Limit the number of items to be matched to ten or less.
        2. Make sure that all items concern a single topic.

     3. Have more answers than questions or stipulate that some answers may be used more than once or not at all.

     4. Arrange options in some logical order.

E. Completion items

     1. Write items that can be completed with a single word or a short phrase.

     2. Be sure that only one word or phrase can correctly complete the sentence.

     3. Put the blanks near the ends of the sentences.

     4. Make all blanks the same length.

     5. Do not put more than two blanks in any one item.

Essay Tests

I. Advantages

A. Allow sampling of students' abilities to create, analysis, synthesize, and evaluate

B. Provide an in-depth sampling of students' knowledge of a specific topic

C. Enable students to develop the skills of organizing pieces of information and demonstrating their understanding of how those pieces interrelate to form a complex whole

D. Help students learn to express themselves coherently and concisely in writing

II. Disadvantages

A. Reduced reliability and validity compared with objective tests

B. Inherently biased in favor of students who write well

C. Time-consuming to grade

D. Increased chance for students to bluff

III. Utilization Factors

A. Be definitive about what kinds of things students are to include in their answers.

B. Make sure that students have sufficient time and materials to do the job.

C. Compare each response with a model response and with a list of grading criteria.

D. Essay tests and objective tests take about the same amount of time in total. With objective tests more time is spent constructing the items than in grading the answers. With essay tests just the opposite is true.

SO HOW DOES THIS AFFECT MY TEACHING?

The single greatest measure of the effectiveness of a teacher is the extent to which his or her students can use what they learned. This was true in 450 B.C., when the Elder Sophists made their living selling their abilities to help students learn to speak in public, and it remains true today. If the students of the Elder Sophists had been unable to successfully speak in public, the teachers would have soon gone out of business. One does not get much more accountable than that.

Teachers today must also be accountable. Helping students learn is just part of the job. To demonstrate that they have learned, you must develop measurement and evaluation techniques that enable them to clearly and adequately demonstrate their abilities. They have to be able to use what they have learned. Their demonstration of their abilities is the way you demonstrate your accountability.

Further, think about the things that you consider when you assess your own instructors. The chances are good that an important point is the ability of the instructor to fairly assess what was taught. Your students will look at this same point when they assess you. Do what you want your instructors to do. Specify, in the objectives, what students are supposed to be able to do after instruction, provide appropriate instruction, and then assess the extent to which students have achieved the objectives. This is the honest and fair way to do business and it provides the greatest opportunity for you and your students to be successful.

KEY TERMS, PEOPLE, AND IDEAS

Tests = Samples
Measurement = Assigning numbers
Evaluation = Value Judgments
Validity = Measures what was taught—Content or Face, Predictive, Construct
Reliability = Consistency of test results, 1.00 to .00, and –1.00 to .00
Criterion-referenced—Pass or Fail
Mastery Learning—allowing students to redo work—average the original and redo grades.
Norm-referenced—Performance relative to performance of a norming group
Objective tests—No value judgments required with respect to answers
Stem—that part of the question that poses the problem
Visual Package—Listing all choices for multiple-choice questions under one another and keeping the stem and all choices on a single page.
Subjective tests—Value judgments required with respect to the answers.

SUGGESTED READINGS

Additional information concerning the construction of objective and subjective tests can be found in the following sources.

Thorndike, Robert L., and Elizabeth Hagen, *Measurement and Evaluation in Psychology and Education,* 5th ed. (New York: Macmillan, 1991).

Linn, Robert L., and Norman E. Gronlund, *Measurement and Assessment in Teaching,* 7th ed. (Englewood Cliffs, N.J.: Prentice-Hall, 1995).

13

CALCULATING, INTERPRETING, AND COMMUNICATING GRADES, AND TEACHER EVALUATION

RATIONALE

Once tests are given or projects completed, grades must be calculated and assigned and the grades must then be communicated so that students and parents can make sense of them. It is important that students and parents understand that you do not "give" grades, you report student achievement and progress. Those reports are likely to please some and discourage or possibly anger others, but accurate reports must be made.

Although much is said about learning for the sake of learning, students, parents, and administrators all take grades seriously, and so should you. Any teacher who consistently records many more As, Ds, or Fs than most other teachers, courts disaster. Fortunately, there are ways of calculating, assigning, and reporting grades that are well tested and generally accepted as being fair and appropriate. This chapter will explain some of the most useful of these. Their consistent use can help minimize problems related to grading.

Since it is likely that your performance as a teacher will be continually evaluated by yourself and by others, this chapter also includes a section dealing with teacher evaluation. The information in this section can help you earn high ratings and continually improve your own effectiveness.

SAMPLE OBJECTIVES

You will be able, in writing, to:

1. Explain what information is provided by conducting an item analysis on a test, and how the results of an item analysis might be used to adjust the grades on the test. (Comprehension)
2. Given a set of scores, and either the traditional grading scale in which the lowest A ≥ 90 percent of the total points, the lowest B ≥ 80 percent, etc., or a curved scale; properly assign letter grades to the scores. (Application)
3. Compare traditional and curved grading scales by explaining at least two advantages and two disadvantages of each. (Comprehension)
4. Explain at least three procedures teachers can use to assess their own effectiveness, including both process and product assessments. (Comprehension)

ITEM ANALYSES

Item analyses enables makers of objective tests to assess the effectiveness of each question and of each option. Although item analyses can be conducted by hand, many high schools have equipment that can read answers recorded on mark-sensing forms, print the number of correctly answered questions on the form, and automatically conduct and print out an item analysis. As a student teacher or a new teacher, it would be appropriate to ask if your school has such equipment, or ready access to it. If so, have students record their answers on mark-sensing forms and use the equipment. It will save you a great deal of grading time and will automatically produce an item analysis. A typical item analysis might appear similar to the one shown in Table 13.1.

The item analysis in Table 13.1 shows that everyone answered item 1 correctly. If the test was strictly criterion-referenced (pass or fail), this is not a problem. However, if the test was norm-referenced and a spread of scores

TABLE 13.1   Item Analysis

Item Number	Correct Answer	Options				
		A	B	C	D	E
1	A	20				
2	C		20			
3	E	10	1	5	2	2
≈						
49	D	4	4	5	7	
50	B	2	15	1	1	1

was expected (which is usually the case), item 1 one was of little value. It did not help differentiate between those who knew and those who were pretending to know. For purposes of building morale, a teacher may choose to leave one or two such questions on a test, but most such questions should be replaced with questions that do a better job of differentiating among students.

The analysis shows that not only did everyone miss item 2, but that they all selected the same incorrect option. One possible explanation is that there is a mistake on the answer key. A more likely explanation is that something was said in class or appeared in what students read that misled them. The latter explanation is also the likely explanation for the spread of choices in item 3. In both cases, the choices students made are more likely to be at least partly due to a mistake on the teacher's part than to lack of knowledge on the students' part. This being the case, serious consideration should be given to awarding credit not only to the correct answer, but also to the answer selected by the majority of the students. Doing this will eliminate much of the ill will that might otherwise be generated, and the few points involved will make little or no difference in semester grades.

Item 49 shows such an equal distribution of choices that the power of the item to discriminate is lost. The item should be reworded so that the distribution is closer to that shown in item 50. Option E in item 49 was not selected by anyone, so it may be too obviously wrong. Consideration should be given to changing it.

Item 50 shows that most of the students answered the question correctly, but some students chose each option. From a test-maker's viewpoint, this is the ideal situation.

An added benefit to examining each item and option on a test is that it enables the teacher to polish those items. As polished test items are accumulated, the length of time needed to construct future tests will continually decline, allowing more time for other things.

With essay tests, when you grade all the answers to one question before going on to grade all answers to the next question, you make it possible to conduct an ongoing item analysis. If expected facts or explanations fail to appear on a significant number of papers, or if wrong information appears, it will be noticed and grades can be adjusted accordingly.

RECORDING AND POSTING GRADES

The easiest way for students and parents to interpret the grade on a given test or paper is to see the number of points earned, in relation to the number of points possible. For example, 85/100. Letter grades such as B, B+, A–, and A, cannot provide the useful X out of Y information. Further, at some point, letter grades need to be converted into numbers in order to calculate statistics such as the mean and the median. Reserve letter grades for use on report cards, where they are typically required. Further, if extra credit is earned on a particular assignment, keep those points apart from the points for achievement, both on the papers returned to students, and in your grade book. You need to be able to differentiate between the two sets of points.

It is a good idea to date and initial each paper as you grade it. This eliminates any question of who graded it or when. These may sound like bothersome steps, but they tend to eliminate problems and they take little time or effort.

Confidentiality is important. When graded work is returned to students, the teacher should hand each student's paper or test directly to the student. The quality of each student's work is a confidential matter between each student and the teacher. For this reason it is *not* a good idea to have students grade each other's work. If you make an assignment, you should grade it. Doing so protects the confidentiality of grades, lets you provide appropriate encouragement and reinforcement, and enables you to more quickly identify, and help students deal with, problems.

Students and parents get upset, and justly so, when they see a grade on a report card that is unexpectedly low. (They rarely get upset if the grade is unexpectedly high.) Students should know, at all times, where they stand with respect to grades. If you recall, it was suggested that on the last page of the course syllabus, space be provided for students to keep a running record of the points possible for each assignment and the points they actually earned. You can, however, do more.

Teachers who take time to learn how to use a grading or spreadsheet program will not only save themselves hours of work, they will also be able to easily post grades. After the first assignment is graded, grades should be posted and left up until the next assignment is graded. At that time the printout should be replaced with one showing the grades for all past assignments and those for the latest assignment. If such a cumulative printout is continually posted, all students will have access to all relevant grading information. Everything will be public.

Whether grades are kept in a grade book or in a computer program, most teachers list their students in alphabetical order according to last names and record grades for each student as they are earned. A computer can easily generate a printout of names and the associated grades (see Figure 13.1). Such a printout or listing, however, could not be posted without compromising grade confidentiality.

One way around this problem is to assign each student an identification number, such as the last four digits of their Social Security Number. When the printout is generated, leave off the column with the students' names and arrange the ID numbers from high to low or low to high. Unless a student deliberately gives his or her identifying number to others, confidentiality is assured while, at the same time, grades are publicly posted. See Figure 13.2.

FIGURE 13.1 Grade Sheet for Teacher's Use (with Names)

Session: Fall, 199___
Professor: Lorber
Class: 216
Section: 001

Current Date

Acad. Major	Student Name	SSN	Rat.	Cog. Obj.	Goal Test	Med. Test	Microteaching Plans 1	2	3	4	TPSA – Lesson 1	2	3	4	Lab School Field Exp. Plans 1	2	3	Obj. Test	Ess. Test	Meas. Test	Man. Test	Sup. Pts	Quizzes 1	2	3	4	Ex. Cr.	At tend.	Total Points	High to Low
History	Adams, John	1695	94	95	78	74	95 +	100	70 +														0	10			10	10	636	636
History	Baily, Beetle	5253	88 +	98 +	88	80	95	100	82 +														25	20			10	10	696	696
Math	Black, Tim	2749	75 +	85 +	88	80	80	95	95 +														5	20			10	10	643	688
Business	Brown, Charlie	6532	73	90 +	78	74	90	90	85 +														20	10			15	10	635	671
Phy. Ed.	Brown, Joan	6823	73	87	62	68	70	65	70 +														5	10			15	10	535	657
History	Brown, Tim	3294	96	79	66	78	93	85	90 +														5	15			20	10	637	649
Art	Bumstead, Blondie	1993	81	77 +	64	68	88	88	85 +														5	0			20	5	581	643
Phy. Ed.	Cat, Garfield	6358	66	95 +	82	92	84	85	86 +														5	5			5	6	611	637
Math	Clinton, Bill	2223	51	85	100	100	78	63	80 +														5	15			5	7	589	636
Music	Confucius	7950	36	75	50	95	92 +	94	100														5	10			5	8	570	635
Soc. Sci.	Dog, Snoopy	2048	51	43	100	38	79 +	99	90 +														5	5			10	9	529	632
Speech	Eddie, Lucky	8825	66	65	86	28	34	65	0 +														5	20			10	10	389	618
Math	Gorbachev, Mike	6503	81	100 +	64	68	73	85	60 +														5	15			15	11	577	612
German	Green, Joe	3031	96	83 +	80	86	80	95	55 +														20	0			20	12	612	611
Soc. Sci.	Green, Mary	1028	85	87	86	74	89 +	98	100 +														15	20			15	10	688	607
English	Horrible, Hagar	4653	84	68	68	66	100	95	60 +														0	15			15	10	607	589
English	Hun, Attila	3157	78	97 +	74	66	100	95	82 +														5	5			20	10	632	581
Phy. Ed.	Jordon, Michael	3674	78 +	86 +	66	76	100	100	100 +														15	15			25	10	671	577
Business	Key, Don	2631	83	100 +	90	68	88	88	90 +														10	10			20	10	657	570
Biology	Louis XVI	7080	86	45 +	76	68	85	70	50 +														5	15			10	10	520	570
Chemistry	Quayle, Dan	4260	83 +	77 +	46	76	78 +	75	58														0	0			15	10	528	535
French	Smith, Mary	1777	77	85 +	76	76	100	100	90 +														5	20			15	10	649	529
Phy. Ed.	Student, General	4951	90	70 +	74	78	90	90	91 +														5	25			10	10	618	528
Health	Tut, King	8270	75	68	46	52	70	70	65 +														0	5			15	5	471	520
																														471
																														389
Mean =		77	77	82	75	72	84	87	76							####	####	####	####	####	####	####	####	6	12	##	##	14	10	595	
Median =		80	85	85	76	74	87	90	84						####	####	####	####	####	####	####	####	5	13	##	##	15	10	612	
Poss. =		100	100	100	100	100	100	100	100	5					####	####	####	####	####	####	####	####	25	25			25	10	760	

Number of Students = 24

Do Not Post

Percentage Grade

Lowest A = 760 × .90 = 684
Lowest B = 760 × .80 = 608
Lowest C = 760 × .70 = 532
Lowest D = 760 × .60 = 456

Point Ranges for Standard Deviation Scale

A ≥	685	M + 1.25 SD	(10%)
B ≥	613	M + 0.25 SD	(30%)
C ≥	523	M − 1.00 SD	(44%)
D ≥	452	M − 2.00 SD	(14%)
E <	452	M − 2.00 SD	(02%)

SD = 72

Approximate Percentages When Applied to a Very Large Population

Percent Grade

Number of Students

F D C B A

Curved Grade

Number of Students

F D C B A

FIGURE 13.2   Grade Sheet for Posting (without Names)

Session: Fall, 199___   Class: 216
Professor: Lorber   Section: 001

Current Date

SSN	Rat.	Cog. Obj.	Goal Test	Med. Test	MT 1	MT 2	MT 3	MT 0	TFSA-Lesson 1	2	3	4	Lab Field Exp. Plans 1	2	3	Obj. Test	Ess. Test	Meas. Test	Man. Test	Sup. Pts	Quiz 1	Quiz 2	Quiz 3	Quiz 4	Ex. Cr.	At tend	Total Points	High to Low
8825	66	65	86	28	34 +	65 +		0 +													5	20			10	10	389	696
8270	75	68	46	52	70 +	70 +		65 +													0	10			15	5	471	688
7950	36	75	50	95	92 +	94 +		100													5	10			5	8	570	671
7080	86	45 +	76	68	85 +	70 +		50 +													5	15			10	10	520	657
6823	73	87	62	68	70 +	65 +		70 +													5	10			15	10	535	649
6532	73	90 +	78	74	90 +	90 +		85 +													20	10			15	10	635	643
6503	81	100 +	64	68	73	85		60 +													5	15			15	11	577	637
6358	66	95	82	92	84	85		86 +													5	15			5	6	611	636
5253	88 +	98 +	88	80	95	100		82													25	20			10	10	696	635
4951	90 +	70	74	78	75 +	90 +		91													5	25			10	10	618	632
4653	84	94 +	68	66	100 +	95 +		60 +													0	15			15	10	607	618
4260	83 +	77	46	76	78 +	95 +		58 +													0	10			15	10	528	612
3674	78 +	86 +	66	76	100 +	100 +		100 +													15	15			25	10	671	611
3294	96	79 +	66	78	93 +	85 +		90 +													5	15			20	10	637	607
3157	78	97 +	74	66	100 +	95 +		82 +													5	5			20	10	632	589
3031	96	83 +	80	86	80 +	95 +		55 +													5	0			20	12	612	581
2749	75 +	85 +	88	80	80 +	95 +		95													5	10			10	10	643	577
2631	83	100 +	90	68	88 +	88 +		90 +													10	10			20	10	657	570
2223	51	85	100	100	78	63 +		80 +													5	15			5	7	589	535
2048	51	43	100	38	79 +	99 +		90 +													5	5			10	9	529	529
1993	81	77 +	64	68	77 +	88 +		85 +													5	0			20	5	581	528
1777	77	85 +	76	76	100 +	100 +		90 +													0	20			15	10	649	520
1695	94	95	78	74	95 +	98 +		70 +													0	10			10	10	636	471
1028	85	87	86	74	98 +	98 +		100 +													15	20			15	10	688	389
Mean	77	82	75	72	84	87		76	####	####	####	####	####	####	####	0	0	####	####	####	6	12	##	##	14	10	595	
Median	80	85	76	74	87	90		84	####	####	####	####	####	####	####	####	####	####	####	####	5	13	##	##	15	10	612	
Poss.	100	100	100	100	100	100		100	####	####	####	####	####	####	####	####	####	####	####	####	25	25	##	##	25	10	760	

Percentage Grade

Lowest A = 760 × .90 = 684
Lowest B = 760 × .80 = 608
Lowest C = 760 × .70 = 532
Lowest D = 760 × .60 = 456

Point Ranges for Standard Deviation Scale

A ≥ 685	M + 1.25 SD	(10%)
B ≥ 613	M + 0.25 SD	(30%)
C ≥ 523	M − 1.00 SD	(44%)
D ≥ 452	M − 2.00 SD	(14%)
E < 452	M − 2.00 SD	(02%)

SD = 72

Approximate Percentages When Applied to a Very Large Population.

Percent Grade — Number of Students (0, 5, 10, 15) by grade F D C B A

Curved Grade — Number of Students (0, 2, 4, 6, 8, 10) by grade F D C B A

CALCULATING GRADES

Once students get their grades on a particular test or assignment, they typically want to know how they did in relation to the rest of the class. To explain this properly to them, to parents, and to administrators, you need to understand and use a few key terms.

Raw Score. This is the number of points, for example, 18, earned on a test or paper. By itself, a raw score is useless because there is no reference point. There is no way to know if the 18 is out of 20 or out of 100. Expressing a grade as a fraction such as 18/20 adds meaning to the raw score.

Mean. This is the arithmetic average. Students can compare their own score with the mean to get an idea of how well they did in comparison to their peers. To calculate the mean, add together all the scores and divide the sum by the number of scores. The smaller the number of scores, the more the mean will be affected by one or two extreme scores. See Table 13.2.

All scores are the same except for the last one. However, because of that one score the mean for Class B drops by six points. It should be noted that as the number of scores increases, the effect of any one score is lessened. This factor is known as regression toward the mean.

Median. After the scores are listed from high to low, the median is the score that divides the distribution in half. The distributions in Table 13.2 each

TABLE 13.2   Effect of Extreme Scores

M = Mean,	Σ = Sum of scores,	N = Number of scores		
Class A			Class B	
90			90	
85			85	
75			75	
75	$M = \Sigma/N$		75	$M = \Sigma/N$
72	$M = 730/10$		72	$M = 670/10$
70	$M = 73$		70	$M = 67$
68			68	
65			65	
65			65	
65			5	
730			670	

have an even number of scores, ten. In such cases, the median is the mean of the two middle scores. In Class A the median is 71 ($\frac{72 + 70}{2}$). If there is an odd number of scores, the median is simply the middle score.

Mode.   The mode is the most frequently occurring score. In Table 13.2, the mode in Class A is 65. Class B has a bimodal distribution with 75 and 65 occurring with equal frequency.

Range.   The number of points between the highest and lowest scores is the range. In Table 13.2, the range of scores in Class A is 90−65 = 35. In Class B, the range of scores is 90−5 = 85.

Percentile Point versus Percentile Rank.   Percentile scores are expressed either as a percentile point or a percentile rank. A percentile *point* is a number representing the percent of scores that a particular raw score *exceeds.* It is computed by counting the number of scores that are *lower than the score in question,* dividing this number by the total number of scores, and multiplying by 100. For example, in Table 13.2, the score of 85 is higher than eight other scores. Since the 85 exceeds eight other scores, we divide eight by ten (the total number of scores), and get .8. We then multiply the .8 by 100, and get 80. This means that, in Table 13.2, the score of 85 represents a percentile point of 80. The score of 85 is, itself, *not* included in the 80 percent of lower scores.

A percentile *rank,* by contrast, is a number representing the percent of scores that a particular raw score *equals or exceeds.* It is computed by counting the number of scores that are *equal to, or lower than, the score in question,* dividing this number by the total number of scores, and multiplying by 100. For example, in Table 13.2, the score of 85 is equal to, or higher than, nine other scores. Since the 85 is equal to, or higher than, nine other scores, we divide nine by ten (the total number of scores), and get .9. We then multiply the .9 by 100, and get 90. This means that, in Table 13.2, the score of 85 represents a percentile *rank* of 90. The score of 85 *is,* itself, included in the 90 percent of lower scores. The median of a distribution has a percentile rank of 50.[1]

ASSIGNING GRADES

The Traditional A–F Scale

Grades in schools are typically assigned on an A–F scale. This scale is based on the idea that a grade of A represents outstanding work, B represents above average work, C represents average work, D represents below average work, and F represents failing work. Unfortunately, there is a phenomenon known as **grade inflation.** Essentially this means that many people now expect, and receive, grades of A or B for average work, and C for below average work. Virtually no one receives a grade of F.

Grade inflation causes a number of problems. First, it makes it impossible to recognize truly outstanding students, because so many less able students also receive grades of A. Second, if students start off believing that a grade of C is "no good," they are likely to become discouraged and stop trying, when their performance is, in fact, average. Third, inflated grades mislead students into believing they are more competent than they really are. Fourth, inflating grades makes liars out of teachers. Think about the stories of high school graduates who cannot read or do simple arithmetic. Assuming that such stories are true, the only way those students could have passed the courses necessary to graduate, is if their grades were falsified—if teachers gave them passing grades when they earned failing grades. Grade inflation is still very much with us and you can be part of the problem or part of the solution. That choice is yours.

One way to begin dealing with grade inflation is to point out to students that the objectives in the course syllabus represent D-level work, the minimal acceptable standard. Explain also that students who keep up in class will have little difficulty meeting those standards and that most students will likely end up with grades of C or higher. Students who want to earn the higher grades must meet higher standards. That choice is theirs.

The most common way to use the traditional A–F scale is to have the lowest A equal 90 percent of the available points, the lowest B equal 80 percent, the lowest C equal 70 percent, and the lowest D equal 60 percent. Some teachers raise or lower the cut-off points for various grade categories, but the basic approach remains the same.

The greatest advantage of this approach is that virtually everyone understands it. It is the traditional approach to grading. Another advantage is that it is administratively convenient; a whole semester's work is summed up and recorded with a single letter.

A significant disadvantage is that the letter grades have no relationship to the complexity of the work required. For example, there is a significant difference between the level of work required for an A in a regular history class and that required for an A in an advanced placement class, yet the best students in both classes will get As.

The Curve

Another approach to calculating grades is to use a curve. The curve refers to a mathematical construct known as the normal, bell-shaped, curve. See Figure 13.3.

This bell-shaped curve results when a graph is plotted based on the distribution of some characteristic such as height, weight, or intelligence quotient (IQ), among a very large population, such as the population of Chicago.

FIGURE 13.3   Normal, Bell-Shaped, Curve

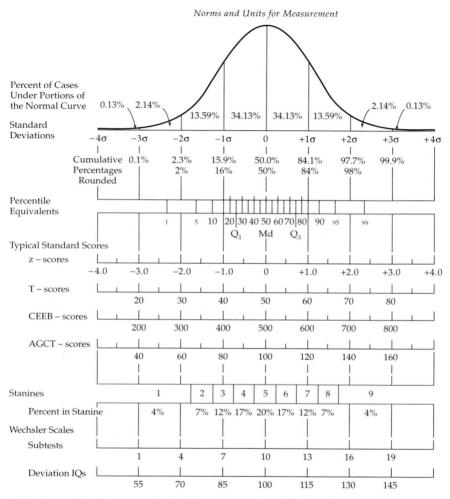

Various types of standard-score scales in relation to percentiles and the normal curve. Reproduced by permission of the Psychological Corporation.

For example, the mean on the Wechsler Scales (an established IQ test) is 100. If the IQs of all the people in Chicago were plotted, 100 would be at the center of the baseline (abscissa) under the highest point of the curve. To the left of the high point, and sloping down toward the baseline, would be successively lower scores, and to the right, again sloping down toward the baseline, would be successively higher scores. Neither end of the curve touches the baseline, showing that some extreme scores, not shown, might exist.

When basing grades on a curve, one needs to know the mean score and how far each score deviates from the mean. The statistic used to express this is the **standard deviation** (SD). The size of the SD depends on how much the people in the sample are alike or different. In heterogeneous classes, the SD tends to be relatively large because the range of abilities is relatively large. In homogeneous classes, such as advanced placement classes, the range of abilities, and the SD, are relatively small.

The Wechsler Scales have a standard deviation of 15 points. Figure 13.3 shows that about 34 percent of the scores fall between the mean score and one SD above the mean. This means that if all the people in Chicago were tested with the Wechsler Scales, about 34 percent of them would have IQs between 100 and 115. About another 34 percent would fall between the mean and one SD below the mean and have IQ scores between 85 and 100. However, for these distributions to hold true, the population must be very large—high school classes do not qualify.

Grades could be based on the normal curve and the standard deviation cut-off points shown in Figure 13.3, but consider the consequences. About 68 percent of the students would get Cs, 14 percent Bs, 14 percent Ds, 2 percent As, and 2 percent Fs. If there were 25 students in the class, about 17 would get Cs, four would get Bs, and four would get Ds. There would be no As or Fs. It would be hard to justify a grading system in which it was mathematically impossible to earn a grade of A. There is a better way, but before looking at it, it might be a good idea to look at why some teachers choose to use SD cut-off points in the first place.

Advantages of Using SD Cut-off Points for Grading

The main advantage of using SD cut-off points is that the grades are based on the mean performance of the class rather than on some arbitrarily fixed point such as 60 percent or 70 percent of the total points available. Using the traditional grading scale, if the low score on a 100-point test was 10 and the high score was 50, everyone would fail. If an SD cut-off scale is used with modified cut-off points, the teacher could still assign A–F grades by calculating how far above or below the mean each score is, and then applying a scale of SD cut-offs.

For example, if the teacher had decided previously that a grade of A was going to be any score one and one-quarter standard deviations above the mean, it would not matter whether the mean was 23 or 83. One and one-quarter standard deviations would be calculated from that point, and the grade assigned. Further, there is no magic in any particular SD cut-off point. Most statistics books include tables that show area under the curve for specific standard deviations. All that is needed is for the teacher to decide on some acceptable percentage of As, Bs, Cs, Ds, and Fs, find those percentages as areas under the curve in the appropriate table, and use those SDs.

Calculating the SD is not difficult. Most calculators and computers have built-in functions to do the job. However, one can estimate the SD very closely, with paper and pencil, by using a formula developed by W. L. Jenkins.[2]

$$\text{Est. SD} = \frac{\text{Sum of top } \frac{1}{6} \text{ of scores} - \text{Sum of bottom } \frac{1}{6} \text{ of scores}}{\frac{1}{2} \text{ the number of scores in the total distribution}}$$

The steps to this procedure are as follows.

1. Arrange all the scores from high to low.
2. Divide the number of scores by six to find out how many scores are in the top $\frac{1}{6}$ and the bottom $\frac{1}{6}$.
3. Calculate the sums of the top $\frac{1}{6}$ of the scores and the bottom $\frac{1}{6}$.
4. Subtract the sum of the bottom $\frac{1}{6}$ from the sum of the top $\frac{1}{6}$.
5. Divide the difference by $\frac{1}{2}$ the number of scores in the total distribution.

Suppose that a class of twelve students was given a twenty-item test worth 100 points. After 5 points were deducted for each incorrect response, the scores were calculated to be 95, 90, 85, 75, 75, 75, 70, 70, 65, 65, 60, and 40. Suppose further that the teacher had decided on the following standard deviation cut-off points (where M = mean):

A $\geq$ M + 1.25 SD
B $\geq$ M + 0.25 SD
C $\geq$ M − 1.00 SD
D $\geq$ M − 2.00 SD
F $<$ M − 2.00 SD

Grades for the class of twelve, based on a curve, could be estimated by the following procedure, using Jenkins' formula:

Example 1

$$\text{Est. SD} = \frac{\text{Sum of top } \frac{1}{6} \text{ of scores} - \text{Sum of bottom } \frac{1}{6} \text{ of scores}}{\frac{1}{2} \text{ the number of scores in the total distribution}}$$

$$= \frac{(95 + 90) - (60 + 40)}{6} = \frac{185 - 100}{6} = \frac{85}{6} = 14$$

Next, calculate the mean.

$$\text{Mean} = \frac{\text{Sum of scores}}{\text{Number of scores}}$$

$$= \frac{95 + 90 + 85 + 75 + 75 + 75 + 70 + 70 + 65 + 65 + 60 + 40}{12}$$

$$= \frac{865}{12} = 72$$

Now, calculate the point equivalents to the standard deviation cut-offs by adding the approximate SD to, and subtracting it from, the mean score. Since an A is any score 1.25 SDs or greater above the mean, the point equivalent is found by multiplying the estimated SD (14), by the 1.25 cut-off, and adding the product (17.5) to the mean (72). The lowest A is therefore 72 + 17.50, or 89.5. This would be rounded *down* to the next *lowest* whole number in order to have the cut-offs work to the advantage of the students.

The lowest B is 0.25 SD above the mean, so its point equivalent is found by multiplying 14 by 0.25, and adding the product (3.5) to the mean (72). The lowest B is therefore 72 + 3.5, or 75.5, which would round to 75.

Similarly, the lowest C is found by subtracting one SD (14) from the mean. The lowest C is therefore 72–14, or 58.

The lowest D is found by subtracting two SDs from the mean. The lowest D is therefore 72–(2 × 14 = 28) or 44. Scores less than 44 would be graded as F. The actual test scores might then be determined by using the following scale.

The grade distribution for the scores given at the beginning of this problem would then be

95 = A	75 = C	65 = C
90 = A	75 = C	65 = C
85 = B	70 = C	60 = C
75 = B	70 = C	40 = F

Practice Problems for Assigning Marks Using a Curve

Calculate the mean score and estimated standard deviation (using the Jenkins' formula), to the nearest tenth, for the following 24 test scores:

24, 22, 20, 19, 19, 18, 17, 17, 16, 16, 15, 15, 15, 14, 14, 13, 13, 13, 13, 12, 12, 12, 11, 11.

Step 1   Calculate the mean by adding all the scores and dividing the sum by the number of scores. Compare your calculations to the following:

24 + 22 + 20 + 19 + 19 + 18 + 17 + 17 + 16 +16 + 15 + 15 + 15 + 14 + 14 + 13 + 13 + 13 + 13 + 12 + 12 + 12 + 11 + 10 = 370
M = 370/24 = 15.42

Step 2   Calculate the estimated standard deviation. Compare your calculations with the following.

A. Arrange all the scores from high to low: 24, 22, 20, 19, 19, 18, 17, 17, 16, 16, 15, 15, 15, 14, 14, 13, 13, 13, 13, 12, 12, 12, 11, 10.

B. Divide the number of scores by six to find out how many scores are in the top $1/6$ and the bottom $1/6$: $24/6 = 4$

C. Calculate the sums of the top $1/6$ of the scores and the bottom $1/6$:

Top $1/6$ = 24 + 22 + 20 + 19 = 85
Bottom $1/6$ = 10 + 11 + 12 + 12 = 45

D. Subtract the sum of the bottom $1/6$ from the sum of the top $1/6$:
85−45 = 40

E. Divide the difference by $1/2$ the number of scores in the total distribution:

40/12 = 3.33 = 3 (round down to next lowest whole number)

Step 3   Assign grades using the standard deviation cut-offs shown below:

A ≥ M + 1.25 SD
B ≥ M + 0.25 SD
C ≥ M − 1.00 SD
D ≥ M − 2.00 SD
F < M − 2.00 SD

A ≥ 15.45 + (1.25 × 3.3 = 4.13) = 19.58 (round to 19)
B ≥ 15.45 + (.25 × 3.3 = 0.83) = 16.28 (round to 16)
C ≥ 15.45 − (1.00 × 3.3 = 3.30) = 12.15 (round to 12)
D ≥ 15.45 − (2.00 × 3.3 = 6.60) = 8.85 (round to 8)
F = Fewer than 8 points

The assignment of grades would look like this:

A   24, 22, 20, 19, 19
B   18, 17, 17, 16, 16
C   15, 15, 15, 14, 14, 13, 13, 13, 13, 12, 12, 12
D   11, 10

Disadvantages of Using SD Cut-off Points

Aside from the additional decisions and calculations needed to use SD cut-off points, the fact that grades are based on mean scores is a serious problem. For example, in an advanced class, a student might have to get a 95 to get an A, whereas in a slower class a student might need only a 65. Since an A is an A on a grade transcript, many educators have reservations about grading on a curve. Many bright students have the same reservations and think twice before enrolling in advanced placement classes. They know that if the advanced class is graded on a curve, the same work that would earn them an A in the regular class might earn them only a C or B in the advanced class. Some schools try to work around this by weighting grades in regular and advanced classes differently, but those efforts are only partially successful. On a transcript, an A is an A and a B is a B.

GRADING SUBJECTIVITY

All grading methods have one point in common: they all depend on some subjective decision—what percent to use as the lowest A, B, C, or D, or what SD cut-off points to use. Some educators argue that since all grading methods ultimately depend on subjective decisions, none is any better or worse than any other. The advantages and disadvantages balance out. However, unless your school has a policy concerning grading, you will have to make some choices, and there are some crucial points you should consider.

Perhaps the most important factor is fairness. Students should be confident that everyone in the class will have their achievement reported on the same basis. Explaining how the grades will be determined, and keeping a cumulative grade list posted, do much to generate that feeling of confidence.

Closely associated with fairness is consistency. Once you decide on a grading system, you need to use it consistently so that students know that the established procedures are followed for everyone, all the time. Changing grading procedures capriciously would have the same effect as changing course objectives capriciously. No one would know what to expect or how to prepare and they would soon stop caring; the rules might change again next week.

The grades should be relatively easy to calculate, explain, and understand. As a conscientious teacher, you will have more to do than you will have time in which to do it. There is, therefore, no point in developing a complex grading scheme that requires a great deal of calculation time on your part, or that will take you a relatively long time to explain to students or their parents. The less complex it is, the less time you will need to devote to it and the easier it will be for everyone to understand it.

Students need to understand one other point. The point total they accumulate represents their lowest possible grade, but not necessarily the grade they will receive. For example, if the cut-off for a B was 900 points, and a student ended up with just 900, that student would get the B even though he or she might have been obnoxious throughout the semester. However, if a student ended up just a few points short of the cut-off, say with 895 points, and had earned all or virtually all of the extra credit points available, you might exercise your professional judgment and also award that student a B.

The question of just where to draw the line between one grade and the next may not be clear-cut. Once the student has clearly achieved all the objectives necessary for a D, if you believe that the number of points keeping the student from the next higher grade is relatively inconsequential given the total number of points involved, give the student the benefit of the doubt. You and the student will sleep better.

AFTER THE TEST

This chapter began with a discussion of item analyses and, from that point to here, we have dealt with grade calculation. Now that the item analysis has been conducted, the grades calculated, and the graded tests handed back to students individually, the next step is to go over the test with the students. This is a good idea for a number of reasons. First, it provides an opportunity to call to students' attention any questions the item analysis identified as causing problems to many students. A good approach here is to explain what the right answer is and why it is right, and then explain why each of the wrong answers is wrong. If students have further questions about these items, answer them.

Then, encourage students to ask questions about any other questions, but establish a ground rule. Explain that you are quite willing to consider answers other than the ones keyed as correct. However, you want to ensure that only those students who have particularly strong and relevant explanations to support alternative answers get credit for those alternative answers. Therefore, if a student believes he or she has a strong and relevant explanation for an alternative answer, he or she should see you after class or after school to discuss the matter. This policy provides for needed flexibility yet prevents all students who chose a particular wrong answer from getting credit for it if only one student is able to build an adequate case for that option. After going over the test, it and the answer sheets should be collected. This will help ensure test security, thus enabling the teacher to use some or all of the items in the future.

REPORTING GRADES

There are three basic ways of reporting students' achievement. The most effective method is in a parent–teacher conference. Such a conference allows two-way communication, lets you show examples of the student's work, and allows discussion of other relevant issues with parents. Most schools have time set aside for parent–teacher conferences, but relatively few parents attend. One way to encourage attendance is to involve parents early, and a good way to do this is to mail home a copy of the course syllabus. Parents may not take the time to carefully read either the syllabus or the cover letter that you send home with it, but the fact that you took the time to send it, and to solicit their involvement, will tell parents that you care and want to see their son or daughter do as well as possible. This realization may prompt some parents who might otherwise have stayed home to come to a parent–teacher conference.

A somewhat less effective method is a phone call. Phone calls still allow for two-way communication and they do not take very long. In fact, some teachers make it a point to call each student's parents once or twice a semester to report on something good that the student did. Such a phone call can pay big dividends. Imagine yourself as a high school student who comes home to have Mom say, "I got a call from your teacher today." Your first question, probably with some dread, is likely to be, "What did he (or she) want?" If Mom says that the call was to let her know that you had done something particularly well, think of your reaction. You will be pleased, and you are likely to think well of the teacher. Students who think well of their teachers rarely cause classroom management problems.

A still less effective reporting method is a letter. By using a word processor, you can write a general letter describing what objectives students were working toward during the marking period. Then, as you print the letters, and with little effort, you can personalize each one by adding information concerning the achievements and efforts of that student. This method allows for only one-way communication, but it enables you to better explain what the student has been doing, better than the use of a report card.

Report cards are the most common, and least informative, way to report student achievement. All that parents see is a list of courses and a corresponding list of letter grades. By themselves, report cards provide no insight as to what is being learned in each course and, consequently, no insights as to what parents might do to help their children be more successful. The best one can hope for is that, if a parent sees a grade lower than they would like, they will call the teacher for more information. It does not happen often.

Stanines

When it comes to reporting, or helping students and parents understand, the results of standardized tests, it is often necessary to understand **stanines.** The term is an acronym that stands for "standard nine," a structured distribution that consists of nine intervals. These intervals are shown, in relation to areas under the normal curve, in Figure 13.3.

Stanines are used to minimize the misinterpretations associated with exact scores. By placing a score into one of nine intervals you lose some precision because you do not know where the score falls in that interval. The trade-off is that, because the intervals are so large, you can be fairly certain that any given student's true score falls into the stanine interval indicated by the test score.

Standard Scores

Another kind of score used in interpreting scores is the **standard score.** There are two basic standard scores, the z-score and the T-score. Referring to Figure

13.3, you can see that **z-scores** are identical to standard deviations. This means that if scores on two different tests are expressed as z-scores, you can compare the two. A z-score of 1 is equivalent to a percentile rank of about 84 percent regardless of whether the mean on the test was 10 or 110.

Referring again to Figure 13.3, you can see that a **T-score** is simply a z-score that has been multiplied by 10 and to which 50 points have been added. These few manipulations rid the z-scores of negative numbers and move the mean to 50. As is the case with z-scores, expressing scores as T-scores makes it possible to compare scores on tests such as the ACT and the SAT, which have different means.

TEACHER EVALUATION

Process

There are two major ways by which teachers are evaluated—process and product. Process evaluation is the more common because it focuses on what is going on in the classroom. Evaluators can make judgments about what they see then and there. While some evaluators look to see if the blinds on the windows are evenly raised or if the chalkboard is clean, most use evaluation forms containing questions most of us consider reasonable. A small sampling of such questions follows.

1. Are the course and lesson objectives clearly understood by the students?
2. Does the lesson focus on a planned and identifiable objective?
3. Are students asking, or responding to, thought-provoking questions?
4. Are students actively, as opposed to passively, involved in the lesson?
5. Does the teacher encourage students to think for themselves?
6. Does the teacher provide helpful comments on returned papers and tests?
7. Does the teacher seem well prepared?
8. Are appropriate instructional aids used?
9. Is there sufficient stimulus variation to stimulate and maintain interest?
10. Does the teacher seem genuinely interested in each student's progress?
11. Are the skills and knowledge to be learned relevant to out-of-school life?
12. Is the room appropriately decorated—relevant bulletin boards, appropriate resources, etc.?

Product

One of the reasons process evaluation is so common is that its counterpart, product evaluation, must wait until learning has taken place. Product evaluation focuses on how well students are able to achieve the stated objectives.

To determine this, evaluators can look at such things as student products and demonstrations, and at test scores, but they cannot look at these things as often as they can observe the instructional process. It is wise to remember that regardless of how well you do on process evaluations, if your students are not able to achieve the approved objectives, if they cannot produce the expected products, you are not likely to be rehired.

Administrative Evaluations

When administrators (or anyone else) evaluate, they tend to do so from a particular perspective. As a consequence of their educational philosophy and their experiences, they have a mental picture of how the ideal teacher should look and operate. A good part of your rating will depend on the extent to which that picture is matched by you and your performance.

It is common for the evaluator, often the principal, to meet, beforehand, with the teacher. One of the things discussed during this preconference is the evaluation form. If you are in this position, be sure to go over the form carefully so you have a clear idea of what is expected. If the kinds of things on the evaluation form do not lend themselves well to your style of teaching, ask if you can share your lesson plans with the evaluator, and if those plans can be the basis of the evaluation. If the course objectives have already been approved and the plans look reasonable, the evaluator may be quite willing to base the evaluation on them. This will enable you to be evaluated on how well you do what you say you intend to do, rather than on a generic evaluation form alone.

You may also be given the choice of having the evaluation on a predetermined day or having the evaluator come in unannounced. If given this choice, it is wise to choose the unannounced visits. If the visit is announced, the evaluator will expect to see you at your very best. If you have heard of "Murphy's Laws," one of them says that if anything can go wrong, it will, and at the worst possible time. It is wiser to tell the evaluator to come in unannounced, and to see you as you are. If you do the kinds of things recommended so far, the evaluator will find few faults.

Peers

As a beginning teacher it will not take long for you to identify at least one other teacher in the building who you believe is doing an exceptionally fine job. When that happens, it is appropriate to ask that teacher to sit in during some of your classes and suggest ways in which you might improve. You are likely to have more confidence in the suggestions of a person of your own choosing than in suggestions provided by an administrator who may or may not be familiar with your subject area.

Students

No one sees your day-to-day performance more frequently than your students, so it makes good sense to ask them to evaluate you. Forms for evaluations by students typically include questions similar to those listed previously in the Process Evaluation section, but teachers are free to develop their own forms. Students can also be asked to bring in written or typed evaluations that focus on what they like most and least about the teacher and the course.

It is common for student evaluations to vary widely, and you need not be devastated if a student says things that are unkind or even untrue. The power of student evaluation is in their sheer numbers. If one or two students mention a particular problem, you may choose to ignore it. It is more difficult to ignore that problem if it is cited by many students, particularly if the same problem is cited over the course of two or three semesters. However, unless you ask for student input, you might never know what problems are interfering with student learning. Getting student input gives you one more basis for analyzing, and improving, your own teaching, and thus being better able to help your students succeed.

There is a difference of opinion about whether students should be asked to sign their evaluations. Some educators believe that if students are asked to sign their ratings, they will not rate a teacher poorly or cite problems, even if such a rating is deserved, for fear of having their grade lowered. Other educators argue that students are likely to take the evaluation more seriously if they have to sign their name. If students' grades are kept public (using ID numbers to protect confidentiality), students should have little to fear by being honest. Nonetheless, they may be fearful. A compromise is to encourage students to sign their evaluations, but make such signing optional.

Teacher Performance Tests

A teacher performance test (TPT) is a test that you, as the teacher, give to yourself. One way to use a TPT is to specify one or two precise instructional objectives that students can achieve within a single class period and which you have reason to believe concern information or skills that are new to the students.

Next, establish a minimum acceptable level of class performance. This standard is different from the minimum acceptable standard specified in the objective(s). Here, you use your own judgment to decide on a minimum percentage of students who must be able to demonstrate the objective(s) before you will consider the lesson a success. There is no one "right" percentage.

The final step is to go ahead and teach the lesson. If the minimum number of students established as a cut-off point are able to demonstrate the objective, you have reason to believe that, for those students, under the conditions that existed, you did an effective job. Reach over and pat yourself on the back. Of course, success with one lesson might have been a matter of luck, but you can verify the findings by using the same process frequently. If the expected number of students are unable to demonstrate the objective(s), you will know to look more closely at what actually took place during the lesson and to try some other procedures.

Audio and Video Recordings

So much takes place during a typical lesson that it is difficult to recall, afterwards, all that went on. Let machines help. Most schools have audio tape recorders and many have video tape recorders as well. Taping the TPT (or any other lesson) can provide highly useful information. You may find, for example, that you talk too fast, tend to cut off students' responses, or neglect to reinforce students for their contributions. Because of the wealth of information that can be gleaned, many educators believe that the most effective form of self-evaluation is to view a video tape of a lesson while checking what you see against the plan for that lesson. This enables you to see how well you were able to do what you planned to do, and how much students were actively and appropriately involved.

Interaction Analysis Techniques

In addition to simply listening to or watching a playback of a lesson, you could utilize an interaction analysis technique. One of the most common of these was developed by Edmund J. Amidon and Ned A. Flanders and is known as *Flanders' Interaction Analysis*.[3] This technique is based on the delineation of nine categories of student and teacher verbal behaviors. The analyst uses the numbers assigned to each category of verbal behavior to encode, every three seconds, the kind of interaction (if any) that is taking place at that moment. The list of numbers can then be analyzed to determine if particular interaction patterns are used to the exclusion of other patterns and whether the interaction pattern recorded was what the teacher intended. The technique is useful for quantifying verbal interaction patterns and it is not intended as a technique for determining whether those patterns are good or bad. Judgments of that sort should depend more on the kind of interaction intended and the extent to which the interaction pattern facilitates students' achievement of the specified objectives. Another interaction analysis system was developed by Morine, Spaulding, and Greenberg.[4] Either system can help ascertain what actually transpired during the lesson and help to quantify that information.

SUMMARY

Immediately after a test is administered, the teacher should conduct an item analysis to determine which questions and choices help differentiate among students of differing abilities and which do not. Then the teacher must assign grades using whatever system was decided on. The traditional A–F scale with the lowest A equal to 90 percent of the possible points, the lowest B equal to 80 percent of the possible points, etc., has the advantage of being easy to understand. It does not, however, make it possible to clearly see differences in students' abilities if tests or assignments prove to be particularly easy or difficult. Further, the traditional scale poses problems in equating grades in general courses with those in advanced courses. Grading on a curve, such as one based on standard deviation cut-off points, provides for tests of differing difficulty levels since the scale moves up and down with the mean, but it opens the possibilities for awarding passing grades for work that is, in fact, unacceptable.

All grading systems have strengths and weaknesses. If the school does not mandate a specific system, you are free to adopt or adapt one that you feel reasonably comfortable with and can defend. That system should be one that is fair to students, can be applied consistently, is easy for students, parents, and administrators to understand, and is relatively easy for you to use.

Grades must eventually be reported to parents, and the best way to do this is through parent–teacher conferences during which questions parents have can be answered and examples of the student's work can be shown and discussed. Reporting progress via telephone allows for two-way communication, but not for responses to facial expressions or the examination of written work. Letters are one-way communicators, but they enable the teacher to provide parents with some idea of what objectives students were working toward and how successful they were. Report cards are the most common, and least effective, way of communicating what a student has achieved. The work of weeks is summarized, supposedly, in a single letter. Its convenience accounts for its popularity.

Teacher evaluation is just as important as student evaluation. A particularly useful approach is to videotape a lesson and then assess the extent to which it followed the lesson plan and the extent to which students could achieve the lesson's objective. Other techniques, such as student, peer, and administrative evaluations, may provide useful information, but no single piece of information should be considered conclusive. A good teacher is continually trying to improve and is continually seeking feedback. The single best feedback is the success of the students. A teacher's success is dependent on the success of his or her students.

SO HOW DOES THIS AFFECT MY TEACHING?

Becoming familiar with some basic statistical terms and procedures enables you to calculate, interpret, and communicate grades effectively. This is particularly important today because people seem most interested in the "bottom line," and, in education, for better or worse, the grade represents the "bottom line." Since grades are of such crucial interest, you should go out of your way to ensure that not only is your grading system fair, but that students and parents understand why it is fair. To help them understand you often have to explain and use some basic statistical terms and procedures, so taking the time to understand them now will make things easier later.

With respect to self-evaluation, little needs to be said. Improvement is always possible and there are procedures that can effectively aid in this continual effort. The very fact that you make the effort to improve your effectiveness has value. It helps students, parents, and administrators see you as a professional who is continually trying to learn and improve. Such an image provides a good model for students to follow.

KEY TERMS, PEOPLE, AND IDEAS

Item analysis
Raw score
Measures of central tendency
    Mean
    Median
    Mode
    Range
    Percentile Point versus Percentile Rank
Confidentiality
Assigning Grades
    Traditional grading scale (A–F where lowest A equals 90 percent, etc.)
    Grade inflation
    Curved grades
    Normal, bell-shaped curve
    Standard deviation
    Standard deviation cut-off scale
    Jenkins' formula for estimating standard deviation
    Round down to next lowest whole number when calculating cut-off
        points
Reporting Grades
    Go over the test with students
    Two-way communication is best when reporting grades
    Stanines
    Standard Scores—z-scores and T-scores
Teacher Evaluation
    Process versus Product evaluations
    Random, rather than planned, evaluation by administrators work to the
        advantage of the teacher

Teacher Performance Test
Flander's Interaction Analysis

ENDNOTES

1. Ferguson, George A., *Statistical Analysis in Psychology and Education,* 2nd. ed. (New York: McGraw Hill, 1966), pp. 256–262.

2. Diederich, Paul B., "Short-Cut Statistics for Teacher-Made Tests," *Evaluation and Advisory Series,* No. 8 (Princeton, N.J.: Educational Testing Service, 1960), p. 23.

3. Amidon, Edmund J., and Ned A. Flanders, *The Role of the Teacher in the Classroom* (Minneapolis, Minn: Association for Productive Teaching, 1967).

4. Morine, Greta, Robert Spaulding, and Selma Greenberg, *Discovering New Dimensions in the Teaching Process* (Scranton, Penn.: International Textbook, 1971), p. vi.

14

CLASSROOM MANAGEMENT

RATIONALE

One of the greatest concerns felt by most beginning teachers is whether they will be able to establish and maintain a classroom atmosphere conducive to effective teaching and learning—in short, whether they will be able to control their classes. Actually, the issue of classroom control is larger than maintaining a good classroom atmosphere. It involves what you can do to help students learn to be responsible for their own actions.

This chapter examines principles of classroom management, how helping students meet some basic human needs can help minimize or eliminate problems, some approaches to dealing with problems if they arise, and some of the legal terms and factors that may help guide your actions in the classroom. The intent is to provide you with information and techniques that you can use to prevent most common classroom management problems and to deal humanely and effectively with any that do arise.

SAMPLE OBJECTIVES

You will be able, in writing, to:

1. Explain at least two basic management principles and their supporting rationales. (Comprehension)
2. Select any two levels of needs described by A. H. Maslow and explain at least two things that can be done to help students satisfy those needs in a classroom. (Application)
3. Given a video tape, or a written description, of a classroom management problem, determine whether an operant conditioning, reality therapy, or

Limiting Involvement approach is most appropriate and cite specific factors from the tape or description to support your decision. (Analysis)
4. Define terms such as *in loco parentis,* case law, slander, libel, extortion, assault, and battery. (Knowledge)

BASIC MANAGEMENT PRINCIPLES

There are many classroom management rules and principles, but the following are likely to prove particularly useful to you.

The Goal Is Self-Control

One of the primary missions of all teachers is to help students learn to control their own actions and take responsibility for those actions. Young children lack the foresight to anticipate the consequences of many of their acts, so parents and primary-grade teachers assume much of that responsibility. This helps protect youngsters from impetuous actions that might be harmful. As children get older and more experienced, they mature—they become more able to anticipate consequences and, thus, more aware of the need for self-control. Parents and teachers who, for various reasons, are slow to give up the control they have, hinder the maturation process. The situation is analogous to learning to ride a bicycle. It is helpful to have someone hold the bicycle when you are first learning to balance, but if the helper does not let go, you will never master the skill or be able to use the bicycle to its fullest advantage. Teachers need to let go of some control in order to provide opportunities for students to practice the skill of self-control. If students do not practice the skill, it will be difficult for them to master it.

One way to "let go" is to minimize the number of rules imposed. Teachers are required to enforce all rules set forth by the school board and the school administration. These are usually written in a handbook that is given to each student at the beginning of the school year. All teachers, and particularly beginning teachers, should read the school rules carefully because they are contractually obligated to enforce them, and they should make that point clear to students. Beyond those rules, however, teachers have a great deal of latitude. Some teachers, for example, find that they need just one rule: *You may do whatever you like as long as you do not disturb anyone else.*

Such a rule may sound like an invitation to chaos, but it is not. One reason for this is that the rule is so reasonable that students are reluctant to violate it. Teachers who take such an approach might find the following steps useful:

1. Before the semester begins, construct a syllabus and supporting unit plans that focus on the acquisition of useful information. Be sure that you can show students the personal and social significance of the mate-

rial to be learned. Build a rationale that answers the question "Why should I learn this stuff?"

2. On the very first day of class, distribute, and then discuss, the course syllabus. The discussion of the objectives and week-by-week schedule will communicate to students that you have done your homework, that you have thought seriously about the course and its relevance to the students, that you have confidence in them, and that the plan is workable— it will enable them to achieve worthwhile goals.

3. Explain that you will help students learn the skills and information described in the syllabus, but that you can control only your own actions, not their actions. Therefore, although you intend to do your best to conduct interesting and informative lessons and to help each student achieve useful objectives, students must each decide whether they want to learn. In order to get anything out of the class, they have to put something in: effort.

    While the choice to learn or not learn, to put forth effort or to coast, is up to each student, the choice to disturb others is not. Students who do not want to learn can do other work, doodle, or daydream, as long as neither you nor students who wish to learn are disturbed or distracted. This is not really much of a concession, because if students choose not to learn they will do these other things anyway. You are simply recognizing a fact and trying to impose a condition on it. However, because you give students the option of simply sitting quietly and doing nothing, if they choose to cause a problem, their choice makes them seem unreasonable. Since few students want to appear unreasonable to their peers, the rule acts as a deterrent against disruptions.

Rely on Natural Consequences

A natural consequence is one that follows an action without the necessity of human intervention. For example, if you continually consume more calories than you expend, you will put on weight. If you fall asleep while driving on the highway, you are likely to have an accident. If you daydream during class, you may miss some information and may not be able to perform tasks requiring that information.

Schools do not deal with life-and-death issues, and failing a course does not condemn a person to a life of abject slavery. Nonetheless, many students and parents expect that if a student is not doing well, the teacher will come up with some way to save the day. Do not do it. At the beginning of the semester, explain that you have no intention of trying to live students' lives for them and, in part, this means that you will not shield them from the consequences of their own actions. If they do not pay attention, do not complete assignments, or miss class because they are discussing their unacceptable behavior with an administrator, their grades are likely to suffer and they may end up failing the course. You will not fail them, they will fail themselves.

This approach to classroom management shifts responsibility for proper student behavior from the teacher to each student, where it belongs, and it gives students the opportunity to develop self-control. That opportunity is denied them if you closely supervise and control their every move.

Helping Students Succeed

People would rather be successful than unsuccessful, and to the extent that you can help students succeed, they will tend to be cooperative. Success means the achievement of some goal or the satisfaction of some need or desire, so the first thing teachers must do in order to help students be successful is to identify some of the basic needs and desires that motivate their behavior. As it happens, the groundwork has already been done.

MASLOW'S HIERARCHY OF NEEDS

In 1943, Abraham H. Maslow described a hierarchy of human needs beginning with basic physiological needs and extending through needs for safety, love, esteem, and self-actualization. He theorized that people would devote their attention to at least partially satisfying their most basic needs before they diverted their efforts to satisfying less basic needs.[1] For example, you might, at one time or another, have had to miss part of a play or movie in order to use a restroom. The physiological need was more powerful than the desire to watch the entertainment. Teachers can make use of Maslow's work because the needs he described are the motivating forces behind many student actions. Understanding the hierarchy of human needs may help teachers understand how they can help students meet those needs in the classroom. This will help minimize or eliminate many classroom management problems.

One word of caution. In thinking about why particular students may be causing problems, you need to keep your own qualifications in mind. Unless you are a certified psychologist or a licensed physician, you should not try to diagnose or treat any suspected psychological or physical problem. Teachers are employed to teach the content they are certified to teach, not to play amateur psychologist, physician, or minister. Any attempts to do so may do more harm than good (regardless of good intentions), and they may delay or prevent the proper thing from being done.

Physiological Needs

Maslow identified physiological needs as the most basic and powerful of all human needs. For example, the first concern of a person who is drowning, starving, or dying of thirst is to satisfy that crucial need for air, food, or water. Teachers do not often encounter situations involving actual survival; nevertheless, physiological needs can prompt behavior problems.

Air

People work best when they are reasonably comfortable. If a room is too cold or too warm, smells bad, or simply lacks adequate air circulation, students will soon begin paying more attention to the discomfort than to the lesson. Teachers who ignore such problems will appear to be unreasonable or unaware of the world around them. Neither image is helpful. A better course of action is to acknowledge the problem and to try to solve it. Sometimes it helps to simply open a window, but in some cases it might be necessary to move to a different place. In any case, the acknowledgment of the problem, and the effort to solve it, are important. These steps show students that the teacher cares about them, and this alone will help minimize potential behavior problems.

Food

One could argue that it is the responsibility of parents to feed their children, but since the passage of the National School Lunch Act in 1946, schools have taken on part of that responsibility. Most students come to school adequately fed, but they are in a period of rapid growth and are frequently hungry. Do not be surprised, therefore, if students are somewhat less attentive toward the end of the period immediately preceding lunch. Hunger is a powerful force, and hungry students would rather contemplate a hamburger than an algebraic equation. This does not mean that teachers should allow students to snack during class (since that would be likely to disturb the teacher and the rest of the class), nor does it mean that a teacher should end instruction early. What is does mean is that if you are aware of basic human needs, you are more likely to understand students' actions—in this case, why they may be less than fully attentive.

If you suspect that a student is getting too little to eat or is suffering from malnutrition (perhaps from dieting too rigidly), the proper course of action is, first, to discuss the issue privately with the student and then, if necessary, to alert the appropriate school administrator. Your primary function is to provide food for thought. Others are employed to deal with the question of food for the body.

Water

The need for water is not usually a great problem, but callous teachers can make it into one. If a student asks for permission to get a drink of water and is refused for no good reason, you will appear to be unreasonable. If students believe that you are unreasonable, you will find it difficult to elicit student cooperation and can expect continual challenges to your authority.

On the other hand, some students use requests for drinks as a way of avoiding work or disrupting the class. One effective way to handle this problem is to meet with such students privately and express concern for their health. Tell students that you will keep track of their requests and, if there seems to be a problem, that they will be referred to the school nurse. If the requests were just excuses, the idea of having to talk with the school nurse will quickly end the problem—people like to keep their personal habits personal. If the requests continue, there might, in fact, be a problem and a visit to the nurse would be appropriate.

Using the Bathroom

The need to eliminate bodily wastes is a very real and basic need and requests to go to the bathroom should be granted immediately. If you suspect that students are making the request in order to avoid work or to disrupt class, the same strategy as used with the excessive water-drinkers should be used. You should meet with such students privately and express concern for their health, and explain that if they cannot attend to their needs before or after class, an appointment will be made for them to see the school nurse. Students are even less likely to want to discuss their toilet habits with a nurse than to discuss their requests for drinks, so the problem will quickly end. If the need is real, a referral might result in finding and treating a disease or malfunction at an early stage.

Sleep

Today's teenagers have full schedules. In addition to attending school and doing homework, many students engage in extracurricular activities and some hold part-time jobs. As a result of trying to attend to so many things, some students do not get the sleep they require and may therefore doze during class. Certainly such students are less likely to sleep if a class is interesting and informative, but even when it is, some students may still get drowsy. One way to help students fight drowsiness is to announce to the class that anyone who feels sleepy should feel free to get up and stand in the back of the room for awhile.

Unfortunately, some students may fall asleep in your class and, even though they may not be snoring, the very fact that they are sleeping will distract you and, as they become aware of it, it will distract other students. You will need to take some action.

The first time a student falls asleep, it would be appropriate to indicate, via nonverbal cues, that someone nearby should awaken the student. It is important to avoid embarrassing the sleeper. Once awake, the student can be brought into the class activities by being asked a not-too-specific question or by being asked for an opinion. If the problem persists, you should meet with the student privately, express concern, and use the referral strategy. In some cases, students may not be able to control their amount of sleep—they must work late to help support their family, or it is impossible to get to sleep at a reasonable time because of noise. These problems should be referred to an appropriate administrator. Your primary responsibility is to teach. Others are employed to deal with out-of-school problems.

Interest in the Opposite Sex

Interest in the opposite sex is normal, and it begins to manifest itself during the early teen years. Educators are well aware of the hormonal changes affecting students, and they try to help students adjust to their new needs by providing instruction about reproductive systems, social expectations, and how to avoid sexually transmitted diseases. This instruction provides students with useful information, but in some cases the hormones appear to override the thinking process.

You need to be aware that teenagers are sometimes preoccupied with sex. They have just undergone pubescence, and they are naturally curious about their bodies and their attractiveness to the opposite sex. Some concern about physical development and some flirting is to be expected. If the interest interferes with academic performance, then the teacher needs to intervene. The intervention should take the form of a private conference to discuss with the student the need to separate physical concerns from academic concerns. Since the issue is a sensitive one for most students, one conference is usually enough. If the preoccupation continues or if the student brings out a concern that may reflect a physical problem, referrals to appropriate school staff may be in order.

Safety Needs

Once physiological needs are at least partially met, Maslow contends that people will turn their attention to the next most powerful need, physical safety. As was the case with physiological needs, safety needs refer to survival—not being killed by wild animals or by other people. In today's schools there are three main sources of physical harm.

Other Students

The U.S. Department of Education estimates that each day about 100,000 students carry guns to school and that each hour more than 2,000 students are physically attacked on school grounds.[2] Further, more than 400,000 crimes are reported in and around our schools and many more go unreported.[3]

There is little that teachers can do to protect students against violence by other students, because most of that violence takes place when teachers are not present, as in restrooms, before or after school, or in congested, hectic situations, such as crowded hallways or lunchrooms. If such violence is a serious problem in your school, the school administration may decide to have police patrol the school grounds and hallways and/or to install metal detectors. Having to take these steps is unfortunate, first because it is an admission that education alone is not sufficient to induce social order and, second, because it is expensive. It reduces the number of dollars available to meet other educational needs. In some cases, however, there is no choice. Without that protection, education in some schools is not practical.

While you may not be able to do much about violence outside your classroom, you can take steps to prevent it in your classroom. One step is to establish and follow a routine. If you begin each class on time, greet students, take attendance, make announcements, and then move directly into the lesson, students will understand what to expect in that class and what is expected of them. This understanding will help generate among students a sense that the classroom is a special place, a place to learn, not a place to continue out-of-class discussions or fights. The classroom becomes more of a safe and secure haven.

The Curriculum Itself

A second source of safety concerns for students is the curriculum itself. Handling a welding torch in a shop class, putting a cake into a hot oven in a home economics class, or jumping off a diving board in a physical education class, are activities that may, depending on the previous experiences of individual students, cause them great concern. It does not matter that the activity is one that can easily be performed safely; what is important is the student's perception of danger. It is the perception that must be dealt with because that is what the student sees as real.

It is best to avoid problems, so it is wise to examine planned activities and to identify any that have caused concern for students in the past or that might cause concern for students now. If any such activities are identified, it makes sense to make a special effort to show students how those activities should be done and how to avoid common mistakes. While you do not want to generate fears where none exist, students need to know that having concerns about some things is not wrong or "dumb," and that if they have such concerns you are willing to work with them, individually, to help them get the job done.

It may happen that a student does not ask for extra help, but shows great reluctance to engage in an activity during class. The student should not be pressured, either physically or by fear of ridicule, to engage in the activity. You should move on to another student and discreetly arrange to talk with the fearful student after class or after school. Great care should be taken to avoid embarrassing the student. Most of us are fearful of one thing or another, but none of us would want that fear to be the source of public ridicule or embarrassment. If you handle the problem with sensitivity and tact, you will do much to strengthen your rapport with the class.

When meeting with the student privately, discuss the problem and offer additional time and help. It should be made clear, however, that credit for achieving the objective can be given only if the objective is, in fact, achieved. The student's fear may be so great that he or she chooses to lose credit for the objective rather than attempt the activity. Make it clear that this is an acceptable choice. There is no point in telling the student that unless that particular objective is achieved, his or her academic career is ruined. First, such a statement is not true. There are other objectives that can be achieved and other things the student can learn. Second, an understanding attitude may, over a little time, help the student overcome the fear and achieve the objective. Your job is to help students succeed. Helping them overcome fears helps them succeed.

Corporal Punishment

A third source of student concern for safety is physical punishment. Although hundreds of years ago teachers, such as Hillel and Comenius, argued that physical punishment has no place in the instructional process, the practice is still with us. In fact, as recently as 1988, 50 percent of 2,118 adults surveyed approved of the use of physical punishment.[4]

The legality of corporal punishment is in the hands of each state, because there is nothing in the U.S. Constitution about education. In April of 1977, the U.S. Supreme Court, in *Ingraham* v. *Wright,* ruled that the provision against cruel and unusual punishment does not apply to school children.[5] Nonetheless, many state boards of education have banned the use of corporal punishment, some for pedagogical reasons, and others out of fear of lawsuits. Within those states that have not formally banned corporal punishment, many local school boards have done so. Even in districts that have not banned it, many principals have done so. It is important to keep in mind that once a rule or law is passed at one level, no one at a lower level has the right to unilaterally change or ignore that rule.

It is reasonable to ask why so many teachers favor corporal punishment, and the answer is not hard to find. Imagine yourself as a primary grade teacher who has just told a student, for the third or fourth time, to stop poking other students. The student looks up at you and says, "No." After your attempts, and perhaps the attempts by the principal or school counselor to reason with the student have failed, what would you do? You are charged with the education of 20 or 30 small children. Students such as your poker have apparently not learned appropriate social skills at home, and they see no reason to listen to you or to anyone else. The problem is that there is no natural consequence for their continued misbehavior. Lacking other workable alternatives, many teachers see corporal punishment as the most appropriate substitute for a natural consequence.

You, however, will not be teaching primary grade students and, at the high school level, the arguments against physical punishment are strong.

First and most important, using force rather than reason contradicts the intent of the educational process. Educators are trying to help students learn to solve problems by using brains rather than brawn. If educators themselves use force, the brains versus brawn argument is seriously weakened. This, of course, is equally true at the primary grade level, but there the students may be too young to understand the concepts involved.

Second, although physical punishment may be expedient and may provide some immediate satisfaction to the punisher, it teaches the student very little other than not to get caught. If a teacher is unable to explain the rationale for or against a particular act with sufficient clarity to convince a student, it is unlikely that a session with the paddle will do the job.

Still further, while educators might be able to use physical punishment in the lower grades, because they are so much bigger than the students, older students are unlikely to submit meekly to such treatment. In the interest of self-preservation, teachers should abstain from physical punishment.

If a student is subjected to physical punishment, you should not administer it. Your role as a concerned helper is too important to jeopardize by assuming the role of bully. Further, if physical punishment is administered, it should be done in the presence of at least two adults. Lawsuits are likely to arise out of charges of physical abuse, so a witness may be needed in court. Avoid the problems. With the exception of occasional congratulatory pats on the back, teachers should keep their hands off students.

Love Needs

Maslow's description of love needs centers on the love that usually exists between husband and wife, between parents and children, and among siblings. The need for this kind of nurturing love and sense of belonging is only indirectly related to classroom management, because a teacher's sincerest concern for a student cannot replace the love and concern of a mother, father, brother, or sister. Further, you are not employed to act as a substitute mother, father, brother, or sister, you are employed to teach.

Nonetheless, you should recognize that students who are deprived of love at home suffer a deficiency as debilitating as that resulting from the deprivation of food or sleep. Students who suffer from a lack of parental concern, nurturing, and love are likely to be less stable emotionally and more easily depressed than their more typical peers. A teacher who learns of such a problem can make special efforts not to amplify the problem at school.

While it is not true that all students who come from single-parent homes suffer from a lack of love, the following statistics are not encouraging.

About 24 percent of single women age 18 to 44 had borne a child (as of June 1992), compared with 15 percent a decade earlier. The proportion of single mothers more than doubled among women with one or more years of college (4.4 percent in 1982; 11.3 percent in 1992) and nearly doubled among women with a high school diploma, 17.2 percent in 1982; 32.5 percent in 1992.

Out-of-wedlock childbearing increased among all racial and ethnic groups between 1982 and 1992. About two-thirds (67 percent) of births to black women in 1992 were out of wedlock, compared to 27 percent for Hispanic women and 17 percent for white women. Comparable figures in 1982 were 49 percent, 16 percent, and 10 percent, respectively.

In 1992, about 65 percent of teenage (15–19 years old) births were out of wedlock. Ninety-four percent of black American teenage births were out of wedlock, compared to 60 percent of Hispanic and 56 percent of white teenage births.[6]

Nearly 30% of all family groups with children were maintained by single parents in 1993, a significant increase from 12% in 1970. A child in a one-parent situation was just slightly more likely to be living with a divorced parent (37%) in 1993 than with a never-married parent (35%).

Although two-thirds of all single parents were white, one-parent situations are much more common among black American, than whites. About 65% of all black family groups with children were maintained by single parents versus 25% of comparable white family groups. Among Hispanics, single parents represented 35% of family groups with children.[7]

The statistics just cited make it clear that many students have less than an ideal family life and are, in many cases, parents themselves. One thing you *can* do with respect to love needs is to maintain your classroom as a place where students are safe from physical abuse and from psychological abuse such as ridicule and embarrassment. This can be done, in many cases, by generating among students a sense of unity and security. This, in turn, can be facilitated by having a set of common goals, treating students with respect and insisting that they treat you, and each other, with respect. If these things are done, your room is likely to become an island of calm and sanctuary. Students will know that when they are in your room, they are safe and that you care about them as individuals. In an otherwise threatening and turbulent world, students would value such a place.

Esteem Needs

The need for self-esteem is the need for a sense of worthiness in one's own eyes and in the eyes of others. Although this need is less basic than the preceding needs, it is more directly related to classroom management and more amenable to teacher manipulation.

One aspect of self-esteem is one's sense of oneself as a person—the need to be accepted as one is. You should make it clear by words and actions that your first, and greatest, concern is for each student as a person. People are not perfect, and it is reassuring for students to know that when they make a mistake, they will not be regarded as inherently bad. It is the act, not the person, that rates the disapproval. This stance enables you to continue working with students who sometimes cause problems. It becomes a matter of "John, I do not like what you did, but I believe that you have done better and will do better," rather than, "John, I do not like what you did and therefore I want as little to do with you as possible." The first stance allows for cooperation in the future, whereas the second tends to end the relationship.

The same is true if students do poorly in your class. It is important to remember that despite your best efforts to demonstrate the usefulness and relevance of what you are teaching, not all students will recognize that usefulness and relevance. Consequently, those students may not put forth the effort required to learn, although they may go through the expected motions of working on projects, doing library work, or even sitting with the book in their laps for hours. Their poor performance means only that they are not doing well in your class. It is likely that those students have a host of talents that you, yourself, lack. For example, they may be better than you at playing basketball or football, cooking or taking care of a house, or stealing cars. Low grades do not necessarily reflect stupidity.

Internal Recognition

Self-esteem has two parts. The first and most important part is the recognition, by individuals, that they are being successful—that they are developing new abilities, new knowledge, or new control over their lives, or are acquiring some other desired thing or state. Think back to the time you learned to ride your bicycle or to swim. The chances are good that one of the first things you did after learning the new skill was to show off your new ability to Mom or Dad. You were proud, and you felt good about yourself. That is what self-esteem is all about—earning a sense of accomplishment.

Earning the sense of accomplishment is crucial. Students are unlikely to feel good about themselves if they get high grades for relatively simple work. The symbol (whether it is a gold star, a high grade, money, or some other reinforcer) is not sufficient, by itself, to produce the feeling of pride and accomplishment that builds self-esteem. To exist at all, the feeling must be earned: it must be based on having made a real gain.

One way teachers can help students achieve is by helping them help themselves. For example, if a student is having difficulty learning a skill, it might be useful for the teacher to break the skill into separate components and encourage the student to work on each component independently, with minimal teacher assistance. This "systems analysis" approach should help the student eventually overcome the larger problem. The procedure requires careful monitoring of each student's progress, but it helps students more accurately perceive their abilities, and it builds their self-esteem as they see their abilities increase through personal effort.

Allowing students to redo all or some assignments is another way to help them develop self-esteem. No one feels good about doing poorly, but if you provide a second chance and additional guidance, it is likely that the students' competence will increase and it will take their self-esteem with it.

Sometimes students are so caught up with their failures that they lose sight of the fact that they are making some progress. When students are not doing well, examine their overall performance and isolate the things that they do well. If you then take those students aside, and point out the progress they have made and the likelihood that more can be made, they are more likely to develop a feeling of accomplishment. Such students may not feel great about their work, but they will not feel hopeless either. You cannot give students a sense of accomplishment as you might give a five-dollar bill, but you can help students realize their actual achievements, and that is important.

External Recognition

A second part of self-esteem is having other people recognize your accomplishments. Remember running to show Mom or Dad that new ability? You did not do that until you were confident that you had acquired the skill; that had to come first. Immediately thereafter, however, you wanted everyone to know. Much the same is true of your students. Having worked and practiced to develop new skills that they perceive to be important, they will want others to know of their accomplishments. Acknowledging students' achievements boosts their self-esteem. Posting good work on bulletin boards is a common way elementary school teachers share students' achievements, and grades on report cards are common at all levels. However, if you are serious about helping students feel good about themselves, a phone call to their parents once in a while to tell them about a piece of good work or some good class participation, will go a long way. The parent will certainly tell the student about the call, and the student will feel good. Most people feel awkward about blowing their own horns, but few object if someone else does it for them. Take the time to point out the accomplishments of students to parents, other teachers, and administrators, making sure that the accomplishments represent real gains in skills and abilities. The better students feel about themselves, the better work they are likely to do. The more successful they are, the more successful you will be.

The need for peer acceptance is great among teenagers. If they cannot satisfy that need by doing well in some socially accepted arena (such as school, music, or sports), they may try to satisfy the need by demonstrating to peers that they can challenge an authority figure—you—and win. From the students' standpoint, winning may be measured by the degree to which they can get away with some rule infraction, by publicly proving that some rule is outdated or logically inconsistent, by causing a teacher to lose patience, or by using up class time. Regardless of the outcome, such students accomplish part of their goal simply by focusing attention on themselves.

Challenges and confrontations can be minimized if teachers follow a routine of beginning class promptly, explaining the objective, and moving directly into the lesson. This routine focuses the attention of the class on a specific objective. Once the lesson is underway, any issue raised that is not relevant to the work at hand should be deferred. Students raising such issues should be told that the work at hand must continue, but that the issue can be discussed immediately after class. By refusing to argue during class, the teacher minimizes the peer reinforcement that the student might get. Further, and equally important, deferment provides a cooling-off period. This increases the likelihood that the issue can be discussed objectively.

Teachers need to be careful not to use sarcasm, ridicule, or humiliation, for any reason. It is particularly important to guard against sarcasm. Teachers have many opportunities to make remarks that seem clever, and perhaps even funny, but that may offend some students. Think twice before speaking. A sharp tongue can inflict deep and lasting wounds, and it can surely destroy any rapport that might be developing.

Keeping grades confidential helps minimize student embarrassment and humiliation, and it protects your own integrity. It is generally no secret who is doing well in a class and who is not, but if you become the source of information about who is and is not doing well, you are betraying a trust. Further, many schools have strict rules prohibiting the sharing of confidential information such as grades.

Perhaps the best advice is the oldest. "Do not do unto others what you would not have them do unto you."

Self-Actualization Needs

The last need described by Maslow is the need for self-actualization, or the need to develop as fully as possible.[8] This need is directly related to classroom management. Students who believe that their time and efforts will help them make useful and relevant gains in abilities or will open up new areas of personal development, are likely to be more willing learners.

One of the most crucial steps you can take to help students meet their need for self-actualization is to ensure that the course objectives focus on the higher levels of the cognitive or psychomotor domains. Such objectives require the integration of skills and knowledge and usually reflect abilities relevant to life outside of school. Discuss these abilities with students and, further, show how the content clearly relates to current events in business, industry, research, the arts, or some other human endeavor. These steps will help students see that they will be learning interesting and valuable information and that they are, in fact, enhancing their own abilities.

It is also important for students to use their newly acquired abilities. Individual or group projects can provide opportunities for students to utilize new skills and to see how their study has paid off. Further, to the extent that the projects involve people other than the teacher, students will be demonstrating their abilities to different adults, thus helping build their self-esteem.

In review, many classroom management problems can be avoided if teachers recognize that, in most cases, students' actions are motivated by basic human needs. By consciously helping students satisfy those needs, teachers will eliminate many of the causes of classroom management problems.

GUIDELINES FOR MINIMIZING DISCIPLINE PROBLEMS

Using the background information on human needs, along with other psychological principles and common sense, the following set of ten guidelines can be helpful in organizing to preclude discipline problems.

1. *Minimize Physical Distractions.*

   Students who are concerned about their physical well-being are likely to pay less attention to the classwork at hand. Simple steps, such as assuring a continual flow of fresh air through the room, maintaining a comfortable temperature, eliminating glare on the chalkboard, and establishing a reasonable policy concerning leaving the room for drinks or trips to the restroom, can help eliminate the causes of many "discipline problems."

2. *Treat Students with Respect.*

   Remember that students are fellow human beings and deserve to be treated with the same degree of respect and courtesy that adults extend to any of their peers. Students are likely to treat you the same way you treat them

3. *Explain the Big Picture.*

   Taking the time to explain to students what the course is about, what skills and abilities students will gain, and how those skills and abilities can be of practical utility to them, helps give students the big picture. Letting students know what will be happening and when, treats them like adults. They have a sense of direction and a timeline to use in assessing progress.

4. *Maintain Reasonable Expectations.*

Your expectations of students, and your confidence in your own ability to help them succeed, will have an effect on their performance. Many teachers, hoping to ensure student success, have expectations that are far too low. They have the effect of cheating students by depriving them of the opportunity to truly excel. At the same time, teachers should not set unreasonably high expectations. The solution is not complex. Set expectations that you believe are reasonable even if they are higher than most students originally think they can achieve. Present them with a mountain, not a mole hill. Further, do not feel guilty if it is necessary to expect more work from students than they think should be required. Make it clear that it requires hard work to achieve most worthwhile goals.

At first, this step will not make you popular, but you are not in a popularity contest. You are in business to help as many students as possible become as competent as possible. If you are willing to work with students individually, you will find their frustration at having to work hard seems to speed learning. The mildly uncomfortable feeling that students get when their initial efforts do not always lead to immediate success continues until they achieve the objective. The sooner the task is completed, the sooner the frustration ends. If you expect too little from students, this sense of frustration will be lacking, the work may be viewed as busywork, and the final sense of achievement students could otherwise have experienced will be minimized. At the same time, unattainable goals or artificial barriers to goal achievement must be eliminated or students will become overly frustrated, and this frustration may be manifested in the form of discipline problems.

When students successfully complete your course it seems more desirable for them to say, "I worked like a dog, but I really learned useful stuff," as opposed to "We had a lot of fun, but we didn't learn much." Your students may be young, but they are not stupid. They do not want to waste their time and effort. They may not love you for making them work hard, but they will take pride in their accomplishments, and they will respect you for doing what you were supposed to do.

5. *Use a Variety of Instructional Experiences.*

A frequently cited cause of discipline problems is student boredom. You can combat this by building into your lessons a variety of learning experiences. Not every student will be equally interested in each experience, but by having a number of different experiences, you increase the probability of gaining and holding the interest of students more of the time. Interested students are less likely to cause discipline problems.

6. *Provide Prompt Feedback.*

Students are generally very interested in finding out how they did on any given task, and they are young and do not have a lot of patience. If feedback is not forthcoming fairly soon after the task is completed, students are apt to think that the teacher did not regard the task as very important. This feeling will continue to grow as such instances multiply, with the eventual result that students will feel that whatever they do in that particular class is of little value. Such an environment is open to the generation of discipline problems. As a general rule, a second assignment should not be given until the first is corrected and handed back. That is one reason why it is a good idea to have written assignments turned in on Fridays. You then have the weekend to correct the work.

7. *Provide Positive Reinforcement.*

When evaluating students' work, many teachers concentrate on the identification and correction of errors. This is useful in that if you do not point out mistakes, students will not know about, or be able to correct, them. However, if you do not also recognize those things students have done well, they may become discouraged and resentful. Their needs for esteem and self-actualization will go unsatisfied and they may seek other, undesirable sources of satisfaction. It is a good idea, therefore, to point out sections of students' work that are well done and to encourage students to use those sections as models for the less well-done portions. Sincere, positive reinforcement can go a long way toward making corrections more palatable and toward satisfying student needs.

8. *Be Consistent.*

If students perceive inconsistencies in a teacher's reactions to problems, or if they believe a teacher is being unfair, their respect for that teacher will decrease. Once a teacher loses the respect of his or her students, discipline problems will begin to increase.

9. *Foster Peer Approval.*

As was pointed out earlier, peer approval or disapproval is an important element in the life of most adolescents. At times this force may motivate students more than any other single element. If you are able to gain the respect and approval of the majority of your students, potential trouble-makers will recognize that they risk peer disapproval if they cause problems.

It must be pointed out that, although teachers can accept most forms of student support and can allow most forms of peer pressure to bear on students causing discipline problems, the tool cannot be used indiscriminately. Peer pressures such as physical reprisals, ridicule, sarcasm, and humiliation cannot be tolerated. If teachers condone the use of such measures, the very student respect that generated the support in the first place will be lost.

10. *Avoid Punitive Action.*

This principle is one of the most difficult for beginning teachers to follow. Many people have become accustomed to an eye-for-an-eye philosophy. When a student causes a problem for a teacher, that teacher's first inclination may be to cause at least as great a problem for the student. There is, however, little evidence to support the idea that punitive action will have any lasting effect on deviant student behavior. Nonetheless, what follows is an examination of common punitive actions.

A. *Detention.*

This option punishes teachers as much as students, since someone must supervise the detention. Often the student is bused to and from school or has an after-school job, and the hardship caused makes the punishment excessive. In other cases, students may be involved in sports or some after-school club and the detention may therefore deprive them of one of the few school experiences that is keeping them from dropping out.

B. *Extra schoolwork.*

There seems to be no evidence to support the idea that assigning extra schoolwork is helpful in eliminating discipline problems. In fact, it is likely that the assignment of such work will cause students to associate all schoolwork with unpleasant experiences and thus cause more harm than good.

C. *Repetitive sentences and the like.*

The use of repetitive sentences and similar busywork assignments has been widespread among teachers for years. There must be teachers somewhere who have found this device effective in maintaining good discipline, but locating such a teacher proves to be difficult. Such tasks are likely to cause students to equate schoolwork with busywork and to dislike both.

D. *Special seating assignments.*

Special seating assignments usually take one of two forms. In the first form, a seat is isolated from the rest of the class and students are assigned to it essentially as objects of ridicule. Ridicule is not acceptable as a discipline device.

Another form of special seating is to attempt to separate friends or arrange seats in a way that will minimize student interaction. This procedure is less satisfactory than using friendships in a positive way to foster intrinsic motivation. Further, if they want to, separated students will still find ways to communicate despite the teacher's efforts.

E. *Physical labor or exercise.*

The use of physical work or exercise is fraught with danger. A student who is asked by a teacher to do as little as move a desk, and who is hurt in the process, is in a position to sue the teacher. In some schools, asking or telling students to engage in physical labor is specifically forbidden.

Exercises, such as running the track, doing push-ups, and so on, are sometimes used in physical education classes as punishment. The same reservations apply here that applied in the assignment of schoolwork as punishment. How are students going to build an intrinsic desire for exercise if the teacher considers it distasteful enough to use as punishment?

F. *Lowering of grades.*

In some school districts there are policies that condone the lowering of an academic grade for disciplinary reasons. This practice is analogous to withholding a diploma as punitive action, when all necessary requirements have been met. In this case the courts have ruled that the diploma must be awarded.[9] In the case of grades, unless the grading criteria are clear and public, a teacher may be accused of lowering a grade because a student caused discipline problems. Lowering grades is difficult to defend logically because once a student has achieved an objective and demonstrated a competence, it is senseless to deny the accomplishment. Teachers who engage in this practice will be deemed unfair by their students and will quickly lose a large measure of student respect.

G. *Banishment from the classroom.*

Sending a disruptive student from the room may solve a problem for the moment, but it definitely causes another problem, and may cause still more. The immediate problem caused by sending a student from the room is that it denies the student access to ongoing instruction. Forget, for the moment, that the student obviously did not want the ongoing instruction. If that student's academic achievement is considered important, the teacher will eventually need to spend extra time helping that student learn the missed material. Further, you are legally responsible for your students while class is in session. By sending a student from the room, you remove that student from your direct supervision and may, therefore, be held liable if the student is injured or gets into additional trouble.

BEHAVIOR MODIFICATION: OPERANT CONDITIONING

All learning is intended to modify behavior, but the term **behavior modification** is most commonly used in reference to classroom management. A more exact term would be **operant conditioning,** a term made popular by B. F. Skinner. Operant conditioning is a behavior modification approach that centers on the belief that behavior is modified more by its consequences than its causes. Therefore, if one wishes to increase a particular behavior or cause it to continue, one provides a **positive reinforcer,** some immediate reward. For example, suppose some students were not doing their homework well. If those students were given a piece of candy every time their homework was done well, and they began to do their homework well more often, then the candy would be functioning as a positive reinforcer.[10]

Negative reinforcement occurs when something a student does not want, such as nagging or the revocation of the right to park in the student parking lot, is withdrawn, and the desired behavior increases. If you continually ask certain students about their homework, or lack of it, and they start doing the homework simply to "get you off their backs," the principle of negative reinforcement is at work.

Punishment occurs when the presentation of a stimulus results in a decrease in the *undesired* behavior. If students are required to stay after school if they forget to do their homework, and they do their homework in order to avoid staying after school, then staying after school is a punishment.

Care must be taken not to make assumptions about reinforcers or punishments. For example, if some students were particularly conscious of their weight, candy would probably not function as a positive reinforcer. In fact, it might even be seen as a form of sarcasm or punishment. In the case of negative reinforcement, some students, those who receive little if any attention, might feel that the nagging was better than no attention at all. In the case of punishment, if the student was scheduled for some activity that was disliked even more than school, a detention might function as a positive reinforcer rather than as punishment. The point here is that the only way to determine whether an action is a positive reinforcer, a negative reinforcer, or a punishment, is to see its effect on the target behavior.

Use

One can use operant conditioning to initiate or continue desirable behaviors. All that is necessary is to find something that the individual(s) value, and make attainment of that thing contingent on achieving some desired behavior. Pizza Hut® conducts a nationwide program known as Book It.© This program is designed to encourage reading among elementary school students. Each teacher who chooses to participate sets reading goals for each student. Every month that the students reach their individual goals they are rewarded with a coupon for an individual pizza at a Pizza Hut® restaurant. If all the students in the class reach their goals, the class gets a pizza party from Pizza Hut.®

When used to end undesirable behaviors, operant conditioning usually involves the following steps:

1. *The teacher identifies the behavior to be changed.*

   Care needs to be taken here. Behaviors, by themselves, are neutral. They become misbehaviors when someone, in this case you, decides that at the time and in the place the behavior was demonstrated, it was inappropriate. Since you decide what constitutes a misbehavior, you have the option of considering every glance out the window and every whisper to be worthy of immediate intervention on your part, or of choosing to overlook behaviors that are not truly disruptive.

2. *Devise and try countermeasures.*

   Countermeasures will depend on the misbehavior. For example, if a student, Tom, whispers only occasionally, ignoring it might be appropriate. However, while this option might work, it might also result in other students' misinterpreting your lack of action for approval.

   A second option would be to move Tom to a different seat where neighbors would be unlikely to whisper back. This option might work, but it may be less desirable than other possibilities because it is unlikely to bring about a lasting modification in Tom's behavior.

   A third option would be to try to determine why Tom was whispering. For example, it may be that he frequently fails to prepare adequately, and whispers prior to discussions in an attempt to acquire needed information. In this case, you could wait for a time when Tom *was* able to participate in a discussion of homework and then praise him for his good work and valuable contributions. If the praise or other positive reinforcement is forthcoming each time he contributes to discussions without whispering beforehand, the whispering might soon cease. This procedure, while effective, depends on waiting until the student is adequately prepared, so it could turn out to be a long-term approach.

A fourth option to speed up the reinforcement process could be initiated. The teacher could:

a. Make specific homework assignments for each student.
b. Privately encourage Tom to do the assignment.
c. Call on some students to discuss their homework, but call on Tom the first day only if he has done his homework, and ignore whispering if it occurs.
d. Again make specific assignments and privately encourage Tom to do his.
e. As soon as Tom has made an effort to do the assignment even if it came only as the result of heavy prompting, call on him during the discussion and praise his contribution. Again ignore his whispering if it occurs.
f. Repeat steps d and e each day, praising Tom's contributions and ignoring his whispering. The whispering should decrease and disappear within a few days. If it does not, the analysis must be reexamined for alternative explanations for the behavior.

The point of the operant conditioning process is to focus attention on desired behavior and to provide an incentive for students to engage in that behavior. The incentive may be praise, points, or any other reward valued by the student, and the expectation is that the desired behavior will soon become self-reinforcing and will replace the undesirable behavior, which is never reinforced.

Keep in mind that sometimes the removal or withholding of a stimulus (for example, the denying of an opportunity to receive attention and reinforcement from peers) is as effective as the presentation of a stimulus (for example, the giving of praise or rewards). Once the right stimulus is found for any individual, a procedure can be established to help bring about lasting behavioral changes via operant conditioning.

Reservations about Operant Conditioning

This emphasis on rewards rather than causes seems superficial to many educators, and has caused many to express reservations about using operant conditioning techniques. Among the arguments used by opponents of operant conditioning is that the process may cause as many problems as it solves. When teachers use operant conditioning, the basic process is to identify the specific behaviors they wish to increase, and reward the student when the desired behavior is demonstrated. It is usually not long until other students observe that one way to get extra attention or rewards from the teacher is to misbehave and then behave properly on cue. If this happens, operant conditioning techniques can be unfair to those students who behave properly.

Still another concern of many educators is that operant conditioning techniques imply that appropriate behavior should be demonstrated only because such behavior will generate an **extrinsic reward** such as praise, candy, money, or free time. They maintain that the use of rewards for appropriate behavior obscures the fact that such behavior has its own *intrinsic rewards,* such as the feeling of having done the right thing, and will not, in fact, bring extrinsic rewards in the "real" world. They claim, therefore, that operant conditioning techniques mislead students by giving them a false impression of reality.

There are other reservations concerning operant conditioning, including where to draw the line between creativity and exuberance, and the need for an environment conducive to learning. However, most of the attacks on operant conditioning have been prompted by aversion to its abuses by individual teachers who use it indiscriminately and without regard for its ramifications. When used properly, the rewards often pertain to student fulfillment of basic needs, such as the needs for esteem and self-actualization. Further, when teachers fully understand the ramifications of the technique, they are quick to point out to students the intrinsic rewards of the desired behavior and thus lead students away from continued dependence on extrinsic rewards.

BEHAVIOR MODIFICATION: REALITY THERAPY

Reality therapy is a behavior modification technique pioneered by Dr. William Glasser in his work as a psychiatrist.[11] It utilizes student needs, but its philosophical orientation is significantly different from that of operant conditioning. In operant conditioning, individuals undergoing the conditioning are often unaware that their behavior is being manipulated. No attempt is made to treat individuals as responsible people, to make them partners in a joint effort to modify behavior, or to help them see the cause–effect relationships between their behavior and its long-term consequences.

Reality therapy, on the other hand, makes individuals the prime movers in the modification of their own behavior. Reality therapy is predicated on the idea that people engage in those behaviors they believe will satisfy one or more perceived or unperceived needs, but that some individuals have either a distorted idea of what their goals are or a distorted idea of how to achieve them. Reality therapists see their role as a "perception sharpener"— one who attempts to help the individual perceive the reality of the situation. The assumption is made that the students know right from wrong.

Reality therapy begins with the current situation. Although reality therapists are well aware that many problems have roots in past events, they are not willing to allow those past events to become excuses for future actions. The individual's attention is focused on the behavior to be modified, not on the root causes of that behavior, and the individual is helped to see the consequences of continuing the undesirable behavior as well as the consequences of modified behavior. The basic reasoning is not to dwell on the past since the past cannot be changed. Instead, think about the future; you *can* shape that. The following step-by-step procedure is illustrative of how a teacher might use reality therapy to deal with Tom's whispering.

1. *Help the Student Identify the Undesirable Behavior.*

   In this case, the teacher would arrange to see Tom privately. The teacher would first get Tom to identify the problem. It is important that Tom identify the problem, because then he is taking the first step toward its solution. If the teacher makes the identification, Tom is likely to look to the teacher for the solution rather than to seek that solution for himself.

   Care is exercised not to ask Tom why he is engaging in the undesired behavior (whispering). To do so would provide him with an opportunity to offer an excuse for his actions and to focus attention on the excuse rather than the action. The reality therapist does not deny that there may be legitimate reasons for inappropriate behavior—he or she simply insists on beginning with the inappropriate behavior rather than with a series of antecedent events. Nothing can be done about the past, but something can be done about the future.

2. *Help the Student Identify the Consequences of Undesirable Behavior.*

   It is important that the consequences identified be real and logical. If the environment is manipulated so the consequences of a particular action are unreasonably harsh or virtually meaningless, the situation becomes contrived and irrelevant to the real world. In such a situation, no technique is likely to be effective. In this case, for example, telling Tom that he will be suspended from school if whispering continues is unreasonable. Similarly, it would be unreasonable to tell him that inappropriate behavior will have no consequences. It is appropriate, however, to point out that consequences are often cumulative and tend to get more and more severe.

3. *Help the Student Make a Value Judgment about the Consequences.*

   The purpose of this step is to help the student see that the inappropriate behavior is contributing more to eventual unhappiness than to immediate or long-range happiness. The student is likely to have inaccurate perceptions about the effects of the behavior and may need help in making a value judgment about its desirability or undesirability. In this case, continued whispering will, because it interferes with the learning of others, cause Tom to be removed from the room, and possibly to miss so much work that he will fail the course. If Tom says that he understands all that and has no problem with it, the discussion is at an end. The student may have, in your opinion, made a terribly unwise choice, but you must res-pect his right to make the choice. Everyone has the right to live their life as they see fit, providing they do not interfere with the lives of others. Hope-fully, however, Tom will decide that the consequences are undesirable.

4. *Have the Student Formulate a Plan for Changing the Behavior.*

Once Tom has concluded that the behavior is not, in fact, in his own best interests, the next step is for him to suggest alternatives to that behavior. If possible, he should be encouraged to propose an alternative behavior, for example, that he will:

a. Simply stop whispering.
b. Admit to not knowing an answer or not doing his homework, rather than trying to acquire last-minute information via whispering.
c. Tell the teacher before class when he is not prepared and then he will not be called on to answer questions.

Of these three alternatives, the last is the least acceptable, and the teacher should reject it if Tom does not see its inappropriateness, because it forces the teacher to share responsibility for his actions when, in fact, that responsibility belongs to him alone. It is important that Tom recognize that (1) the current situation is a result of his own behavior, and (2) he can extract himself from the situation by engaging in behaviors that are both socially acceptable and conducive to achievement of his own, and other people's, success and happiness.

5. *Have the Student Select and Implement a Specific Plan.*

After Tom (perhaps with the teacher's help) has generated alternatives, he should decide which one to implement. At this point, the teacher's role is to monitor Tom's behavior, to see how well he is following the plan, and to provide appropriate reinforcement.

The differences between the operant conditioning approach to behavior modification and the reality therapy approach are many and significant. It is unlikely that both approaches will appeal to all teachers, or that all teachers will be able to use both with equal effectiveness. It is suggested, therefore, that before either approach is decided on, teachers assess their own philosophical position concerning classroom control and behavior modification. Haphazard or indiscriminate use of either or both of these procedures can not only be frustrating and futile, it can also harm a teacher's rapport with students. Used properly, however, these procedures may bring about lasting behavioral changes.

BEHAVIOR MODIFICATION: THE "LET'S KEEP IT SMALL" APPROACH

In the mind of every teacher is a conceptual model of an "ideal" teaching–learning environment. You may prefer a highly structured environment and someone else, a loosely structured environment, or just the opposite may be true. Similarly, you may be willing to tolerate a much broader range of deviant student behaviors than other teachers. Nonetheless, regardless of how carefully you plan and how skillfully you conduct your classes, there may still be minor disruptions that can develop into major classroom management problems. The best way to deal with such problems is to keep them small.

Jacob S. Kounin reports that teacher-initiated disciplinary acts (which he and his associates labeled "desists") can have significant effects on the other students in the class who are not the target of discipline. These effects have been called "ripple effects." In one study it was found that teachers who use angry or punitive desists often cause other students in the room to refocus their attention from the work at hand to the disturbance and the teacher's reaction to it. Simple reprimands, on the other hand, tend to have a smaller ripple effect.[12] Kounin also reported that interviews with high school students indicate that, for a teacher viewed as fair and generally liked by the students, desist actions are less likely to cause ripple effects destructive to the teaching–learning environment.[13]

One could conclude, therefore, that to deal successfully with most discipline problems, teachers should establish good rapport with their students and should use simple reprimands to deal with occasional deviant behavior. Mild desists can include actions such as moving toward disruptive students, standing by them, glancing at them, and directing questions at them, as well as direct reprimands. Further, reprimands should be in the form of direct statements rather than questions. "Would you please stop talking?" is less desirable than "Please stop talking," because it does not invite a verbal response from the student.

If mild desists are not effective, and the previously discussed preventive measures are being used, or if reality therapy or operant conditioning techniques have failed, the teacher needs a plan of action. In some schools, teachers are told exactly what disciplinary procedure to use. If such a policy exists, it should be followed precisely. If no policy exists, the teacher should develop one based on whatever policies do exist. The following procedure is based on the belief that most people already have more problems than they want and that they will not choose to complicate their own lives if they can avoid doing so. It is called the "Let's Keep It Small" approach because the idea is to solve the problem with the involvement of as few people as possible. Here are the steps.

1. If a student engages in behavior that interferes with the teaching–learning process, politely tell the student to stop.
2. If the deviant behavior persists, tell the student to remain in the room for a short meeting after the class is dismissed. Keep the meeting brief, businesslike, and to the point. Explain to the student that such behavior is unacceptable. At the very least, it was keeping other students from learning because it was taking your time and attention away from help-ing those students. Try to get a commitment from the student that such misbehavior will not reoccur. Most importantly, have a note card at hand, let the student see you noting the problem, who was involved, and the date, and ask the student to initial the entry. The purpose of the anecdotal record is to help convince the student that you are serious and intend to follow through. You want the student to realize that coopera-tion will be far less troublesome than non-cooperation.
3. If the offending student continues the disruptive behavior, schedule a mutually convenient time for a longer meeting with the student. The rea-son for ensuring that the time for the meeting is mutually agreeable is that students will find reasons why they cannot meet at teacher-decided times. You should be willing to meet before, after, or at an appropriate time during the school day. Make sure that the student understands the commitment to meet. If there is any doubt about the student's showing up, make two copies of the time and place and mutually initial each copy.

   It should be made clear to the student that such a meeting is not synonymous with detention. The purpose of the meeting is to review the student's offenses and to outline the consequences of future offenses. The teacher should explain why the offenses cannot be tolerated (because they disrupt the teaching–learning process and keep other students from learning). The focus of the meeting should be on identifying and elimi-nating the misbehavior, not on excuses, and not on the student person-ally. A record of the meeting, offense, date, and so forth should be added to the anecdotal record card and the student should be asked to initial the entry.

   At this point, even the slowest student should begin to feel that the procedure and meetings are a bother (or even a little embarrassing), and will also realize that you mean what you say, you intend to see the problem ended. Notice that no punitive action has been taken. The emphasis is on changing the behavior of the students, not on punishing them. Students should be told that further problems will result in your contacting their parents; the choice of involving others is theirs.

4. If the problem persists, enlist the aid of the student's parents. This step may or may not help, but taking it is important in any case. At the next offense, as the student is leaving the room, note that you will be contacting the student's parents. Once this step is announced, it is important that the contact with the parents be made as soon as possible, preferably before the end of the school day. If this is not done, the student may arrive home before the teacher's call and set a stage that is difficult or impossible to cope with. Once the contact is made, go through the anecdotal record explaining the actions taken, enlist parental support, and explain that if the problem continues you will need to refer the student to the school administration. A record of the home contact should be made on the anecdotal record card.

5. If the problem persists, refer the student to the school disciplinarian but, before making the referral, contact the disciplinarian and discuss the anecdotal record with the list of offenses and corrective efforts. This is important because the disciplinarian must understand that you have tried to deal with the problem professionally. You had a minimum of two conferences with the student, you talked with the parents, and you are now hoping that the disciplinarian can help resolve the problem. Once the disciplinarian understands that the problem is not superficial, work with the student can be attempted by this new party. If the disciplinarian decides on some punitive action, the choice will not be yours.

6. In most cases, if you have made a professional, but unsuccessful, attempt to deal with a disruptive student, the administration will be willing to help. Administrators will be less willing to help if you charge into the principal's office screaming that student X is impossible, incorrigible, and ought to be thrown out of school immediately, preferably minus a head. Typically, the administrator will try essentially the same steps you tried. However, the administrator might also impose detentions, suspensions, and might even go so far as to recommend that the Board of Education expel the student.

One advantage of the "Let's Keep It Small" approach is that you are, at no point, threatening punitive action. You are simply trying to get students to control their own behavior so that teaching and learning can take place effectively in the room. Others may impose punishments, but you do not. In fact, you are doing all you can to keep the student from reaching the point at which punishment might be administered.

Another advantage is that you are acknowledging that only the student can solve the problem. You can steadily involve more people, which will probably make things increasingly unpleasant for the student, but only the student can choose to end the problem. This is the true state of affairs and you want the student to know that you know it.

POTENTIALLY DANGEROUS SITUATIONS

At some point, you may face a potentially dangerous situation. Some of the more obvious examples include students who are armed, verbally abusing you or other students, drunk, high on drugs, overtly defying authority, or maliciously destroying property. In such situations your first obligation is to do what you can to keep students from harming themselves or others. This does not mean that you are expected to throw yourself between a drunk student's gun and the class. It does mean that you will remain calm, that you will notify the administration of the problem either by intercom or by sending a student to the main office, and that you will try to contain the situation until help arrives. Keep in mind that you are responsible for all of the other students in the class. If you send them from the room or leave them alone, perhaps in order to escort the offending student to the main office, some provision must be made for their supervision.

SPECIAL CASES

Hyperactivity/Attention Deficit Hyperactivity Disorder

Sometimes when teachers see a student who is continually restless, given to sudden outbursts, or unable to concentrate on the work at hand, they attribute it to **hyperactivity** or, as it now called, **Attention Deficit Hyperactivity Disorder** (ADHD). Without hyperactivity, the problem is called **Attention Disorder Deficit** (ADD). Hyperactivity was, at one time, thought to be caused by the inability of an individual to assign priorities to the many sensory inputs constantly bombarding the brain. Then it was thought to be caused by a chemical imbalance in the brain. Today, doctors are still not sure just how to define or treat hyperactivity or attention deficit disorder, but experts believe that as many as three and a half million students under the age of 18 suffer from it.[14] However, one thing is certain. You, as a classroom teacher, are not qualified to diagnose such problems and attempting to do so may cause harm. What occasionally happens is that a teacher mistakes lapses of attention, restlessness, or even the normal exuberance of youth for hyperactivity or attention deficit disorder. Having "diagnosed" the problem, the uninformed teacher may call the student's parents (or have the school nurse call them), and suggest that they take the student to a physician and "have the doctor give him something."

Unfortunately, some physicians will, after only a cursory examination, accept the teacher's "diagnosis" and prescribe a treatment on that basis. The typical treatment for hyperactivity is the prescription of amphetamines such as Ritalin and Dexedrine. Although these drugs act as stimulants for adults, they act as depressants for children. It is difficult to predict accurately the exact effect of any specific drug on any specific child, and many children are being adversely affected by such chemotherapy. Even worse, because of the increasing instances in which drugs are prescribed for students on the basis of inadequate diagnoses, many students are exposed to drugs who do not need to be.

If you suspect that a student may be hyperactive or suffering from attention deficit disorder, the initial step should be to double-check the basis for the suspicion. The procedure is to keep a written record of the frequency of each "hyperactive" act, check with other teachers to see if the student is demonstrating similar behavior in other classes, and engage in discussions with the school nurse and guidance personnel to see if they have been told of any specific problems the student may be having.

Dyslexia

Dyslexia is a medical problem that hinders one's ability to learn to read and it is estimated to affect between five and ten percent of the U.S. population.[15] In some cases, dyslexia causes people to see certain letters or words transposed. In 1994, it was discovered dyslexia is not so much a vision problem as it is a hearing problem. Dyslexics cannot process sounds properly. If students cannot hear what sounds certain letters make, they cannot sound out words. This, in turn, hinders their ability to learn to read.[16] As is sometimes the case with hyperactivity and attention deficit disorder, students with dyslexia may, mistakenly, be thought to be lazy, obstinate, or simply misbehaving.

If the suspected behaviors are persistent and not just isolated examples, the collected data should be discussed with the guidance department and nurse. If the results of this conference indicate that an examination by a physician is in order, then the parents should be involved in a separate conference in which such an examination is recommended. At this conference the parents should be provided with a copy of the list of incidents without any diagnosis of the source of the problem. The *doctor alone* should diagnose the problem and prescribe any treatment.

Assuming that the teacher is informed of treatment, it is then the teacher's responsibility to continue to monitor the student's behavior. In this way, the effectiveness of the treatment can be determined and its eventual elimination hastened.

It should be noted that differentiating between real and imagined problems is not easy. Sometimes students will, in fact, have medical or psychological problems that account for their problems at school. More often, however, students and parents will look for, and accept, any rationale to excuse disruptive behavior or poor performance. Citing a medical or psychological problem makes a particularly good excuse because it tends to generate sympathy, but claims that "the devil made me do it" have also been heard. In any case, it is best to avoid diagnosing a problem or labeling a student. Your diagnosis may be incorrect and a label does not help. It may, in fact, be used as an excuse.

LEGAL TERMS AND ISSUES

In most cases, teachers are able to resolve classroom management problems quickly and easily. Few problems require the involvement of parents and even fewer require the involvement of school administrators. Nonetheless, situations that have legal ramifications may arise, so it is useful to know some of the legal terms that might be encountered.

"*In loco parentis*" is Latin for "in place of the parent." Courts of law generally recognize that a teacher acts in place of a parent during school activities. If a question is raised about the propriety of a given action, such as breaking up a fight or detaining a student to prevent a harmful act, the question that is most likely to be asked is whether the teacher acted as a *reasonable and prudent* parent would have acted. A judge or jury would answer that question on a case-by-case basis (case law), because each situation is likely to be unique.

In loco parentis offers you some protection as you go about the task of helping students, but it does not offer immunity to bad judgment. For example, if a student mentions taking drugs, you are placed in an uncomfortable position. A reasonable and prudent person would be expected to try to get help for the student, perhaps by notifying parents, a counselor, or a school administrator. If you do not do this, and the student dies from a drug overdose, how would you feel? Your active intervention might have saved a life. If it is school policy to report such situations, and you do not do so, you might be charged with **negligence**: "the omission to do something which a reasonable man, guided by those ordinary considerations which ordinarily regulate human affairs, would do, or the doing of something which a reasonable and prudent man would not do."[17] On the other hand, if you do notify someone, students might perceive that action as a betrayal of trust, and that perception would seriously weaken your rapport with all students. The choices are not always easy.

Sometimes teachers witness illegal acts. For example, if a student is forced or frightened into giving lunch money to another student, that action is not just "a shame," it is **extortion**: "the obtaining of property from another induced by wrongful use of actual or threatened force, violence, or fear, or under color of official right."[18] A student might also **menace** someone by showing a, "disposition to inflict an evil or injury on another."[19] Some teachers, if menaced, immediately report the situation and many administrators, choosing to be safe rather than sorry, immediately notify the police.

A more serious threat is an **assault**: "any willful attempt or threat to inflict injury on another, when coupled with an apparent present ability to do so (or) any intentional display of force such as would give the victim reason to fear or expect immediate bodily harm."[20] If the student actually carries out the threat and makes bodily contact, the offense of **battery** has been committed.

Teachers are sometimes the victims of slander. **Slander** is "the speaking of base and defamatory words tending to prejudice another in his reputation, office, trade, business, or means of livelihood."[21] Students sometimes say things about teachers that are not true. To the extent that such comments do not go beyond one or two students, they may be no cause for concern. However, if such comments or rumors become widespread they may result in a formal or informal inquiry about the teacher. Depending on how much trouble the comments or rumors cause, the teacher might consider filing charges of slander against the perpetrators. **Libel** is essentially slander in writing.

Sometimes, despite the best efforts of a teacher, it is necessary to remove a student from the classroom. A teacher usually has the right to remove a student for part or all of a class period by having the student go to some other supervised place in the school such as a detention room or the main office. A principal usually has the right to suspend a student from all activities for up to a week. The suspension may be an in-school suspension (the student comes to school, but spends the time in a detention area usually away from other students) or an out-of-school suspension (the student is not allowed into the school during the suspension period). In-school suspensions are most often used when there is doubt as to who would be supervising the out-of-school student.

Students who commit serious breaches of school rules are sometimes expelled. Expulsion is such a serious matter that most school boards take it on themselves to impose that penalty. When a school board expels a student, it generally bans the student from attending school or school functions for a specified period of time and establishes the conditions on which the student may return to school after the expulsion period.

LAWSUITS

Historically, laws have been passed to ensure the greatest happiness for the greatest number. The laws provide a structure and element of stability that is analogous to a curriculum in schools. At the same time, laws must also be applied so as to ensure that everyone has equal rights and protection. Sometimes the two goals conflict as, when in a school, a teacher claims the right, as part of academic freedom, to deviate extensively from the established curriculum. It is from conflicts such as these that lawsuits arise.

Student Suspensions

In January of 1975, the U.S. Supreme Court ruled, in *Coss* v. *Lopez,* that if a student is to be suspended from school for more than a week (this varies from state to state), school administrators are obligated to (1) inform the student that a hearing will be conducted at a particular time and place, (2) explain what the charges will be, (3) show or explain the evidence used to justify the suspension, and (4) listen to the student's side of the story.

In February of 1975 the U.S. Supreme Court, in *Wood* v. *Strickland,* held that if students were to be expelled from school, they were entitled to face their accusers, cross-examine witnesses, introduce witnesses of their own, be represented by counsel, and to appeal. The court also ruled that individual teachers could be held personally liable in monetary damages if they knowingly, or reasonably should have known, that what they were doing would deprive an individual of a civil right.

Teacher Negligence

Cases involving allegations of teacher negligence are most often associated with situations in which students suffer actual, physical harm. In deciding such cases, the court generally uses a three-point test. The first point that the plaintiff (the person bringing the complaint) must demonstrate is that *the defendant* (in this case, the teacher), *had a legal obligation to perform a particular duty,* such as to provide adequate supervision. The second point that the plaintiff must demonstrate is that *the defendant willfully failed to carry out that obligation.* The third point is that *the defendant's failure to carry out this legal responsibility was the proximate cause of the student's injury.*

Suppose, for example, that a teacher spent four or five minutes writing something on the blackboard, and during this time John and Sam were silently sword-fighting with their pencils and John's pencil ended up in Sam's eye. It is quite possible that a court would rule that the teacher had a legal obligation to provide adequate supervision, that such supervision was not provided because the teacher's back was to the students for so long and that, therefore, the teacher's failure to provide adequate supervision was the proximate cause of the injury. If the teacher had been watching the students, the "sword-fight" would never have taken place. Is the use of overhead projectors beginning to sound better and better to you?

Generally, teachers have little to fear from the courts, but being the litigious society that we are, it pays to take precautions. Read your teacher's handbook carefully and follow its rules. Further, although you are unlikely to ever need it, consider the benefits of the malpractice insurance offered as part of membership in both the National Education Association (NEA), and the American Federation of Teachers (AFT).

SUMMARY

The goal of classroom management procedures should be to help students develop self-control. This development is facilitated by freeing students from as many restraints as possible and expecting them to think about, and control, their own behavior rather than mindlessly following rules. Some teachers find that they can extend student freedom to the point of needing only one classroom rule: You may do whatever you like as long as you do not disturb anyone else.

The key to helping students develop self-control is to help them be successful. The first step in this process is to recognize basic human needs and plan the instructional program so that students can satisfy as many of those basic needs as possible. Abraham Maslow identified the following basic human needs: physiological, safety, love, self-esteem, and self-actualization. Physiological needs refer to the maintenance of life and may be reflected in a classroom by a student's need for a drink, for sleep, or to visit a restroom. Physiological needs are powerful enough to override other needs and often must be met immediately. Students sometimes use these same needs as excuses to avoid work or to disrupt class. In these cases, the teacher may speak privately to the student, expressing concern over the student's repeated need for water or the bathroom, and offer to refer the student to the school nurse (or a similar staff member) for a checkup.

Safety needs refer to physical safety. Concern over physical safety may surface in a class where a student refuses to participate in a particular activity, or it may relate to a fear of physical abuse from peers. It is important to remember that regardless of whether a student's fear is real or imaginary, it is real to the student. Students are often embarrassed about being afraid. The teacher should minimize the potential for embarrassment by working privately with the student to help overcome the fear, step by step. If fear keeps a student from completing a required objective, however, the student cannot be given credit for achieving that objective. With respect to safety, students should know, by the words and actions of the teacher, that they are safe both physically and psychologically in the classroom. Teachers can help students meet safety needs by establishing a routine and treating students as people with feelings.

Love needs refer to the kind of love shared by parents and children and as such has little relevance to the classroom. There is, however, at least one point of relevance. With the increasing amount of violence, the high number of divorces, and the high mobility of the population, the classroom may be the only social unit in which the student can be safe from both physical and psychological abuse.

The need for self-esteem refers to the development of a positive self-concept, and teachers are in an ideal position to help students meet that need. Self-esteem is founded on a sense of satisfaction about oneself. Teachers can help students achieve this sense of satisfaction by conveying to students that the work they are doing is serious and worthwhile. This can be done by developing a course syllabus that contains relevant objectives; setting up a calendar showing when various topics will be covered, due dates for papers, and test dates; and selecting appropriate grading criteria. On the first day of class this syllabus should be distributed to students and discussed. This approach lets students know that the teacher has given serious thought to the course and has outlined a reasonable plan for helping them achieve the objectives.

A student's sense of achievement is fostered by internal and external recognition of achievement, premised on the student's attainment of some significant goal. The teacher, therefore, must be sure that the objectives of the course are set at a reasonably high level. If students feel they are improving their skills, abilities, or knowledge in ways that seem valuable to them, they receive the internal recognition of achievement necessary for meeting self-esteem needs. External recognition refers to having others (such as parents, peers, or authority figures) acknowledge a student's achievement. Favorable grades, phone calls to parents (giving good news), and the sharing of students' work are ways of attending to the need for external recognition.

The highest need, self-actualization, refers to lifelong continual growth and improvement. Once again, the course objectives play a central role. If those objectives were formulated with long-term utility in mind, they will be seen as contributing to the satisfaction of the need for self-actualization.

Regardless of how diligently a teacher tries to help students meet their needs, classroom disruptions may still occur. Operant conditioning is one way to deal with disruptive students, but it puts the teacher, not the student, in control of solving the problem. Another approach, reality therapy, puts the student in control, but works only if the student wants to change the behavior.

A third way to deal with such problems is to use the "Let's Keep It Small" approach. To use this approach, explain to students why disruptions will not be tolerated and explain the procedure that will be used to handle them. That procedure consists of first telling a student to stop the undesired behavior. If the behavior continues, the teacher begins an anecdotal record, which will document the student's name, the date, the problem, and what was done. The student may be asked to initial the entry to show awareness of it. If the problem persists after two or three private meetings with the teacher (each with its own entry in the anecdotal record), the student's parents will be contacted. If the problem persists after that, the school administration will be brought in. This course of action demonstrates to the students that the teacher means business, it enables the teacher to follow a consistent, nonpunitive procedure, and it documents the history of the problem and the attempts made to solve it.

With respect to legal issues, teachers will find that if they fulfill the responsibilities assigned to them and act as reasonable and prudent parents would act, they have little to fear from the courts. For example, the usual test applied in negligence suits is whether the teacher had a clear responsibility to the student, whether the teacher willfully failed to fulfill that responsibility, and whether the student suffered actual harm as a consequence of the teacher's failure to fulfill the responsibility. Teachers should not utilize corporal punishment because it is educationally unsound even if it is legal in their school district.

If teachers are humane and recognize that students have basic human needs that must be at least partly fulfilled, and if they establish and maintain a classroom management program aimed at helping students learn to control their own behavior so they can function as effective citizens in a democratic society, they will have few, if any, classroom management problems.

SO HOW DOES THIS AFFECT MY TEACHING?

Each of us should have the right to live our lives as we see fit. However, since we are social animals and interact with others, we sometimes have to control our first impulses and desires in order for the larger group to function. Your job, with respect to classroom management, is to help students recognize these truths. Further, you will have all you can do to live your own life successfully; do not try to live your students' lives for them. Help them learn to take responsibility for their own actions. If they learn nothing else from you other than that, they will have learned something of incalculable value. Further, if they learn that, they are also likely to achieve the other course objectives and, for the last time, their success is your success.

KEY TERMS, PEOPLE, AND IDEAS

Self-Control
You may do whatever you like as long as you do not disturb anyone else.
Natural Consequences

Maslow's Hierarchy of Needs
 Physiological—air, food, water, using the bathroom, sleep, interest in the opposite sex
 Safety—other students, the curriculum, corporal punishment
 Love
 Self-Esteem—internal and external
 Self-Actualization
Behavior Modification
 Operant Conditioning—B.F. Skinner—Teacher is the primary mover
  Positive and Negative reinforcement
  Punishment
  Intrinsic and Extrinsic Rewards
 Reality Therapy—William Glasser—Student is the primary mover
Let's Keep It Small
Hyperactivity, Attention Deficit Hyperactivity Disorder, Dyslexia
In loco parentis, In place of the parent
Negligence, Extortion, Menace, Assault, Battery, Slander, Libel

ENDNOTES

1. Maslow, A.H., "A Theory of Human Motivation," *Psychological Review,* 50 (1943), pp. 370–396.

2. Lantieri, Linda, "Waging Peace in Our School," *Phi Delta Kappan,* Vol. 76, no. 5 (January 1995), p. 386.

3. Chancellor's Working Group on School-Based Violence Prevention, "Draft Report" (New York City Board of Education, July 1994), as cited in Lantieri, p. 386.

4. "20th Annual Gallup Poll of the Public's Attitudes Toward the Public Schools," *Phi Delta Kappan,* Vol. 70, no. 1 (September 1988), pp. 32–46.

5. *Ingraham et al. v. Wright et al., United States Reports,* Cases Adjudged in The Supreme Court at October Term, 1976, Vol. 430 (Washington, D.C.: U.S. Government Printing Office, 1979), p. 651.

6. Farnighetti, Robert, *The World Almanac and Book of Facts, 1994,* (New Jersey: World Almanac, an imprint of Funk and Wagnalls, 1993), p. 957.

7. Farnighetti, Robert, *The World Almanac and Book of Facts, 1995,* (New Jersey: World Almanac, an imprint of Funk and Wagnalls, 1994), p. 960.

8. Maslow, p. 382.

9. Flowers, Anne, and Edward C. Bolmeier, *Law and Pupil Control* (Cincinnati, Ohio: W.H. Anderson, 1964).

10. Skinner, B.F., "The Evolution of Behavior," *Journal of Experimental Analysis of Behavior* (March 1984), pp. 217–212.

11. Glasser, William, *Reality Therapy—A New Approach to Psychiatry* (New York: Harper and Row, 1965).

12. Kounin, Jacob S., *Discipline and Group Management in Classrooms* (New York: Holt, Rinehart and Winston, 1970), p. 49.

13. Kounin, p. 142.

14. Wallis, Claudia, "Life in Overdrive," *Time*, Vol. 144, no. 3 (July 18, 1994), p. 43.

15. Begley, Sharon, "Why Johnny and Joani Can't Read," *Time*, Vol. 144, no. 9 (August, 29, 1994), p. 52.

16. Begley, p. 52.

17. Black, Henry Campbell, *Black's Law Dictionary*, 5th ed. (St. Paul, Minn.: West, 1979), p. 930.

18. Black, p. 525.

19. Black, p. 1137.

20. Black, p. 105.

21. Black, p. 1244.

15

MULTICULTURAL CONCERNS
by Dr. Joe Parks

RATIONALE

By the year 2020, it is estimated that the population in U.S. public schools will have moved to a division by thirds among white, Black, and Hispanic students. According to Thomas, "by the year 2000, one out of every three U.S. residents will be non-white. In addition, U.S. African Americans and Latinos (primarily Mexican/Chicano Americans) presently account for 25 percent of the school-aged population and will comprise approximately 47 percent of that group by the year 2020."[1] It follows, therefore, that some of your students will have a skin color or ethnic background different from yours. Should this make any difference in the way you teach? Theoretically, no. All students should be treated equally and all should be working toward the same objectives. Of course, theoretically, a bumblebee cannot fly, but it does, so we know that theoretical models do not always work in real life. Racial, ethnic, and other cultural differences might affect the teaching–learning process. The question is how, and the answer to that question is dependent on how much you know about racial, ethnic, and other cultural differences.

This chapter is intended to help you understand some of the pressures faced by students who do not fit the traditional white, middle-class stereotype of the American teenager. For example, the chapter will help you better understand the pressures facing biracial students, one of the fastest growing minority groups. Knowing more about the characteristics of, and social pressures facing, minority students will enable you to better help them succeed, and their success is no less important than the success of the majority group—whatever it may be.

SAMPLE OBJECTIVES

You will be able, in writing, to:

1. Describe at least three characteristics that differentiate a given category of minority students from the stereotypic majority. (Comprehension)
2. Define multicultural education and cite at least three ways in which you could modify your content and/or instructional procedures to better accommodate a diverse student population. (Analysis)
3. Determine to what extent, if any, you should adjust your instructional practices to accommodate cultural differences among your students and cite at least three relevant facts, or use cause–effect reasoning, to justify your position. (Evaluation)

MINORITY STUDENTS IN THE CLASSROOM: SIMILARITIES AND DIFFERENCES

Individuals preparing for a career in teaching during the 1990s will encounter a different type of student than those of us who prepared to be teachers during the 1960s and 1970s. The K–12 students of the late 1990s and the 21st century will be more culturally diverse and ethnically different than the K–12 students of the 1960s, 1970s, and 1980s. According to Garcia and Pugh, "While predictions vary, demographers agree that the racial and ethnic proportion of the U.S. and of the world will change in the 21st century. In his introduction to the published proceedings of a conference on the national need for minority scholars, Robert Lichter, executive director of the Dreyfus Foundation, recounts often-cited statistics to emphasize the changing complexion of American society. By the year 2000, Lichter writes, whites will constitute only 55.9% of the U.S. population, down from 75.5% in 1980. Internationally, similar populations trends are predicted for the 21st century. Gwendolyn Baker estimates that, at the turn of the century, five billion of the six billion people on earth will be non-white."[2]

According to Henry, "In New York State, some 40% of elementary- and secondary-school children belong to an ethnic minority. Within a decade, the proportion is expected to approach 50%. In California, white pupils are already a minority. Hispanics (who, regardless of their complexion, generally distinguish themselves from both blacks and whites) account for 31.4% of public school enrollment, blacks add 8.9%, and Asians and others amount to 11%—for a nonwhite total of 51.3%. This finding is not only a reflection of white flight from desegregated public schools. Whites of all ages account for just 58% of California's population."[3] Because the California trend concerning multicultural growth seems to be taking root in every major city in America, the need for educational institutions to address multicultural and multiethnic and educational concerns is apparent. The preparation of new teachers in teacher preparation institutions must involve an understanding and clarification of the rapidly changing demographics and ethnic diversity in America as we enter the 21st century.

Given the fact that there is no one concise definition for multicultural education, it can be stated with reasonable accuracy that multicultural education is *not* intended to teach students about one specific race, culture, or national origin. In the opinion of Cottrol, "multicultural education should include, as part of its fundamental corpus, the teaching of the democratic ideas—tolerance, justice, rule by law, individual rights, majority rule, and more—that have made possible our incredibly diverse, prosperous and—relatively speaking—amicable society."[4] The research literature suggest that multicultural education should include a wealth of information about various cultures on a global scale that allows students to make intelligent conclusions through analysis, synthesis, and evaluation of their society and to develop critical interpretations and arrive at a contextual understanding. It is further suggested in the literature that the academy (universities) should take the lead in establishing a "canon" or knowledge base on which to build a consensus opinion or opinions concerning multicultural education. According to Gordon,

> *In order for the academy to implement a multicultural curriculum it may be necessary to agree on what the canon should embody. What is acceptable knowledge within the boundaries of the canon? Gordon and Bhattacharyya (1992) have identified several criteria by which the integrity of the canon can be judged. They assert that the canon:*
>
> 1. *must be viewed as dynamic, responsive to contextual and temporal variance, and subject to change;*
> 2. *should be capable of accommodating diverse and conflicting information, perspectives, and techniques;*
> 3. *should comprehensively reflect the universe of situated knowledges, perspectives, and techniques, as well as those which may be more universal;*
> 4. *should contribute to the conservation and stability of knowledge, techniques, and world views without the imposition of rigidity;*
> 5. *should be accessible to and engageable by a wide range of audiences;*
> 6. *should reflect functional and meaningful relationships between prior knowledge and the requirements of learning to understand available knowledge and the construction of new knowledge; and*
> 7. *should enable imagination, reflection, accommodation, and transformation as active and creative processes in the service of understanding and human action.*[5]

Gordon is suggesting that university professors and preservice teachers focus their attention on developing a multicultural learning environment that encompasses a broad range of concepts that include the behaviors of all diverse populations within the society. Furthermore, professional educators, old and new, must adopt multicultural curriculums that are inclusive of many different diverse cultures.

During the past thirty years, there has been a move away from the one-dimensional view of the American educational system that was predicated on a "middle-class" Caucasian model. A multicultural and multiethnic understanding of the American society has been prompted because of the rapidly changing diverse make-up of the American population. No longer can one ethnic model (i.e., the white middle class) be used to paint the picture of American society as we begin the 21st century.

Public school teachers and public school curriculums must reflect the "true" American society. Our 21st century K–12 public school teachers must be able to teach and function in culturally pluralistic classrooms.

According to Gay, "the percentage of students of color in U.S. schools has increased steadily since the 1960s. They now compose 30% of the total population of elementary and secondary schools."[6] New public school teachers will not be required to change their frames of reference or their points of view because of the demographic changes taking place in public school population; however, they will be required to add to their knowledge base cultural information about other cultures and ethnic groups that are different from their own. The current K–12 teaching core remains approximately 87 percent Caucasian and approximately 75 percent female.

The lack of knowledge on the part of 21st century public school teachers will certainly impede effective teaching and learning. Gay suggests that, "teachers spend inordinate amounts of time on classroom control and maintaining the anglocentric cultural hegemonic status quo. Culturally different students spend much of their psychoemotional and mental resources defending themselves from attacks on their psychic senses of well-being. Many find themselves in what Boykin (1986) calls a 'triple quandary,' having to negotiate simultaneously in the often-disparent realism of experience: the mainstream school culture, their natal ethnic cultures, and the status of being members of oppressed, powerless, and unvalued minority groups."[7]

BIRACIAL CHILDREN AND ADOLESCENTS: A "WITHIN-GROUP" MINORITY

As professional educators continue to examine and sort out the demographics of the rapidly changing K–12 student population, there is one group of individuals that does not seem to fit into any of the standard categories of student learners. Biracial and bicultural individuals have increased in number during the past 30 years and have become a "within-group" among our various minority populations. Biracial individuals are defined as those individuals whose parents are from two different racial and/or ethnic groups (e.g., Black/White, Asian/White, Hispanic/White, Hispanic/Black, Black/Asian, and a number of other racial classifications).

The "biracial baby boom" came into prominence about 1970 and has continued to grow at a fast pace. According to Root, "The 'biracial baby boom' in the United States started about 25 years ago, around the time the last laws against miscegenation (race mixing) were repealed in 1967. The presence of racially mixed persons defies the social order predicated on race, blurs racial and ethnic group boundaries, and challenges generally accepted proscriptions and prescriptions regarding intergroup relations. Furthermore, and perhaps most threatening, the existence of racially mixed persons challenges long-held notions about the biological, moral, and social meaning of race."[8]

During the past three centuries, the social identity of racially mixed persons has been based on linear models of social relations that use the Caucasian racial group as the acceptable model. Therefore, social distinctions based on racial heritage become important to the dominant group when several groups enter into economic and/or status competition. The distinction of race is used to subordinate some people into the category of "other." In the case of racial subordination in the United States, African American people have been relegated to the status of other by the dominant White culture. Being categorized as other appears to have produced a negative public image for African American people. Wedged between the larger White dominant culture and the African American culture is a group of biracial or "mixed blood" individuals who may have been cast in the role of "buffer" or "marginal" people by both the White and African American monoracial cultures.

In order to understand the identity problems encountered by biracial individuals, one should understand the process by which individuals develop racial and ethnic identities. Because the predominantly White American society tends to classify its members in monoracial terms, biracial individuals are forced to bridge the "gap" between both Black and White racial and cultural groups or to identify with one specific group. Furthermore, because of the accepted and unofficial "one-drop rule," biracial individuals of African American and Caucasian descent are arbitrarily assigned to the lower social status of the African American racial group. (As defined by Davis, this term means "that a single drop of 'black blood' makes a person black. It is also known as the 'one black ancestor rule'."[9])

During the 50-year period following the Civil War, the question of racial identity and classification became a priority issue for government officials because ex-slaves were now available to compete with the working White poor for the bottom rung jobs. The short-lived reconstruction period was over by the turn of the century, and Jim Crow segregation laws were enacted in the South during the late 1900s and became national law after the court case of

Plessy v. *Ferguson* in 1896. In ruling on the *Plessy* v. *Ferguson* case, the Supreme Court ruled in favor of the state of Louisiana and upheld the Jim Crow statute that required racially segregated seating on interstate transportation such as trains and buses. The Supreme Court finally overturned *Plessy* v. *Ferguson* in its 1954 ruling in the case of *Brown* v. *The Board of Education*. In that case the court ruled that the separate but equal doctrine was inherently unequal.

The research literature generally accepts the following factors as key components in the self-identity development of biracial individuals: (a) self-esteem, (b) family interactions, (c) family social and economic factors, (d) psychological development and state of maturity (age of individual), and (e) geographic location of the individual.

Because many clinical researchers suggest that Black adolescents and biracial adolescents encounter similar problems during adolescent development, it is important to review the empirical data on Black adolescent development. At present, researchers and social science experts from various disciplines continue to automatically classify biracial individuals as Black. Although it seems inappropriate to classify all biracial individuals as Black, it is appropriate to study Black history and culture in an attempt to provide a definitive rationale concerning the impact of the Black culture on the social and identity development of biracial individuals. If in fact the larger dominant society classifies biracial and bicultural individuals in the same manner as Black individuals, then it stands to reason that biracial and bicultural individuals encounter similar assimilation problems as Black people.

Spencer suggested that "Black children are at risk because of structural factors in the society that place limits on their opportunity for optimal development."[10] She further states that "The lack of status, political power, and economic opportunity in the Black community results in outcomes for children that frequently are labeled deviant by the majority culture. Young Black children face prejudice and stereotyping both in personal contacts and in the media. As Black children move into the larger society, they face additional risks if they have not been prepared by parents or other socializing agents to understand and take pride in their own culture."[11] Ogbu indicated that Black people and Native Americans are classified as castelike minorities because they were "incorporated into an existing social system involuntarily and permanently."[12] The involuntary inclusion into the dominant White cultural system has posed self-identity problems for Black and Native American people as well as biracial individuals. There is clear and convincing evidence that Caucasian immigrants did not encounter self identity problems during their assimilation process into the American mainstream.

Root suggested several general assumptions that have in the past clouded the issue of biracial identity development as it relates to the larger society, that is, White society. She stated that, "in the United States, despite our polychromatic culture, we are divided into white and non-white. The positive imagery created by the 'melting-pot' philosophy of the United States [appears to be] relevant to white ethnic groups or immigrants such as the Irish, French, and Scandinavian people [but] not [to] African, Asian, Hispanics, or even on home territory, American Indians. Cultural pluralism is neither appreciated nor encouraged by the larger culture."[13]

Biracial children generally become aware of race at an earlier age than monoracial children because their (biracial) racial status is "called into question" by the majority group. When biracial children are asked the question of "Who are you?" or "What are you?", it suggests to the child an inferior racial status as compared to the majority group. Brown suggests that using mainstream cultural norms as the evaluative criteria presumes the structural inferiority of minority cultures. The presumed structural inferiority of their racial groups is a stigma that biracial and other minority group members carry with them throughout life.[14]

Generally, it is believed that all children demonstrate a racial preference and racial awareness by age five. The question of "Who am I?" seems to cause a problem for biracial children after they become aware of how the majority culture ranks minority groups in terms of social status in the societal "pecking order."

When the biracial adolescents move from junior high school to high school, their close-knit group of peers and friends tends to change. The high school peer group assumes a much greater role in the shaping of social attitudes and behaviors. Furthermore, during the junior high/high school transitional period, adolescents move further away from the protection of their parents, who usually attempt to shield their biracial children from the "bigotries of society."

Many research findings indicated that biracial and bicultural individuals developed defense mechanisms and coping strategies to deal with their racial and social identity problems. "To cope with their conflicts over their mixed racial/ethnic identity and their marginal social status, they used defense mechanisms of denial ('I'm not really black, I'm mixed'), reaction formation ('I avoid the Latino kids at school because they're always getting into trouble'), and overidentification with the idolized racial group ('I prefer to hang out with white kids').... Some teens handled their fears of social rejection by either withdrawing socially or trying too hard to please their peers."[15]

In the area of educational and career aspirations, biracial adolescents adopted patterns of being persistent overachievers or chronic underachievers. The underachievers use various rationalizations for their lack of interest in academic matters and future goals.

In evaluating these defensive strategies, four points can be made. First, teens who expressed a negative identity tended to adopt more primitive defense mechanisms (e.g., denial, acting out) and more dysfunctional cop-

ing strategies (e.g., sexual promiscuity, delinquent behavior). Second, teens with negative identities usually incorporated the most devalued stereotypes about their minority heritage, then behaved in a self-fulfilling cycle. Third, teens who identified more positively with their majority racial/ethnic heritage appeared to be superficially adapted to the majority culture but still experienced some degree of identity diffusion. This was reflected in behavioral or psychological indicators such as sexual and emotional inhibition, overerenmeshment in their families, and overconformity in school and community context. Fourth, many of these teens rejected the racial or cultural identity of both parents and sought an alternative identity through identification with a fringe or deviant social group."[16]

MULTICULTURAL ENRICHMENT SUGGESTIONS FOR PRESERVICE AND NEW K–12 TEACHERS

Although there are numerous ways to include several different cultures in a K–12 school curriculum, the following three ideas are offered as suggestions. First, all students should be inculcated with a sense of empowerment concerning their own worth and value within the context of the overall society. This is especially needed among biracial and bicultural groups. When minority group students believe that they have a "real stake" in their own educational future, they become active learners instead of passive observers. According to Nel, "Empowering relationships [between teacher and learner] depend on the extent to which teachers 1) incorporate students' language and culture into the school program; 2) encourage minority community participation as an integral component of children's education; 3) promote intrinsic motivation in minority students to use language actively to generate their own knowledge; 4) become advocates for minority students in assessment procedures."[17] Second, parents must be sought out and encouraged to participate in their children's education. The involvement of parents fosters a sense of community togetherness and allows parents to learn about and better understand the educational institutions of their children. There are a number of suggested ways parents can become involved in the overall curriculum structure of their children's schools. For example, parents can be volunteers to help plan and implement academic as well as social events for students. Also, faculty might involve parents in the development of student/teacher/parent contracts that outline what is expected of the learner, the teacher, and the parents.

Finally, professional and staff development is an important part of the curriculum structure in providing a diverse educational setting. Teachers, administrators, and other staff members could be encouraged to keep up with the current literature and enroll in classes at local universities that offer courses in multicultural and multiethnic education. Teachers must be included in decisions concerning curriculum changes as those changes pertain to multicultural educational needs. Also, faculty members might institute a collaborative effort among various departments in order to develop a multicultural curriculum that crosses disciplines.

SUMMARY

The research literature reveals that there are a number of commonalties among adolescents of all races. However, it appears that biracial adolescents are somewhat unique in certain areas of identity development. For example, biracial children tend to become aware of their racial distinction earlier than monoracial children because of their physical appearance and being asked questions by monoracial children concerning "What they are" in reference to race. Furthermore, biracial children are made aware very early in life that one dominant racial group is more valued than others. Moreover, the literature suggests that the "linear" model of identity development found in monoracial adolescents was not present in biracial adolescents primarily because of the possible "contradictory cultural frames of reference" of interracial couples regarding their own racial identity as well as that of their children.

SO HOW DOES THIS AFFECT MY TEACHING?

In today's society, K–12 public school teachers are required to know more and do more as professional educators. Given the constantly changing demographics of our current student populations, today's teacher must be a "Jack/Jill of all trades," as opposed to just being content literate. In order to help students learn, the new recruit (novice teacher) must possess the technical as well as mental skills that are required in order to make sense out of our forever changing society. New teachers must be especially knowledgeable about the cultural and ethnic groups that do not look like themselves. Having just a basic understanding of the many different cultural and ethnic groups in the United States will help in devising strategies, objectives, and plans for improving K–12 curriculums.

Furthermore, keep in mind that it will be your former students who will become the politicians and leaders that lead American society through the 21st century. Multicultural education as it relates to the growth and development of student minds suggests that educators need to be at the forefront of the movement of our ever-changing multicultural and ethnically diverse society. Educators have a significant influence on the minds and lives of their students and should use that influence to move their students and the society in general toward a more tolerant and understanding attitude concerning individuals who are from a different cultural or ethnic background than their own.

KEY TERMS AND IDEAS

Multicultural—multi-racial and ethnic grouping
Biracial—Children of parents from two different races
Monoracial—Children of parents from the same race

ENDNOTES

1. Thomas, G. E., "Participation and degree attainment of African-American and Latino students in graduate education relative to other racial and ethnic groups: An update from the Office of Civil Rights Data," *Harvard Educational Review,* Vol. 62, no. 4 (1992), p. 46.

2. Garcia, J., and Pugh, S., "Multicultural education in teacher preparation programs: A political or an educational concept?", *Phi Delta Kappan,* (Nov. 1992), pp. 214–219.

3. Henry, W. A. III, "Beyond the Melting Pot," *Time* (April 1990), pp. 28–31.

4. Cottrol, R. J., "America the multicultural," *American Educator,* (Winter 1990), pp. 25–28.

5. Gordon, E. W., *Forward,* in J. Q. Adams and Janice R. Welsch, eds., *Multicultural Education: Strategies for Implementation in Colleges and Universities* (Macomb, Ill.: Western Illinois University Foundation, 1993), p. ii.

6. Gay, G., "Building cultural bridges," *Educational Urban Society,* Vol. 25, no. 3 (1993), pp. 285–299.

7. Gay, p. 36.

8. Root, M. P. P., *Racially Mixed People in America* (London: Sage Publications, 1992), p. 3.

9. Davis, F. J., *Who Is Black? One Nation's Definition* (University Park: The Pennsylvania State University Press, 1991), p. 5.

10. Spencer, M. B., "Black children's ethnic identity formation: Risk and resilience of caste-like minorities," in J. S. Phinney and M. J. Rotheram, eds., *Children's Ethnic Socialization* (London: Sage Publications, Inc., 1987), p. 103.

11. Spencer, p. 103.

12. Spencer, p. 104.

13. Root, M. P. P., "Resolving 'other' status: Identity development of biracial individuals," in L. Brown and M. P. P. Root, eds., *Diversity and complexity in feminist therapy* (London: The Hawthorn Press, 1990), p. 187.

14. Brown, P. M. "Biracial identity and social marginality," *Child and Adolescent Social Work,* Vol. 7, no. 4 (1990), pp. 319–337.

15. Gibbs, J. T. and G. Moskowitz-Sweet, "Clinical and cultural issues in the treatment of biracial and bicultural adolescents," *Families in Society: The Journal of Contemporary Human Services,* Vol. 72, no. 10 (1991), p. 585.

16. Gibbs and Moskowitz-Sweet, p. 586.

17. Nel, J., "Preservice teachers' perceptions of the goals of multicultural education: Implications for the empowerment of minority students," *Educational Horizons* (Spring 1993), p. 120.

SUGGESTED READINGS

Buttery, T. J. (1987). "Biracial children: Racial identification, self-esteem and school adjustment. *Kappa Delta Pi Record,* 23(2), 50–53.

Capuzza, J. (1922). "Why good intentions aren't good enough: Reflections and suggestions for curriculum inclusion." *SUNY* at Plattsburgh's Faculty Forum 18, 14–17.

Cummins, J. (1992). Forward. in S. Nieto, *Affirming diversity: The sociocultural context of multicultural education.* New York: Longman.

Frances, P. L. (1991). "A review of the multicultural education literature." In J.Q. Adams, J.F. Niss, & C. Suarez, eds., *Multicultural education: Strategies for implementation in colleges and universities* (Macomb, Ill: Western Illinois University Foundation), pp. 1–13.

Frances, P. L. (1993). "Assessing the effectiveness of multicultural curriculum initiatives in higher education: Proving the self-evident." In J.Q. Adams & Janice R. Welsh, eds., *Multicultural education: Strategies for implementation in colleges and universities* (Macomb, Ill: Western Illinois University Foundation), pp. 101–109.

Gibbs, J. T. (1987). "Identity and marginality: Issues in the treatment of biracial adolescents." *American Journal of Orthopsychiatry,* 57(2), 265–278.

Gordon, E. W., & Bhattacharyya, M. (1992). "Human diversity, cultural hegemony, and the integrity of the academic canon." *Journal of Negro Education,* 61(3).

Gordon, M. M. (1964). *Assimilation in American life: The role of race, religion and national origin.* New York: Oxford University Press.

Merton, R. (1957). *Social theory and social structure.* New York: Free Press.

Miller, R. L. (1992). "The human ecology of multiracial identity." In M. P. P. Root, ed., *Racially mixed people in America.* (Newbury Park/London/New Delhi: Sage Publications), pp. 24-36.

Ovando, C. J., and McCarty (1993). "Multiculturalism in U.S. society and education: Why an irritant and a paradox?" In J. Q. Adams & Janice R. Welsh, eds., *Multicultural education: Strategies for implementation in college and universities* (Macomb, Ill: Western Illinois University Foundation), p. 53.

Overmier, K. (1990). "Biracial adolescents: Areas of conflict in identity information." *The Journal of Applied Social Sciences,* 14(2), 157–176.

Parks, J. (1994). *Analysis of factors affecting the development of a social identity for biracial adolescents* (Doctoral dissertation, Illinois State University, 1994). Dissertation Abstracts International, Txu 684–047.

SELECTED QUOTES BY ROBERT HUTCHINS (PERENNIALIST) AND JOHN DEWEY (PROGRESSIVIST)

Robert Hutchins—Perennialism

A modern heresy is that all education is formal education and that formal education must assume the total responsibility for the full development of the individual.... We are beginning to behave as though the home, the church, the state, the newspaper, the radio, the movies, the neighborhood club, and the boy next door did not exist. All of the experience that is daily and hourly acquired from these sources is overlooked, and we set out to supply imitations of it in educational institutions.[1]

The child-centered school may be attractive to the child, and no doubt is useful as a place in which the little ones may release their inhibitions and hence behave better at home. But educators cannot permit the students to dictate the course of study unless they are prepared to confess that they are nothing but chaperons, supervising an aimless, trial-and-error process... The free elective system as Mr. Eliot introduced it at Harvard and as Progressive Education adapted it to lower-age levels amounted to a denial that there was content to education. Since there was no content to education, we might as well let students follow their own bent.[2]

If we are educators we must have a subject matter, and a rational, defensible one. If that subject matter is education, we cannot alter it to suit the whims of parents, students, or the public.[3]

... the curriculum should be composed principally of the permanent studies.[4]

... for general education a course of study consisting of the greatest books of the western world and the arts of reading, writing, thinking, and speaking, together with mathematics, the best exemplar of the process of human reason.[5]

The prospective teacher's general education would be identical with that of the lawyer, doctor, and clergyman. With a good education in the liberal arts, which are grammar, rhetoric, logic, and mathematics, he has learned the basic rules of pedagogy. The liberal arts are, after all, the arts of reducing the intellect from mere potentiality to act. And this is what teaching is. The liberal arts train the teacher in how to teach, that is, how to organize, express, and communicate knowledge. In the university he should learn what to teach.[6]

John Dewey—Progressivism

When speaking of the intellectual growth of children he said that "Growth is not something done to them, it is something they do."[7]

Children proverbially live in the present.... The future having no stimulating and directing power when severed from the possibilities of the present, something must be hitched to it to make it work. Promises of reward and threats of pain are employed.[8]

Every energy should be bent to making the present experience as rich and significant as possible. Then as the present merges insensibly into the future, the future is taken care of.[9]

Isolation of subject matter from a social context is the chief obstruction in current practice to securing a general training of the mind.[10]

The present, in short, generates problems which lead us to search the past for suggestion, and which supplies meaning to what we find when we search."... Education "is that reconstruction or reorganization of experience which adds meaning of experience, and which increases ability to direct the course of subsequent experience.[11]

One who recognizes the importance of interest will not assume that all minds work in the same way because they happen to have the same teacher and textbook.[12]

The problem of instruction is thus that of finding material which will engage a person in specific activities having an aim or purpose of moment or interest to him...[13]

ENDNOTES

1. Hutchins, Robert, *The Higher Learning in America* (New Haven: Yale University Press, 1936), p. 69.
2. Hutchins, p. 70.
3. Hutchins, pp. 72–73.
4. Hutchins, p. 77.
5. Hutchins, p. 85.
6. Hutchins, pp. 114–115.
7. Dewey, John, *Democracy and Education* (New York: The Free Press, 1916), p. 42.
8. Dewey, p. 55.
9. Dewey, p. 56.
10. Dewey, p. 67.
11. Dewey, p. 76.
12. Dewey, p. 131.
13. Dewey, p. 132.

APPENDIX B

ORGANIZATIONS FOR NATIONAL STANDARDS

Arts—*National Standards for Arts Education: What Every Young American Should Know and Be Able to Do in the Arts* (Item number 1605) Note: These standards result from the collaboration of the American Alliance for Theatre and Education, Music Educators National Conference, National Art Education Association, and National Dance Association. They are available from:

Music Educators National Conference Publication Sales
1806 Robert Fulton Drive
Reston, VA 22091–4348 Telephone: (800) 336–3768

Civics and Government—*National Standards for Civics and Government*

Center for Civic Education
5146 Douglas Fir Road
Calabasas, CA 91302–1467 Telephone: (818) 591–9321

Economics

Colorado Council on Economic Education
225 East 16th Avenue, Suite 740
Denver, Colorado 80203 Telephone: (303) 832–8480

Foreign Languages

American Council on the Teaching of Foreign Languages, Inc.
6 Executive Plaza
Yonkers, NY 10701–6801 Telephone: (914) 963–8830

Geography—*Geography For Life*

> National Council for Geographic Education
> Geography Standards Project
> 1600 M Street NW
> Washington, D.C. 20036 Telephone: (202) 857–7000

History

> National Center for History in the Schools at UCLA
> 231 Moore Hall
> 405 Hilgard Avenue
> Los Angeles, CA 90024–1521 Telephone: (310) 825–4702

Mathematics—*Curriculum and Evaluation Standards for School Mathematics*
(Item number 398E1, ISBN 0–87353–273–2)

> The National Council of Teachers of Mathematics
> Order Processing
> 1906 Association Drive
> Reston, VA 22091 Telephone: (800) 235–7566

Science

> National Academy of Sciences
> National Research Council
> 2101 Constitution Avenue NW
> Washington, D.C. 20418 Telephone: (202) 334–1399

For general information about content standards development, contact:

> Office of Educational Research and Improvement/FIRST Office
> U.S. Department of Education
> 555 New Jersey Avenue NW
> Washington, D.C. 20208–5524 Telephone (800) 872–53276

APPENDIX C

PSYCHOMOTOR DOMAIN, HARROW, ANITA J., 1972

3.00 Perceptual Abilities
    3.10 Kinesthetic Discrimination
        3.11 Body Awareness
            3.111 Bilaterality
            3.112 Laterality
            3.113 Sidedness
            3.114 Balance
        3.12 Body Image
        3.13 Body Relation to Surrounding Objects in Space
    3.20 Visual Discrimination
        3.21 Visual Acuity
        3.22 Visual Tracking
        3.23 Visual Memory
        3.24 Figure-Ground Differentiation
        3.25 Perceptual Consistency
    3.30 Auditory Discrimination
        3.31 Auditory Acuity
        3.32 Aditory Tracking
        3.33 Auditory Memory
    3.40 Tactile Discrimination
    3.50 Coordinated Abilities
        3.51 Eye-Hand Coordination
        3.52 Eye-Foot Coordination
4.00 Physical Abilities
    4.10 Endurance
        4.11 Muscular Endurance
        4.12 Cardiovascular Endurance
    4.20 Strength
    4.30 Flexibility
    4.40 Agility
        4.41 Change Direction
        4.42 Stops and Starts
        4.43 Reaction-Response Time
        4.44 Dexterity
5.00 Skilled Movements
    5.10 Simple Adaptive Skill
        5.11 Beginner
        5.12 Intermediate
        5.13 Advanced
        5.14 Highly Skilled
    5.20 Compound Adaptive Skill
        5.21 Beginner
        5.22 Intermediate

JANE'S BABY

TO _Doctor_

DATE _11/6/92_   TIME _3:30 PM_

WHILE YOU WERE OUT

CALLER _Mrs. Barton's OB_

OF

PHONE

TELEPHONED ✓   PLEASE CALL

WILL CALL AGAIN   URGENT ✓

RETURNED YOUR CALL

Message

Mrs. Jane Barton is very concerned about diagnosis regarding her fetus. Test results and social worker's report attached.

Mrs. Barton is scheduled for consultation with you at 3:00pm, Friday, November 13.

CONSULTATION REPORT

Consulting Service _____ Office of Social Services

Consulting Physician ___ D. McMann _____

REASON FOR CONSULTATION REPORT Background would be helpful
in light of the difficult decision the Barton's face.

_____
Signature-Referring Physician

REPORT OF CONSULTANT

Findings and Recommendations

Jane is in generally good physical and mental health; Jane is concerned about
diabetes in her family, her father developed late onset diabetes and began insulin
treatment at age 48. He is still alive and in good health. Jane stopped smoking
at age 28 after being a moderate smoker for 6 years.

Jane works in the home and has a part-time job at the local library. Ralph is a
computer software programmer. He works long hours but enjoys his work and the
couple have adapted to the work schedule without problem.

The Bartons describe themselves as happily married. They have one female
child, age 7. Jane had a miscarriage five years ago. This is her third pregnancy.

The couple is devastated by the possibility of birth defects associated with the
current pregnancy. They are not yet aware of the options they face in this case
but have been reading a little about anencephaly but don't want to worry themselves too much more until they talk with their specialist. They want to have
another child if they can.

Ralph inquired about the possibility of transplanting organs or tissue from their
fetus to another baby in order to "make something good out of this." Abortion is a
possibility for the Bartons. They will discuss it but have concerns based on the sanc-
tity of life issues in their religious background. The couple is concerned about the
risks that an abortion might bring to the chances of another pregnancy. They are also
concerned about the possibility that the present conditions could show up again in
another fetus.

The Bartons describe themselves as doing "ok" in terms of financial status but do
worry now and then about their obligations, they have a mortgage on a small house
and are making payments on a second car. Ralph Barton asked if researchers "buy"
tissue and organs so the costs of the donors are covered.

Ralph's employer provides major medical insurance.

November 7, 1992   _____
Date   Signature Consultant

ALL REQUESTS AND CONSULTATIONS MUST BE SIGNED

CONSULTATION REPORT

Consulting Service ___Radiology_____

Consulting Physician _____Broule_____

REASON FOR CONSULTATION REPORT   Jane Barton is a 35 year old Caucasian female in her third pregnancy (1-viable delivery; 1 spontaneous abortion); estimated due date 2/13/93 Reported for routine prenatal visit at 26 weeks gestation. Decreased uterine fundal height noted. Examination suggests 22-23 weeks and not 26 weeks gestation. Ultrasound requested to verify date of conception (EDC).

_____

Signature-Referring Physician

REPORT OF CONSULTANT

Findings and Recommendations

```
Ultrasound reveals femur length and abdominal
circumference consistent with 26 week gestation.
No cerebral hemisphere demonstrated. Head small
and irregular in appearance.
Amniocentesis performed under ultrasound. Elevated
alpha feto protein present.
DX: Findings consistent with anencephaly.
```

_____   _____
            Date   Signature Consultant

ALL REQUESTS AND CONSULTATIONS MUST BE SIGNED

Jane's Baby

The Center for Problem-Based Learning,
Illinois Mathematics and Science Academy

GOALS AND OUTCOMES

The chief goal of this problem is for students to recognize how emerging scientific and technological discoveries are impacting on existing practices and beliefs regarding treatment of the fetus and the newborn, public policy and scientific research, and definitions of *personhood*. In the pursuit of this goal, students will discover that problems seldom, if ever, reside exclusively in one domain or another. Technological problems often spill over into politics and economics. Business, government, and religious beliefs impact upon science. In addition, resolving problems often leaves the problem solver with choices based upon conflicting ethical appeals. *Science, Society and the Future* uses a decision-making strategy that asks students to assess the applicability and impact of each ethical appeal to the specific situation and then to make a reasoned judgement. *Solution* in the SSF sense is to make the "unacceptable a little more acceptable."

OUTCOMES FOR JANE'S BABY
(Second Draft)

After resolving the problem of "Jane's Baby," the student will:

Science (Medicine)

- have increased understanding of the anatomy and physiology of the brain;
- understand the functions of the brain stem, forebrain and hindbrain and the integrated nature of those functions;
- have a basic understanding of normal fetal development;
- understand the nature of fetal tissue research, its applications, and its status in the United States as compared with that in other countries;
- assess the effects of anencephaly on fetal tissue;
- assess the effects of anencephaly on fetal and/or infant organs and resultant suitability for transplant;
- understand the nature of a second- and third-trimester abortion and the medical risks to the mother of that procedure;
- effectively and humanely communicate to the patient how anencephaly affects the development of her fetus's brain and other vital organs as well as her own health;
- competently and considerately inform the patient of the treatment options and the risks associated with anencephaly;
- understand the definition of death used in Illinois for the purpose of organ donation.

Ethics/Morality

- become familiar with the Hippocratic Oath, its content and the guidelines which it gives for physicians' professional behavior;
- assess the degree of autonomy that the parents should possess when making decisions regarding anencephalic infants;
- help the parents decide, in light of their autonomy, what course of action should be undertaken that will result in the desired consequences;
- understand the application of ethical appeals in consideration of the problem of Jane's baby. The appeals include:

  1) consequences,
  2) personhood,
  3) rights,
  4) benefit/cost,

5) justice,
6) virtue;

- recognize the role a patient's religious beliefs play in such issues as abortion, termination of life support, fetal tissue applications and organ donation.

Law

- identify and understand statutes of the appropriate jurisdiction which apply to abortion;
- identify, understand and apply the statutes which have an impact on fetal tissue utilization;
- identify, understand and apply the elements of law which affect organ donation;
- identify the strengths and weaknesses of the legislative decision making process as a vehicle for creating public policy of fetal tissue research;
- understand the legal definition of death and the legal framework which that definition establishes for patients and health care workers in relation to organ donation and fetal tissue research.

Interpersonal Skills

- communicate accurately and compassionately to the patient the medical and legal complexities of the situation;
- communicate medical options to the patient in a nonthreatening and supportive manner;
- collaborate with other students to evaluate the situation, search for and scan data, share it with others, accept and, when appropriate, delegate responsibility for further data gathering and formulate solutions in a timely manner.

Problem Solving

- develop effective problem solving skills that include:
  — defining a problem before beginning searches for information and solutions,
  — developing and using hypotheses as guides in the search for information during the stages of problem identification and solution building,
  — searching for sources which provide information necessary to further define the problem as well as arrive at solutions,

- — scanning information to determine what is relevant and useful,
- — utilizing information to evolve and refine useful operating hypotheses,
- — realizing that there are several possible solutions to most problems,
- — recognizing that time and other constraints impinge on the decision-making process and require closure and,
- — choosing solutions that are ethical and justifiable.
- blend problem-solving skills with effective and humane interpersonal skills;
- evolve and internalize an approach to problem solving that provides not only skills but also an enduring framework for lifelong, effective, self-motivated learning.

INFORMATION GATHERING

Information to be used in the problem comes from a number of sources. Most frequently, students consult books, articles and other information sources housed in our school library. Their inquiries are guided by the "What do we need to know?" questions that are developed as a class. The questions have been developed in response to working hypotheses that rise out of what students know about the problem. Information gathered in this manner and then analyzed by the students is used to review the working hypotheses.

A second source of information is in the form of conversations with mentors. People on or off campus with something to offer the students are contacted in advance and times are agreed upon when students can call or visit to pursue issues related to the problem. It is our rule that considerable thought must be given to what the student wants to know *before* a contact with a mentor is made. This helps avoid "fishing expeditions" on the part of our students.

The third principle source of information on a problem is *simulated* information pertaining to the situation, characters, or setting of the problem. This information is prepared before the problem opens, if possible, or at the close of a school day if something unexpected is called for by the students. Too much reliance on simulated information is avoided because it is time intensive to prepare and apt to contain mistakes and inconsistencies.

It is our practice to be sure that small groups of students work on separate questions during information search and scan activities. This seems efficient when the goal is to find and analyze a great deal of information in a relatively short period of time. This practice also promotes true collaboration in the classroom because students need to know what other students have discovered in order that understanding of the problem can be expanded. Further, the competition for "air time" is reduced when information is distributed among the students, thus reducing the tendency toward discussions dominated by the fastest hand raisers in class.

ASSESSMENTS OF STUDENT PROGRESS
TOWARD OUTCOMES

Assessment takes two forms if SSF. The first is known as a *problem log*. A problem log is a booklet of activities based upon the outcomes for a problem that takes *core samples* of what's going on in a student's mind at different times during the problem-solving process. The activities or exercises in a log are normally completed by individual students, collected, and evaluated for progress toward the outcome statements.

The second principle means of assessment requires that students *perform* in an activity consistent with their role in the problem. During this performance, they must demonstrate skills, abilities, and acquired knowledge related to the target outcomes of the problem. Performances are usually done for "experts" in the field under study and result in reaction discussions that not only assess progress toward the outcomes but also become rich environments for reinforcement of ideas and/or introduction of new issues related to the problem being studied.

PROBLEM LOG ACTIVITIES FOR *JANE'S BABY*

The following exercises would be found in the student's problem log:

1. (Between the first and second days of activity) In the first space below, list any hunches you have about the situation Jane Barton is in. In the second space, list five (5) key questions you feel need to be answered to better understand Jane's problem. Circle the two you are most curious about.

2. (After approximately three or four days) In the space at the bottom of the page, describe the condition known as *anencephaly*, using each of the terms on the diagram of the human brain at the top of the page. Be sure your description would be understandable to Jane Barton. (A diagram of the human brain is provided with features labeled that are missing or severely malformed in an infant suffering from anencephaly.)

3. (After approximately five or six days) Briefly describe the effect of anencephaly on each of the neurologic functions listed below:
   a. sight
   b. hearing
   c. movement of the extremities
   d. sucking and swallowing
   e. wake and sleep cycles
   f. conscious awareness

4. (After approximately seven to eight days) Assume that you are about to meet the Bartons (and you are!). From your perspective, what choices do they face regarding each of the following:
   a. aborting the fetus before full-term?
   b. continuing the pregnancy to full-term?
   c. providing organs or fetal tissue for transplanting or research?

5. (At the conclusion of the activity) Doctor, suppose the Bartons asked you to abort their fetus now. Could you honor their request?

   Think of each of the letters below as representing a reason why you could or could not honor the Bartons' request. Using the letter "a" first, state your strongest reason for agreeing or disagreeing with their request. Go to "b" next. State another reason that supports your decision regarding the Bartons' request. Continue down the list of letters until your most important reasons have been listed. Lastly, use the next letter in the sequence for the strongest reason that might tempt you to consider taking the opposite action you have taken to this point.
   a.
   b.
   c. (provide about ten spaces)

6. *Performance.* Conduct a 15- to 20-minute *successful* consultation with the Bartons'. What do you want to accomplish?

APPENDIX E

THE FORMING OF THE EARTH'S SURFACE

Lovett, Kenneth
C&I 216 (01)
Nov. 30, 1988
Unit Plan

I. Introduction

    A. Course: Earth Science

    B. Target Population: 9th Grade

    C. Title: The Forming of the Earth's Surface

    D. Overview: This unit deals with the natural and human-made forces that have shaped and are continuing to shape the earth's surface, including plate tectonics, mountain building, erosional processes, and urbanization.

    E. Length of time: Approximately four weeks.

II. Unit objectives

Upon successful completion of this unit, the student will demonstrate each of the following objectives, in writing:

    A. Define and exemplify terms such as: continental drift, Pangaea, mid-ocean ridge, deep-sea trench, sea-floor spreading, geothermal energy, hot spots, asthenosphere, lithosphere, faults, Richter scale, volcanoes, mountain types, erosion, glaciation, and acid rain.

    B. Name the seven major plates that make up the earth's crust.

    C. Describe the process by which continental plates move, citing at least one modern-day example as evidence.

D. Describe what geothermal energy is and how humanity exploits it, citing at least three examples to defend or rebut its usefulness to mankind.

E. Describe the process by which an earthquake occurs, then list two positive and two negative effects an earthquake has on the earth's surface today.

F. List the two types of volcanic eruptions and the resulting landform of each, citing at least three distinguishing characteristics of each volcanic type.

G. List and describe at least three types of mountains and give at least one modern example of each.

H. List the three types of erosion and describe the process by which each transports materials of different size and shape.

I. Given examples of different landforms, describe the process by which each was formed and list at least two examples of the landform's effect on humanity.

J. Given a particular erosional process, such as wind, describe at least two examples of man's successful and unsuccessful attempts to control the process.

K. List at least two examples of humanity's continuing influence on the surface of the earth and logically defend the positive or negative effects this influence has had on the Earth.

L. Describe at least two ways in which modern technology has changed the effect humanity has on the Earth's surface.

III. Content

A. Earth's internal structure

1. Three layers of the earth

a. Crust—the outermost layer of the earth

(1) Composed of silicate (SiO_2, sand) minerals

(2) Thickness: 16 km (ocean floor) to 40 km (continental mountain ranges), (10–25 mi)

b. Mantle—the rock layer beneath the crust

(1) Surrounds the core

(2) Composed of olivine (mixture of magnesium and iron)

(3) Thickness: 2895 km (1800 mi)

c. Core—the center of the earth

(1) Composed largely of iron and nickel

(2) Consists of a liquid outer layer and a solid center

(3) Temperatures lie between 4000° and 5000° F

(4) Diameter: 6950 km (4320 mi)

2. Lithosphere—the part of the earth's crust made up of solid rock. Litho = rock.
3. Asthenosphere—soft, weak layer of rock material, which separates the lower crust and the upper mantle. Astheno = weak.
   a. The rock material present is close to the melting point (2000° to 3000° F)
   b. "Plastic" characteristic
4. Convection cell—areas within the asthenosphere in which the "plastic" rock material circulates as a result of constant heating and cooling.
   a. The hotter material is always rising to the top.
   b. The cooler material is falling to the bottom (this is the basis for sea floor spreading and plate tectonics).

(To illustrate the layers of the earth, make a transparency of a cross-sectional view of the earth depicting the planet's interior. Identify the relative boundaries of each layer and describe how the convection cells work. These terms will be a good introduction to continental drift and plate tectonics.)

B. Plate tectonics
   1. Continental drift theory
      a. Proposed by Alfred Wegener in 1912
      b. The breakup of a parent continent, Pangaea, starting about 230 million years ago, resulted in the present arrangement of the continents and intervening ocean basins

   (A transparency showing historical configurations of the continents and how they have drifted since the formation of Pangaea will give the students an idea of the present movement of the continents.)

   2. Sea-floor spreading—pulling apart of the oceanic crust along the mid-ocean ridges
      a. Convection cells circulate molten rock close to the surface
      b. Molten rock propagates through the cracks along the mid-ocean ridges
      c. Molten rock reaches the surface and cools rapidly, creating new sea floor
      d. Newly formed sea floor causes the plates, which make up the crust, to move
      e. Average rate of sea floor spreading is 6 to 12 cm per year (2.3 to 4.6 in)
      f. Mid-ocean ridges—a great undersea mountain range
         (1) Stretch nearly 70,000 km (43,500 mi) around the Earth
         (2) Rise steeply to heights of up to 3 km (almost 2 mi)

(3) In some places this ridge reaches the surface of the ocean and forms volcanic islands such as Iceland

(4) Largest is the Mid-Atlantic Ridge, which is currently moving the Eurasian and African plates away from the American plates

(A transparency showing the ocean floor and mid-ocean ridge system and another showing the seven major plates will help illustrate this topic.)

3. Major plates of the earth's crust

   a. Pacific—largest plate, covering one-fifth of the Earth
   b. Eurasian—one-sixth of the Earth
   c. Antarctic—almost one-sixth of the Earth
   d. North American—one-eighth of the Earth
   e. African—almost one-eighth of the Earth
   f. South America—almost one-tenth of the Earth
   g. Austral/Indian—almost one-tenth of the Earth

(These are the seven major plates, but there are several minor plates, which play an important role in shaping the earth's surface.)

4. Plate boundaries

   a. Continental rock, due to composition, is less dense than sea-floor rock
   b. As a result of sea-floor spreading, there must also be plate destruction (otherwise the earth would not remain round)
   c. When two plates collide, one of three results may occur

      (1) Continent–ocean plate collision

         (a) The continental plate is lighter than the ocean plate
         (b) The continental plate rides over the ocean plate
         (c) This creates a deep ocean trench

            1. The ocean plate is pushed down, back into the asthenosphere
            2. The rock material is then melted
            3. The molten rock is then recirculated in the convection cells
            4. The deepest of these ocean trenches is the Marianas trench east of the Philippines at the depth of 11 km (almost 7 mi)

         (d) The most common result of a continent–ocean plate collision is a chain of volcanic mountains along the edge on the continental plate

            1. The most notable example is the east coast of South America, the Andes Mountains

      (2) Continent–continent plate collision

          (a) The plates are of relative equal density; therefore each is attempting to override the other

          (b) Results in a huge mountain range made up of the rock that at one time was the edge of the continental plate

          (c) Mountains grow very rapidly (as compared to the other types of mountains)

          (d) Associated with the highest mountains on Earth—Himalaya Mountains in south Asia

      (3) Ocean–ocean plate collision

          (a) The plates are of relatively equal density; therefore both are attempting to push the other plate down

          (b) Deep ocean trench is created

          (c) Undersea volcanic mountain range is created

      (When these volcanoes reach the surface of the ocean, a volcanic island chain is formed, such as the islands of New Zealand.)

  5. Evidence of plate tectonics—three facts supporting the theory of continental drift and plate tectonics:

    a. Similar continental boundaries—"puzzle-piece" match-up can be seen on a globe of the world, looking at the eastern side of Africa and the western side of South America.

    b. Similar fossil types—fossil types of particular regions can be found on both Africa and South America.

    c. Regions that are presently different climatically and geographically show evidence in similarities of climate and geography (plant types and soil profiles). Therefore the continents would have had to be connected in the past. Similar examples can be found on the continents of North America and Eurasia.

    d. Similar rock types—rock layers have been found to be the same in composition and postdepositional deformation in areas of South America and Africa. Similar examples can be found in North America and Eurasia.

C. Other tectonic features

  1. Hot spots

    a. Regions around the Earth where convections cells are located just below the surface of the crust

    b. Not a part of the process of continental drift

    c. Volcanoes or volcanic activity prevalent

d. Spots appear to drift as a result of their location under a moving plate

e. Two notable examples of this activity are the Hawaiian Islands and Yellowstone National Park

(A discussion on the phenomena of the Hawaiian Islands and Yellowstone Park can be based on their formation and their "control center," which is molten rock very close to the surface of these regions that forces its way to the surface. In the Hawaiian region, a volcano is created. If continental drift were not present, Hawaii would be one huge island, like Iceland. In Yellowstone, the hot spot is deeper beneath the Earth's surface than in Hawaii. About 500,000 years ago, this hot spot was much shallower than it is presently, and the molten rock worked its way to the surface, making a ring-shaped cut in the crust. The result was a hole about 500 feet deep, about 50 miles across, and about 100 miles long. Today in Yellowstone, groundwater percolates down through the rock, is superheated into steam and is explosively shot out of cracks in the ground—geysers.)

2. Volcanoes

a. Volcanoes can be created two ways.

(1) Collision of plates

(2) From hot spots

b. The shape of the volcano is determined by the type of eruption, and the type of eruption is dependent upon the composition of the molten rock.

(1) Explosive eruptions

(a) Lighter, continental type of rock

(b) Gaseous and volatile lava

(c) The pressure of the gas forces the molten rock to the surface, causing the lava to explode out of the volcano

(d) Pyroclastic (fire-broken) material, solidified lava, in the form of ash (dust size, under .10 in), cinder (pebble size, .10–.50 in), and bombs (.50–24.0 in), is thrown from the volcano

(The typical lava flow associated with volcanic eruptions is not present.)

(e) An explosive eruption that does not include lava is a *nuée ardente*

1. A super-heated gas cloud containing steam and ash is expelled from the volcano

2. Temperature often in excess of 3000° F
3. Moves at very rapid speeds regardless of slope

(In 1902 an eruption on the island of Martinique in the Caribbean was of this type. All but two of the 30,000 inhabitants were killed instantly.)

(2) Nonexplosive eruptions

(a) Rock material is from the ocean floor
(b) Does not contain the gases and volatile material present in continental rock material
(c) Pressure exerted on the lava is released once the vent of the volcano has been cleared
(d) The lava oozes out of the volcano in large flows
(e) Lava can be classified by viscosity (fluidity)

1. *Aa*

a. Thin
b. Fluid in molten state
c. Forms a jagged layer of broken pieces of lava as it cools
d. Sounds like pieces of glass clinking together as the flow moves

2. *Pahoehoe*

a. Thick
b. Less fluid than Aa in molten state
c. Outer layer appears smooth and billowy (rolling mass, like smoke) as it cools

c. Three types of volcanic cones:

(1) Cinder cone

(a) Small
(b) Steep sided
(c) Composed largely of loose volcanic cinder or ash
(d) Associated with explosive volcanoes
(e) Paricutín in Mexico

(2) Shield cone

(a) Nonexplosive
(b) Broad
(c) Gently sloping
(d) Composed almost entirely of layers of lava
(e) The Hawaiian Islands

(3) Composite cone

(a) Explosive and nonexplosive eruption

(b) Large

(c) Built of alternating layers of lava and cinders

(d) Volcano first erupts violently, sending ash and cinder into the air

(e) Second eruption produces a quiet lava flow covering the ash and cinder layer

(f) Mount Vesuvius in Italy and Mount St. Helens in Washington state

3. Faults and earthquakes

   a. Often associated with volcanoes

   b. Earthquakes can sometimes indicate a future volcanic eruption

   c. Earthquakes are associated with faults

      (1) Fault—a fracture in the ground along which slippage occurs

      (2) Cause: Progression of the following

         (a) Crustal movement due to plate tectonics

         (b) Tension created at a fracture in the crust due to the movement

         (c) Slippage along the fracture occurs as stress factors overcome shear factors

         (d) Slippage creates shock waves, which are interpreted as earthquakes

(Clay models are available to illustrate how tension building up as a result of tectonic activity can actually cause solid rock to move and bend.)

      (3) Types of faults

         (a) Normal fault—hanging wall (side above the fault) has moved down in relation to the foot wall (side below the fault)

         (b) Reverse fault—the hanging wall has moved up in relation to the foot wall

         (c) Thrust fault—a very low angle reverse fault

            1. Rock has been heavily folded as a result of slow, continuous pressure.

            2. Shear factors of the rock have not been overcome due to the gradual application of pressure, therefore the rock folds instead of breaks.

            3. Pressure becomes forceful and the stress overcomes the shear factors of the rock, causing the rock to break and thrusting the hanging wall over the foot wall.

         (d) Strike slip or transform fault—the fault is relatively perpendicular to the surface. Two sides of the fault slide laterally past each other rather than vertically.

(A popular example of this type of faulting is the San Andreas Fault in California.)

(Sketches of the different fault types with a rock bed highlighted will help to show how movement is different in each fault.)

(4) Shock waves

    (a) Measured as seismic (earthquake) waves

    (b) Categorized by the direction in which they travel through the earth away from the fracture

    (c) Three types

        1. L—long waves or surface waves

            a. Slowest of the three waves

            b. Travels no deeper into the Earth than the crustal layer

            c. Resembles the waves on the ocean surface

            d. Causes the major damage during an earthquake

        2. P—primary waves

            a. Fastest of the three waves.

            b. Can pass through solids, liquids, and gases.

            c. Considered push-pull waves because they push the rock ahead of them and compress the rock. When the wave passes, the rock pulls back to its original position.

        3. S—secondary waves

            a. Not quite as fast as P waves

            b. Can pass through solid material, but not liquid or gases

            c. Moves the rock from side to side

(5) Magnitude of an earthquake

    (a) The magnitude of an earthquake is measured by recording the L-waves using a *seismograph*

    (b) Plotted on a logarithmic scale

    (c) *Richter Scale*

        1. Ranks the magnitude of the earthquake from 1 to 10 while it is occurring

        2. Each increment of 1 increases the magnitude of the earthquake by 30 times

        3. Visual criteria used to estimate the magnitude of an earthquake

            1—Not felt at all or felt by few

2—Felt indoors; hanging objects swing

3—Hanging objects shake; windows rattle

4—Felt outdoors; doors swing; pendulum clocks affected

5—Felt by all; difficult to stand; windows break

6—Driving affected; chimneys fall; cracks in wet ground

7—Frame structures shifted off foundation; conspicuous cracks in ground

8—Frame houses destroyed; large-scale landslides; train rails slightly bent

9—Train rails greatly bent; bridges and buildings destroyed

10—Damage nearly total; objects thrown into air; large rock masses displaced

4. Mountain building—combination of continental rifting, faulting, folding, volcanics, and geothermal heat result in the uplifting of the landscape into small hills (30 to 300 m, 400 to 4000 ft) and large mountain peaks that reach up to 9 km (29,000 ft). Five major types of mountains (photographs of major mountain ranges needed).

   a. Fault block

      (1) Created by movement along a fault plane
      (2) Movement is more rapid than the rate of erosion
      (3) The Grand Teton Range and the Sierra Nevada Mountains

   b. Folded

      (1) Created as a result of large-scale folding of the rock layers that make up the crustal surface
      (2) Folding can be the result of other tectonic activity, such as plate collisions
      (3) Colorado Rocky Mountains

   c. Volcanic

      (1) Direct result of volcanic activity
      (2) The continual eruption of one or many volcanoes
      (3) Highest peak usually being the most active volcano
      (4) Mount St. Helens (Washington state), Mount Fuji (Honshu, Japan), and Mount Kilimanjaro (Tanzania, Africa)

   d. Dome

      (1) Formed when molten rock attempts to force its way to the surface, pushing all of the rock layers above it upward
      (2) Solid igneous rock core, under layers of sedimentary rocks

(3) Sedimentary rock has been deformed both by the uplift and also the immense heat of the molten rock mass (temperatures in excess of 1000° F)

(4) The Black Hills of South Dakota

e. Orogenic

(1) Formed as result of continental drift and plate collision

(2) Individual mountains can be the result of any of the other mountain-building mechanisms

(3) The Appalachian Mountains and the Himalaya Mountains (Asia)

D. Geothermal heat and humanity

1. Geothermal heat: heat produced from within the earth's crust

2. This can have both negative and positive impacts on humanity

a. Negative aspects

(1) Destruction of life and property

(2) Modern technology has attempted to reduce the amount of destruction, but has had few positive results

b. Positive aspects

(1) An alternative energy source

(a) Heat from within the crust heats up the ground water

(b) The hot water and steam produced can be used to heat buildings and generate electricity

(c) Used as an alternative energy source for years in Italy and Australia

E. Erosional processes (natural forces continually acting on the Earth's surface in an attempt to attain equilibrium, where everything is flat); three major types

1. Wind—wind performs two kinds of erosional work

a. Deflation—large-scale removal of soil

(1) Loose particles on the ground lifted into the air or rolled along the ground

(2) Occurs wherever the ground is thoroughly dried out: dried river beds, beaches, and areas recently formed by glacial deposits

(3) Transports loose particles in one of three ways depending upon their size

(a) Suspension

1. Very fine particles, such as clay and silt

      2. Particles are lifted and carried in the air

(b) Saltation

      1. Fine particles, such as sand-size grains
      2. Wind cannot lift into air easily
      3. The sand grains are lifted when the wind is strongest and dropped once the wind speed decreases

(c) Traction

      1. Gravel and rounded pebbles
      2. Cannot be lifted by the wind
      3. Moved when wind removes the sand and silt size particles that lay under and in front of these larger particles
      4. Gravel or pebbles, then, roll downwind

(When deflation occurs over a large area, it is called a blowout, or deflation hollow. This depression can be from a few meters to a kilometer or more in diameter, but is usually only a few meters deep. Blowouts form in plains regions where the grass cover is broken through.)

b. Wind abrasion

   (1) Wind drives sand and dust particles across a flat area and drives them against an exposed rock or soil surface
   (2) Slow, continuous process
   (3) The obstruction is slowly worn away by the continual blasting by these particles

c. Man-induced deflation (one example)

   (1) Big move to the Great Plains in the 1930s
   (2) Heavily cultivated by each new inhabitant
   (3) Major drought in the late 1930s
   (4) Resulted in a large-scale deflation of the area
   (5) Known as the Dust Bowl
   (6) Since this time, many improvements have been made to try to reduce the possibility of such large-scale blowouts occurring again

      (a) The use of listed furrows (deeply carved furrows), which act as traps to soil movement
      (b) The use of "no-till" planting, which keeps the plant remains from the previous crop in place to protect the soil through the winter months
      (c) Use of tree belts and wind fences to decrease the intensity of the wind at ground level

(7) Causes of deflation, other than agricultural

    (a) Off-road vehicles, such as trail motorcycles

    (b) Four-wheel-drive recreation vehicles

2. Water

  a. Mechanical or fluvial processes

    (1) Dominates the continental land surfaces world wide

    (2) Almost every area of the earth has been affected by fluvial processes

    (3) Transports particles by the use of suspension, saltation, and traction

    (4) Water has a greater density than wind and can move objects and particles more easily

    (5) Fluvial processes can be separated into two major groups

      (a) Slope erosion

        1. Rain or melting ice provides the water

        2. Water carries particles down slope

        3. Combined with gravity, the water and particles increase speed and density down slope; the result is one of two possibilities

          a. Mass wasting—the whole side of the slope is washed downhill (landslide)

          b. Down-cutting, forming a stream

      (Show photograph of mass wasting.)

      (b) Stream erosion

        1. Streams erode differently depending on

          a. The slope of the stream bed

          b. The amount of discharge

          c. The amount of particles in suspension

        2. Fastest down-cutting occurs when

          a. Stream velocity is high

          b. Banks and stream bed are composed of unconsolidated or loosely consolidated rock material

          c. Stream load (amount of particles in suspension) is high

          d. Stream is at flood stage

      (Show photographs of streams undercutting their banks. Photographs of the Colorado River and Grand Canyon will help illustrate stream load and down-cutting forces.)

  b. Chemical weathering

(1) The alteration and breakdown of rock material
(2) Water can come from

    (a) Rain
    (b) Lakes
    (c) Streams

(3) Water contains two important gases from the atmosphere: oxygen and carbon dioxide

    (a) oxygen—causes oxidation of minerals
    (b) carbon dioxide—(CO_2) forms a weak acid (carbonic acid) that dissolves rock material

(4) Acid rain is formed from the mixing of oxides of sulfur and nitrogen with rain to form solutions of sulfuric (H_2SO_4) and nitric (HNO_3) acids

    (a) Sulfur and nitrogen come from the burning of fossil fuels
    (b) Became a greater problem when smokestacks were built higher to alleviate smog, putting the pollutants higher into the atmosphere
    (c) pH of 4 to 4.5 (slightly stronger than CO_2, pH of 5.6)
    (d) Change in pH affects the calcium in the water which the entire ecosystem relies on
    (e) This acid also dissolves rock more readily than carbonic acid (especially carbonate rock, such as limestone and marble)

(Show photographs of ancient buildings made of limestone and how they have been chemically eroded by sulfuric and nitric acids in rain.)

c. Humanity's effect on water erosion

    (1) Grazing livestock

        (a) Tramples and compacts the topsoil
        (b) Removes protective vegetation

    (2) Lumbering—deforestation

        (a) Exposes large amounts of land to erosional processes
        (b) Demand for timber resources and need for agricultural land
        (c) Tropical rain forests suffer worst destruction

            1. Forests protect tropical soils and water supplies
            2. Tropical rain forests have a sensitive balance that is compromised with heavy lumbering

  (3) Agriculture

    (a) Increases the amount of exposed soil
    (b) Decreases protective wind barriers

  (4) Flood management and energy

    (a) Damming of streams and rivers has altered the rate at which streams can achieve equilibrium
    (b) Hydroelectric dams are created by flooding valleys, causing major changes in the down-cutting forces of the stream or river

3. Ice

  a. Ice propagation

    (1) Water leaks down into cracks of rock and soil
    (2) Water expands as it freezes
    (3) Ice forces the crack to become larger
    (4) Pieces of the rock or soil begin to break off
    (5) Rock or soil pieces are carried away by gravity or water

  b. Glaciation

    (1) Alpine (mountain)

      (a) Snow accumulates in the higher elevations
      (b) Snow is compacted into ice
      (c) Ice becomes "plastic" under the increased weight
      (d) The "plastic" ice sheet moves downhill as a result of increasing weight
      (e) The ice scours the rock material and pushes unconsolidated material

    (2) Continental

      (a) Snow accumulates in higher latitudes
      (b) Snow is compacted into ice
      (c) Ice becomes "plastic" under the increased weight
      (d) The "plastic" ice sheet moves out from the area of accumulation
      (e) The ice scours rock material and pushes unconsolidated material
      (f) As the ice melts (retreats), rock and debris are deposited
      (g) This material is then subject to erosion

(Sketches showing a topography before and after glaciation will help illustrate the erosive power of a glacier.)

F. How the earth's surface has been changed by man

   1. Early travel was restricted to water

      a. Major cities were built along trade routes of rivers

      b. Alteration to stream erosion to keep cities out of the rivers

      c. Damming of streams and rivers for both navigation and power supplies

      d. Excavation of man-made canals to facilitate navigation

   2. Invention of the railroads

      a. Initially restricted to valleys

      b. Development of major cities created need to excavate valleys

      c. Development of more cities along railroad routes due to convenience

   3. Usage of coal and other resources

      a. Mining processes created mass wasting of many areas

      b. Mining removed hills and created unnatural holes in the topography

      c. Burning of coal affected the weather by placing more ash and dust particles into the atmosphere

      d. Burning of coal produced pollutants that killed large areas of forest

      e. Mining changed the amount of material being carried by streams and rivers

   4. Development of cities (urbanization)

      a. Increase in larger and higher buildings has changed the wind patterns of many areas

      b. The need for superhighways has increased the amount of flat land across which wind can have a greater effect

      c. Industrialization has changed the chemical makeup of the air and rain

      d. Urbanization has resulted in the destruction of protective vegetation

G. Society's response to man's impact on the earth

   1. Reforestation

      a. Replanting of lumbered areas

      b. Development of special varieties of trees that grow back faster than original species

   2. Improved refinement of fossil fuels

      a. Unleaded gasoline

  b. Coal sulfur scrubbers

3. Development of national parks and preserves
4. Alternative energy sources

   a. Nuclear
   b. Solar
   c. Electric transportation

      (1) Electric automobiles
      (2) Electromagnetic railroads

5. Rejuvenation of excavated areas

   a. Replanting of strip-mined areas
   b. Replacement of natural wind blocks in open areas

H. Celestial impact

  1. Formation of a crater

     a. Creates changes in topography instantaneously
     b. Can change the drainage patterns of the area.
     c. Sunset Crater, Arizona

  2. Formation of a volcanic island

     a. Possible that a meteor large enough could puncture the earth's crust, resulting in a volcanic island
     b. Iceland—one theory is that it was created by a meteor impact

EARTH SCIENCE UNIT EXAM

Forming of the Earth's Surface

Name: _____   Date:_____

Define the term and give an example for each.

1. Fault
   Answer: A crack in the ground along which there is movement. San Andreas Fault, California.

2. Hot spot
   Answer: A place where molten rock is near the surface of the crust. It is not directly associated with plate tectonics. It stays in one spot as the plate moves over it. Hawaiian Islands.

3. Acid rain

> *Answer:* A solution of rain water and sulfuric or nitric acid kills plants and animals and erodes rock at a faster rate than carbonic acid. Upstate New York.

4. Mass wasting

> *Answer:* The downward movement of soil or rock material covering the slope of a hill or mountain. When heavy rains are the cause, this is considered a landslide.

5. Convection call

> *Answer:* A body of molten rock in which the hotter material, heated from the center of the earth, rises to the top of the cell, and the material being cooled from its contact with earth's crust drops, creating circulation within the cell. Theorized to be below the Mid-Atlantic Ridge.

Multiple-Choice
Circle the response that best answers the question.

1. The term used to describe how wind carries very fine dust particles is:
   A. saltation.
   B. solution.
   C. secretion.
   <u>D</u>. suspension.

2. What result between stress and shear factors must occur to cause slippage?
   A. Shear must overcome stress.
   B. Shear must be equal to stress.
   C. Stress and shear are not related to slippage.
   <u>D</u>. Stress must overcome shear.

3. Refer to Diagram 1.

Diagram 1

Fault "a" is a:
   <u>A</u>. reverse fault because the hanging wall has moved down in relation to the foot wall.
   B. normal fault because the hanging wall has moved up in relation to the foot wall.

   C. normal fault because the hanging wall has moved down in relation to the foot wall.

   D. strike slip fault because the hanging wall has moved down in relation to the foot wall.

4. The cause of the Andes Mountains in South America is the result of:
   A. a continental–continental plate collision.
   <u>B.</u> a continental–oceanic plate collision.
   C. a hot spot under the Pacific plate.
   D. an oceanic–oceanic plate collision.

5. Mountains that are the direct result of a continental–continental plate collision are considered to be:
   <u>A.</u> orogenic.
   B. volcanic.
   C. Andean.
   D. domal.

Short Answer

1. List and describe the three types of volcanic cones, and give an example of each.
   Answer: Cinder cone—small, steep-sided cone comprised of cinder, ash, and bombs, which are expelled from the volcano and land on the slopes of the cone. The result of an explosive eruption. Paricutín in Mexico.
           Shield cone—large, broad-based cone. The result of a nonexplosive eruption, made up of layers of lava. Hawaiian Islands.
           Composite cone—the result of alternating explosive and nonexplosive eruptions. The cone is made up of layers of cinder and lava. Mount St. Helens.

2. Defend your opinion on what society should do or should not do about acid rain. Use at least three logically sequential factual statements to support your opinion.

3. Describe how it would be possible to have a mountain form in Illinois.
   Answer: This could occur as a result of a hot spot locating under the part of the crust called Illinois. Or, as a result of continental drift, collision with another plate would form an orogenic mountain range.

4. An earthquake with a magnitude of 6 on the Richter Scale has just occurred in your neighborhood. Describe the damage you see in your house and throughout the neighborhood that would verify the magnitude rating.
   Answer: Everyone felt this earthquake. It was difficult to stand during the quake. The plaster on the walls has cracked and fallen. Windows

and dishes are broken. The chimney has fallen, and the house has been moved off its foundation. Outside, tree branches have broken off, and cracks have appeared in the banks of a creek behind the house. A car has collided with a tree, because it was difficult to steer during the quake.

5. List at least three effects on the land the Army Corps of Engineers has caused by altering the course of the Mississippi River, and describe how these changes are different from what the river would naturally experience. Answers should include variations of these ideas:

   - A decrease in the discharge of the river because the natural down-cutting has been affected.
   - An increase in the depositing of sediments on the bottom of the channel because the river is still trying to reach equilibrium, even though the river is not down-cutting any more.
   - The channel position does not change because the banks of the river are kept constant.
   - The distribution of sediments on the river's delta has been skewed because the natural migration of the river channel has been controlled.
   - Larger cities can be built along the river because the threat of a large-scale flood has been reduced.
   - A more consistent development of the land along the river because the channel is controlled.

BIBLIOGRAPHY

Coble, Charles R., Elaine G. Murray, and Dale R. Rice. *Earth Science.* Englewood Cliffs, NJ: Prentice-Hall, 1981.

Namowitz, Samuel N., and Donald B. Stone. *Earth Science.* New York: American Book Company, 1981.

Ojakangas, Richard W., and David G. Darby. *The Earth Past and Present.* New York: McGraw-Hill, 1976.

Ritter, Dale F. *Process Geomorphology.* New York: Wm. C. Brown, 1978.

Seyfert, Carl K., and Leslie A. Sirkin. *Earth History and Plate Tectonics.* New York: Harper & Row, 1979.

Strahler, Arthur N., and Alan H. Strahler. *Modern Physical Geography.* New York: John Wiley, 1987.

NAME INDEX

SUBJECT INDEX

Note: Page numbers in italics indicate figures; page numbers followed by *f* indicate tables; page numbers followed by *n* indicate footnotes.